AF606745

KUSAMA

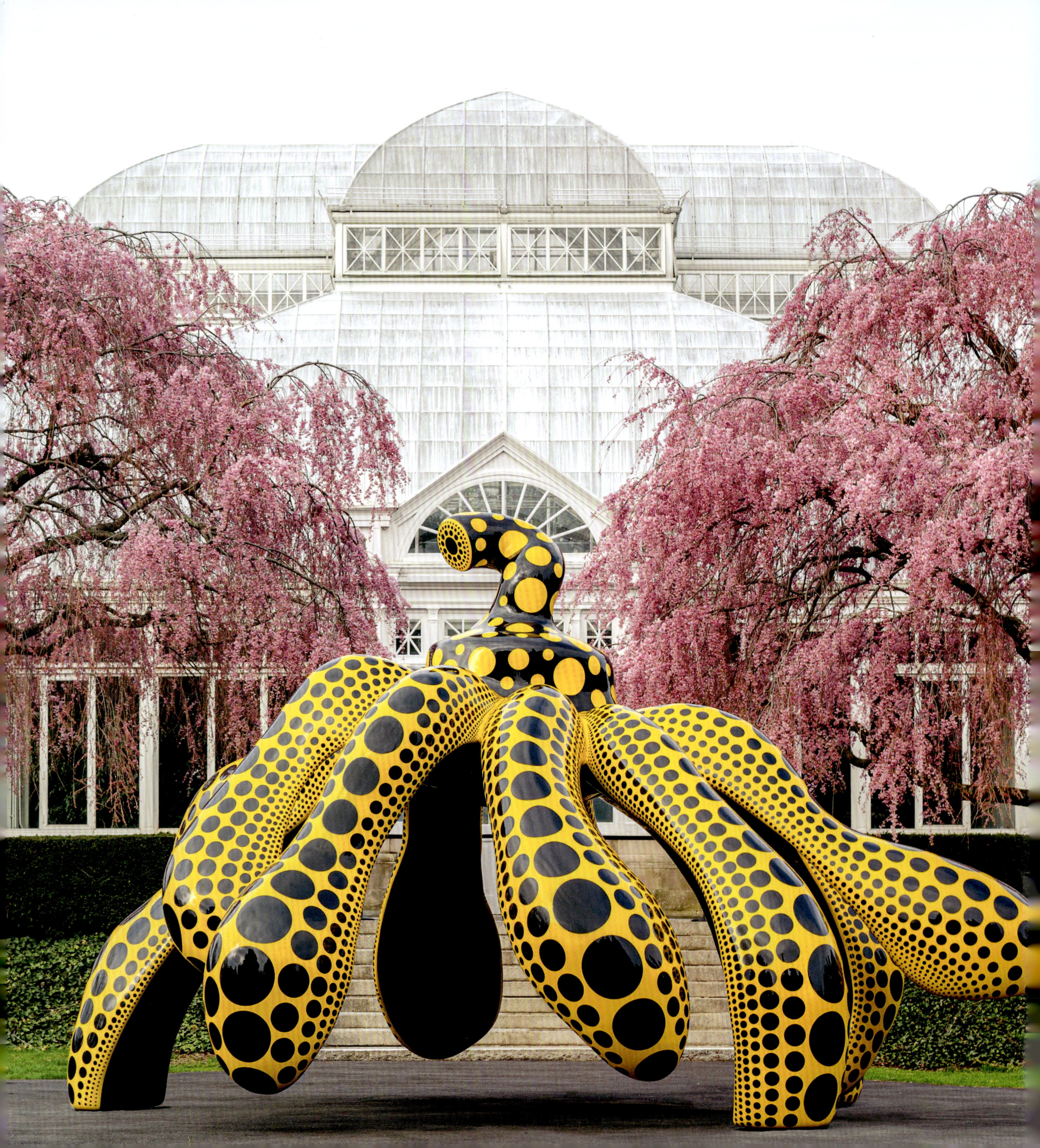

KUSAMA

Joanna L. Groarke and Mika Yoshitake

With contributions by
Barbara Ambrose, Karen Daubmann, Alex A. Jones,
Alexandra Munroe, and Jenni Sorkin

COSMIC NATURE

New York Botanical Garden

Rizzoli Electa

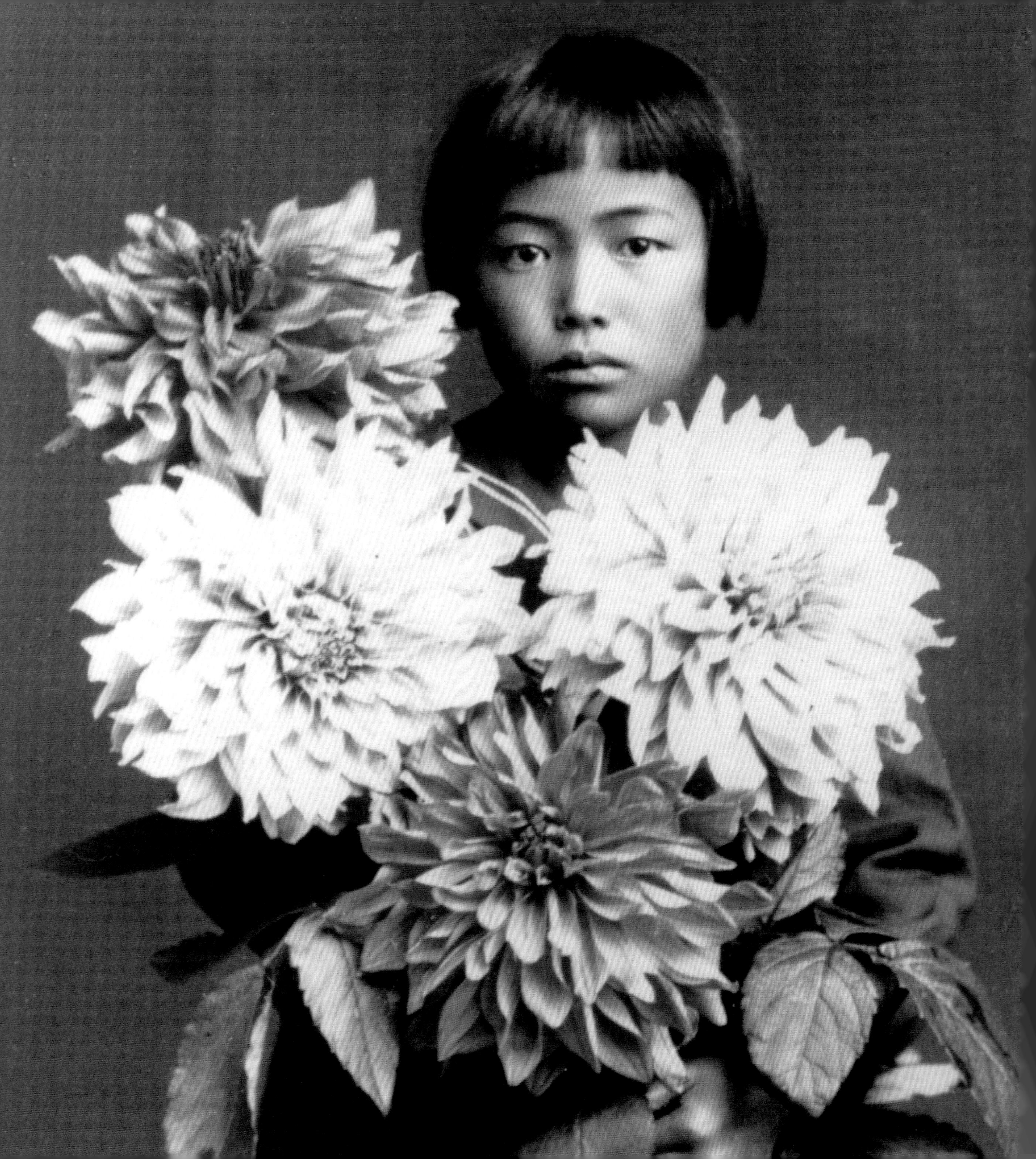

Foreword

KUSAMA: Cosmic Nature is a multi-seasonal presentation of contemporary Japanese artist Yayoi Kusama's profound, lifelong fascination with nature. For the first time, her work is presented extensively in gardens and galleries. Engaging with The New York Botanical Garden's historic landscape, the exhibition explores a life spent revealing the interconnectedness of all living things and presents the artist's work in New York City once again.

The exhibition would not have been possible without Yayoi Kusama's embrace of this ambitious project. We thank everyone at YAYOI KUSAMA, Inc. for their collaboration and for the opportunity to share this exclusive exhibition with our visitors.

For their contributions to the development of the exhibition, I wish to thank numerous individuals: Mika Yoshitake, PhD, guest curator; David Zwirner and Hanna Schouwink, David Zwirner, New York; Hidenori Ota, Ota Fine Arts, Tokyo/Singapore/Shanghai; Glenn Scott Wright, Victoria Miro, London/Venice; Akira Tatehata, director of the Yayoi Kusama Museum, Tokyo; and our colleagues at the Matsumoto City Museum of Art. We are grateful to the lenders of the works of art, YAYOI KUSAMA, Inc.; Ota Fine Arts, Tokyo/Singapore/Shanghai; David Zwirner, New York; Victoria Miro, London/Venice; the City of Beverly Hills; the Takahashi Ryutaro Collection, Yokohama, Japan; and other private collections. We thank our colleagues at Rizzoli Electa, especially Charles Miers, Margaret Chace, and Isabel Venero, for their partnership in producing this publication. I also thank the many talented members of the Garden staff and outside partners who contributed their advice and expertise to help us realize an exhibition of this scale in the midst of historic challenges.

This exhibition would not be possible without the generosity of our sponsors, including Tom and Janet Montag; MetLife Foundation; Veuve Clicquot; Citi; Delta Air Lines; Bloomberg Philanthropies; E.H.A. Foundation, Inc.; Arthur F. and Alice E. Adams Charitable Foundation; National Endowment for the Arts; New York State Council on the Arts; and LuEsther T. Mertz Charitable Trust, which provides leadership support for year-round programming at NYBG.

The New York Botanical Garden presents multidisciplinary exhibitions that explore and reveal the inextricable link between art and nature, often featuring the work of an artist who offers a unique perspective through which to view plants and other living things. *KUSAMA: Cosmic Nature* provides an opportunity for visitors to forge new connections to the living world around them through moments of discovery, reflection, and awe offered by Yayoi Kusama's cosmic view of nature.

J.V. Cossaboom

Interim President & Chief Executive Officer
The New York Botanical Garden

Yayoi Kusama at age ten

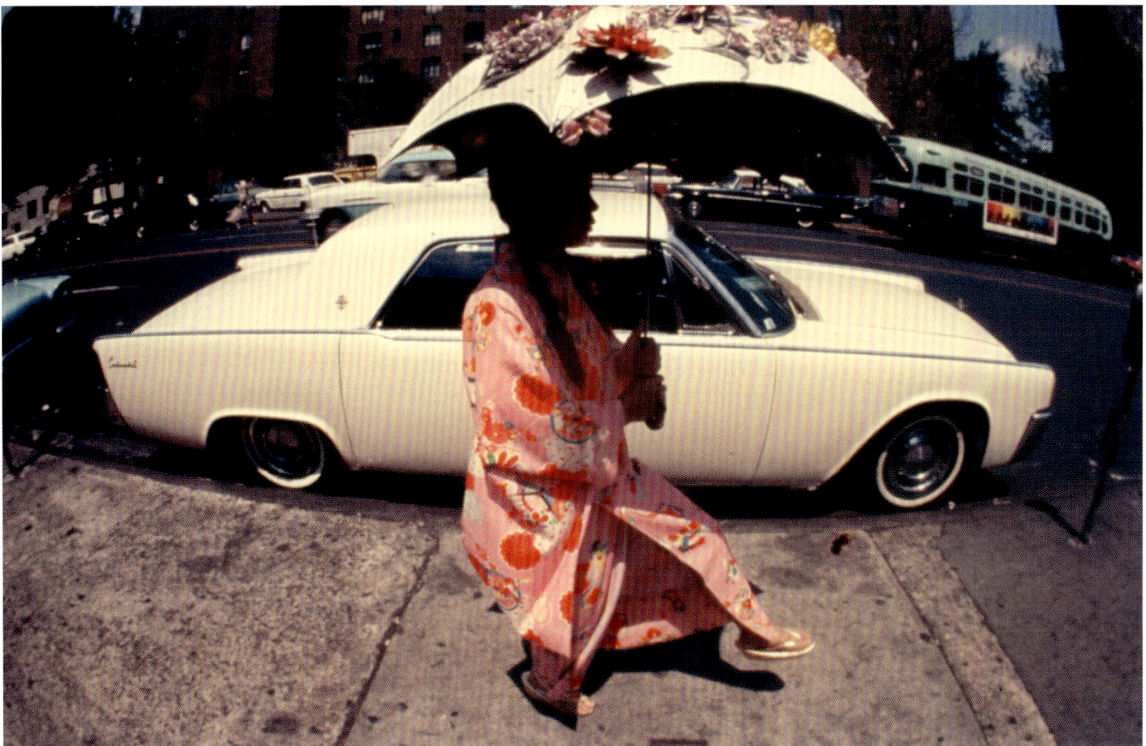

Walking Piece (detail), 1966

Acknowledgments

The New York Botanical Garden wishes to thank the following individuals and institutions for their assistance in the development of *KUSAMA: Cosmic Nature*.

Yayoi Kusama
Mika Yoshitake, PhD, Guest Curator

YAYOI KUSAMA, Inc.
David Zwirner
Ota Fine Arts
Victoria Miro
Cleveland Museum of Art
High Museum of Art

LENDERS TO THE EXHIBITION

City of Beverly Hills
David Zwirner
Ota Fine Arts
Victoria Miro
YAYOI KUSAMA, Inc.
Takahashi Ryutaro Collection, Yokohama, Japan
Private collections

EXHIBITION SPONSORS

Tom and Janet Montag

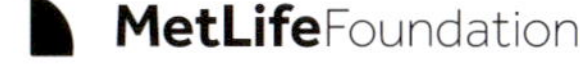

CHAMPAGNE LA GRANDE DAME Veuve Clicquot

citi

Delta Air Lines

Bloomberg Connects
Digital Experience Brought to You by Bloomberg Philanthropies

E.H.A. Foundation, Inc.

Arthur F. and Alice E. Adams Charitable Foundation

NATIONAL ENDOWMENT for the ARTS arts.gov
This project is supported in part by an award from the National Endowment for the Arts.

NEW YORK STATE OF OPPORTUNITY. Council on the Arts
New York State Council on the Arts with the support of Governor Andrew M. Cuomo and the New York State Legislature

LuEsther T. Mertz Charitable Trust
Providing leadership support for year-round programming at NYBG

Exhibitions in the Enid A. Haupt Conservatory are made possible by the Estate of Enid A. Haupt.

Exhibitions in the Arthur and Janet Ross Gallery are made possible by the Arthur and Janet Ross Fund.

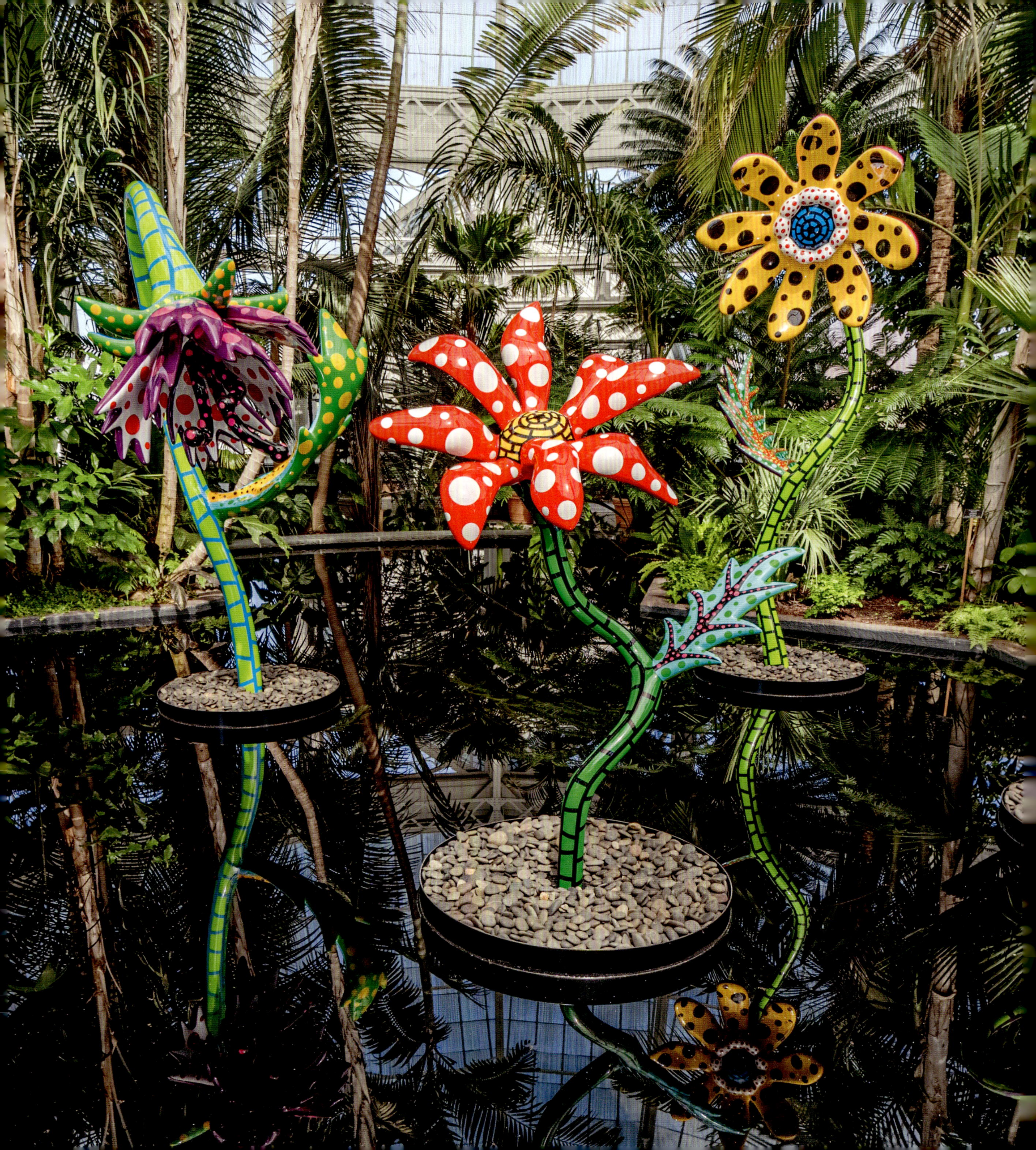

Karen Daubmann

KUSAMA IN THE GARDEN

One day, after gazing at a pattern of red flowers on the tablecloth, I looked up to see that the ceiling, the windows, and the columns seemed to be plastered with the same red floral pattern. I saw the entire room, my entire body, and the entire universe covered with red flowers, and in that instant my soul was obliterated and I was restored, returned to infinity, to eternal time and absolute space.

— Yayoi Kusama[1]

previous
My Soul Blooms Forever
(detail), 2019
Installation view, The New
York Botanical Garden, 2021

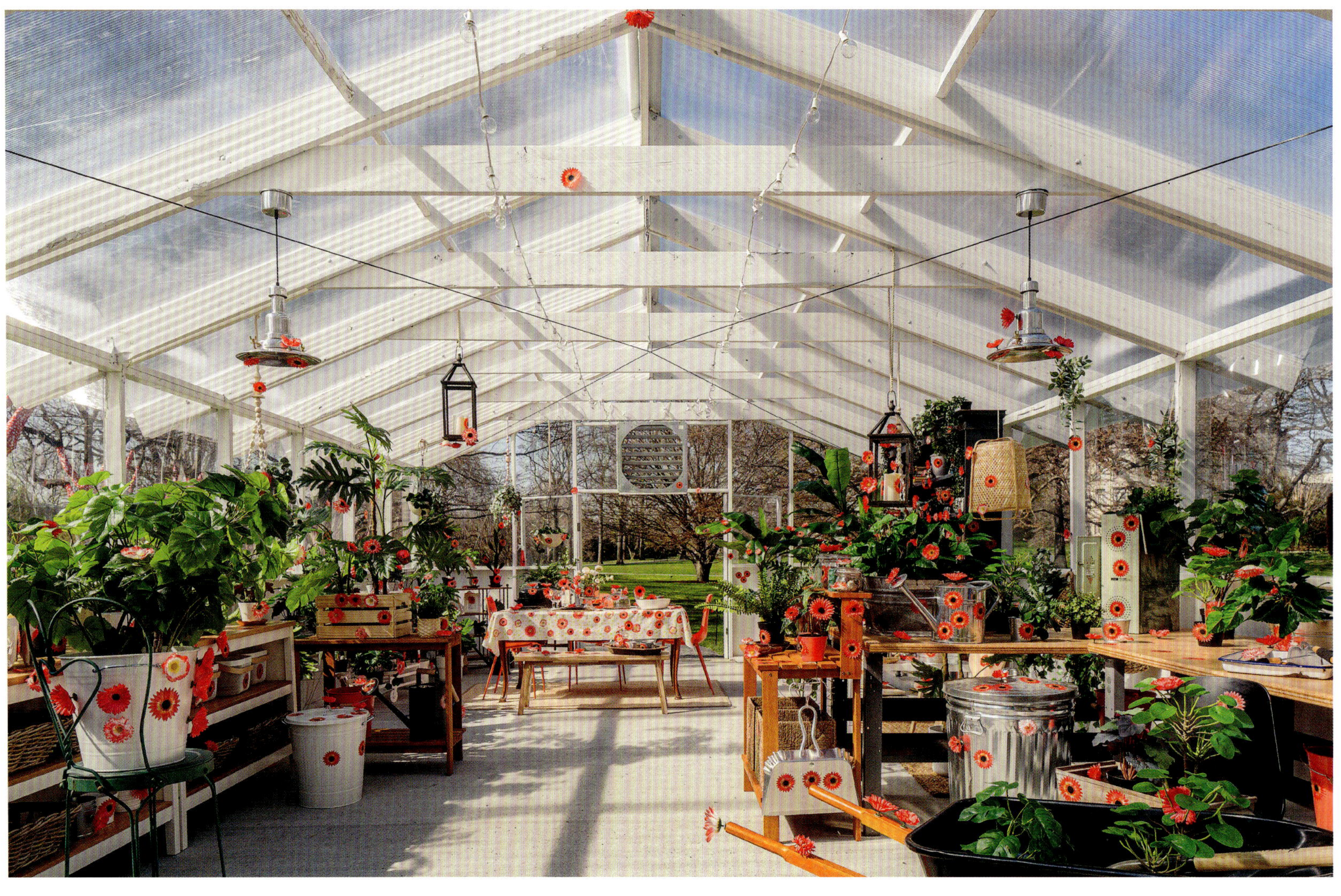

AS A VISITOR ENTERS THE GREENHOUSE, SHELVES ON EITHER SIDE hold potted plants. Pots and other gardening supplies are laid out on a workbench, and a tool cabinet houses trowels and other gardening tools. A table draped with cloth adorned with flowers invites the visitor to take a seat. All around, flowers in shades of pink and coral are gradually overtaking every surface, as if the pattern on the tablecloth has come alive.

Yayoi Kusama's *Obliteration Rooms* enlist the viewer in her artistic practice of enveloping and obscuring the object, generally the contents of a fully furnished domestic space, which are covered with colorful stickers until the entire space dissolves in a sea of polka dots. *Flower Obsession* (2017/2021; **FIG. 1**), shown for the first time in a greenhouse at The New York Botanical Garden, speaks to Kusama's beginnings as an artist and some of the most enduring themes in her prolific body of work. In childhood, she spent her days in the production houses and fields of her family's seed nursery, studying and sketching the plants she observed, as evidenced in archival photographs of her maternal grandfather, her father (**FIG. 2**), and her extended family of nurserymen in greenhouses much like the one on view at the Botanical Garden. Here, each visitor is given a sticker in the shape of a flower and invited to place it anywhere inside the structure. Over the course of the exhibition, every surface will be completely covered with accumulated poppies, gerbera daisies, and other ornamental blooms. The artist has likened her paintings, sculptures, and installations, in which patterns and forms spread to all available surfaces, to a creative embodiment of the vivid hallucinations she has experienced since childhood. In *Flower Obsession*, the visitor becomes a participant, re-enacting the artist's vision in flowers, while conjuring the environment in which the artist's fascination with nature's patterns and proliferations first emerged. In works such as this one, nature is not merely the subject of Kusama's attention, it is a palpable life force.

The New York Botanical Garden, a 250-acre National Historic Landmark site with fifty gardens and collections, is the perfect setting for the consideration of Kusama's cosmic vision of the natural world. The scale of the landscape and the breadth of the living collections complement the variety of forms and subjects in Kusama's art, and together with the Botanical Garden's rich expertise in plant study and cultivation, imbue her art with new meaning. The works in turn cast the landscape in a new light. Velvety green lawns and the scaffolding of historic trees against the wide-open sky create a panoramic backdrop. Kusama's vision is concerned with the patterns found in nature—those that are visible to the naked eye and those that are hidden—in microscopic organisms, in the bark and trunks of trees, in the form and markings on flowers, in the constellations

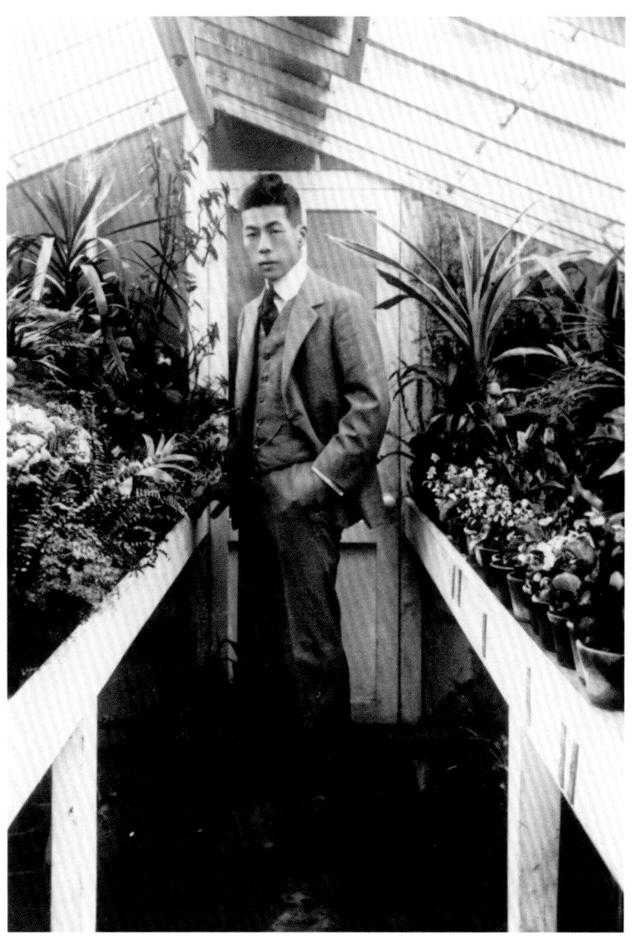

Fig. 1 (opposite)
Flower Obsession, 2017/2021
Interior view, participatory installation in progress, The New York Botanical Garden, 2021
Glasshouse, furniture, household objects, plastic stickers, and silk flowers
Dimensions variable
Courtesy of Ota Fine Arts

Fig. 2 (above)
Kamon, father of Yayoi Kusama, ca. 1920s

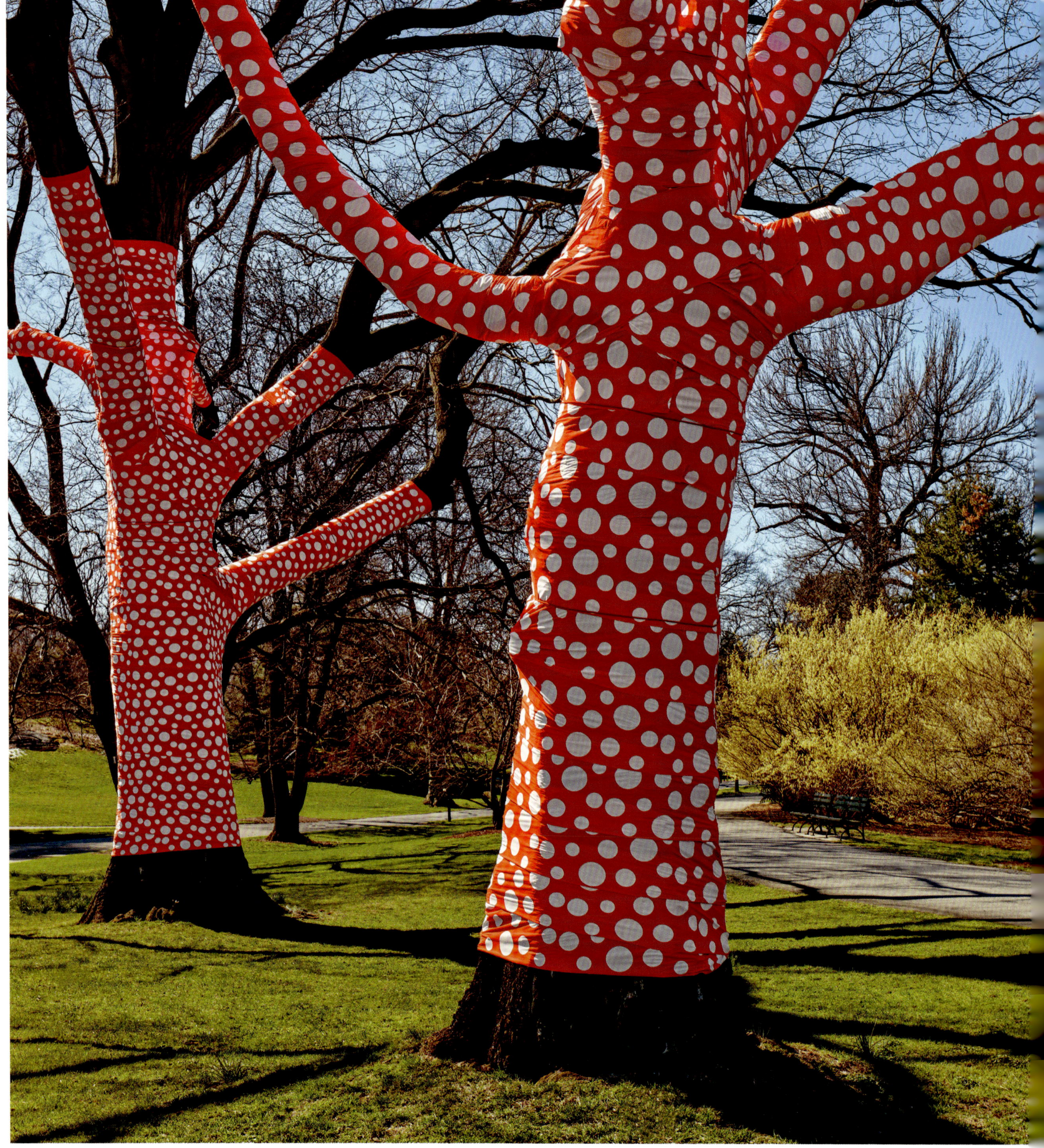

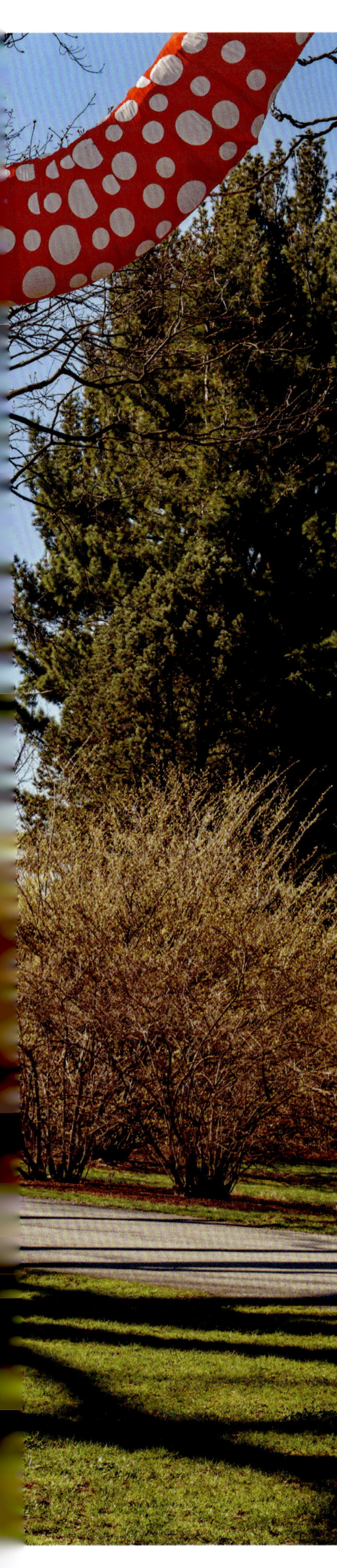

Fig. 3
Ascension of Polka Dots on the Trees, 2002/2021
Installation view, The New York Botanical Garden, 2021
Printed polyester fabric, bungees, and aluminum staples installed on existing trees
Site-specific installation, dimensions variable
Collection of the artist

Fig. 4 (following)
Dancing Pumpkin, 2020
Installation view, The New York Botanical Garden, 2021
Urethane paint on bronze
196⅞ × 116⅞ × 117¼ in.
(500 × 296.9 × 297.8 cm)
Courtesy of Ota Fine Arts, Victoria Miro, and David Zwirner

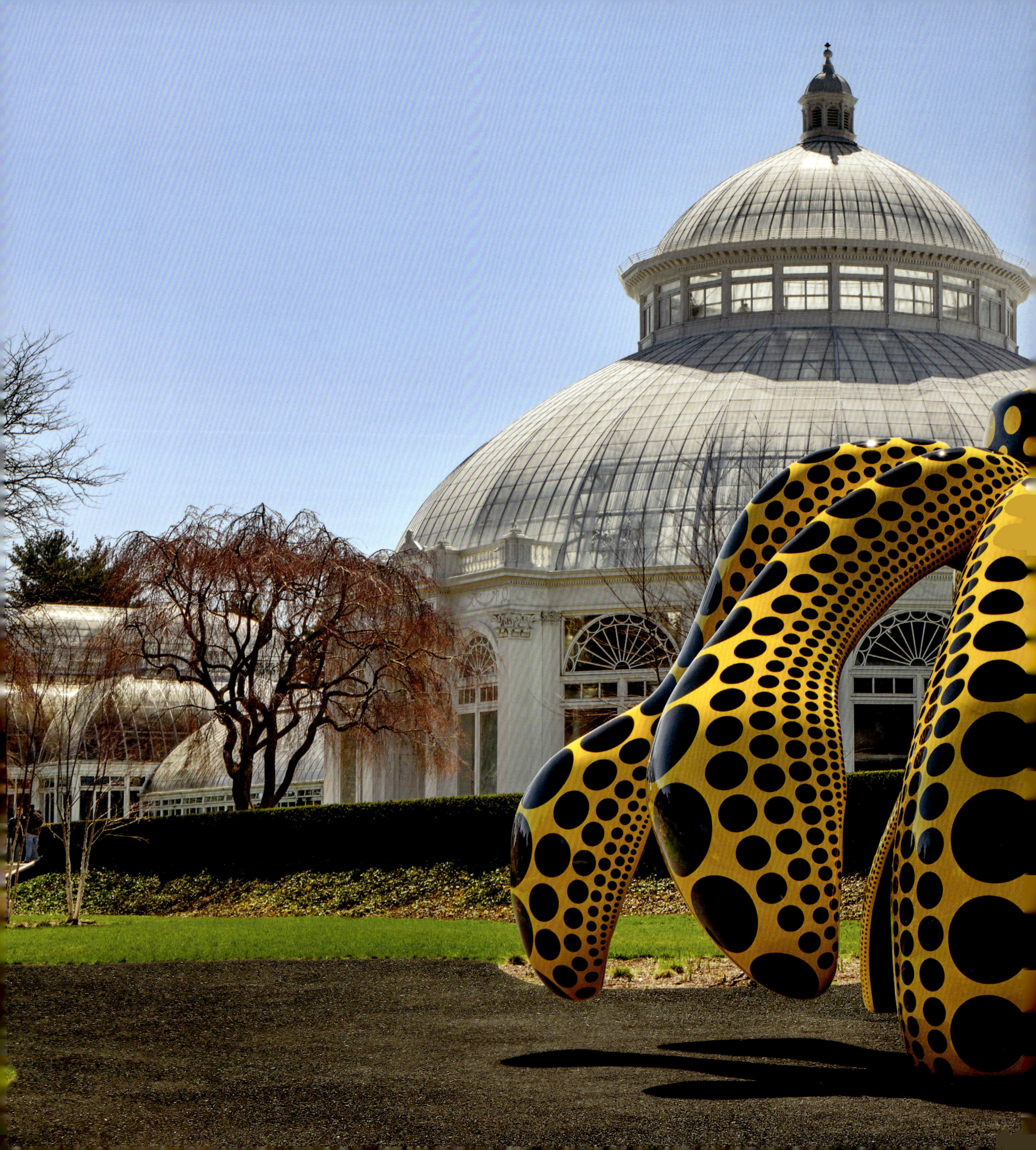

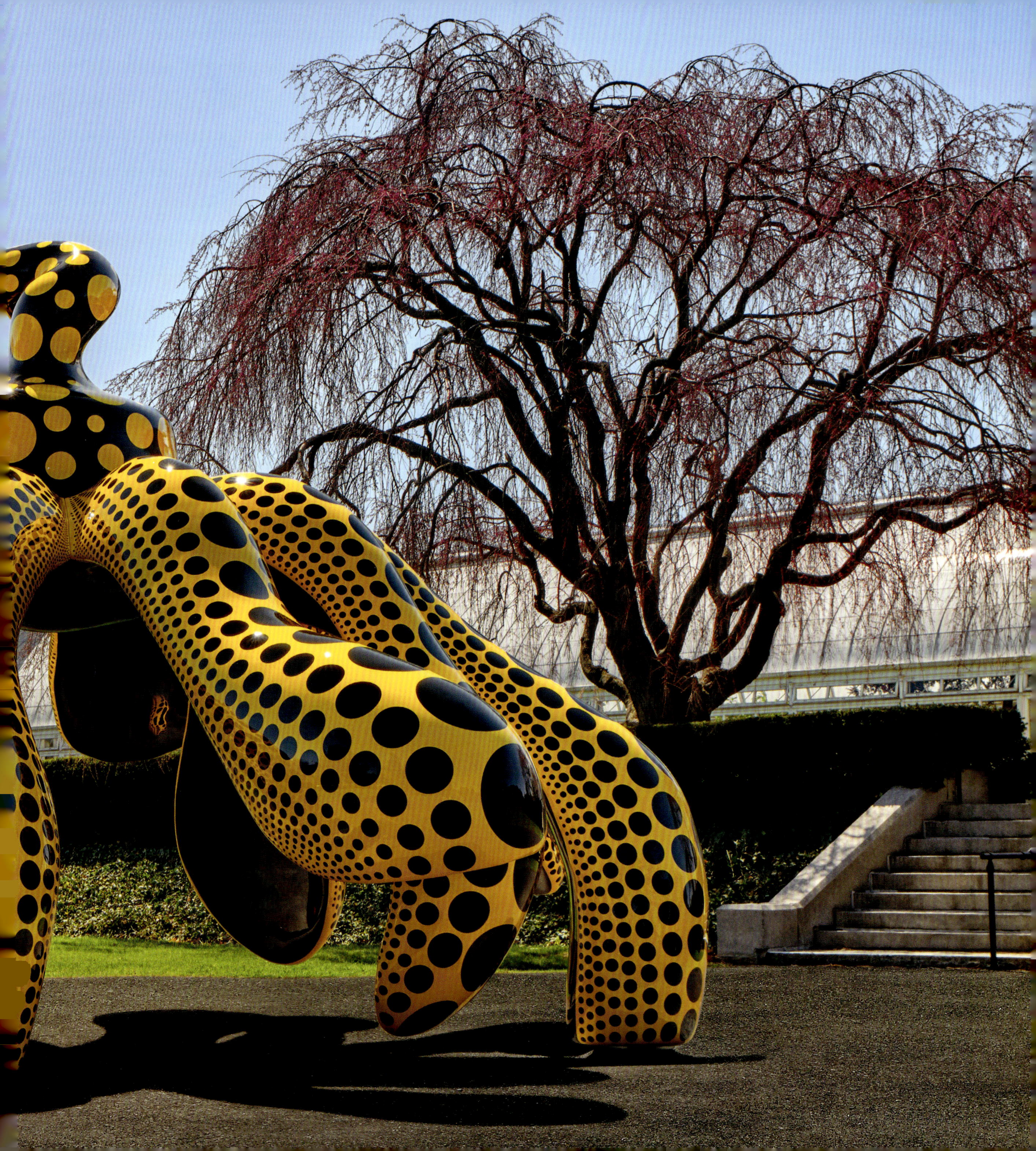

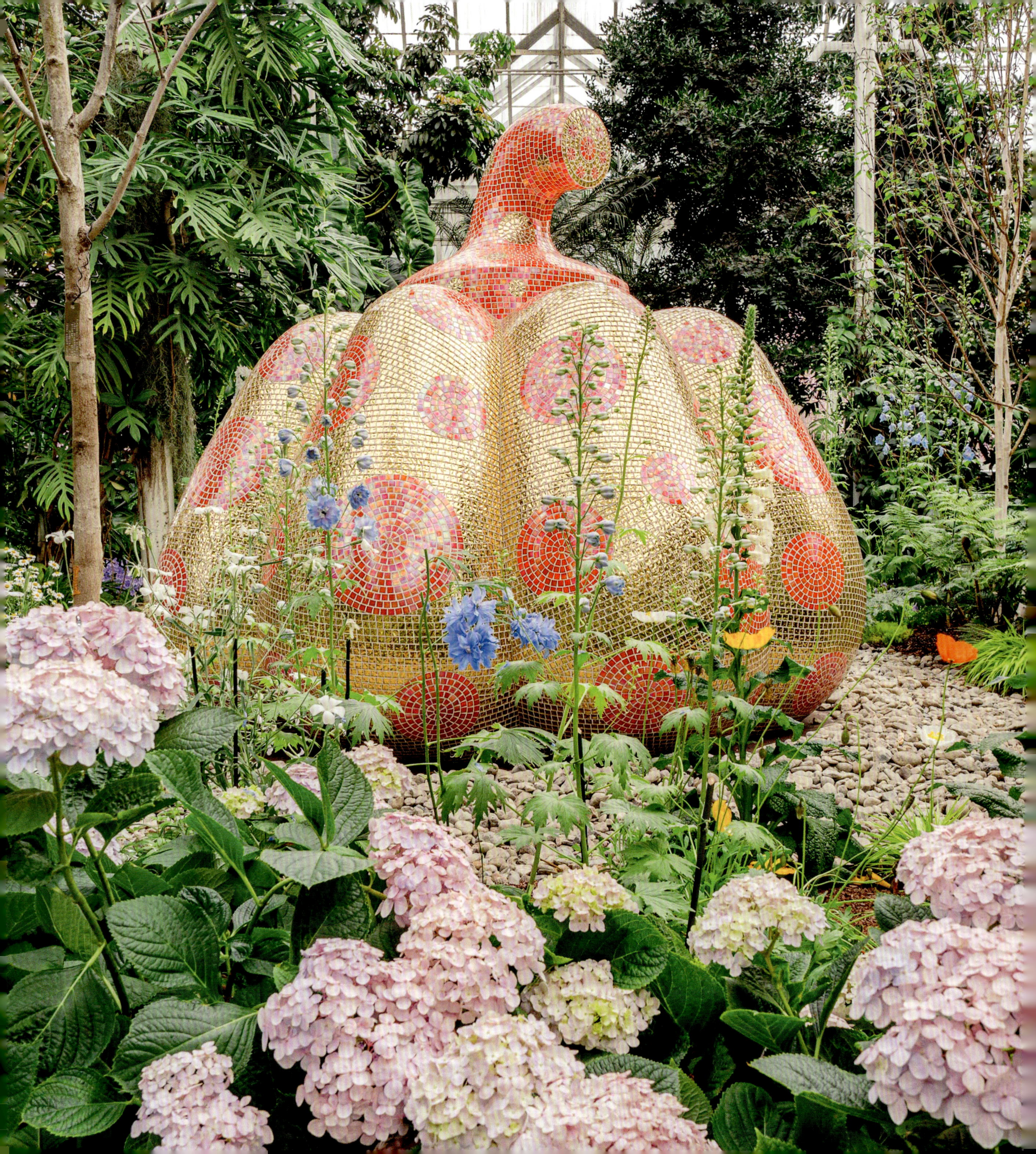

Fig. 5
Starry Pumpkin, 2015
Installation view, The New York Botanical Garden, 2021
Fiberglass-reinforced plastic, tiles, and resin
71¼ × 79½ × 80 in.
(181 × 202 × 203 cm)
Courtesy of Ota Fine Arts

overhead. Wrapping mature specimens of oak and other shade trees in *Ascension of Polka Dots on the Trees* (2002/2021; **FIG. 3**) at the Garden at once emphasizes their forms and obscures their distinguishing characteristics beneath a pattern of dots that overtakes everything in its path, suggesting otherwise invisible, universal cellular structures. Shifts in scale from the micro- to the macrocosmic are a hallmark of Kusama's work, and experiencing them *en plein air* makes them all the more powerful. At the Garden, the exterior of *Infinity Mirrored Room—Illusion Inside the Heart* (2020; pages 118–19) reflects grasses, poppies, verbena, dahlias, and other colorful plants featured in Kusama's work or observed in the archival photos of her family's seed nursery. Ornamental grasses, sky, and towering trees are repeated in the surface of the structure. Stepping inside, visitors are enveloped in darkness punctuated by endlessly repeating constellations of lights in every imaginable color. Unlike many of the artist's other *Infinity Mirrored Rooms*, which incorporate LEDs, natural light entering through perforations in the mirrored surface creates this effect at the Garden, transformed by the moment with the passage of clouds, the intensity of the sunlight, and the angles of shadows, offering ever-changing glimpses of Kusama's view of the cosmos. By placing her work in a garden, nature becomes more than a subject; it is an active, vibrant source of artistic energy and meaning.

Gardens, fields, and greenhouses are where Kusama first discovered plants that tested the bounds of her imagination, and creating for outdoor settings allows the artist nearly limitless freedom of scale. Segmented so that it appears to be balancing on eleven legs, ready to creep away into the surrounding landscape, *Dancing Pumpkin* (2020; **FIG. 4**) towers above visitors amid a planting of white birch trees and alyssum in front of the Enid A. Haupt Conservatory. The setting, achieved in New York's climate with river birch, a North American species of white-barked birch, was inspired by the forests of *Betula platyphylla* in the mountains near the artist's birthplace of Matsumoto, Japan. The pumpkin quite literally assumes the larger-than-life presence it holds as a recurring motif in Kusama's universe. Inside, *Starry Pumpkin* (2015; **FIG. 5**), a pink- and gold-dotted mosaic pumpkin emerges from a clearing in the center of a grove of serviceberry and birch trees, surrounded by an assortment of foxgloves, bellflowers, and ornamental onions in spring, followed later by daisies, blue globe thistle, and pale-purple coneflowers. Inspired by Kusama's earliest memory of coming upon a pumpkin growing among a tangle of zinnias in a field at her family's nursery, this installation allows the visitor to experience the awe of the artist's moment of discovery. As the seasons change, the plantings evolve, with poppies and spring ephemerals transitioning

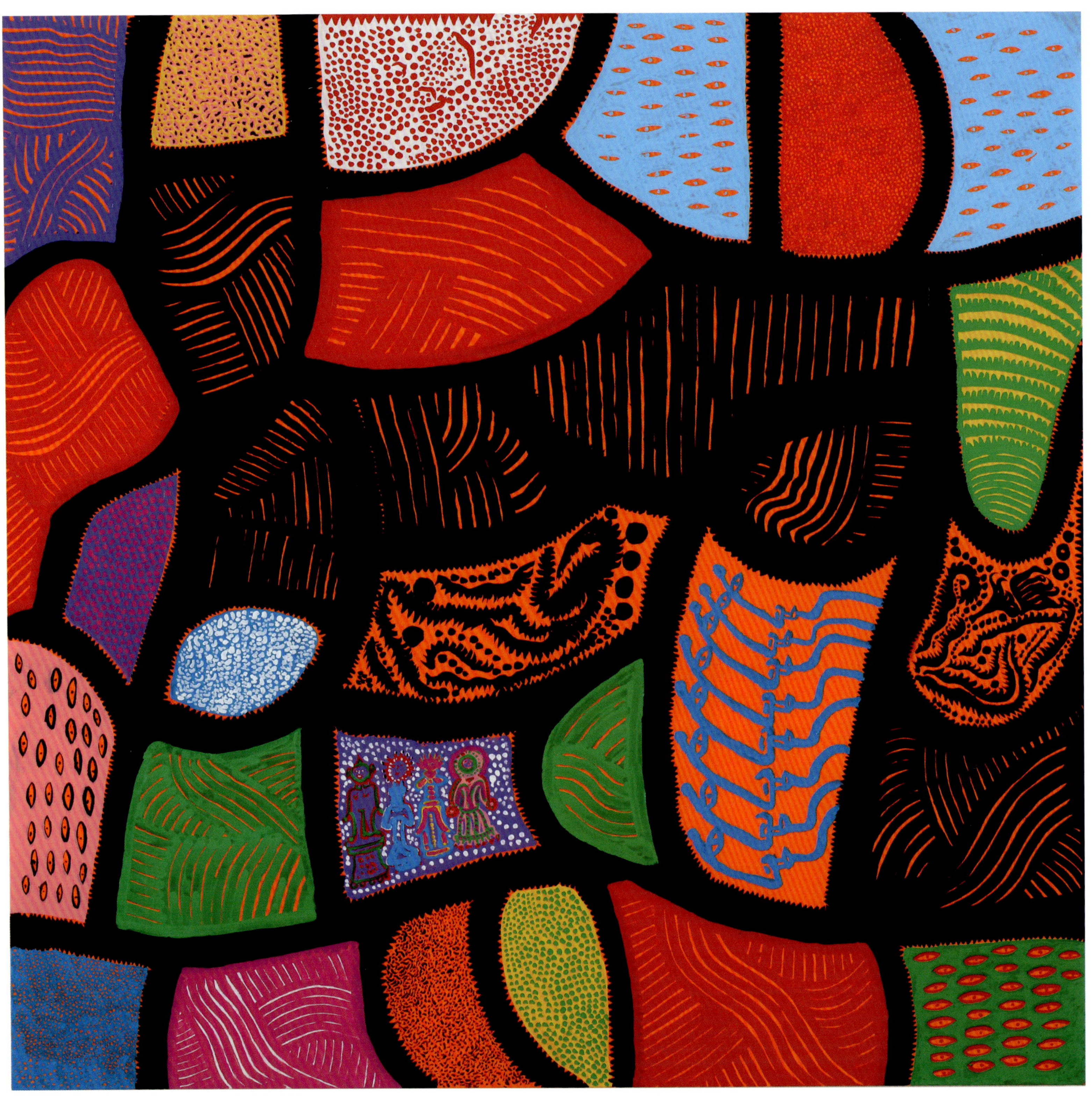

to mullein and sage during the heat of summer. In autumn, pale-pink, buttery-yellow, and creamy-white chrysanthemums trail through the shrubby growth, complementing the iridescent mosaic surface of *Starry Pumpkin*.

Throughout the landscape in autumn, Botanical Garden horticulturists will incorporate displays of pumpkins—from the year's giant pumpkin record holders to the smallest, most colorful, and most unusual squashes and gourds. Taking inspiration from Kusama's preferred palette, displays will include cultivars such as 'Mellow Yellow', a bright-yellow round pumpkin; 'Red Kuri', a teardrop-shaped winter squash; and 'Black Futsu', a deeply ribbed black Japanese squash. Cited by Kusama for their "generous unpretentiousness" and solid "spiritual balance," pumpkins will mark the changing of the seasons across the Garden landscape.[2]

Kusama's *Alone, Buried in a Flower Garden* (2014; **FIG. 6**) inspired a colorful patchwork planting in the Conservatory that changes with the seasons. The painting, from the artist's *My Eternal Soul* series, calls to mind an aerial view of a garden with colorful plots divided by black paths. To design this garden, planting plans that emulate the bold colors, patterns, and textures of Kusama's painting were created for each season. Black charcoal divides the masses of color provided by salvia, ageratum, lantana, and other annuals, while coleus, begonias, and other plants with polka-dotted leaves naturally display the patterns and forms Kusama favors while adding variety and texture. In keeping with the Garden's long-standing cultural partnership with Shinjuku Gyoen National Garden in Tokyo, Japanese-style trained chrysanthemums will be set in fall among brightly colored ornamental grasses such as Japanese blood grass and Japanese forest grass. Red and orange *ogiku*, chrysanthemums trained to yield one large flower atop each long, slender stem, as well as *ozukuri*, thousand-bloom chrysanthemums grown from a single slim stem, will bring a hint of ancient tradition to a garden inspired by Kusama's singular contemporary vision.

Less abstract, Kusama's monumental *Hymn of Life—Tulips* (2007; **FIG. 7**) dominates the Hardy Pool in the Conservatory Courtyard: impossibly colored and patterned, sinewy stems and foliage support equally uncanny flowers. In planters surrounding the pool, thousands of spring tulips will gradually give way to artemesia and salvias as the seasons pass. The flowers of *My Soul Blooms Forever* (2019; page 10) are similarly stunning set against the backdrop of stately trees in the Conservatory's Palms of the World Gallery, larger-than-life flowers beneath an enormous, historic cloche.

Naturalistic settings are where many of Kusama's works are shown to their greatest advantage. In the Native Plant Garden, more than one thousand stainless steel orbs float in the pool, moved by

Fig. 6
Alone, Buried in a Flower Garden, 2014
Acrylic on canvas
76⅜ × 76⅜ in. (194 × 194 cm)
Collection of the artist

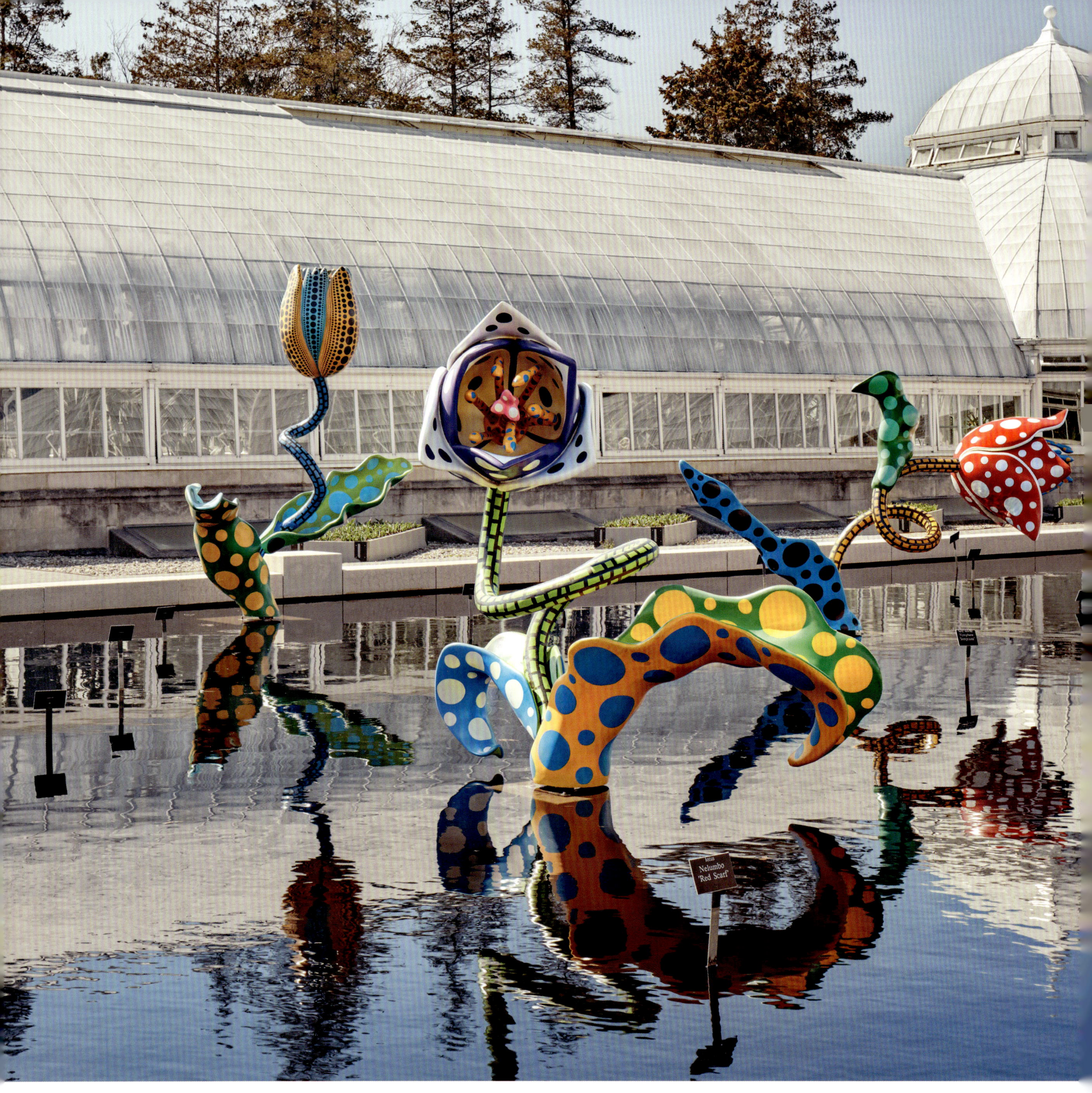
lotus
Nelumbo
'Red Scarf'

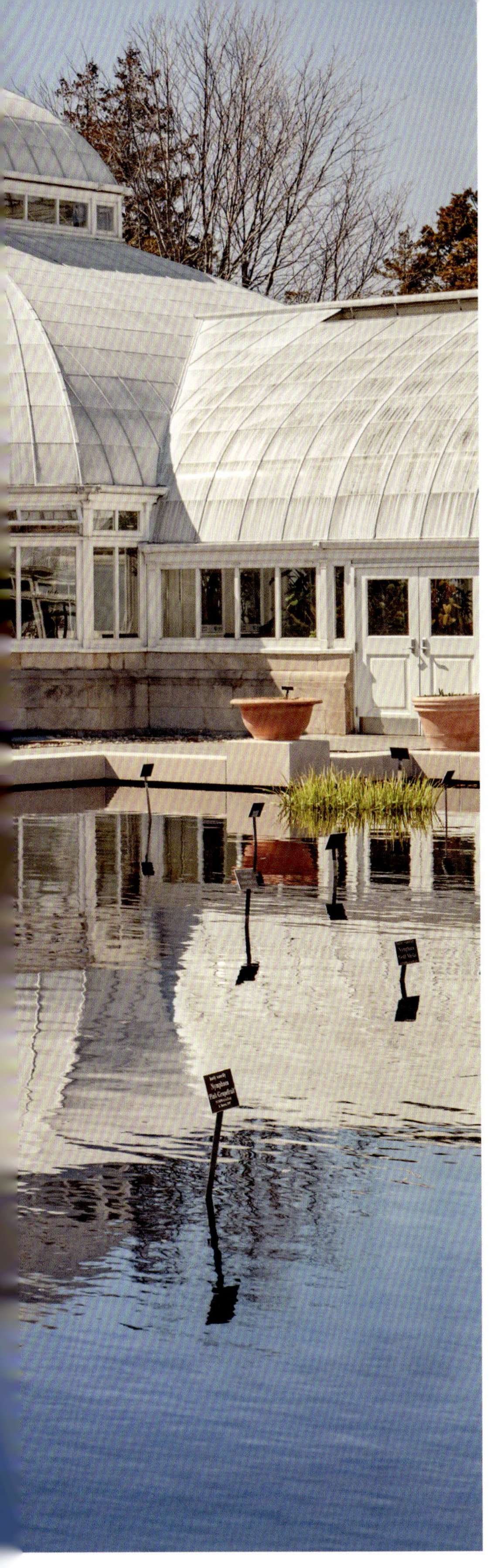

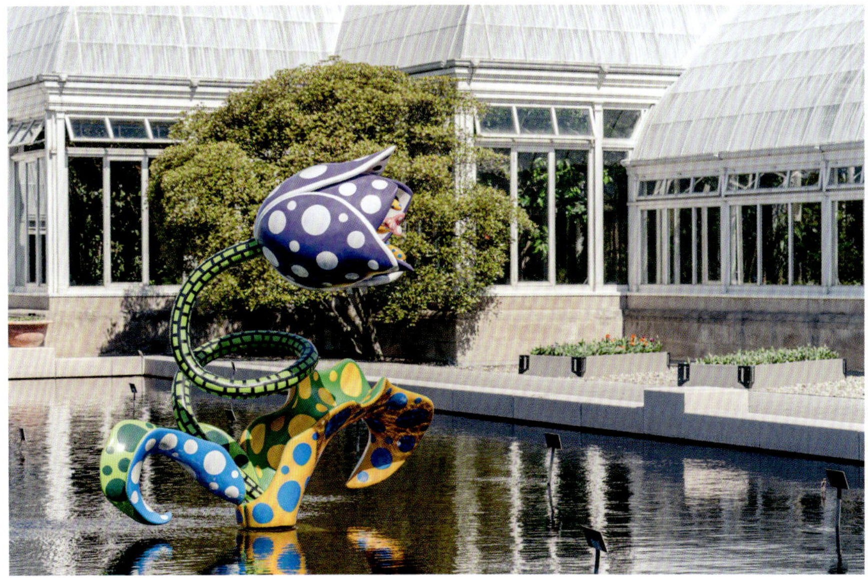

the current and the wind, and reflecting the sky, the water, and the wetland plants swaying at the water's edge (pages 114–15). The sounds of wind in the trees and flowing water are occasionally punctuated by the gentle clinking of the spheres when they are momentarily brought together. Kusama's earliest outdoor work, *Narcissus Garden* was first staged as a critique at the Venice Biennale in 1966. There, mirrored balls were arranged on a lawn near the Italian Pavilion and the artist stood among them with a signboard reading "Your Narcissism For Sale," selling the spheres for two dollars each. Since then, the work has been exhibited around the globe, in galleries and outdoor settings. In the Garden landscape, Kusama's reflective spheres form new patterns and shapes with natural shifts of wind and water, and they offer new, ephemeral reflections with the passage of time. A work that premiered as a pointed critique of the commodification of the art world becomes an immersive meditation on the ever-changing world around us, an opportunity to "forget yourself," in the artist's own words, in a moment of serene contemplation of the wonders of the natural world.

Fig. 7 (opposite and above)
Hymn of Life—Tulips, 2007
Installation view, The New York Botanical Garden, 2021
Mixed media
3 elements, installation dimensions variable
Collection of the City of Beverly Hills

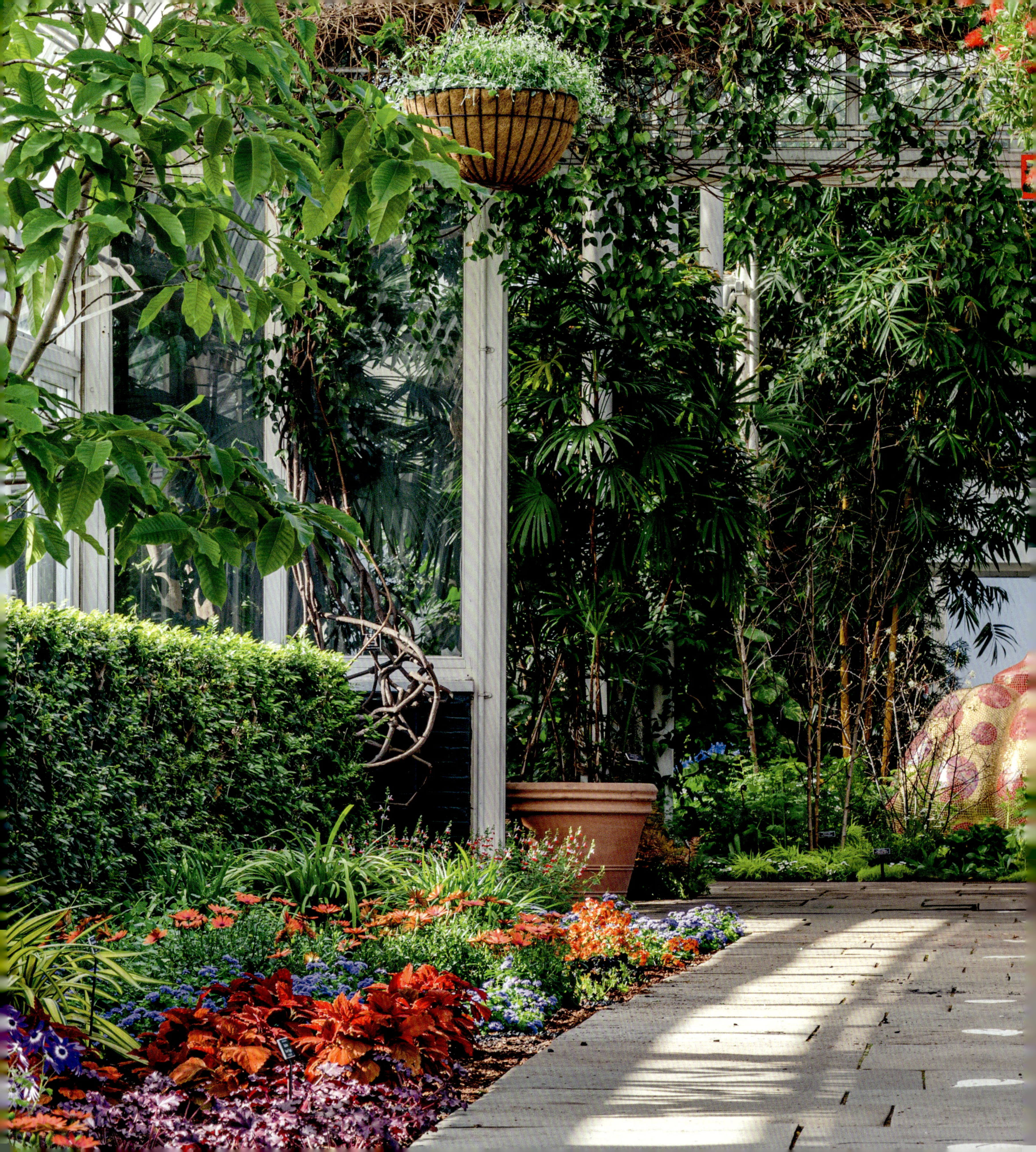

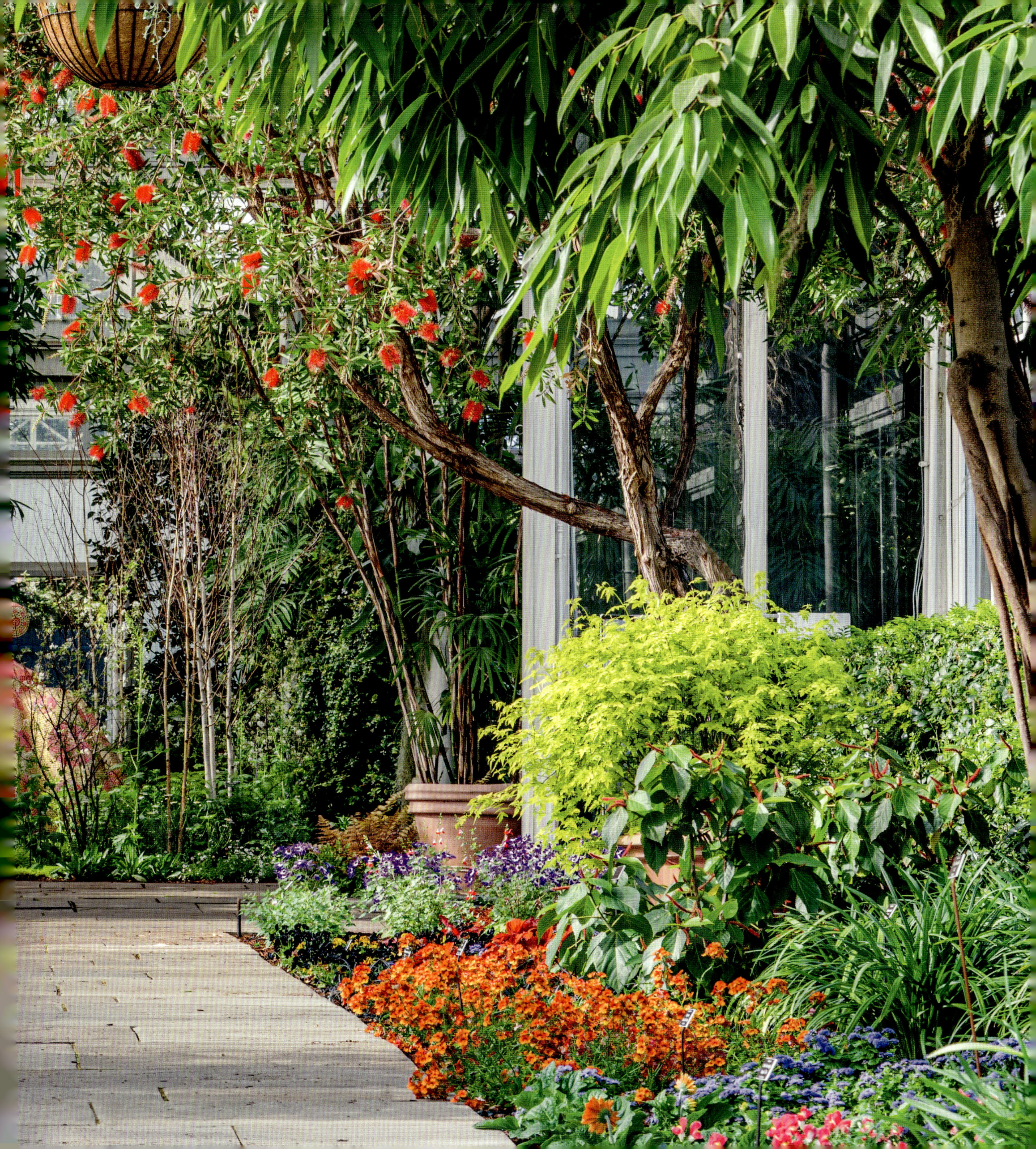

previous
Starry Pumpkin, 2015
Inside the Enid A. Haupt Conservatory, The New York Botanical Garden, 2021

opposite
Pumpkin, 2015
Sewn and stuffed fabric, acrylic, and metal
19⅝ × 25⅝ × 23⅝ in.
(50 × 65 × 60 cm)
Collection of the artist

Early Spring, 1979
Ink and watercolor on paper
20⅛ × 26 in. (51.1 × 65.8 cm)
Collection of the artist

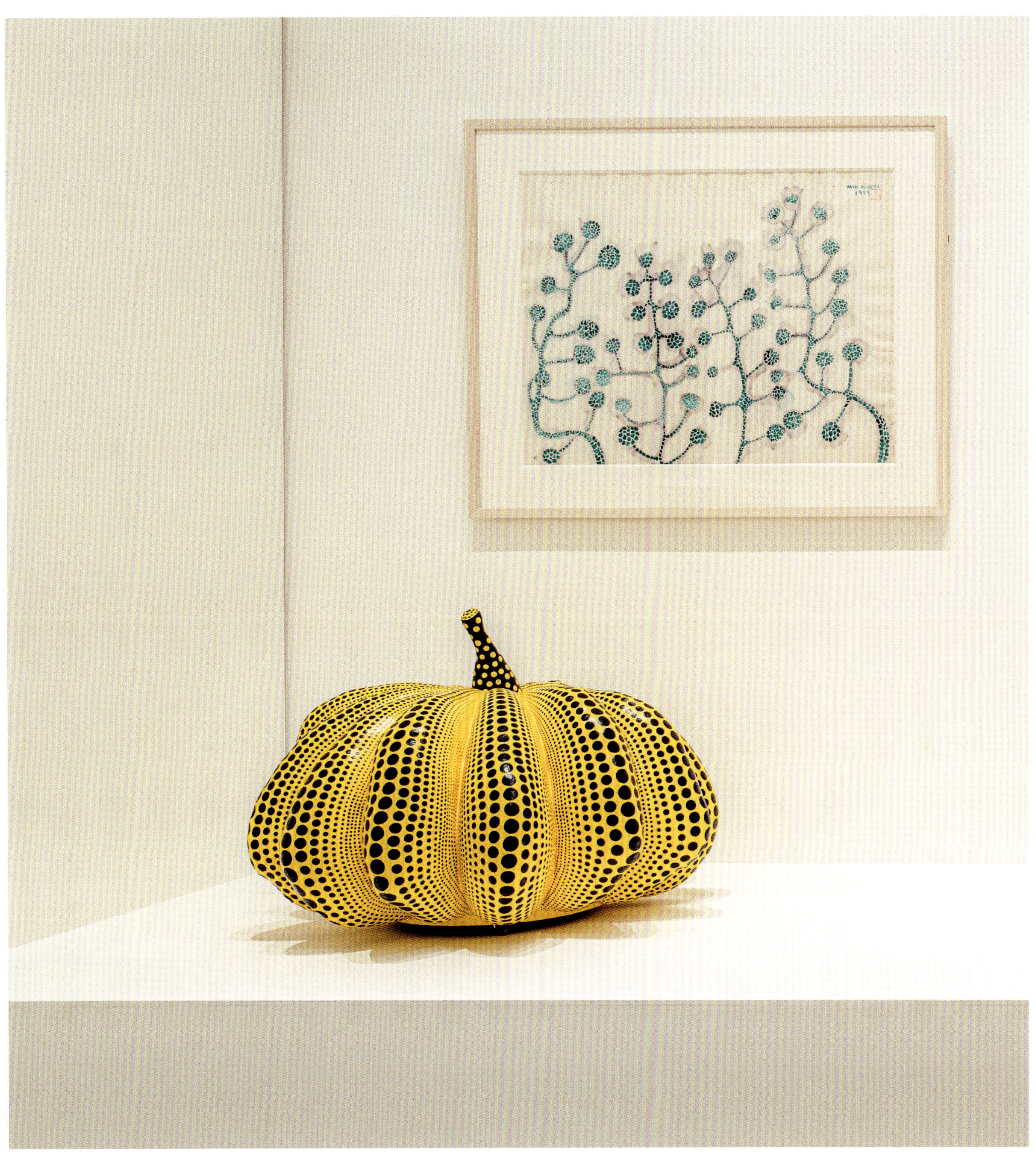

right
The Sun Has Gone Down, I Am Scared as Much as Being Alone, 2016
Sewn and stuffed fabric, acrylic, and metal
18⅞ × 17¾ × 17¾ in.
(48 × 45 × 45 cm)
Collection of the artist

center
Pumpkin, 2016
Sewn and stuffed fabric, acrylic, and metal
18⅞ × 17¾ × 17¾ in.
(48 × 45 × 45 cm)
Collection of the artist

far right
Suppressing the Burning Desire for Death, 2016
Sewn and stuffed fabric, acrylic, and metal
19½ × 19½ × 19½ in.
(50 × 50 × 50 cm)
Collection of the artist

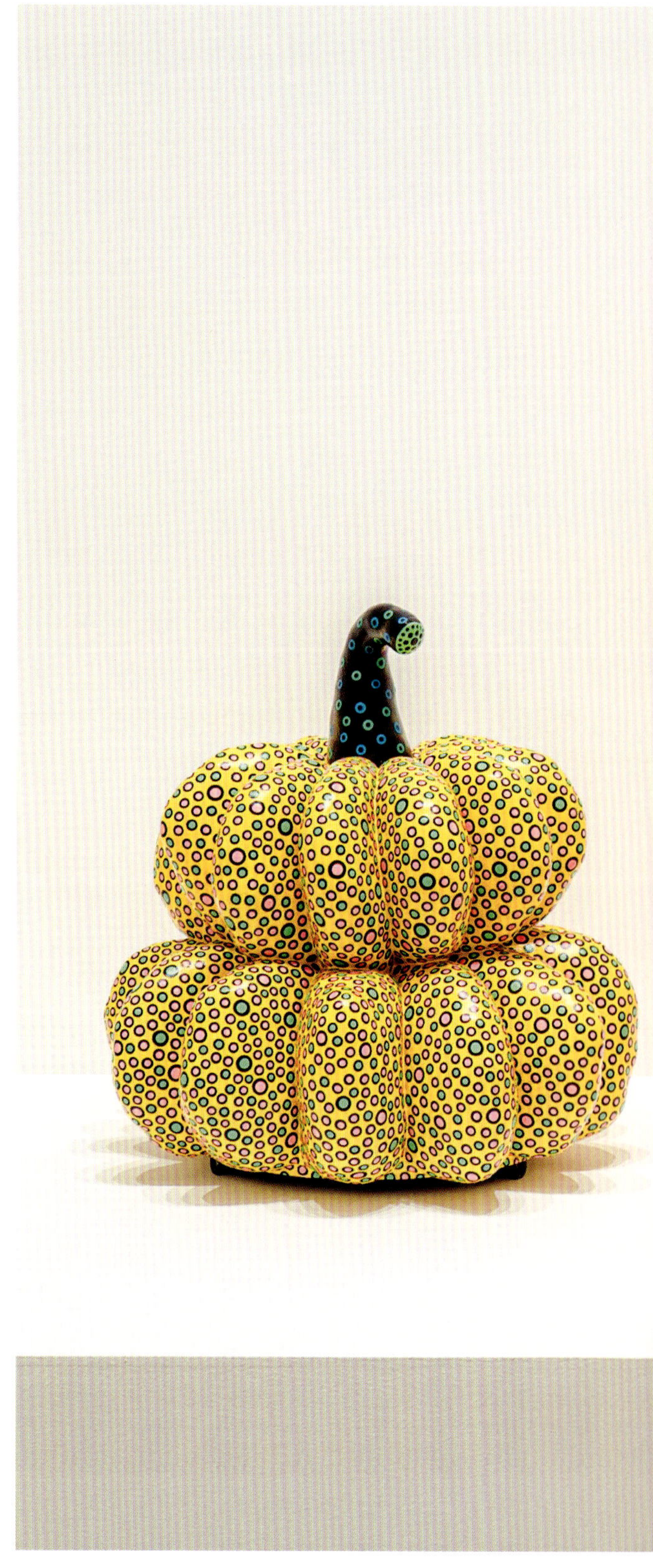

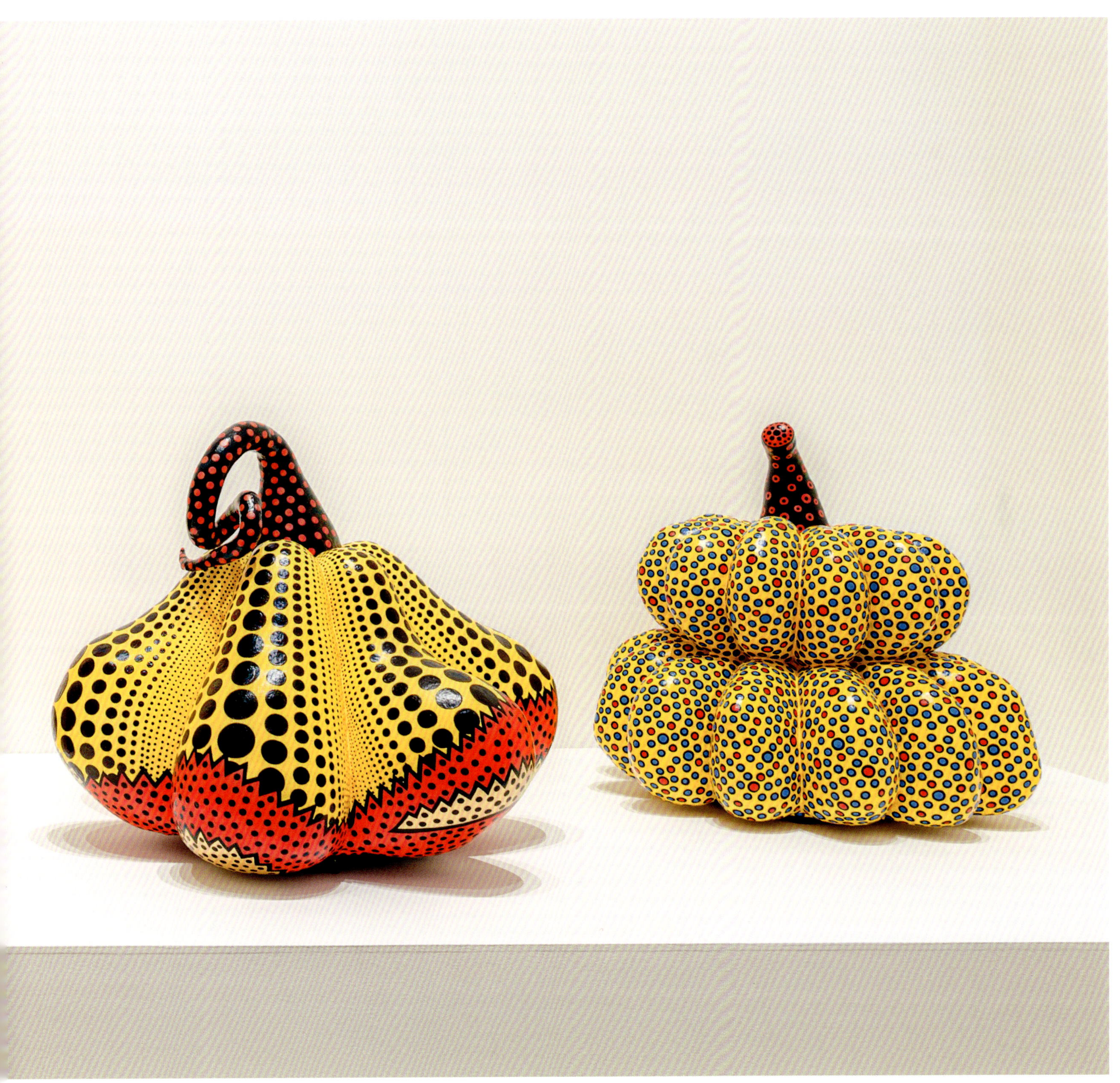

Land of Glory, 2014
Acrylic on canvas
76⅜ × 76⅜ in. (194 × 194 cm)
Collection of the artist

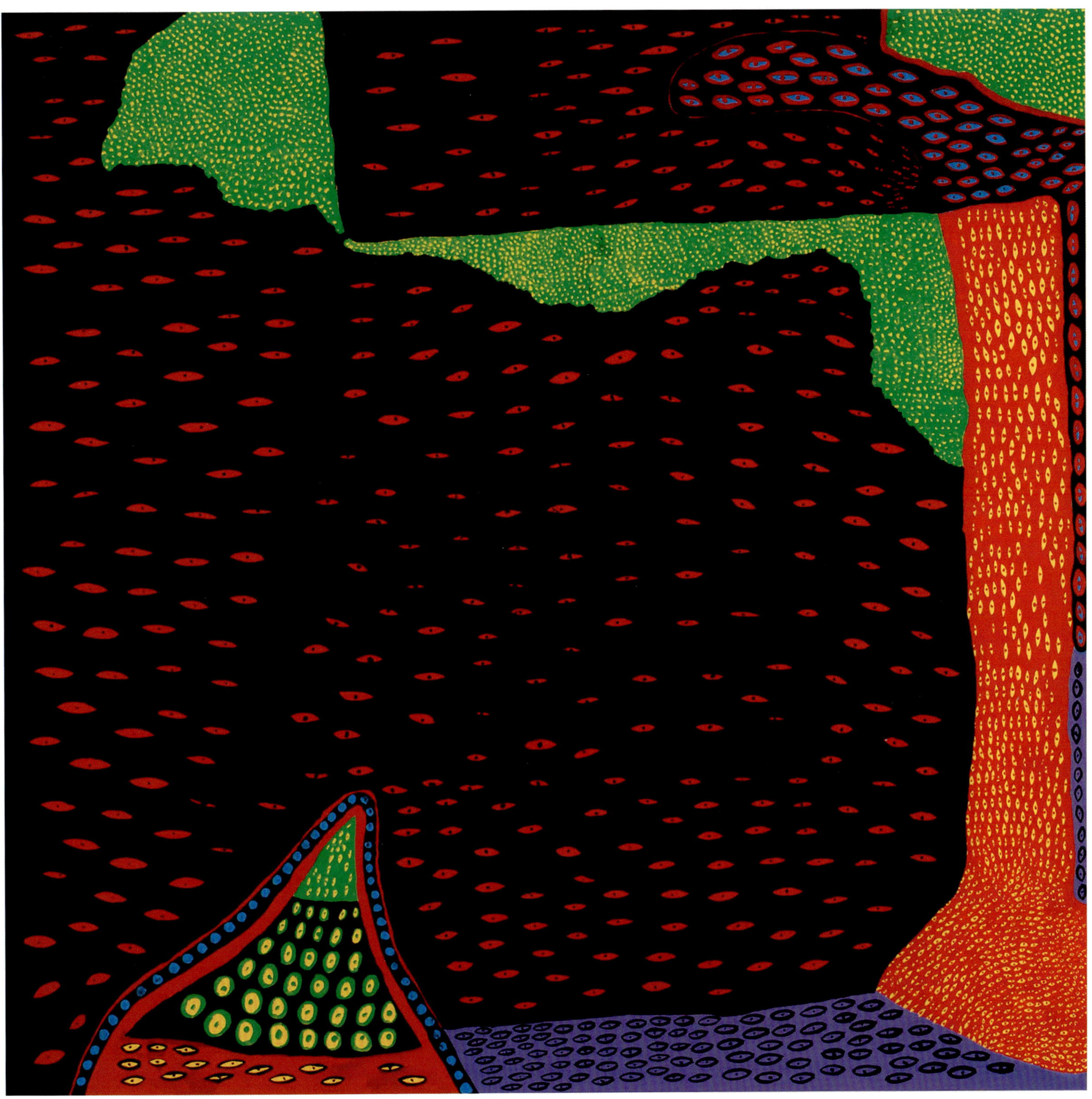

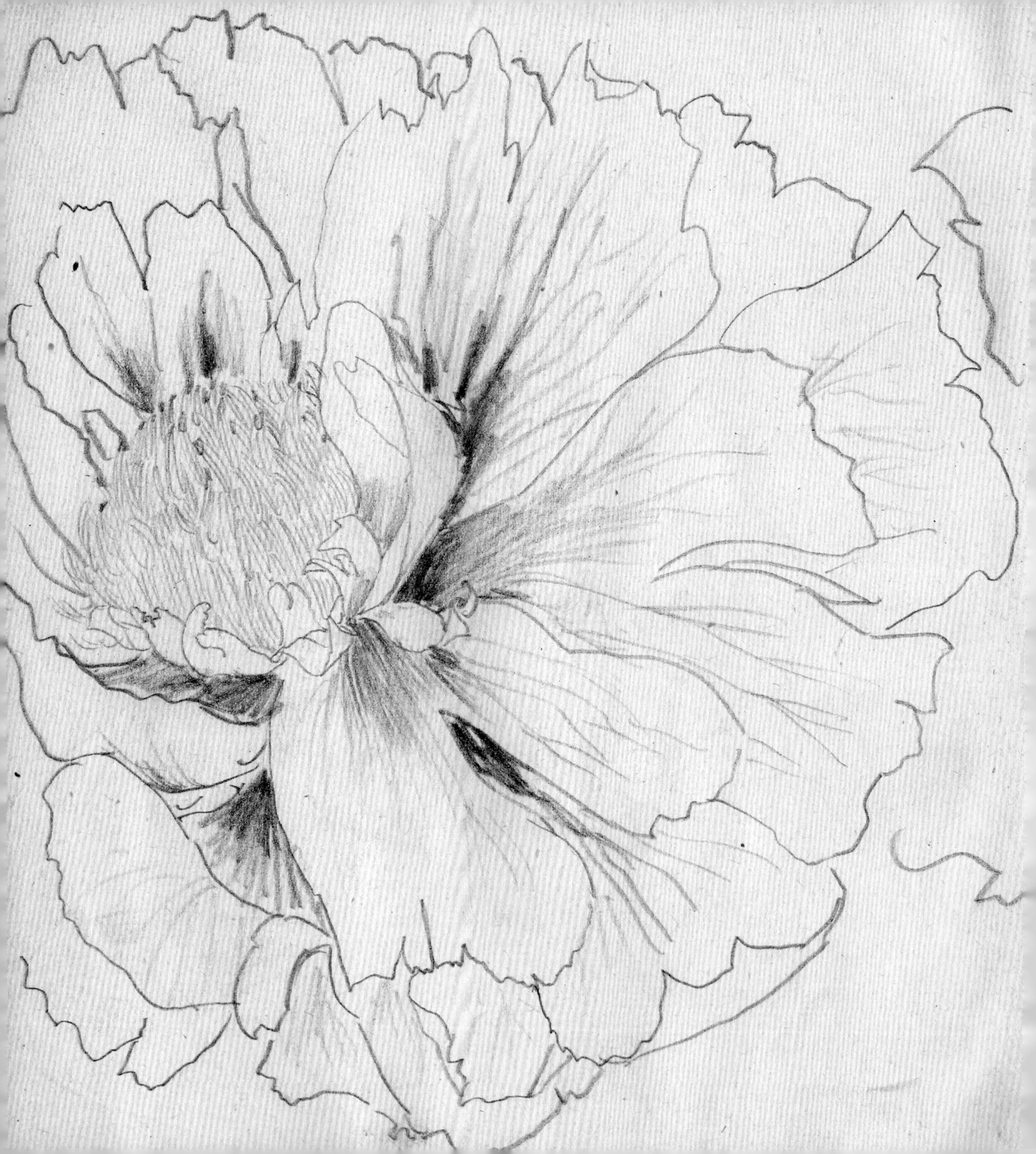

"PROVISIONS OF NATURE"

THE BOTANICAL ART OF YAYOI KUSAMA

The first thing I painted was . . . flowers. There are no objects more interesting. How vast and boundless the provisions of nature!

—Yayoi Kusama[1]

previous
Untitled (Flower Sketches)
(detail), 1945
Pencil in notebook
8½ × 11⅞ in. (21.5 × 30 cm)
Collection of the artist

IN JUNE 1945, SIXTEEN-YEAR-OLD YAYOI KUSAMA FILLED EVERY PAGE of a sketchbook with extraordinarily detailed drawings of the flowers, foliage, and stems of peonies. Kusama's family owned and operated a large regional plant nursery in Matsumoto, the city in the mountains of Japan's Nagano Prefecture, which supplied plants, seeds, and cut flowers to many parts of the country. The artist recalls growing up among her family's glasshouses and growing fields (**FIG. 1**), as well as seminal moments like her first sighting of a pumpkin and vivid memories of flowers, recurring subjects in her extensive body of work.[2] "Each day a crowd of workers came to collect the seeds of violets or zinnias or whatever it might be, for resale all over Japan. We had six large hothouses, which were so rare in those days that sometimes groups of schoolchildren came on field trips to look at them."[3]

Throughout the sketchbook, Kusama exhibits her keen powers of observation and artistic skill in some fifty drawings of peonies. An auspicious flower that is counted among the most beautiful in Japanese culture, peonies have been cultivated in Asia for thousands of years, and they have often been represented in art. While peonies would traditionally have been depicted in peak bloom, Kusama's detailed drawings represent the plants at different phases of their growth cycle, from the unfurling of delicate new leaves to the voluptuous mature flowers to various stages of the wilting, withering, and decay that follow. The young artist captures fleeting moments of extreme beauty and those of gradual deterioration with equally fastidious attention to detail, at times even documenting with small notes the color of petals and stems; changing textures, as when she notes that the "fuzz growing on the blossoms is becoming more obvious" (**FIG. 2**); and the location where a new leaf will emerge from mature wood in a future growing season (**FIG. 3**).[4]

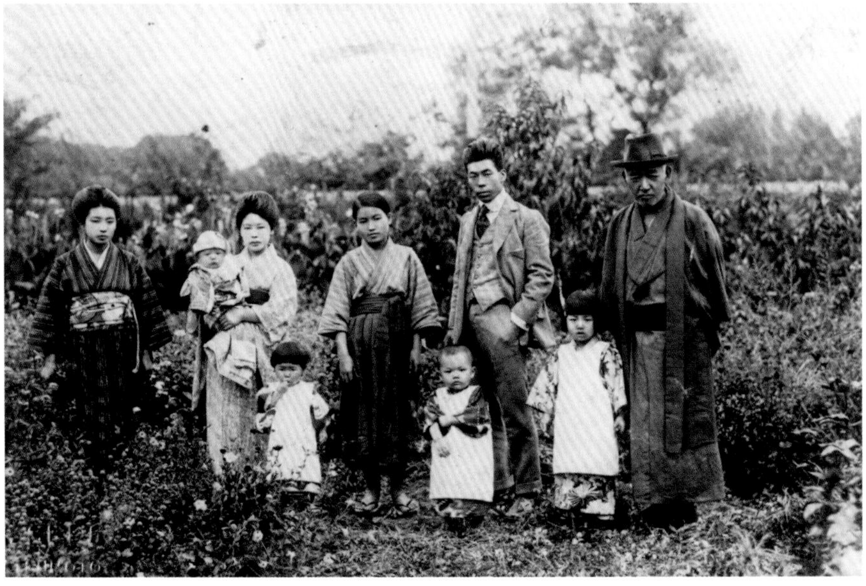

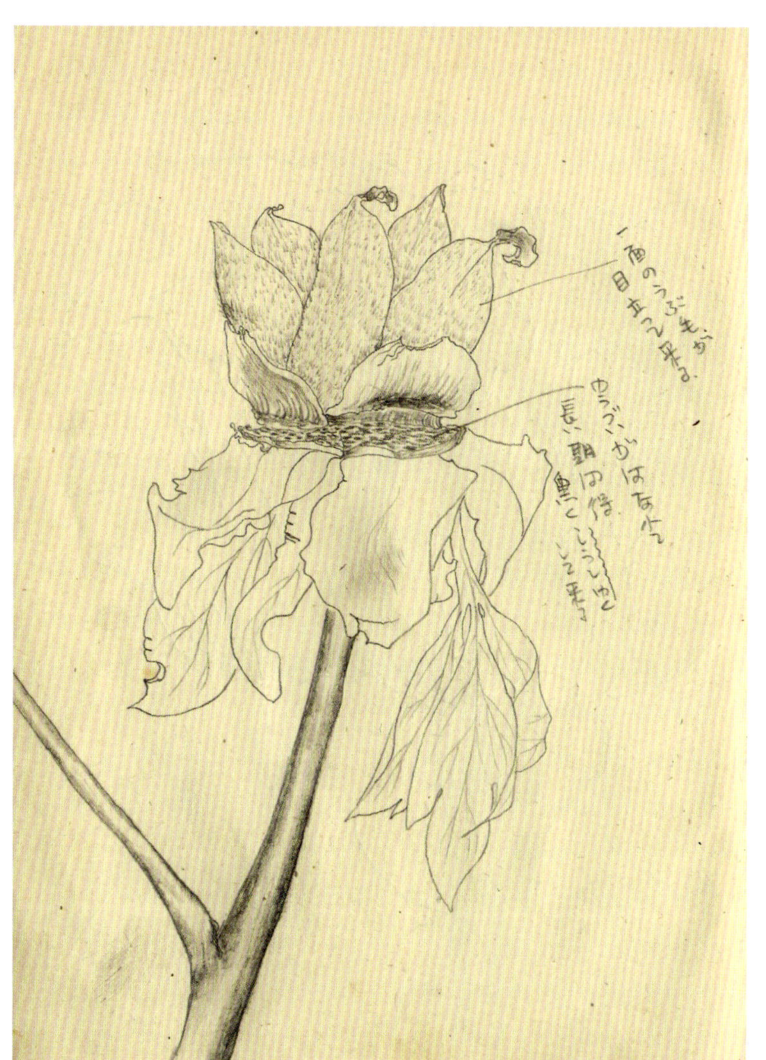

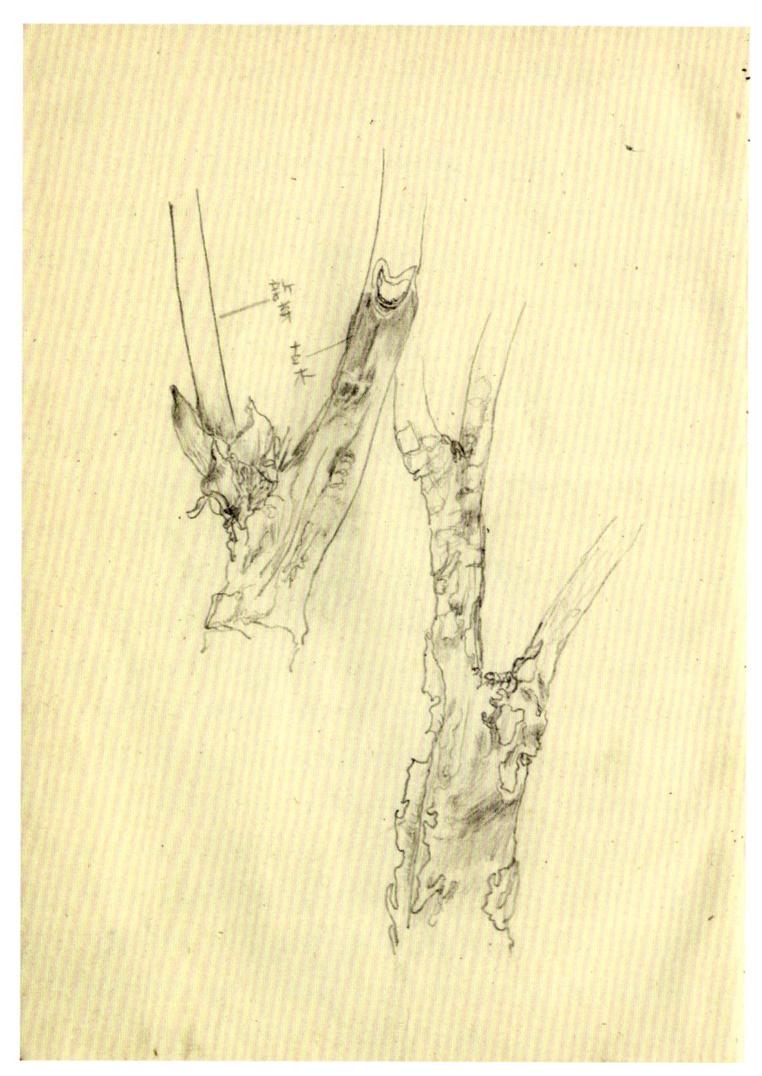

Fig. 1 (opposite)
Kusama family, ca. 1929

Figs. 2 and 3 (above)
Untitled (Flower Sketches)
(details), 1945
Pencil in notebook
8½ × 11⅞ in. (21.5 × 30 cm)
Collection of the artist

Filled during the dark final months of World War II, the sketchbook has been cited in interpreting the young artist's attention to the plants in stages of decline and decay. Kusama has written of her time sketching in nature as a source of solace and inspiration—and also fear and hallucination.[5] Like most Japanese teenagers, Kusama was conscripted to work in a factory making parachutes to outfit soldiers. Many people throughout the Japanese countryside were struggling with hunger during World War II.[6] The artist herself has written of the physical and psychological suffering of this period. Her choice and treatment of subject have also been attributed to the training she received, both at school and in private lessons, from Kakei (Teruo) Hibino, a formally trained *nihonga* artist. The strong contours and careful study that are evident in her sketches, as well her embrace of a more expressive subject and technique that are also seen in a new approach among *nihonga* practitioners, seem to support this theory.[7]

What makes the peony sketches most noteworthy when viewed as a series is what they reveal about not only Kusama's emotional state and her artistic training and skill, but also her deep knowledge of plants and their life cycles. The artist's attention to detail in studies of changing plant morphology throughout every stage of the bloom cycle is remarkable. Accompanying the drawings, her notes, which may indicate that these were intended as preparatory sketches, also permit identification of her subject as tree peonies (*Paeonia suffruticosa*).[8] Perennial shrubs with stout stems, tree peonies are hybrids cultivated from wild species native to the mountains of northwestern China. Herbaceous peonies (*Paeonia lactiflora*), while also perennials, die back in fall, emerging from the ground as fresh shoots each spring. Tree peonies flower and leaf on the previous season's growth. Kusama's drawings and notes demonstrate extensive knowledge of this growing cycle, informed by a childhood spent surrounded by plants.

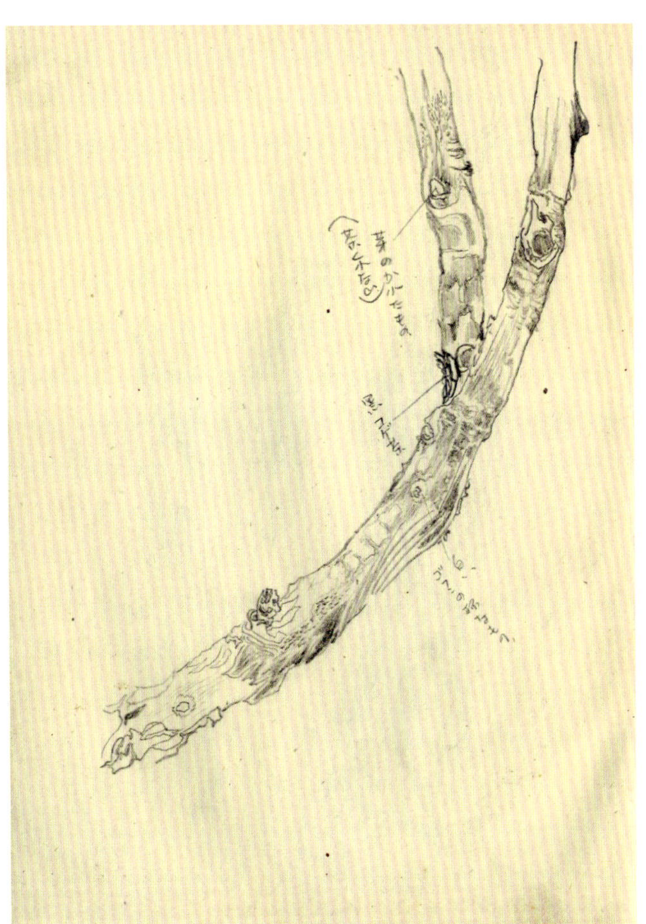

Viewed collectively, these sketches are not merely a student exercise, or a document of plant conditions, or even a glimpse into the artist's inner world. Rather, Kusama's sketches map the themes that would come to dominate her work over the course of the ensuing decades: life and death, accumulation and loss, the awe inspired by the heights of nature's ethereal beauty and the extreme low of decay, and the patterns and connections throughout the universe. Likely produced in the few short weeks of a single peony season, the sketches are an important key to understanding the artist's lifelong artistic practice, an idiosyncratic form of expression grounded in a synthesis of her experiences and careful study of nature and the world around her.

Kusama destroyed most of her existing work prior to leaving Japan to launch her career in the United States in the late 1950s.

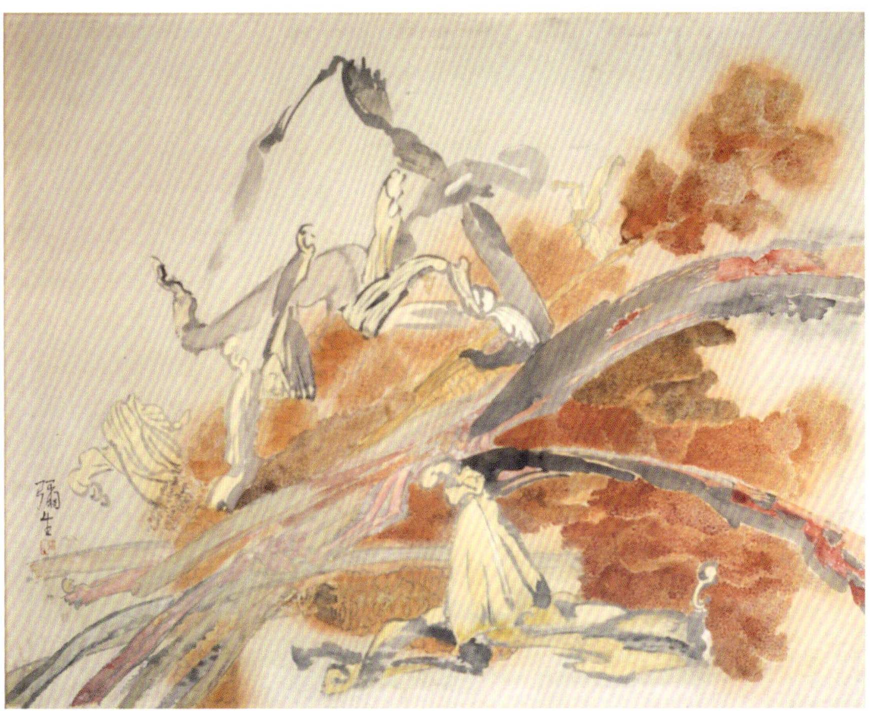

What little survives from this period is primarily drawings and works on paper. Of these, the works dating to the mid to late 1940s—the peony sketchbook and a small number of other works on paper—show evidence of the influence of *nihonga*, a style of painting that arose in the mid-nineteenth century out of a desire to preserve a uniquely Japanese artistic identity in the face of an influx of Western influences (and Western-style painting, known as *yōga*).[9] Traditionally, *nihonga* employs water and mineral pigments (*iwa enogu*) sourced directly from nature, resulting in a finished work that is muted in color and matte, even gritty, in texture. *Nihonga* artists first make studies from observation of their subject, then drawings that are eventually transferred to the final paper support using carbon paper. The mineral pigment is then adhered to the paper with animal glue. An artistic practice that is rooted in appreciation for the natural world, both in materials and in subject matter, at the time of its origin it was a sort of nostalgic hearkening back to Japanese and broader Asian traditions.[10]

Nihonga was developed in response to outside influences; it was a result of looking outward to worldwide art movements and reframing subject matter and technique in a distinctly Japanese mode.[11] Kusama's peony sketches bear a resemblance to *nihonga* preparatory sketches in their strong contours and chosen subjects. Her written notes reveal her engagement with the techniques and materials of this art form. In a sketch of the stems and twigs of the peony plant, Kusama has labeled the parts of the plants with anatomical

Fig. 4 (opposite)
Untitled (Flower Sketches) (detail), 1945
Pencil in notebook
8½ × 11⅞ in. (21.5 × 30 cm)
Collection of the artist

Fig. 5 (above)
Harvest, 1945
Ink and mineral pigments on silk
23 × 28½ in. (58.5 × 72.5 cm)
Collection of the artist

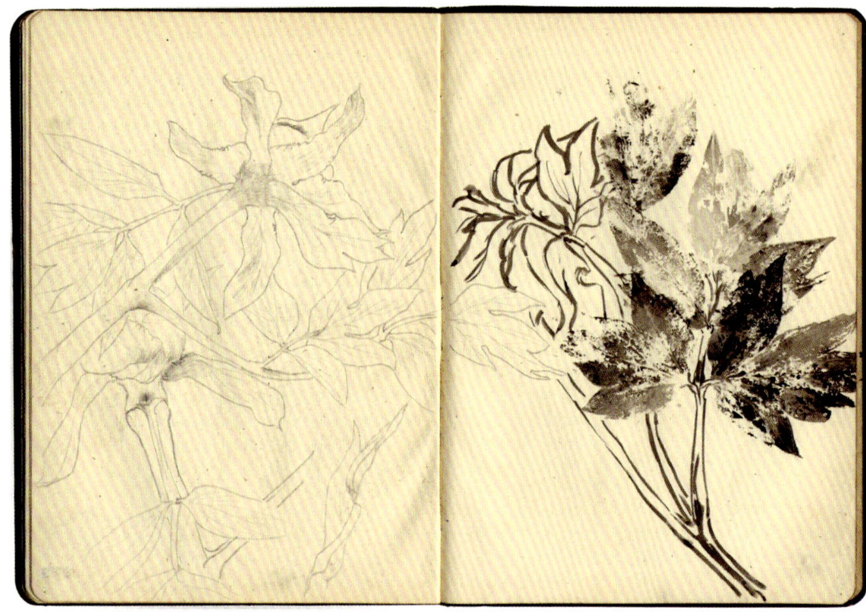

Fig. 6 (right)
Untitled (Flower Sketches) (detail), 1945
Pencil and ink in notebook
8½ × 11⅞ in. (21.5 × 30 cm)
Collection of the artist

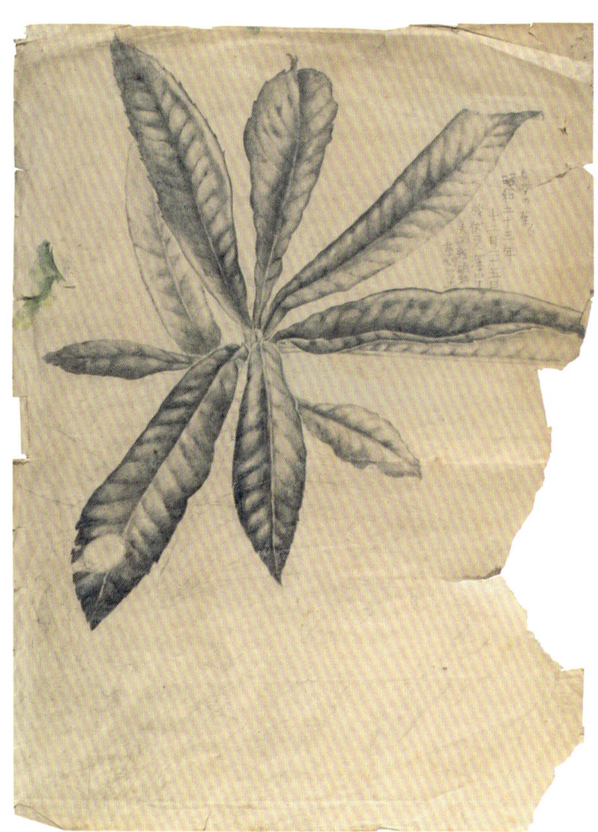

Fig. 7 (below)
Leaf of Japanese Medlar, 1948
Pencil on paper
21⅛ × 15⅜ in.
(53.7 × 39.2 cm)
Collection of the artist

descriptions (**FIG. 4**), "a part of the broken sprout"; the colors she observes, "brownish red" and "very dark brown close to black"; and notes on visible signs of decay and disease, "white powdery thing looking like 'gofun.'" This last observation refers to the shimmery white clamshell gesso that is used to prepare the ground of traditional *nihonga* paintings before any other pigment is applied. Like *nihonga* artists, Kusama's artistic identity was grounded in an appreciation for nature, which served as a means for exploring what was happening around her in the world. In the fall of 1945, Kusama's painting *Harvest* (**FIG. 5**) was displayed at the *All Shinshū Art Exhibition* in Nagano, which traveled to several other cities in Japan. *Harvest* depicts twisted fragments of corn husks and millet—a substitute for rice during the lean years of the war. While employing traditional *nihonga* materials and style, Kusama used an unconventional technique, as she seems to have applied paint directly to the silk substrate in this somber view of wartime provisions.[12] Kusama also experimented with artistic techniques in her sketchbook. On one page (**FIG. 6**), she has rendered the outlines of peony leaves and stems in thick *sumi* (Chinese black ink), creating imprints of some of the leaves in a cleverly composed vignette achieved by applying ink directly to a leaf and transferring it to the blank page.[13] Immediately opposite, the artist's carefully contoured pencil composition of peony leaves and flowers is concentrated on minute details of leaf form and venation. The ink drawing, by comparison, shows a desire to experiment with materials and means of representation.

Kusama's professional artistic training comprised a brief eighteen months at the Kyoto City University of Arts beginning in 1948. Her

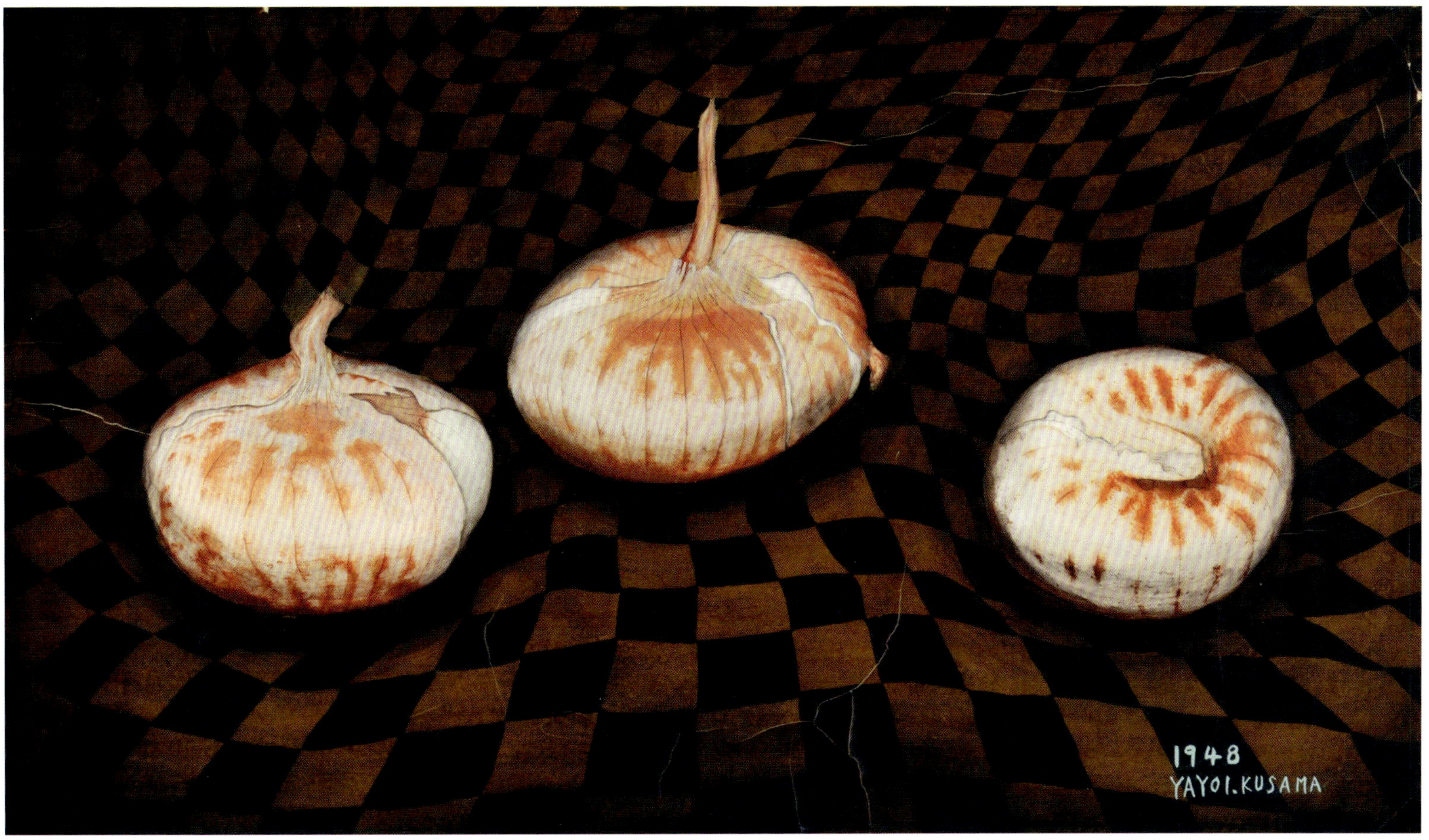

course of study was in *nihonga*—the only art form her reluctant parents would permit her to study formally, likely because they viewed it as an opportunity for her to learn proper etiquette as much as art.[14] *Leaf of Japanese Medlar* (1948; **FIG. 7**) was completed during this period, likely as a school assignment. Kusama's detailed, almost lifelike drawing is easily recognizable as a depiction of a loquat tree.[15] Yet even as she pursued her studies, Kusama forged her own stylistic path. Like other practitioners of *nihonga* at the time, Kusama embraced stylistic changes, favoring heightened color and expression over strict contours, in the development of her own visual language. A carefully executed depiction of a trio of onions (**FIG. 8**) demonstrates her careful observation of her subjects, which are rendered in mineral pigments on paper. The undulating, checkerboard background on which they are displayed creates a disorienting sense of movement. Akira Tatehata, director of the Yayoi Kusama Museum, has noted, "Because these onions hover over a ground delineated in a grid pattern and permeated by strange fluctuations they take on the appearance of a hallucinatory vision severed from reality."[16] In using the traditional techniques of her early training to subvert expectations, Kusama begins to assert her own reality.

Fig. 8
Onions, 1948
Pigment on paper
15½ × 23¼ in. (39.5 × 59 cm)
Collection of the artist

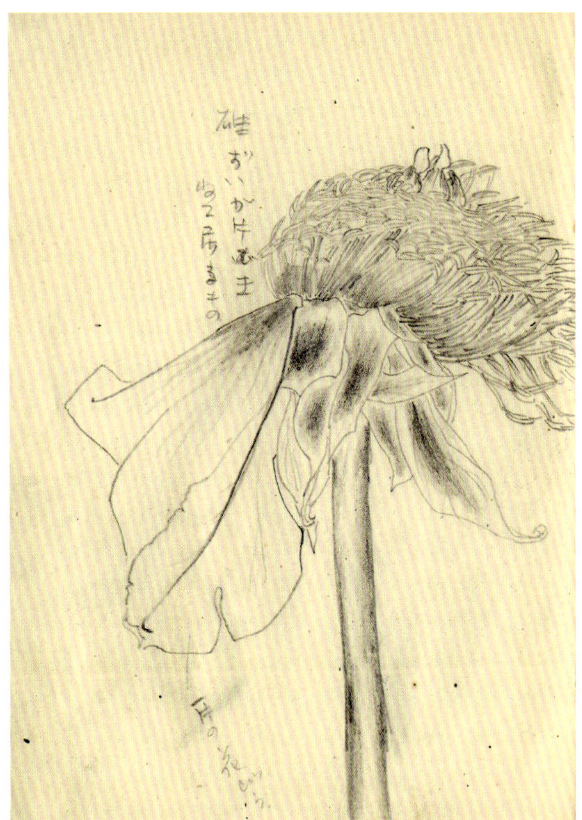

Fig. 9
Untitled (Flower Sketches) (detail), 1945
Pencil in notebook
8½ × 11⅞ in. (21.5 × 30 cm)
Collection of the artist

At one point I went through a phase when I enjoyed snipping off the heads of flowers. I would toss the tight blossoms into a hole I had secretly dug, until I had accumulated hundreds of them. I also drew pictures of flowers in full bloom, the petals of which formed shapes that resembled vaginas. The dots in the centres resembled penises. —Yayoi Kusama[17]

KUSAMA'S UNIQUE PERSPECTIVE—AT TIMES WHIMSICAL, CONTEMPLATIVE, melancholy, and celebratory—is expressed in her botanically accurate drawings of peonies, and later in her fully realized paintings and sculptures. In her depiction of a peony flower in decline (**FIG.9**), nearly all the petals fall away to reveal the slowly wilting stamens, which the teenaged Kusama described as looking like they were sleeping. Pistils and stamens, the female and male reproductive organs of flowers, would recur in Kusama's works on paper (page 70) and sculptures throughout her career, including monstrous, looming flowers (page 55) and immersive installations (page 52). Four decades after completing this sketch, in a work titled *Sleeping Stamens* (1985; **FIG. 10**), Kusama would depict twisting, tangled, tubelike "stamens"—this time enclosed in a series of boxes. Isolated from the rest of the plant, the massed forms of the soft sculptures of this period recall Kusama's stuffed sculptural installations from the 1960s, here more closely resembling carefully observed, magnified plant anatomy, and presented in the manner of contained specimens. Another sketch from 1945 depicts wilting petals and spent stamens falling away to expose the ripening carpel, which contains the fertilized ovary and will begin to give way to the seed pod (**FIG. 11**). Kusama renders the minute hairs that cover the exterior of the carpel, as well as the seeds that are revealed when it splits open (**FIG. 12**), in an extraordinarily accurate drawing that seems to prefigure later works such as *Flower* (1993; page 69), a simplified representation of a flower engulfed in repeating, abstract patterns. Kusama is particularly attentive to the shape and texture of the carpel, correctly labeling it as the "thin skin wrapping the pistils" and noting a "piece of blossom sitting on top." Several decades later, *Flower Bud Opening to the Heavens* (2018; **FIG. 13**), a soft sculpture of a tight seed pod, takes a similar form, here rendered in sewn, stuffed fabric painted with red and black polka dots.

Spreading polka dot patterns, today a signature motif in Kusama's work, have generally been traced to hallucinations the artist recalls from childhood. A small number of surviving artworks from this period, including a 1939 sketch, depict polka dots and flowerlike forms overtaking their surroundings (**FIG. 14**). Tatehata argues that this drawing is important "beyond the unbridled freedom of juvenilia to evoke disquieting, hallucinatory experience," and that these early drawings prefigure works in which proliferating nets

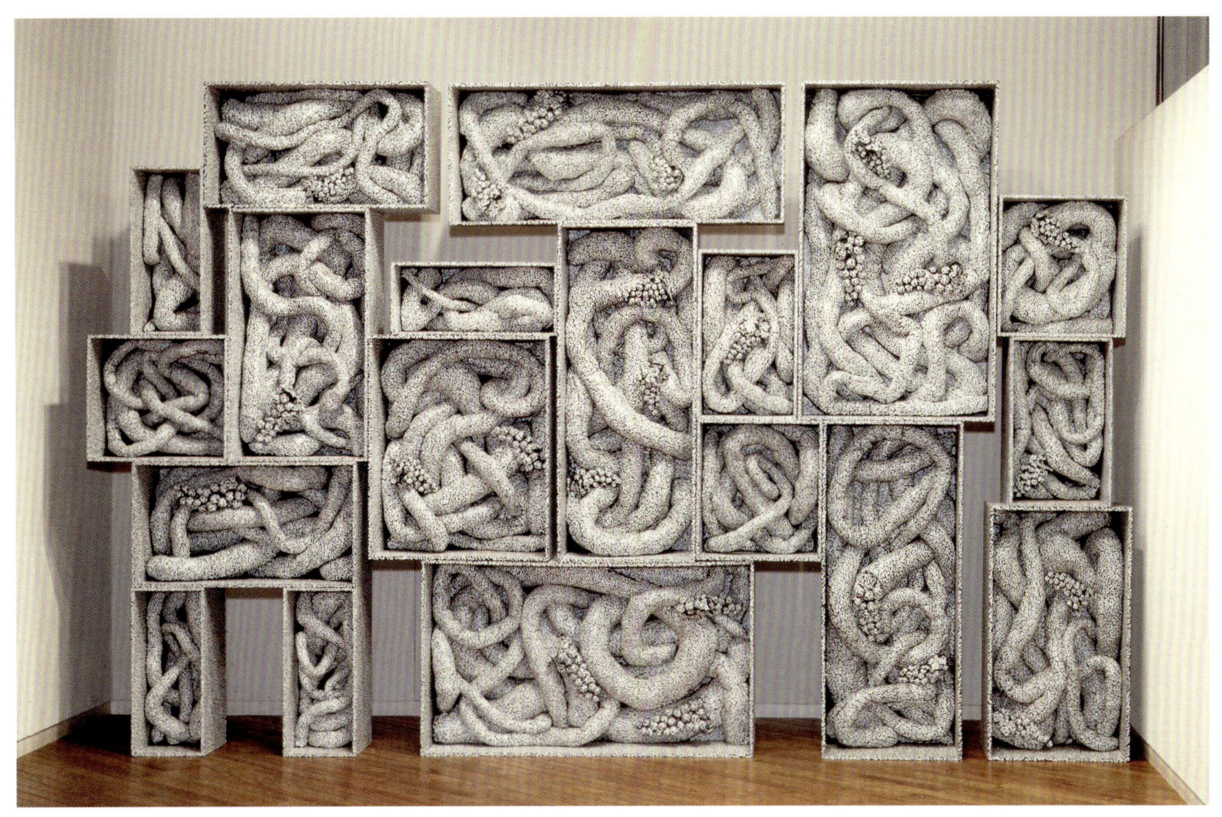

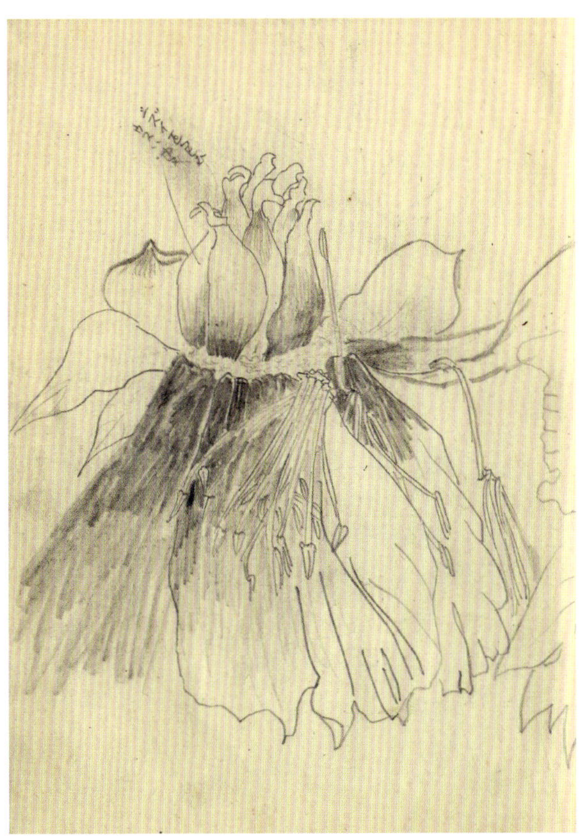

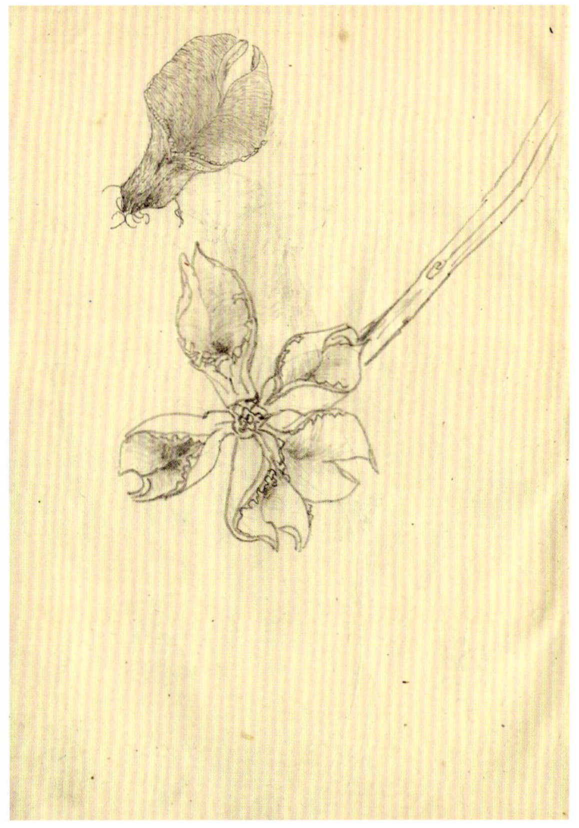

Fig. 10 (above)
Sleeping Stamens, 1985
Sewn and stuffed fabric, found objects, wood, and paint
96½ × 143¾ × 12 in.
(245 × 365 × 30.5 cm)
Private collection

Figs. 11 and 12 (bottom left and right)
Untitled (Flower Sketches) (detail), 1945
Pencil in notebook
8½ × 11⅞ in. (21.5 × 30 cm)
Collection of the artist

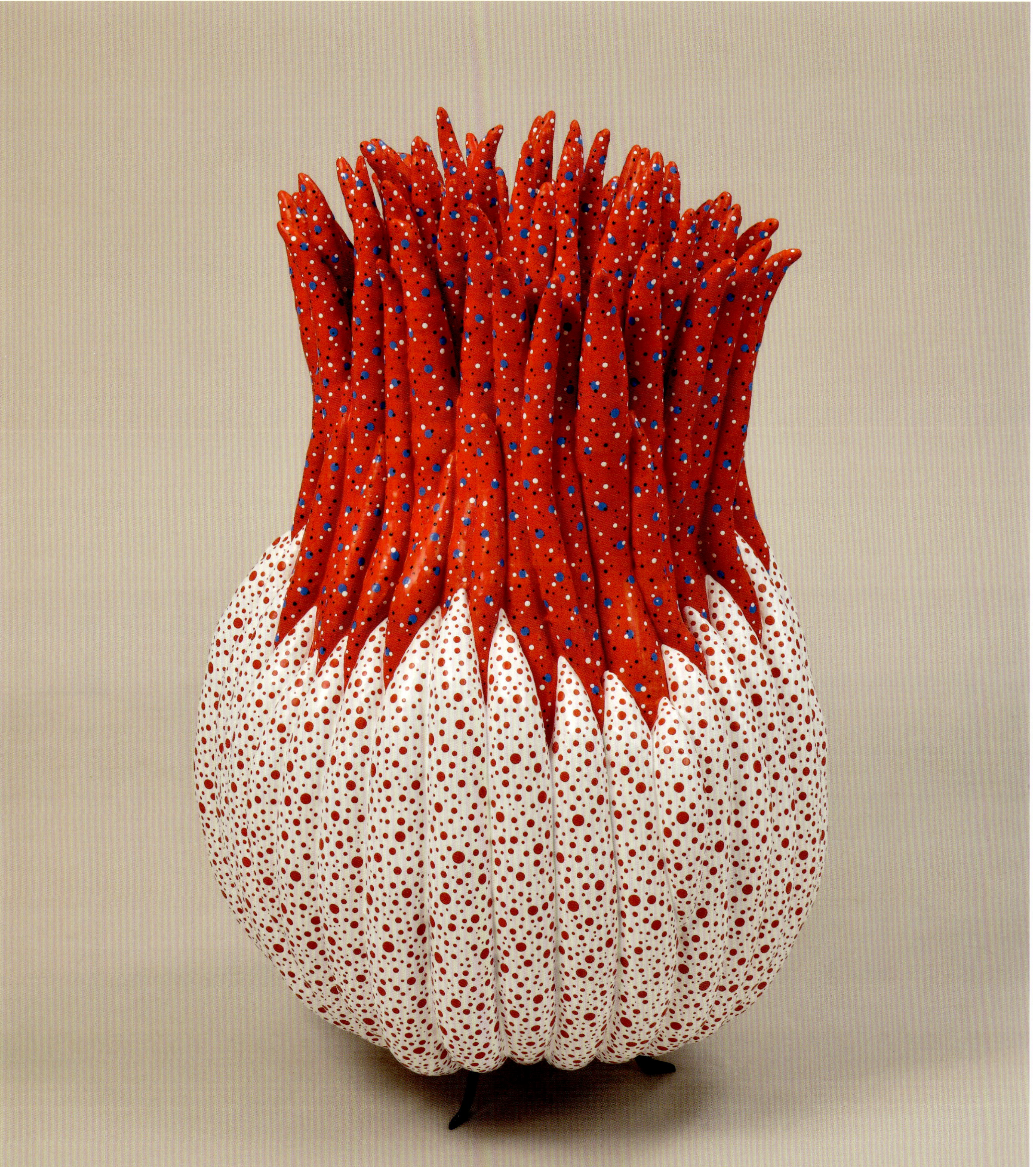

Fig. 13 (opposite)
Flower Bud Opening to the Heavens, 2018
Sewn and stuffed fabric, acrylic paint, and metal
H. 35 ½ in. (90 cm);
Diam. 28 in. (71 cm)
Collection of the artist

Fig. 14 (right)
Untitled, 1939
Pencil on paper
9¾ × 8⅞ in. (24.8 × 22.5 cm)
Collection of the artist

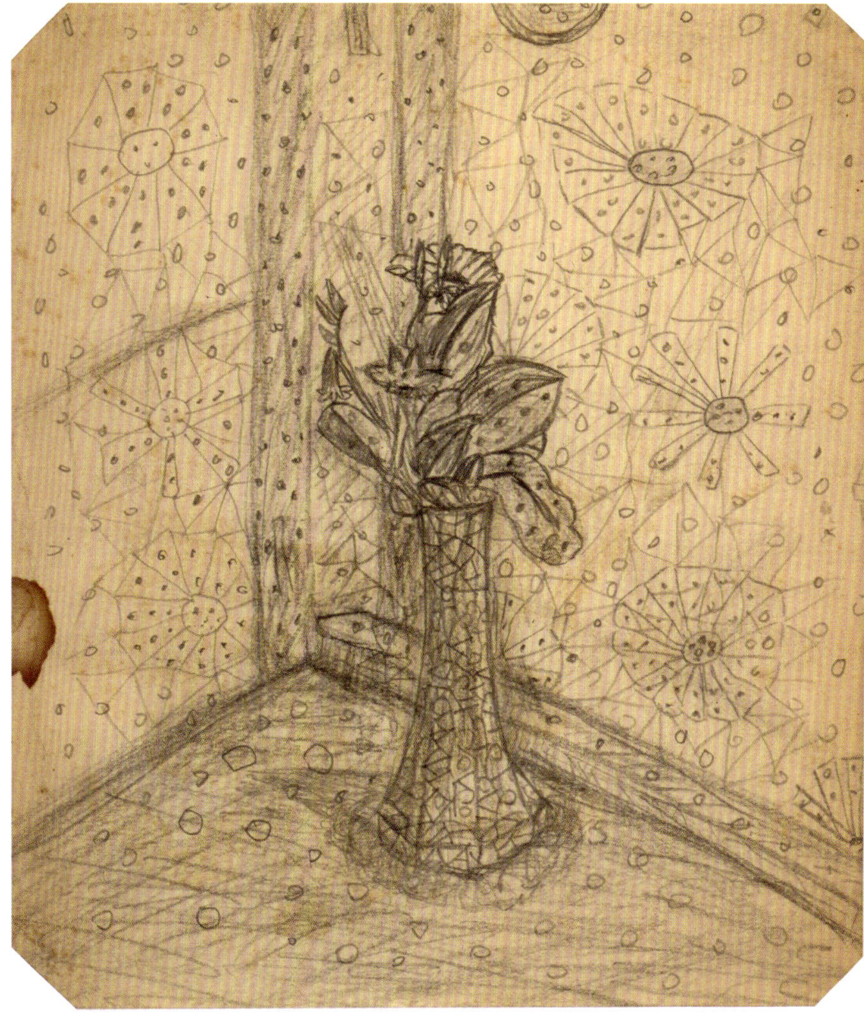

and dots become the primary focus.[18] Leaves speckled with holes and spots also appear in her 1945 peony sketches (**FIG. 15**), here likely indicating insect damage or fungal disease. Viewed with an eye to the dualities represented in so many works to follow, what if the polka dots overtaking the vase of flowers and all its surroundings in Kusama's 1939 sketch evoke not only the proliferation of healthy organisms, but also the diseases and decay that can plague them? As a child of a nursery family, Kusama would have known the signs of crop failure just as well as the names of plants and their bloom cycles, and they would have been of equal interest to the artist's keen eye—and just as evocative of the many cycles and forms of life—as the withering, failing blooms she also documented.

Polka dots figure prominently in early abstract works that bear names suggesting botanical subject matter such as *A Seed* (1952; page 128). Looking back, Kusama wrote, "Deep in the mountains of Nagano, working with letter-size sheets of white paper, I had found my own unique method of expression: ink paintings featuring

Fig. 15
Untitled (Flower Sketches) (detail), 1945
Pencil in notebook
8½ × 11⅞ in. (21.5 × 30 cm)
Collection of the artist

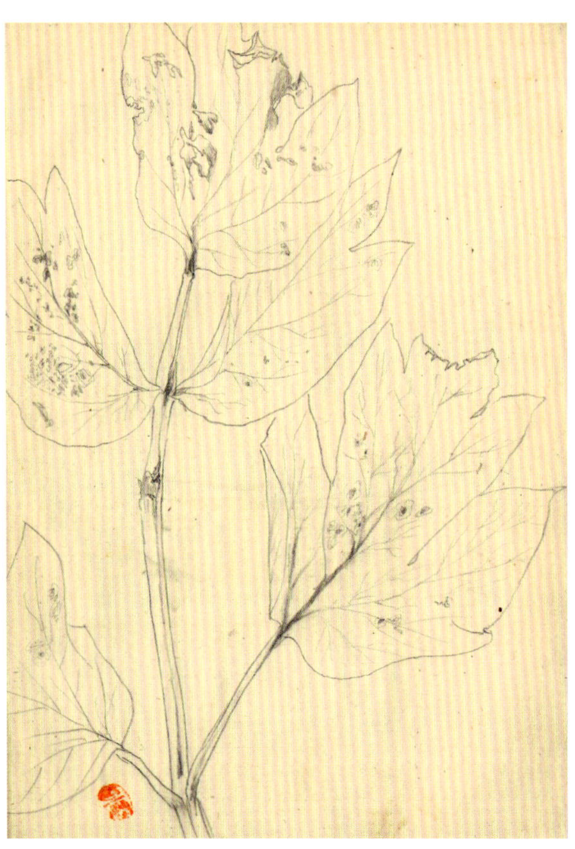

accumulations of tiny dots and pen drawings of endless and unbroken chains of graded cellular forms or peculiar structures that resembled magnified sections of plant stalks."[19] Polka dots are even more prominent in *Early Spring* (1979; **FIG. 16**), a little-known series Kusama painted on paper. Clusters of green polka dots become the subject, arranged to form the branches, buds, and discs of flowers; the polka dots are outlined with faint washes of ink, giving the appearance of cells or segments. The poppy-like blossoms of *Summer Flowers* (1988; pages 46–47) are rendered using vibrant polka dot patterns densely packed into boldly contoured shapes of blooms, stems, and leaves. The patterns even continue into the bright blue and green weblike background. In contrast, the subject of *Flower Bloomed in My Heart* (2004; page 122), rendered entirely in polka dots, is at times hard to distinguish from the similar speckled background. Here the spreading polka dots threaten to obscure the central flower, much as the spreading fungus in the artist's peony sketches threatens to subsume the form of the host plants, and the polka dots Kusama employs on the surfaces of canvases and sculptures, and even on the exteriors of the buildings themselves in which her work is displayed, threaten to overwhelm and overtake their hosts, demonstrating the unstoppable life force of nature itself.

Few studies have been carried out on what remains of Kusama's work from the period prior to her departure from Japan. The artist's training in *nihonga* and her early recollections of hallucinations, both from the same period, are often examined in considerations of this period, cited as key factors in the development of Kusama's worldview. Discussions of her 1945 sketchbook have generally positioned it as a relic of a fleeting moment in time—the exercises of a student learning to look carefully and render natural subject matter in drawing and painting.[20] Yet Kusama's decision not to destroy this series of drawings seems anything but accidental, and it suggests that they warrant closer consideration.

Nowhere else in the artist's known body of work are the cycles of growth and decline, life and death, examined in such minute detail or with such extreme fidelity to reality. Her repeated renderings of peony blooms, stamens, seed pods, stems, and twigs suggest that Kusama was carefully studying her subject from all angles in order to better understand it. She celebrates the beauty of the peony flowers at the height of their bloom, closely examines the reproductive organs throughout the bloom cycle, and meticulously notes the nascent signs of life—new growth and emerging buds that will mature with the passing of time—after the flowers have faded and died. Kusama's sketches reveal the repeating forms found in nature—the venation of leaves, the circular holes formed by insect damage, the speckled surface of fungus, the texture of bark. Through these

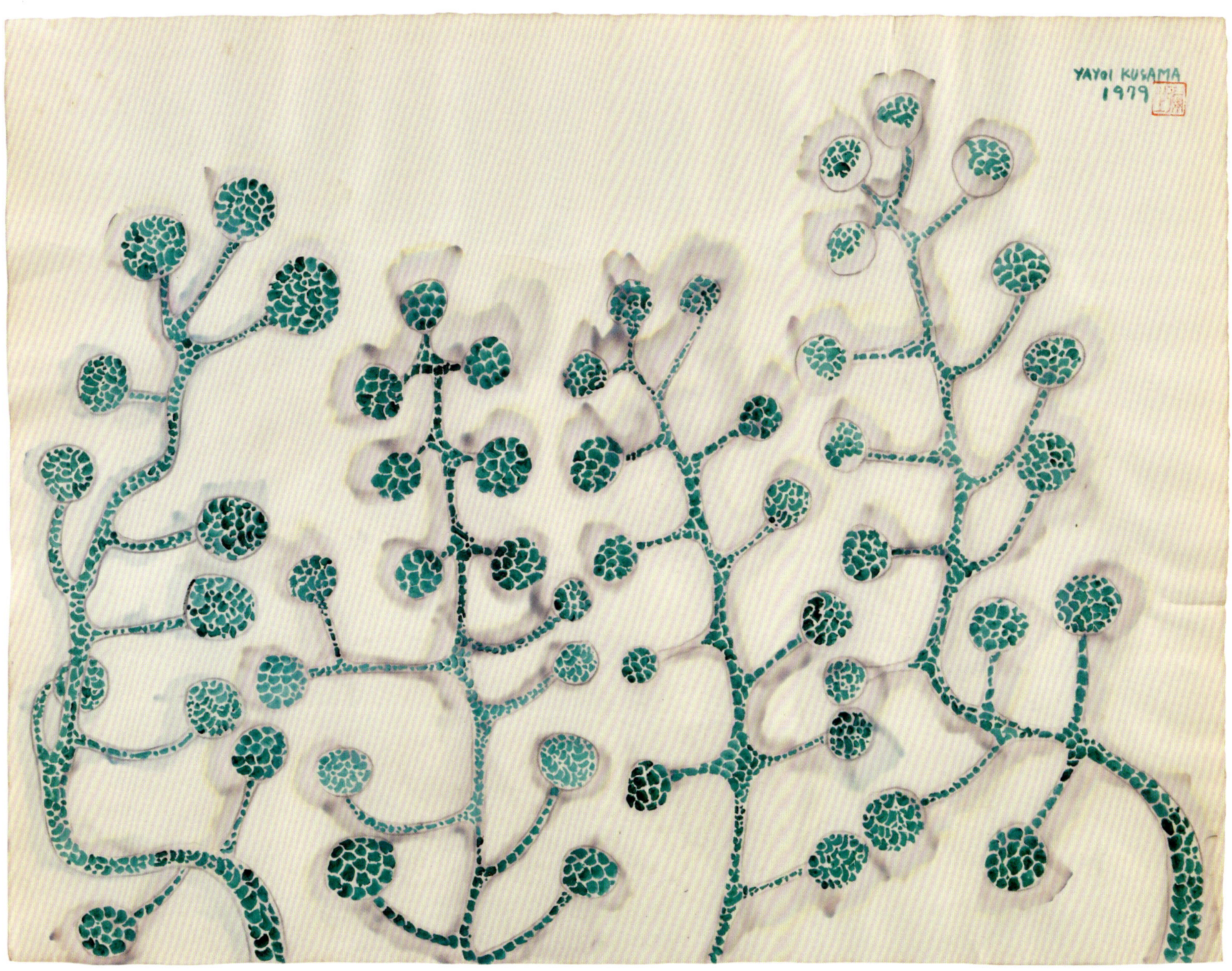

painstaking studies, Kusama begins to engage with the natural cycles of seasons, life cycles, and the passage of time. Looking back, her careful documentation of the peonies can also be viewed as the earliest mapping of the themes that would prevail throughout her career. Though she would soon move away from the realist depictions found in the sketchbook, Kusama's appreciation for the patterns revealed in nature—and the promise and energy they represent—continues to be a powerful presence in her work today.

Fig. 16
Early Spring, 1979
Ink and watercolor on paper
20⅛ × 26 in. (51.1 × 65.8 cm)
Collection of the artist

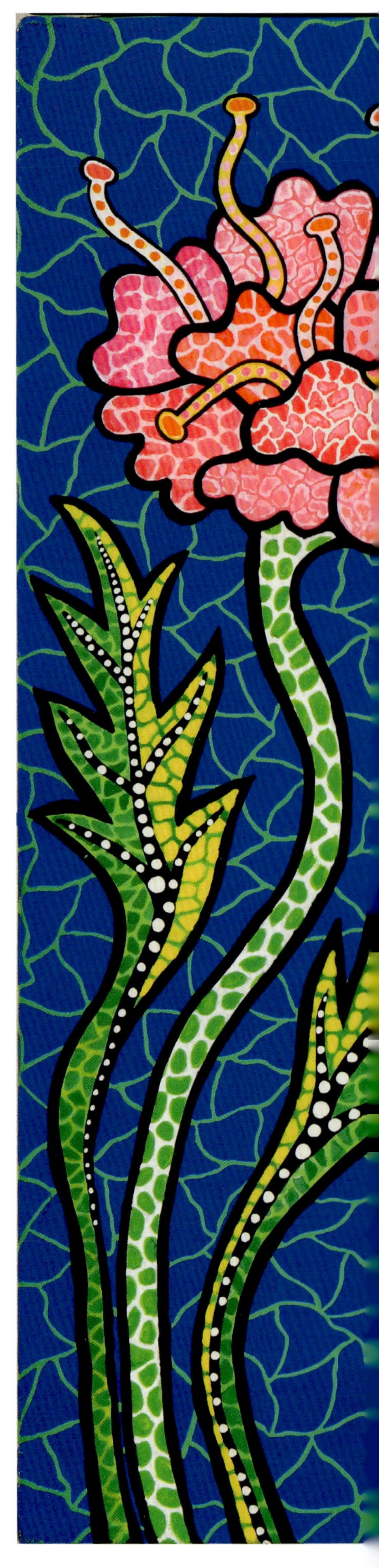

Summer Flowers, 1988
Acrylic on canvas
17⅞ × 20⅞ in. (45.5 × 53 cm)
Collection of the artist

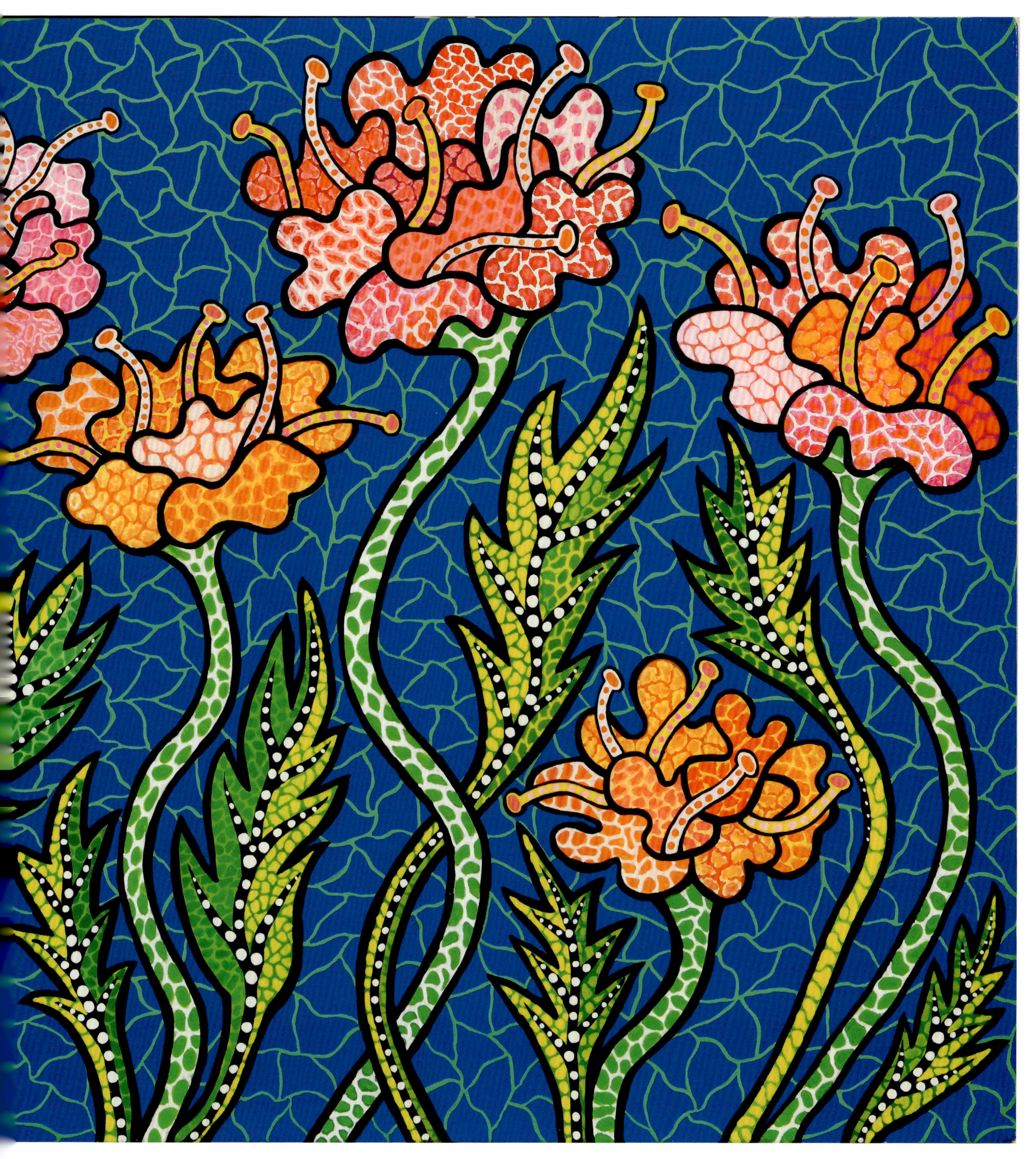

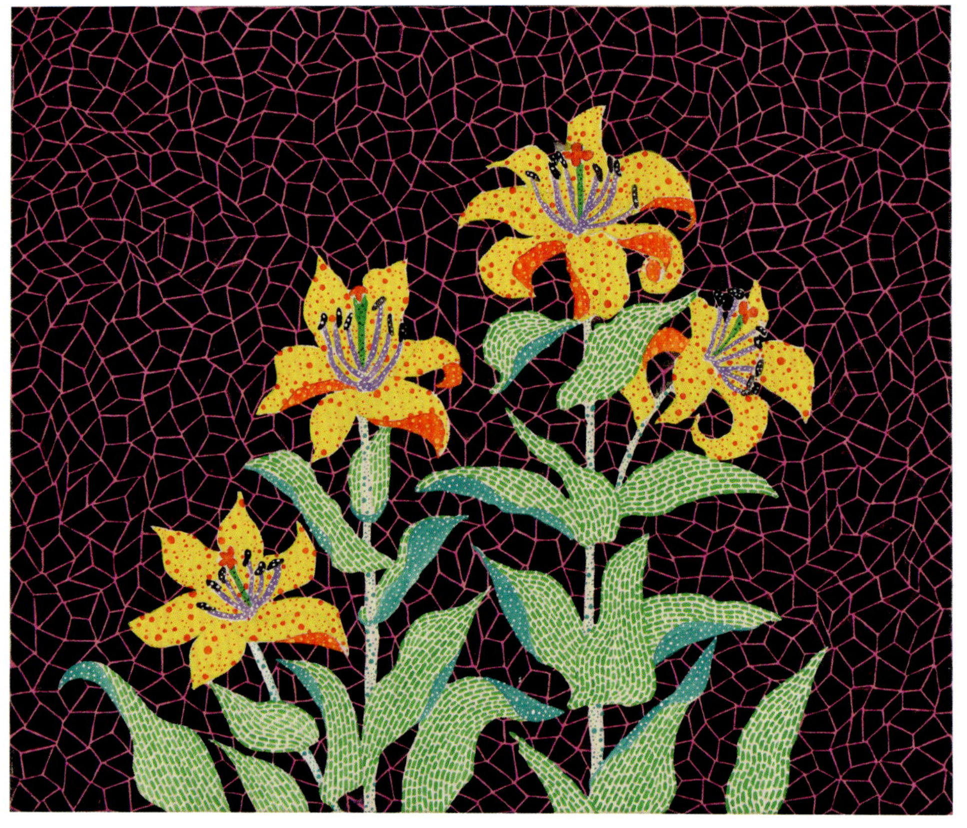

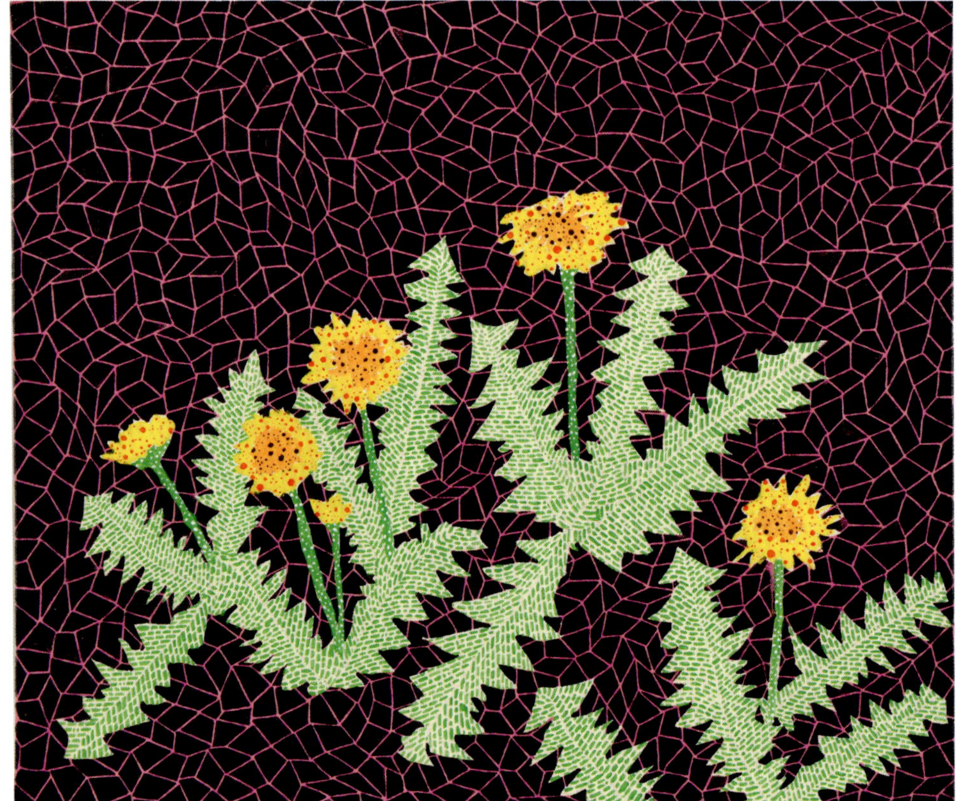

left
Lilies, 1984
Acrylic on canvas
17⅞ × 20⅞ in. (45.5 × 53 cm)
Collection of the artist

below
Dandelions, 1984
Acrylic on canvas
17⅞ × 20⅞ in. (45.5 × 53 cm)
Collection of the artist

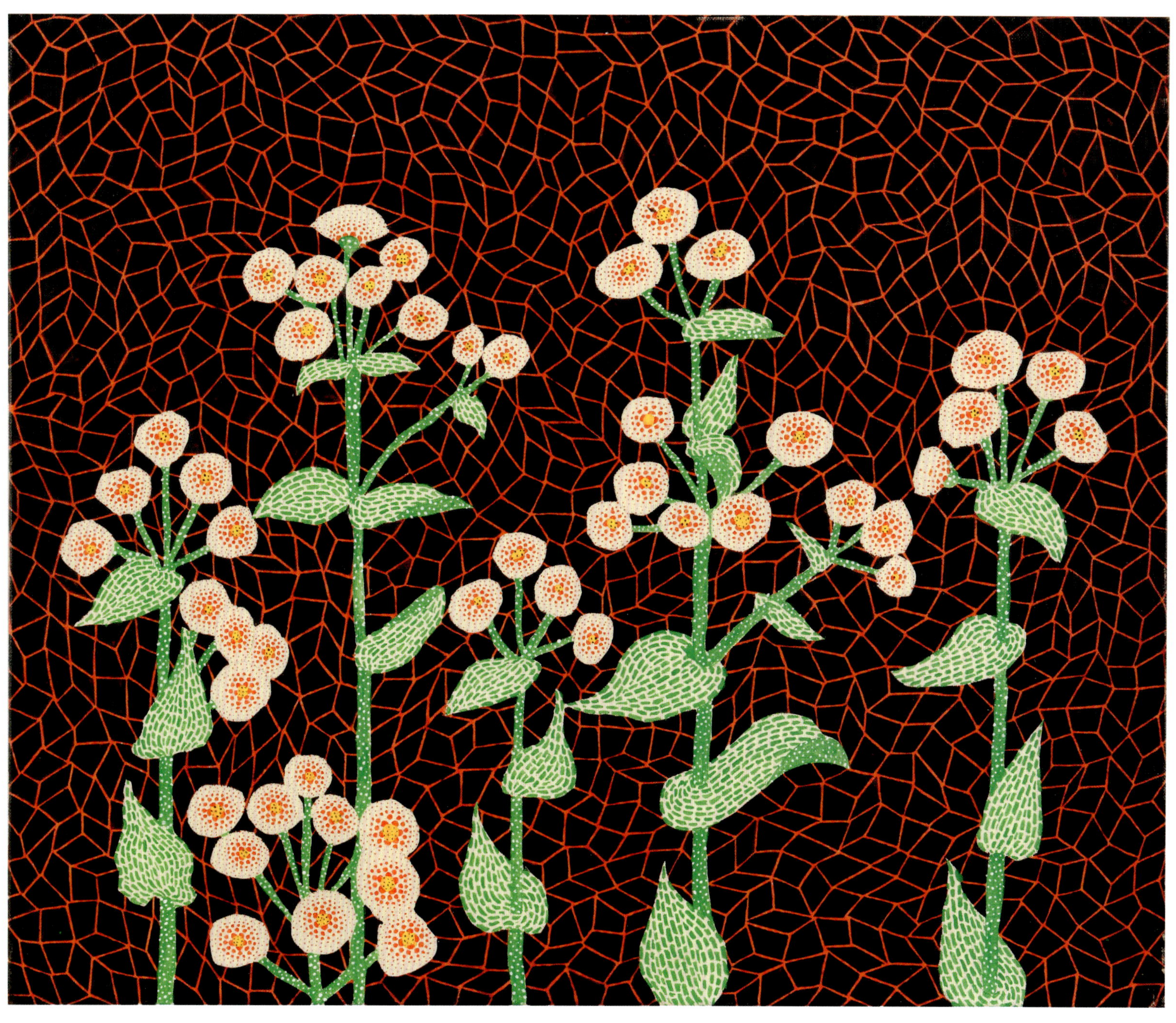

Wild Flowers, 1984
Acrylic on canvas
17⅞ × 20⅞ in. (45.5 × 53 cm)
Collection of the artist

right
Flower Bud Opening to the Heavens, 2018
Sewn and stuffed fabric, acrylic paint, and metal
H. 35½ in. (90 cm); Diam. 28 in. (71 cm)
Collection of the artist

center
Flower E, 2018
Sewn and stuffed fabric, acrylic paint, and metal
H. 19⅝ in. (50 cm); Diam. 16⅞ in. (43 cm)
Collection of the artist

far right
Flower F, 2018
Sewn and stuffed fabric, acrylic paint, and metal
H. 30¾ in. (78 cm); Diam. 26¾ in. (68 cm)
Collection of the artist

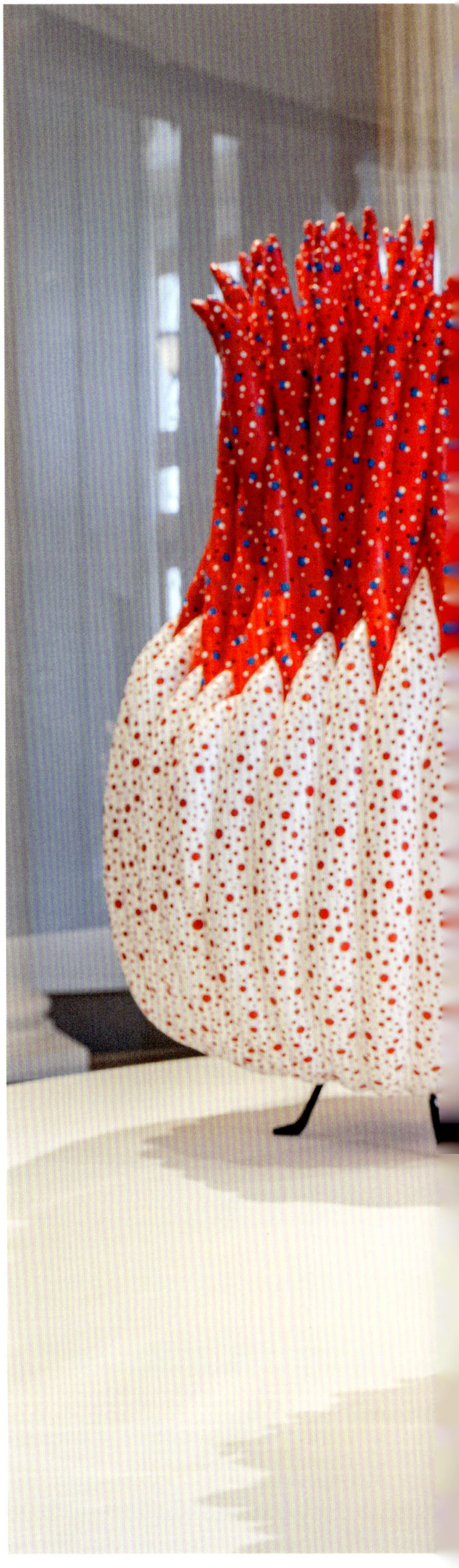

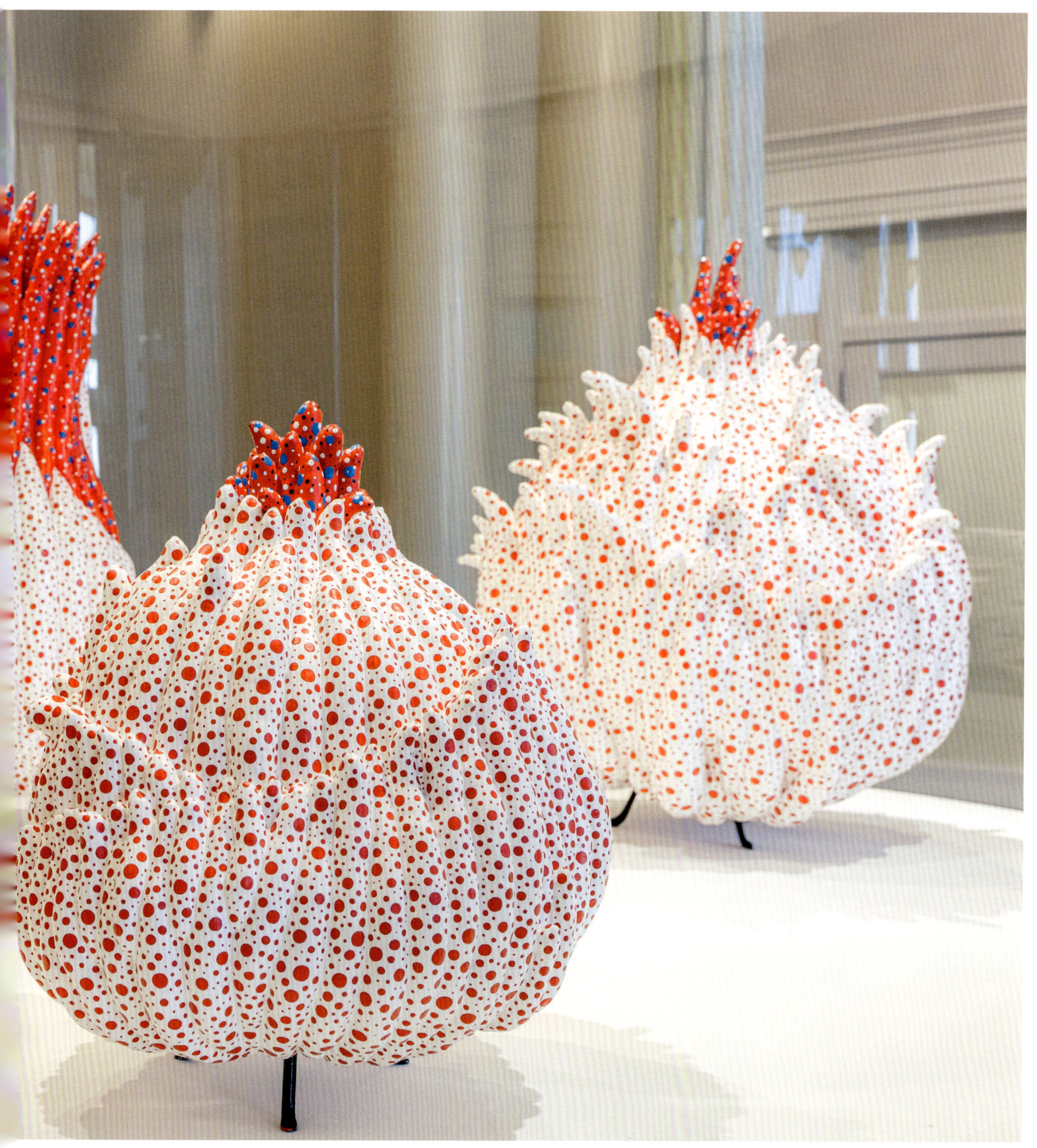

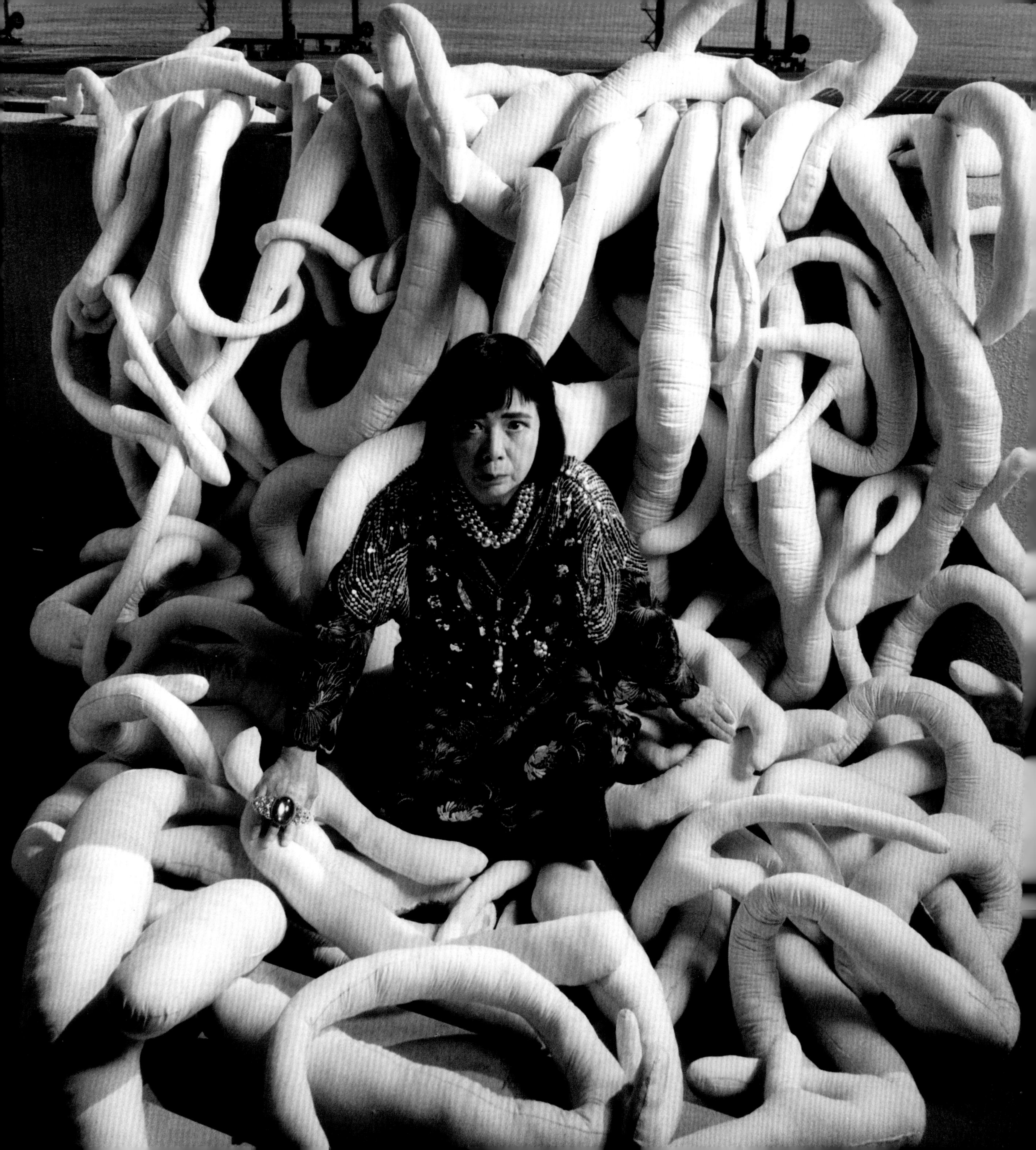

COSMIC NATURE

EMBRACING THE UNKNOWN

Before our very eyes, [Kusama] has returned as a great contemporary artist who creates the most unfathomable emotions of the future.

—Félix Guattari, 1986[1]

Affect spreads out of her . . . . Overwhelmed by illusion and fear . . . , the affect machine, Yayoi Kusama continues to turn her jack towards a "cosmic nature." In her case, her jack is deeper than anyone else. She herself is "nature."

—Shinichi Nakazawa, 1987[2]

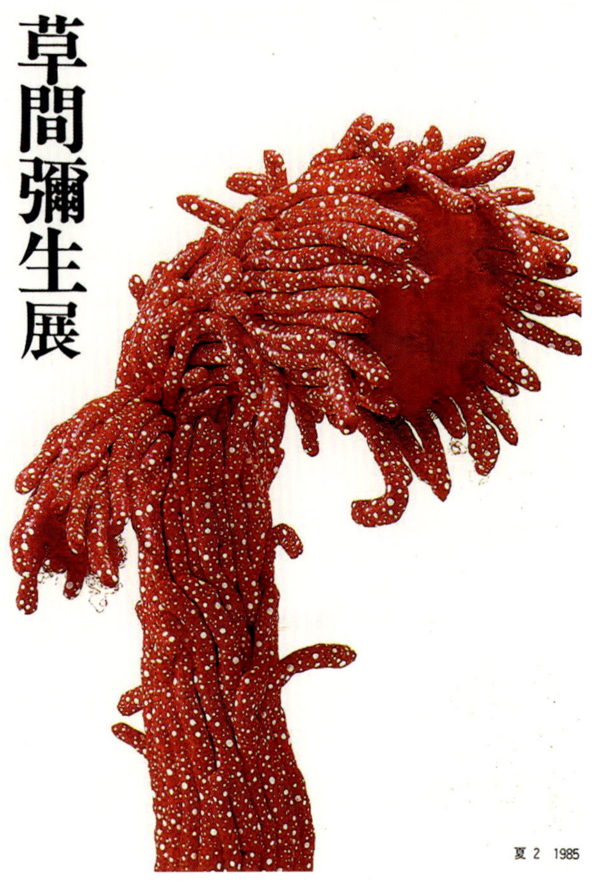

previous
Kusama with soft sculpture in Tokyo, 1993

Fig. 1 (above)
Yayoi Kusama-ten [Yayoi Kusama exhibition] announcement card, 1987. Kitakyushū Municipal Museum of Art, Kitakyushū, Japan

Fig. 2 (opposite)
Kusama with *My Flower Bed* (1962) and accumulation sculptures in her New York City studio, 1965

IN 1987 YAYOI KUSAMA PRESENTED A SERIES OF SOFT, OTHERWORLDLY, psychosexual sculptures—including *Summer II* (1985) and *Sleeping Stamens* (1985; page 41)—in her first museum survey at the Kitakyushū Municipal Museum of Art (**FIG. 1**). The genealogy of these monstrous botanical creatures and wild white tentacles contained inside multiple boxes can be traced to a much earlier sculpture, *My Flower Bed* (1962; **FIG. 2**), captured in a memorable photograph in which a wildflower head made of hundreds of spray-painted fire-red gloves hovers over the artist, a carnivorous plant about to swallow her. The massive forms of these sculptures can feel active, even threatening to the viewer. In his essay "Jōdō shokubutsu (Les végétaux affectives)" [Affective plants] for the exhibition catalogue, philosopher Shinichi Nakazawa asserts the importance of botanical forms in her work, describing the role of nature in Kusama's practice as one tied to human affect. Citing Johann Wolfgang von Goethe's *Theory of Colours* (1810), Nakazawa defines affect as "a productive activity that occurs when nature in general is embodied in a special form of *human* nature. . . . There is an even larger 'cosmic nature' at work hidden inside the affect machine of humans."[3] Affect is the way we experience, connect, and make sense of the world and its aftermath. Nakazawa employs this key philosophical concept of affect to define Kusama's vision of nature as something that is not objectified through representation, but embodied through a visceral transformation that connects the botanical world to the tactile sensations of human nature and even to the sublime feeling of cosmic expansion.

This key concept of affect helps us understand Kusama's central artistic strategy as linking nature, mankind, and the cosmos. From her earliest botanical sketches of the 1940s to her present-day outdoor flower sculptures, nature is the pivotal idea in Kusama's artistic practice, which consistently refers to patterns of organic growth and the biological cycles of life and death. Nature is not a mere source of inspiration, but viscerally embodied in her artistic language. Herein lies Kusama's life force, a cosmic nature that integrates terrestrial and celestial orders of the universe, and signals an ethical stance—a lifelong journey of embracing the unknown (nature, the universe, infinity, death)—in order to form a radical connectivity, a central theme in the artist's philosophy of self-obliteration that equalizes nature, humanity, and the cosmos.

While there have been many efforts to interpret Kusama's practice as an art historical enigma, the artist has staunchly positioned herself both within and outside its vernaculars: *nihonga* (Japanese-style painting), *yōga* (Western-style painting), Surrealism, Abstract Expressionism, Minimalism, Group Zero and Dutch Nul, assemblage, installation, Pop, performance, expanded cinema, and immersive

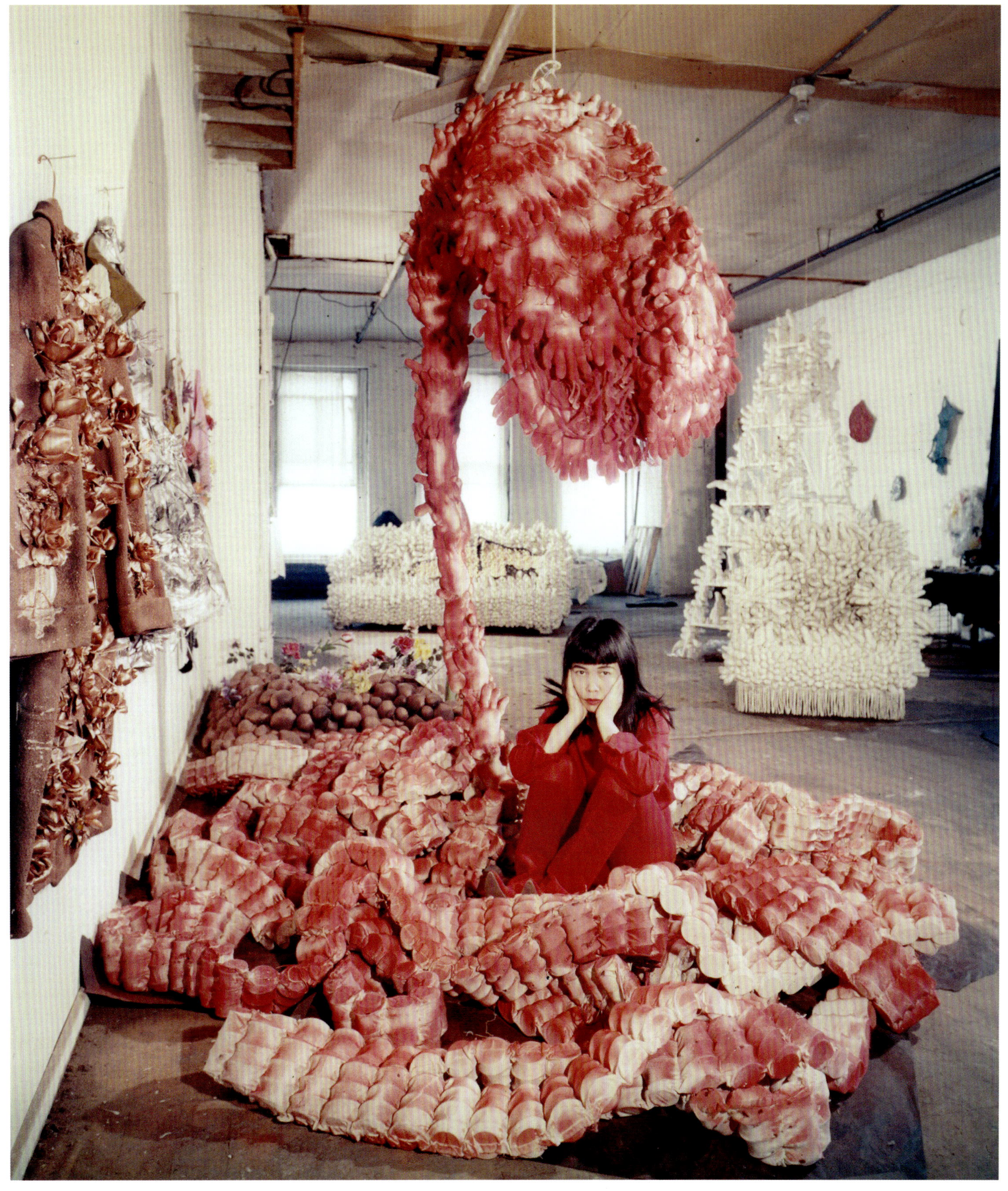

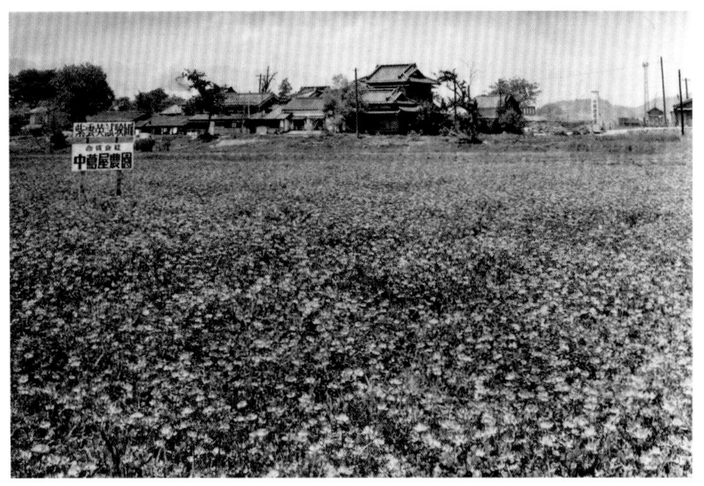

environments. In efforts to classify her work, the consistent presence and examination of organic life are most often overlooked. For Kusama, nature is *alive*, in a perpetual process of becoming, disintegration, and rebirth, and part of a larger cosmos. Throughout her life, she has illustrated both microcosmic and macrocosmic views of the universe, from amoebic works on paper, to biomorphic assemblages and sculptures, to infinitely expansive mirrored installations. What is the relationship of these cosmic-scale shifts to nature and organic growth? How do her works embody the unique affects that we sense through our experiences in nature? Within the context of a botanical garden, Kusama's art takes on new meaning. Three concepts through which to explore this new meaning are anthropomorphism, faciality, and the bio-cosmic. Kusama wrote:

> *There are ten billion bubbles inside my body. Which is precisely why I feel at one with the ten billion stars that twinkle in the heavens, and why I talk to the clouds made up of ten billion tiny drops of water and why I hear the voice of the wind carrying ten billion atoms.*[4]

ANTHROPOMORPHISM

My home is Matsumoto, a mountain village 200 miles northwest of Tokyo. I live with the forest, the birds, the insects, the streams and the things of the earth. I have always lived this way and I always shall. When I wish to paint a bird, I try to place myself inside the character of the bird and speak as I imagine the bird would speak. I do the same for a rock, a fish, a tree. So you see, I talk to you and others through my paintings. If you understand what I am trying to say, then you have heard me speak.

—*Yayoi* Kusama, 1957[5]

Plants entered Kusama's subconscious during her childhood. She was born in the mountainous central Japanese prefecture of Nagano, known for abundant root vegetables and mushrooms, and grew up in her maternal grandparents' massive seed nursery (**FIG. 3**).[6] She recalls her first encounter with a pumpkin growing amid an abundance of zinnias and periwinkles.[7] She thrust her hands through the flowers and pulled out a pumpkin by its stem. She was immediately fascinated by the pumpkin's anthropomorphically large "head," recalling that it began to "speak" to her with all its might, and she felt drawn to the pumpkin's winsome form, in particular its "fat belly and unadorned features" and its "burly, psychological power."[8] She

Fig. 3 (above)
Flower field in the seed nursery owned by Yayoi Kusama's family, Matsumoto, Japan, 1920s

Fig. 4 (opposite)
Lingering Dream, 1949
Pigment on paper
53¾ × 59¾ in.
(136.5 × 151.7 cm)
Collection of the artist

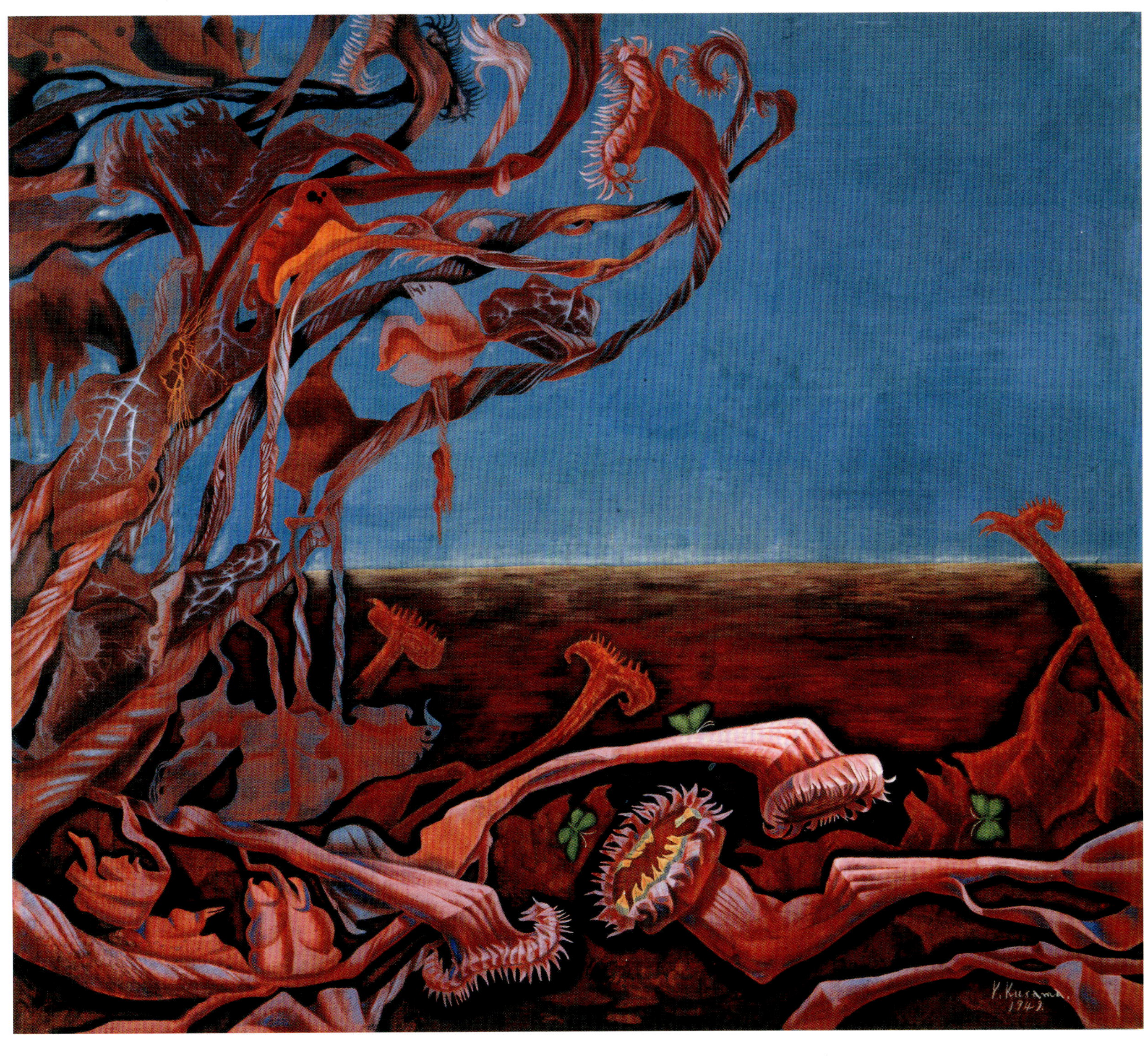
Y. Kusama.

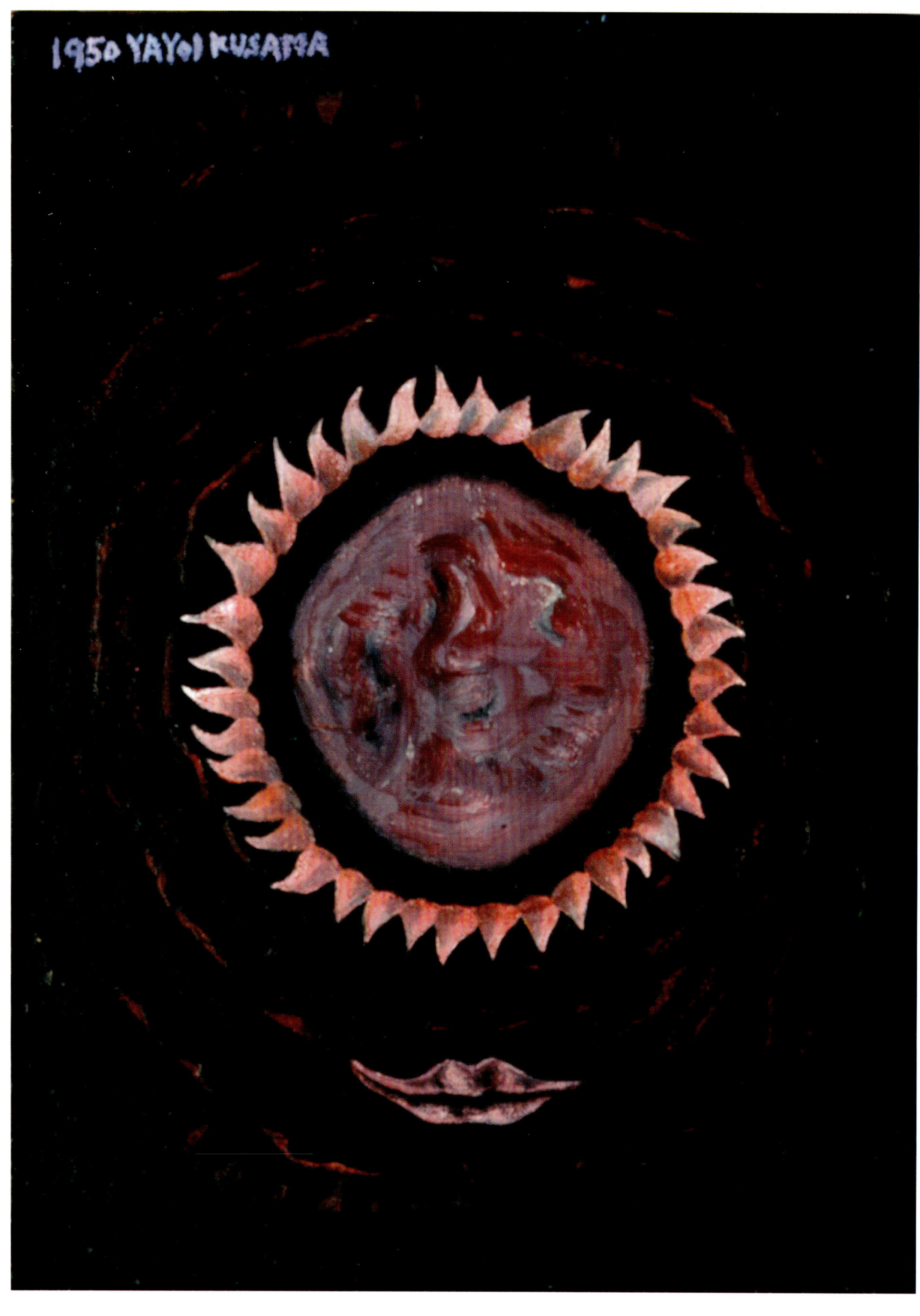
1950 YAYOI KUSAMA

Fig. 5 (opposite)
Self-Portrait, 1950
Oil on canvas
13⅜ × 9½ in. (34 × 24 cm)
Collection of the artist

Fig. 6 (right)
The Bud, 1951
Oil on jute seed bag
36 × 28¾ in. (91.5 × 73 cm)
Collection of the artist

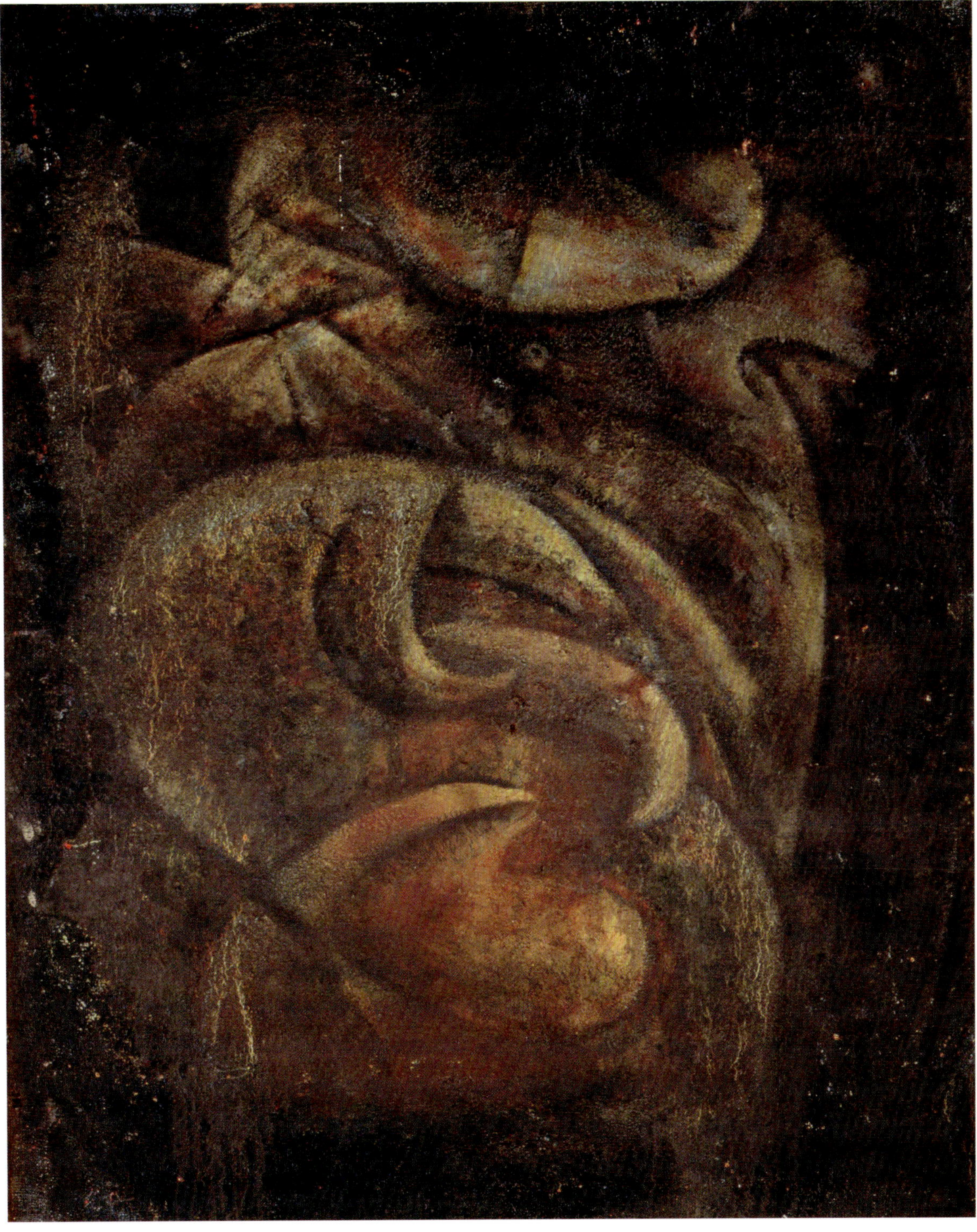

remembers a feeling of endearment when touching its surface with her hands, and the sensation of sap droplets oozing out of the freshly separated stem. Later Kusama spent a month refining a single work depicting a pumpkin, likening the experience to the process of Dharma's enlightenment, while in Kyoto training in *nihonga*.[9]

Kusama, like other progressive postwar artists, was drawn to the power of plants as a vital life force. Organic life was highly symbolic for both Surrealist and *nihonga* painters alike, who sought in different ways to overcome chaos and nihilism in the aftermath of World War II. "The veins of a leaf, grain of a tree, exotic patterns of southern succulents and expressions of tree barks, were a site of competition for artists' originality and expression; plants mediated *nihonga* and surrealist-type expressions and reflected themes of transformation and change."[10] *Lingering Dream* (1949; **FIG. 4**), one of Kusama's final *nihonga* paintings, depicts dry and withered sunflowers in a stark red desert, which one may perceive as symbolic of the dire conditions of food scarcity and desperation during World War II. Working outside the confines of *nihonga*'s symbolic standards of beauty (peonies in full bloom, chrysanthemums in flower, and the like), Kusama, similar to other *nihonga* artists, experimented with an individualized abstraction during a time when expression began to precede representation, and colors were preferred over the technical facility of outlines.[11]

Kusama's unique development during this time consists of an anthropomorphic process in which plants take on a distinct animality or even a human quality. In an early oil painting, *Self-Portrait* (1950; **FIG. 5**), a dark sunflower with bluish-pink petals floats in the center of a dark abyss, with broken concentric lines whirling around it like a vortex.[12] A pair of closed lips in the same pink hue turns the flower into an otherworldly, faceless head. This is a significant shift from the stark, surreal desertscape of *Lingering Dream*. In *Self-Portrait*, the shifting of images between a figurative sunflower and an abstract human face points to a dark apparition that is activated through a heightening of senses. Kusama transforms the sunflower into a site of raw affect, where its "face" takes on a human emotion, in much the same way the artist would often place herself inside the character of "a rock, a fish, a tree," *becoming* a flower and seeking through her work to communicate as she imagined "these things of the earth" would speak.[13] Like a ghost, this anthropomorphic "emergence" subsequently reappears in other paintings, such as *The Bud* (1951; **FIG. 6**), which was painted on jute seed bags. The Cubist shape of the bud, its parts reduced to barely perceptible geometric fragments on the dark ground plane, appears as if it is about to break through the surface of its fetal, shell-like form.

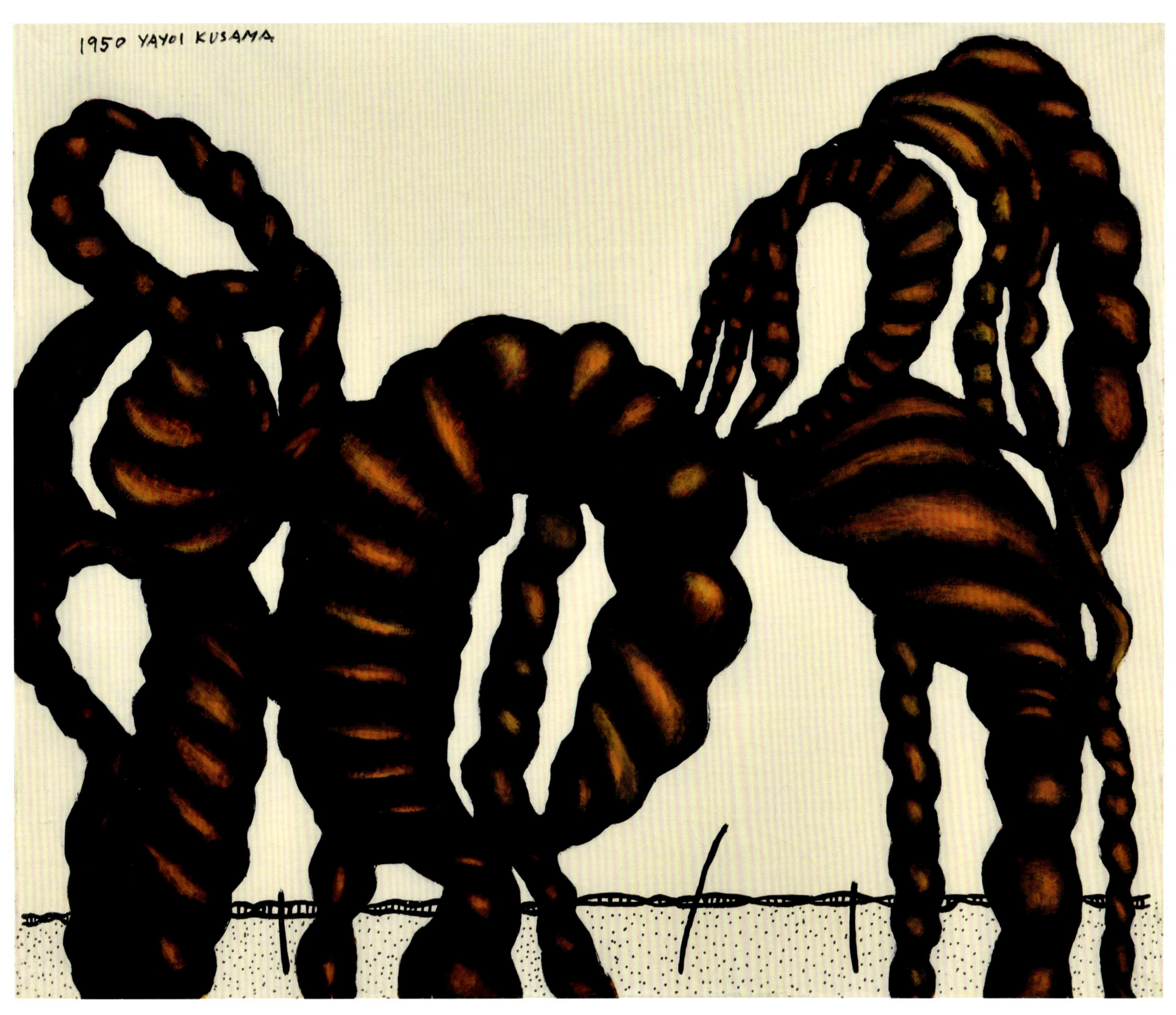

Fig. 7
Accumulation of Corpses, 1950
Oil on canvas
20⅞ × 18⅛ in. (53 × 46 cm)
Collection of the artist

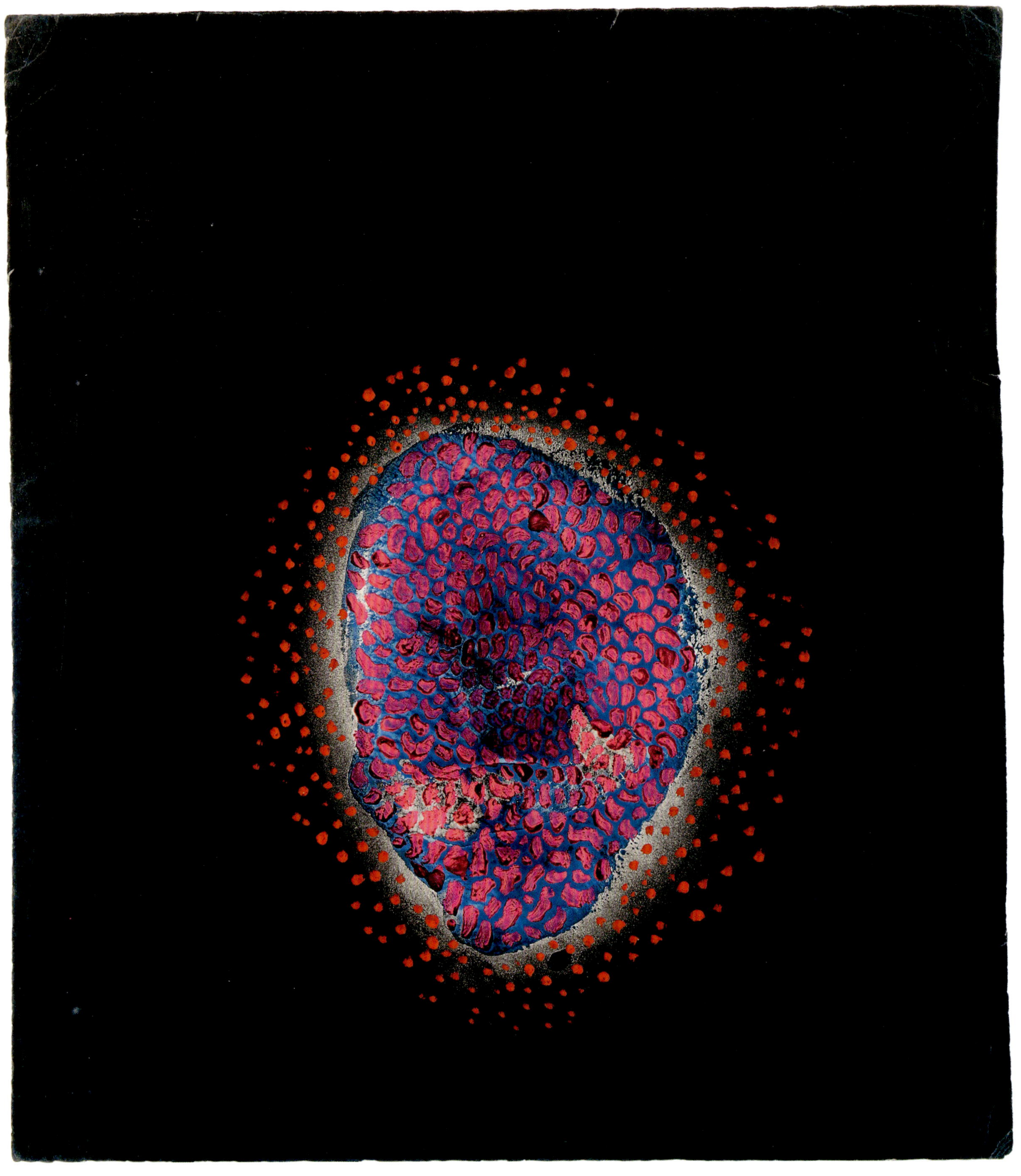

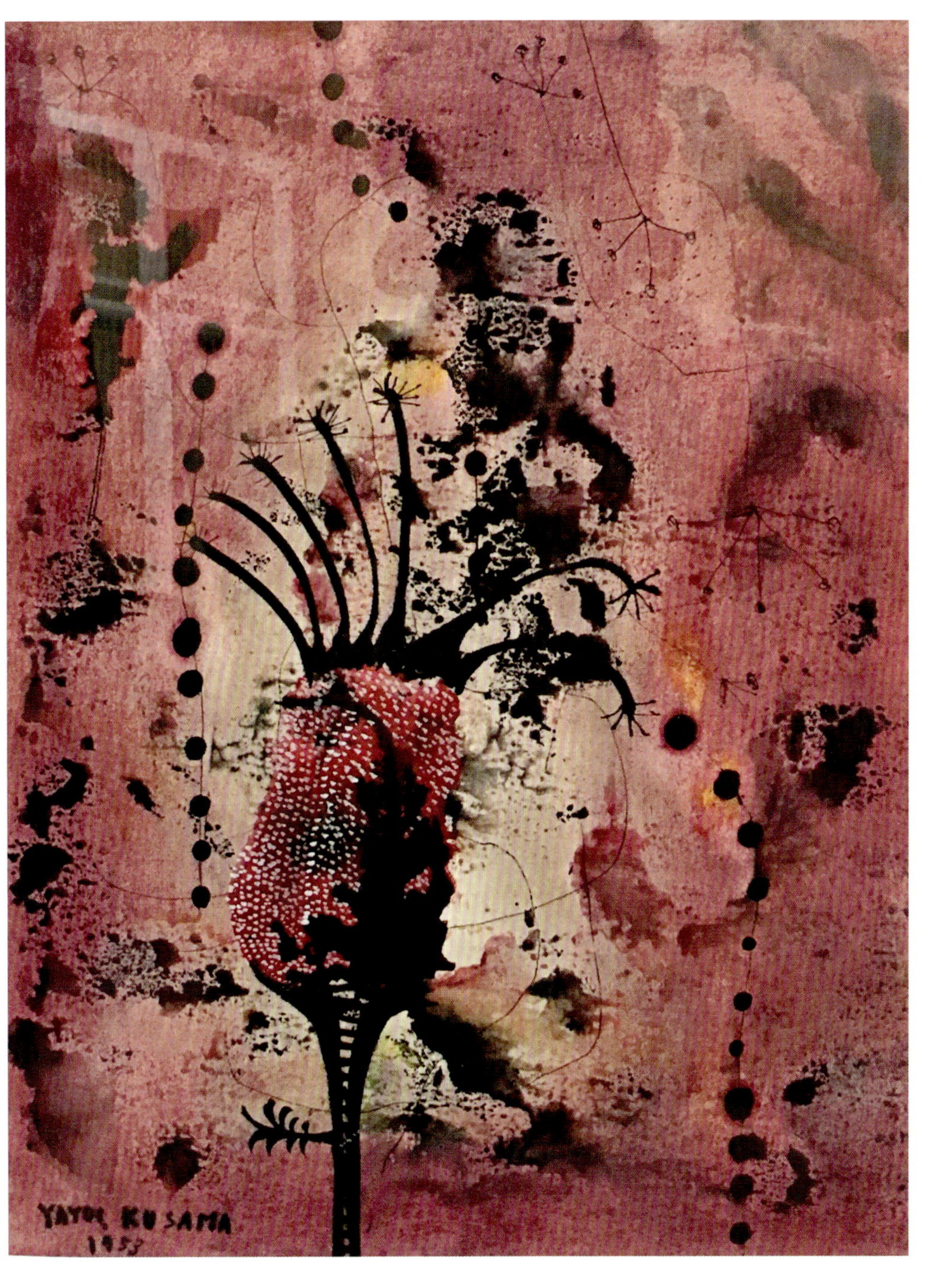

Fig. 8 (opposite)
The Night, 1953
Pastel and gouache on paper
$15 \times 12\frac{1}{8}$ in. (38 × 30.8 cm)
Collection of the artist

Fig. 9 (above)
Untitled, 1953
Ink, pastel, and gouache on paper
$11\frac{5}{8} \times 8\frac{7}{8}$ in. (29.5 × 22.5 cm)
Collection of the artist

In these early experiments, Kusama plays with the Surrealist strategy of doubling—the oscillation between two appearances—that relies on the threshold between emergence and disappearance. This is predominant in *Accumulation of Corpses* (1950; **FIG. 7**), a painting on canvas featuring thick, tightly braided, hairlike ropes emerging in the foreground before a distant fence, which may be an abstraction or could be interpreted as a reference to the Allied Occupation of Japan between 1945 and 1952. (The work was previously known as *Accumulation of Plants.*) The spiraling lines simultaneously conjure aggressive growth patterns of stems, tree bark, or gnarled roots, which emerge as abstract expressions of the fear, rage, desperation, and residual violence that lay submerged within the silent and barren landscape of war's aftermath. Kusama's repeated use of the term "accumulation" in the title of several paintings produced that year—including *Earth of Accumulation*, in which tentacles emerge from a barren field, and *Accumulation of the Corpses (Prisoner Surrounded by the Curtain of Depersonalization)* —attests to her interest in proliferation itself as a living organism, a slowly accruing outburst of raw human emotions that becomes uncontrollable as one faces death.

Art historian Izumi Nakajima has recently described how Kusama's writings of the time critique the hierarchical power of Japanese art critics who looked down on her work as stereotypically feminine, describing it as a "direct expression based on bodily sensation."[14] Taking critics to task, Kusama shifted dramatically between 1952 and 1955, particularly in her works on paper, which Nakajima divides into three categories: automatic drawings, in which she uses bold ink gestures; works employing allover dots and organic, symbolic imagery; and works featuring a balance of mystic, spatial depth and emerging organic elements.[15] Kusama felt a resonance between the "mystic" qualities of her own work and that of American artists based in the Pacific Northwest such as Morris Graves (1910–2001) and Mark Tobey (1890–1976), recognizing that "their power is in their (search for) the eternal liberation of the psyche."[16] Compared to her early paintings, her works on paper employ a less heavy-handed approach in favor of an airy, kinetic shifting or coexistence of organic forms that seem to alternate between abstraction and discernible living forms. This is explored in several works on paper such as *A Seed* (1952; page 128), in which an eye doubles as a seed superimposed on a face, and *The Night* (1953; **FIG. 8**), where a floating orb surrounded by red dotted particles doubles as a pulsating heart. Through this anthropomorphic treatment of plant life, Kusama's early visceral paintings are dark expressions of apparition, premonition, and emotion, yet we also witness a marvelous embrace of light, a celestial nature that integrates the earthly and the cosmic.

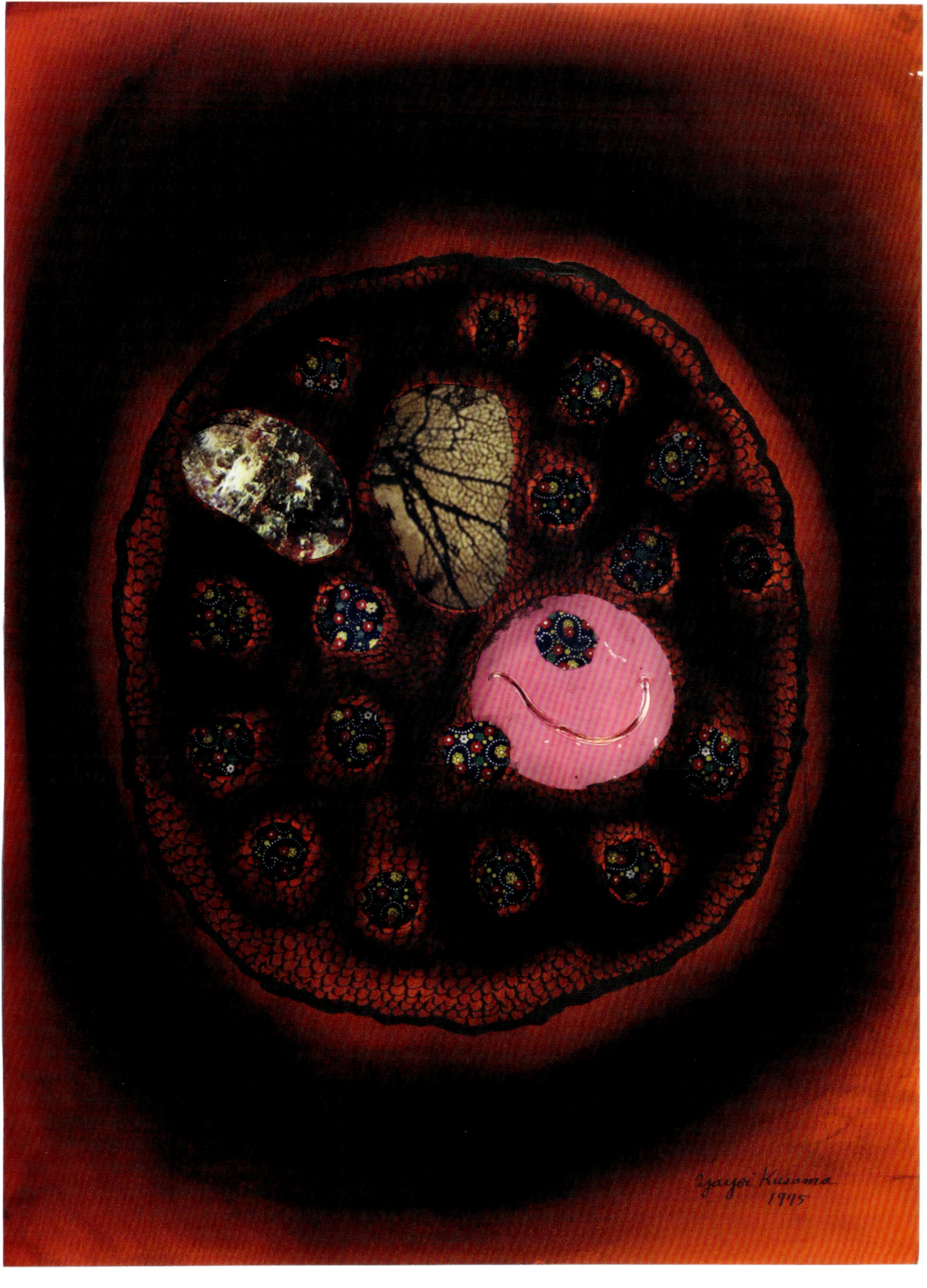

Fig. 10
Flower Petals, 1975
Pastel, ink, and fabric on paper
21½ × 15¼ in.
(54.5 × 38.6 cm)
Collection of the artist

VISAGÉITÉ (FACIALITY)

Polka dots are the "face" of affect. Affective nature (which of course is a complex act of production invisible to the eye) is a "face" that outcrops from the world of vision, and a multitude of "faces" are abstracted into the eye of the polka dot net. This is where the phenomenon of *visagéité* (faciality) that lies hidden at the root of art is taking place. . . . The work of affect, which is not visible to the eye, becomes visible. And because "distance" is introduced inside consciousness, an original fissure is formed between affect and consciousness. Kusama's production of infinity nets from polka dots attempts to capture that moment when the "faciality" of affective nature appears.

—Shinichi Nakazawa, 1987[17]

Kusama's polka dots originated from a hallucination that the artist experienced as an adolescent, in which she saw red flower patterns on her tablecloth spreading from her body onto the environment surrounding her. "I saw the entire room, my entire body, and the entire universe covered with red flowers, and in that instant my soul was obliterated and I was restored, returned to infinity, to eternal time and absolute space."[18] The artist's desire to confront this vision of proliferation manifested into an uncontrollable artistic production and labor of repetition, especially in her works on paper and paintings from the late 1950s titled *Interminable Nets*. Recalling the waves of the Pacific Ocean that she witnessed on her flight from Japan to Seattle in 1957, these works developed later into her signature *Infinity Nets* (page 131) during her time in New York City (1958–73). The infinity net is not a chaotic mass, but an orderly logic that rhythmically proliferates to fill the canvas, forming the negative space of her polka dots.

When considering the anthropomorphic quality of Kusama's early organic works, a related phenomenon introduced here by Nakazawa as *visagéité*, or faciality, emerges in the artist as she develops her *Infinity Net* paintings. Originally derived from a concept developed by philosopher Gilles Deleuze and psychoanalyst Félix Guattari, the term refers to the power of facial images in which multiple modes of affect occur, producing a feeling of intensity.[19] Nakazawa employs the term to refer to the life force that lays embedded in the abstract network of Kusama's motifs, which, not unlike a facial expression, brings forth a much larger, complex entity. Many of Kusama's contemporaries associated with Minimalism, light and space, and the late 1960s postwar Japanese art movement Mono-ha, engaged with the idea of the dot. Robert Irwin (b. 1928) and Bridget Riley (b. 1931) were interested in the haptics of optical perception. Lee

Ufan's (b. 1936) conception of the dot (*ten*) marks time, the beginning and end of the universe, while Jirō Takamatsu's (1936–98) notion of *ten* centered on physics. Kusama's polka dot is analogous to an index of trained pressure points felt in peripheral areas of the body that are interconnected with cosmic life. The polka dot can be perceived not as a single, flat, circular form, but instead as a complex, boundless, spherical entity on the verge of explosive expanse, like a sun. Nakazawa states that "Kusama's ability to make us feel like there is a universal life in her polka dots is undoubtedly due to the way she touches upon the essence of an anomalous 'logic' that brings forth an affective life."[20] One is able to visually perceive this "face" of energy in Kusama's early works on paper, such as *The Night*, in which an infinity net appears inside an orb that radiates with red dots, and *Untitled* (1953; **FIG. 9**), depicting a chain of black dots that dangles into and around a fuchsia-like tubular flower covered with tiny white dots. In later collage works like *Flower Petals* (1975; **FIG. 10**), the "face" emerges as a pink embryonic cell that floats in a glowing red net containing what looks like images of a fossilized leaf vein and an iridescent shell. Despite their distinct periods—the works on paper made in the aftermath of war and the collages during one of the darkest periods of her life, after her permanent return to Japan in 1973 (when she experienced the deaths of her father and her great friend Joseph Cornell)—both bodies of biomorphic works reflect a profound moment in which a fissure between affect and consciousness takes place.

We also witness the emergence of this "face" in her *Infinity Net* paintings. Nakazawa points to how "the eye of the infinite net holds an eerie twist like Felix Klein's bottle," referring to the mathematician who, in 1882, proposed a concept of space in which Möbius strips are joined together, so that the inner and outer surfaces are continuous and interchangeable.[21] This idea is derived from topology (from the Greek *topos*, "place," and *-logy*, "study"), the mathematical concept of geometrical transformation, in which space and shape can be continually expanded, contracted, distorted, and twisted while the structure of the object remains constant throughout. While Kusama's *Infinity Nets* have conventionally been interpreted within the context of the sublime monochrome or Minimalist abstraction, Nakazawa's notion of the "eye" of the net introduces an anti-subjective stance in which, rather than the artist generating meaning, the work itself creates a physical, experiential affect. This idea is best represented in a double exposure photograph in which a portrait of Kusama is superimposed with an infinite net of dots (**FIG. 11**). Her face and body have been consumed by a pixelated mosaic that surrounds her like an enveloping veil that emerges as a "face."

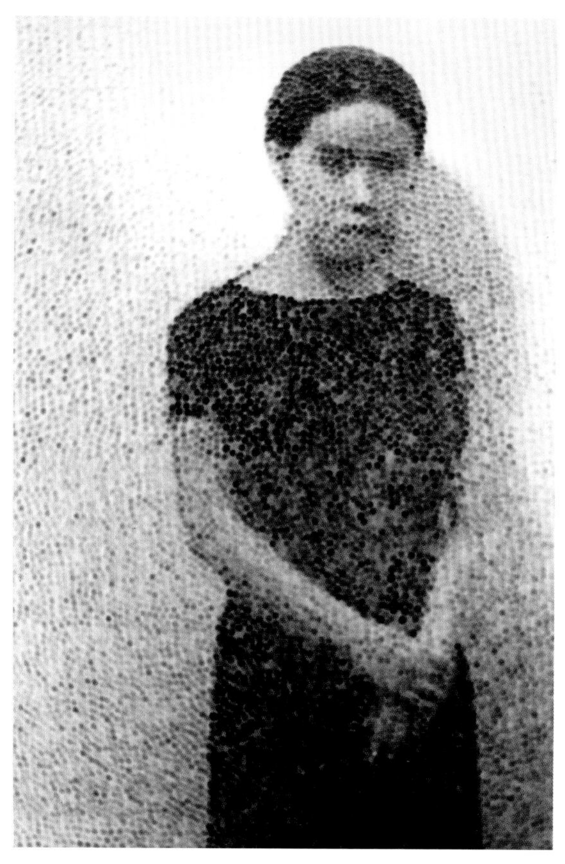

Fig. 11
Kusama with *Infinity Net* painting, double exposure photograph, early 1960s

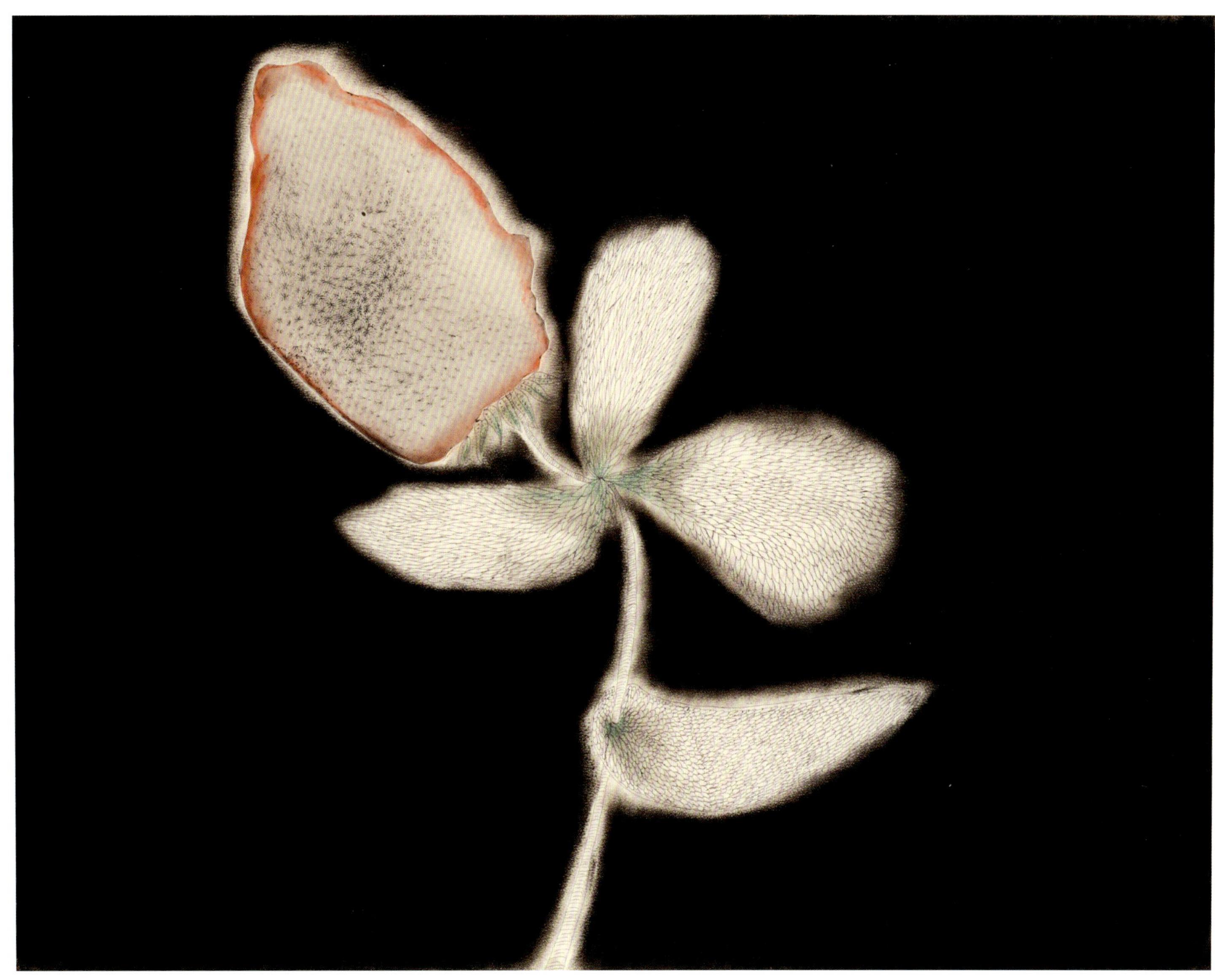

Fig. 12 (opposite)
No. 3 P.B., 1960
Oil on canvas
62¾ × 56¼ in.
(159.4 × 142.9 cm)
Private collection, Chicago

Fig. 13 (above)
Flower, 1993
Pastel, acrylic, pen, and collage on paper
21¼ × 26¾ in.
(54.1 × 67.8 cm)
Collection of the artist

Kusama's nets create an effect of stretching beyond the canvas into a multitude of dimensions, in which the viewer is immersed inside a topological space. At the apex of Kusama's transformative series from this period is *No. 3 P.B.* (1960; **FIG. 12**), one of the earliest large red *Infinity Net* paintings, which Kusama exhibited at the 1961 *Whitney Annual* in New York. Invited by curator John Gordon, a longtime supporter of her work who had previously included her in the *International Watercolor Exhibition, 20th Biennale* (1959) at the Brooklyn Museum, Kusama contributed a breakthrough work of interconnected arcs that spread indefinitely beyond the edge of the canvas. It is possible to discern waves of dense foam undulating beneath the surface, each flowing in a different direction, its abstracted "face" emerging as a glowing red halation like cosmic light about to encapsulate the viewer.

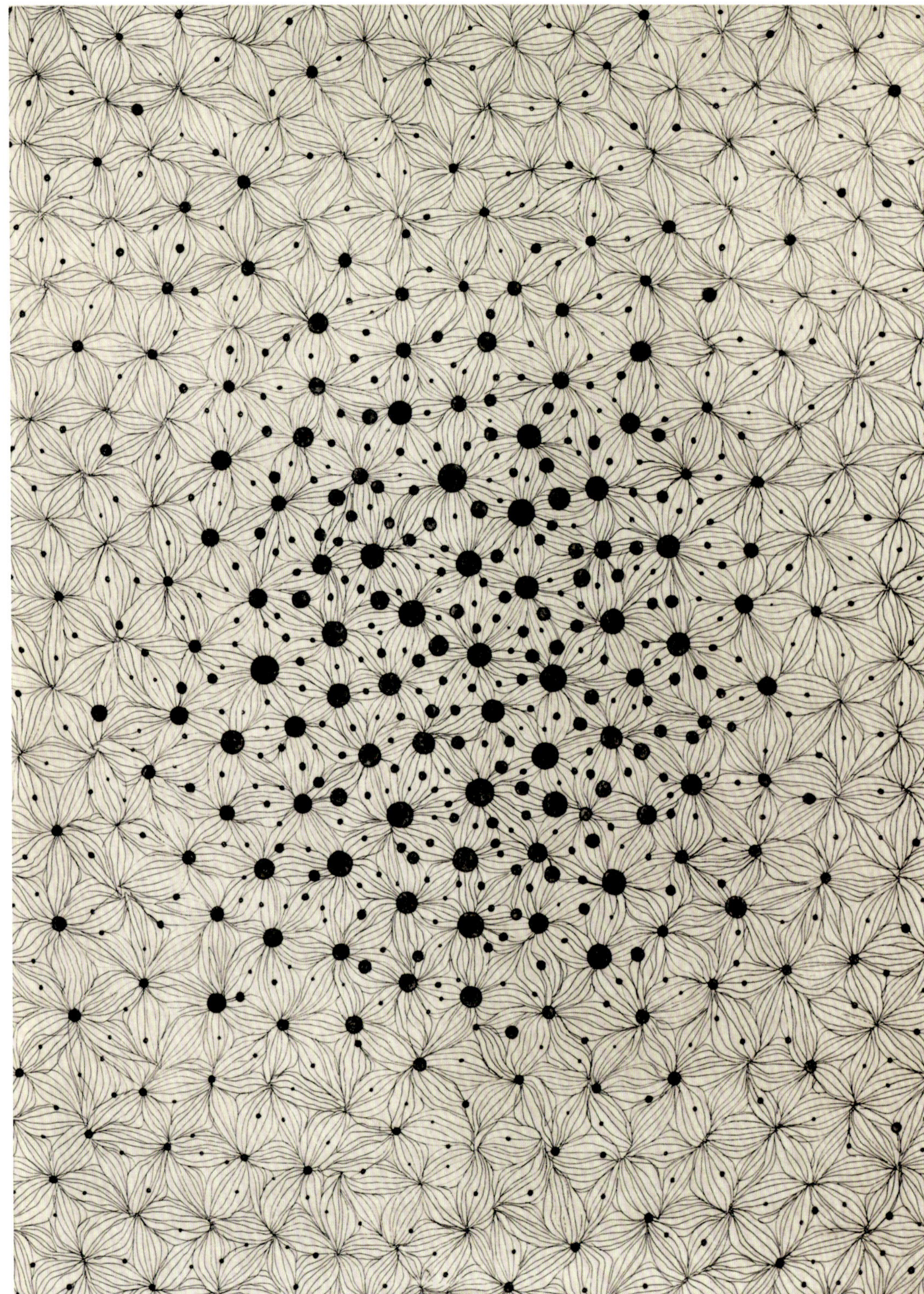

Fig. 14 (left)
Pistils and Stamens, 1994
Etching on paper
16½ × 11⅝ in. (41.7 × 29.5 cm)
Collection of the artist

Fig. 15 (opposite)
Galaxy, 1993
Acrylic on canvas
Collection unknown

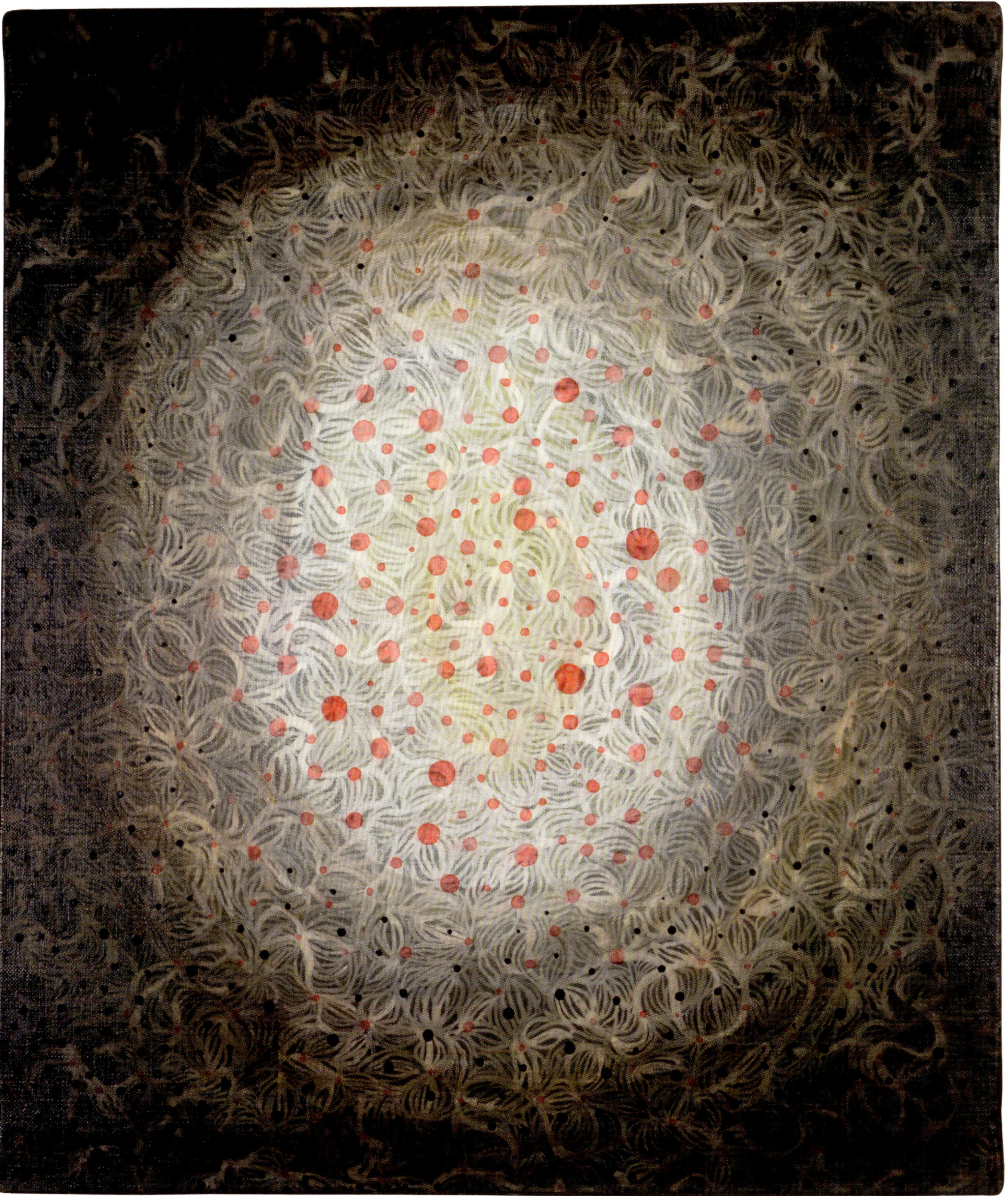

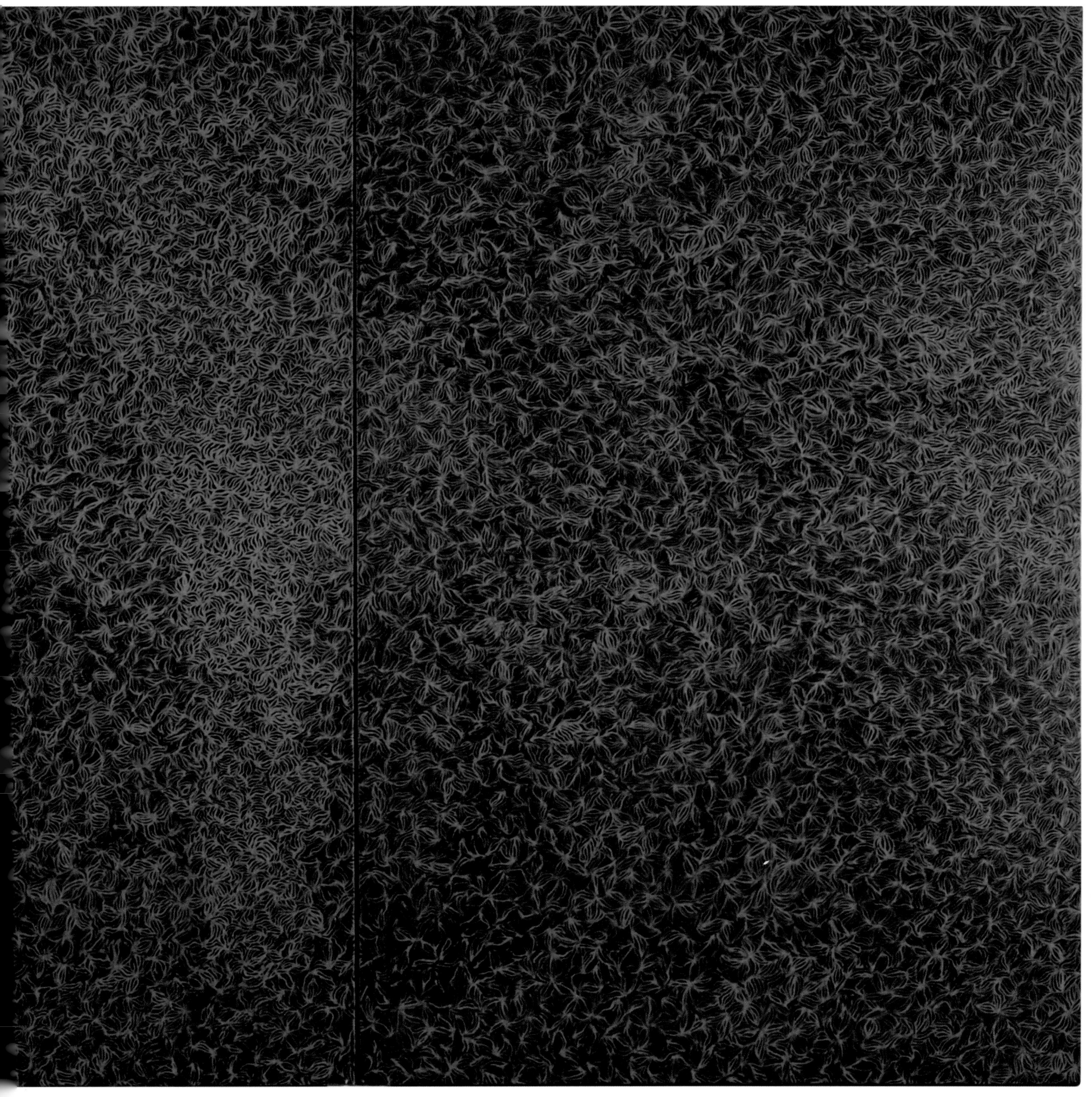

Fig. 16 (previous)
Weeds, 1996
Acrylic on canvas
57¼ × 114½ in.
(145.5 × 291 cm)
Forever Museum of
Contemporary Art, Japan

The *Infinity Nets* evolved in the 1980s and 1990s. Kusama's paintings and works on paper from this period retain the core element of the infinity net, but they feature botanical themes and titles more explicitly. Small-scale paintings, such as *Signs of Life* (1987) and *Multiplication of Life* (1988), accentuate the cell-like structure of the infinity net. *Flower* (1993; **FIG. 13**), a white-on-black collage, depicts a swaying white flower outlined in peach with white leaves patterned with delicate rendering of nets, recalling the hairlike fungal structure of mycelium. Critic Sir Herbert Read first made reference to mycelium in describing the artist's *Infinity Nets* in 1964.[22] The "eye" of the net is perhaps most clearly pronounced in her etching *Pistils and Stamens* (1994; **FIG. 14**), in which black dots (likely pistils) accumulate toward the center of the composition, connected by a net of stamen-like filaments. This centrifugal composition is typical of works from this period that also reference the cosmos, such as *Galaxy* (1993; **FIG. 15**). In this work delicate, white microbial hairs radiate outward from a central light source upon which red dots float—triggering the beginning or the end of the world. *Weeds* (1996; **FIG. 16**), a large-scale green triptych, features hairlike nets that suggest patterns of raindrops on glass. Rather than a drawn gesture, the dark-green expanse and ephemerality of the wet, slippery weblike forms conjure a base materiality that creeps up one's spine; in this sense, the work succeeds in showing the invisible "face" of affect as it emerges through a multitude of proliferating "weeds."

BIO-COSMIC

Yayoi Kusama deconstructs materials, forms, colors, and meaning in order to reconstruct a powerful emotion and perspective much deeper than the foundation with which she began. . . . Her selected path toward non-differentiation and displaced accumulations is none other than to engage us more than ever before toward a process of heightened differentiation.

—Félix Guattari, 1986[23]

In a rare performance, *Infinity Nets* (1983; **FIG. 17**), at Tokyo's Video Gallery SCAN, an untitled Kusama ceramic with white stamens entwined in a circular form was displayed on multiple closed-circuit monitors while the artist drew lines with black markers on the walls and proceeded to wrap participants in white string hung from the ceiling until they were completely entangled.[24] This act of connection was an expression of the philosophy of self-obliteration espoused by the artist since the 1960s. Intended to free oneself of ego and

Fig. 17
Two views of *Infinity Nets*, 1983
Performance video
Video Gallery SCAN, Tokyo

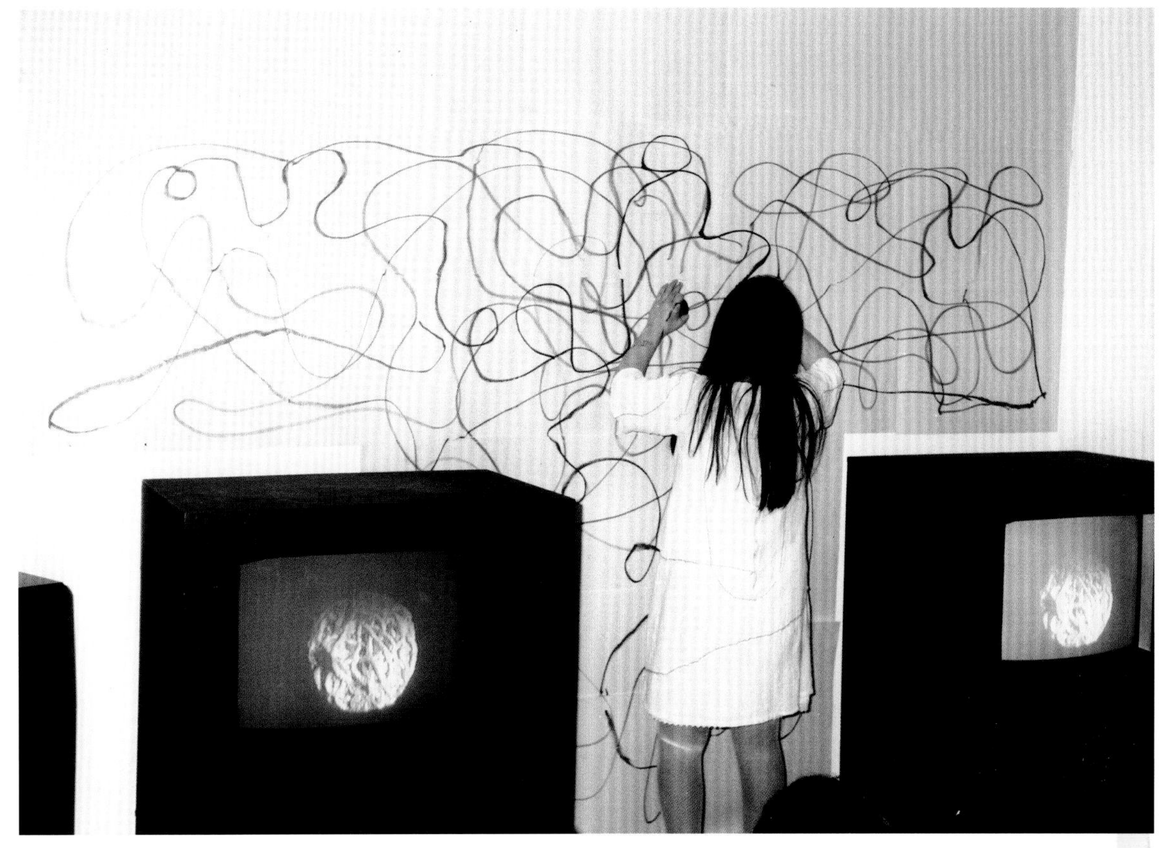

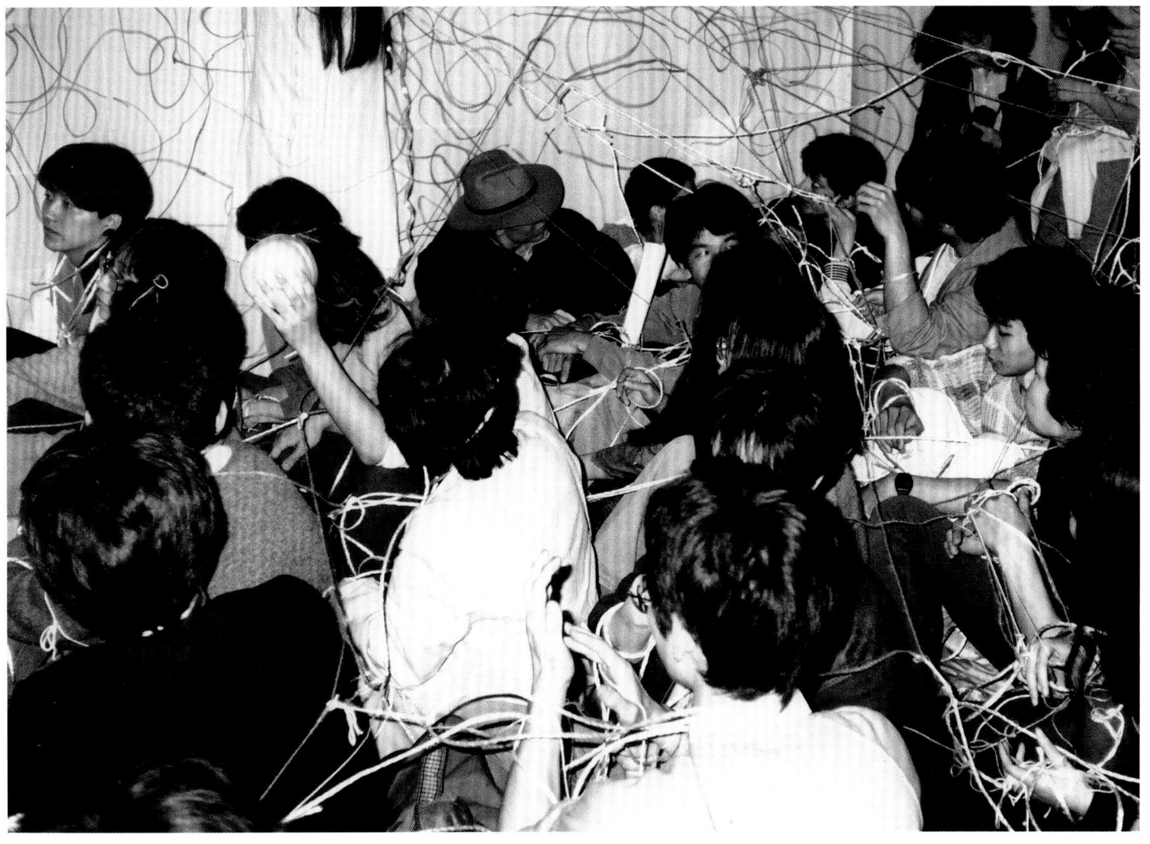

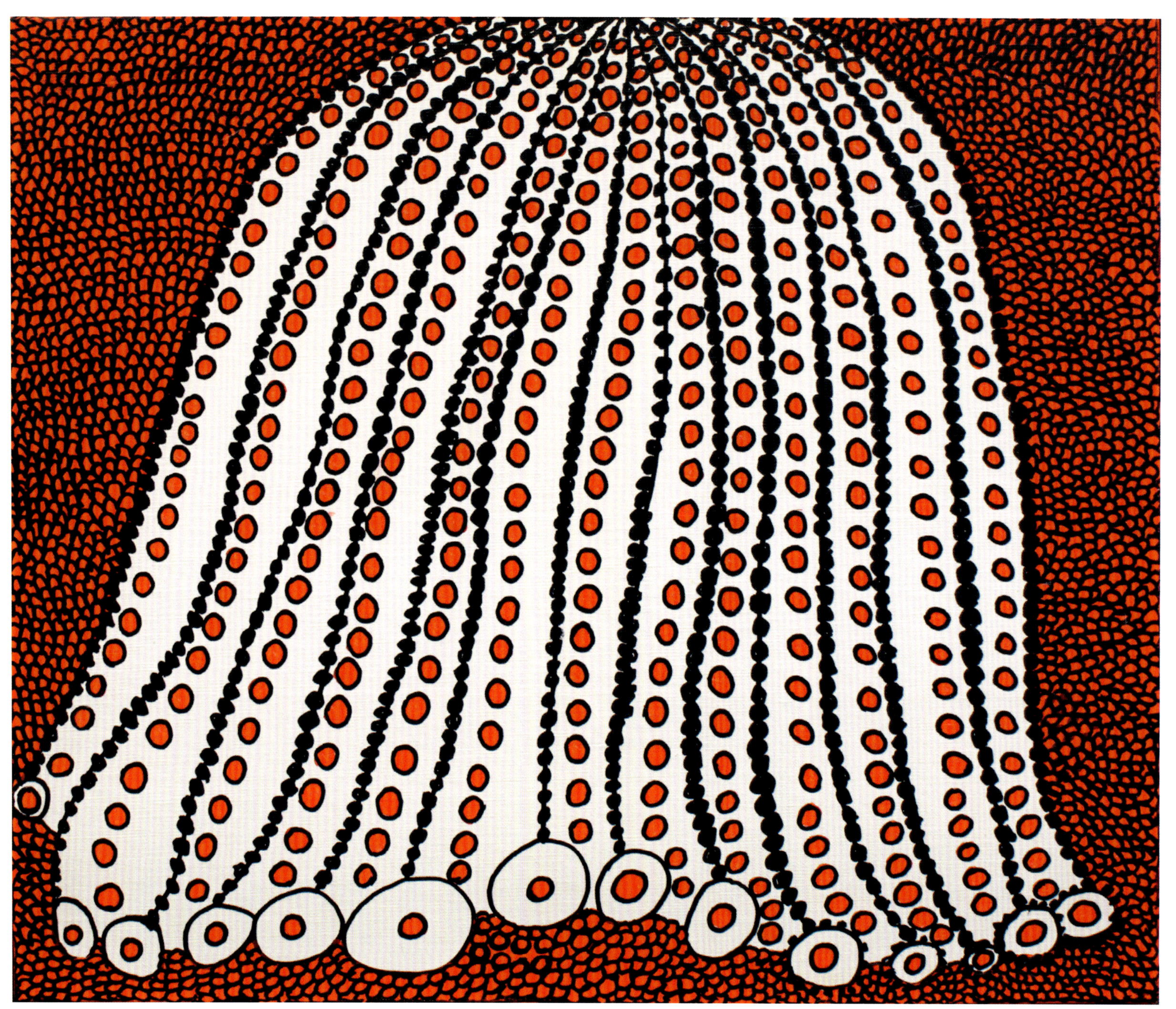

Fig. 18
Pumpkin TWOTOEL, 2004
Acrylic and felt pen
on canvas
17⅞ × 20⅞ in. (45.5 × 53 cm)
Collection of the artist

foster experiencing one another as equals, this was a powerful call for peace during protests against the Vietnam War. In the context of the 1980s, however, the connectivity that is suggested in a live activation of the infinity net is juxtaposed with the artist's psychosexual sculptures, in which one witnesses a process of deconstructing and then reassembling the reproductive organs of flowers, forming intense, organic bodies composed of many repetitive forms. Her assemblage boxes shift between floral and vaginal references, such as the white, spindly hairs that shroud a central, egg-like nest in *Flower* (1985; page 86), and red-dotted phallic forms, drawn from Kusama's *Infinity Mirror Room—Phalli's Field* repertoire, which reappear enveloping white pistils and red, stringlike "stamens" in *Moonlit Bedding* (1988; page 87). Kusama's 1983 performance can be understood as an expression of her unique vision of and engagement with nature at large. Attributing memory to plants, one may conceive this engagement as bio-cosmic. As Nakazawa has noted, "The memory of affect when plants were 'primordial plants' (Goethe) that contained minerals and animals inside itself has not yet been lost. Such bio-cosmic plants search their own 'face' and stand up toward the light."[25]

Around 2003 Kusama began working on a series of paintings that would lead to her present-day *My Eternal Soul* series, in which organic elements—both mineral and animal forms—are employed as recurring bio-cosmic motifs. The artist uses a bright, at times fluorescent, palette and bold outlines. *Pumpkin TWOTOEL* (2004; **FIG. 18**) depicts an octopus-like form in an infinite bed of red arcs, while in *Conversations in Heaven* (2004; **FIG. 19**) flower heads double as the eyes of two silhouetted faces that meet in the center, flanking a set of blue flowers. The negative spaces of polka dots have morphed into bold tentacles that emanate from a brazen red sun in *Tribute to the Sun in the Cosmos* (2010; **FIG. 20**). Fernlike forms, suggestive of curly Japanese sago palm leaves in *The Prairie in the Summer* (2004; page 82) reappear in large scale as leaves borne on a stream of blue water in *The Path of Life* (2017; page 83) and *All About the Appearance of the Heart* (2018; page 89). Sunflowers with radiating, tentacle-like petals appear in *Flowers Speak* (2016; page 147), and are adorned with faces in *I Want to Go to the Universe* (2013; page 139). These form the basis of her new outdoor sculpture, *I Want to Fly to the Universe* (2020; page 140), a bright, purple-tentacled floral form that has morphed into a monumental starfish with a primordial face. The title of this work suggests the imaginary desire of the artist, disguised as a fantastic plant-animal taking a lightning-speed leap into outer space.

Linking human nature to cosmic nature, Nakazawa states that Kusama "stands in a consistent place. That place is one in which 'nature at large' catapults a leap inside 'human nature,' and the

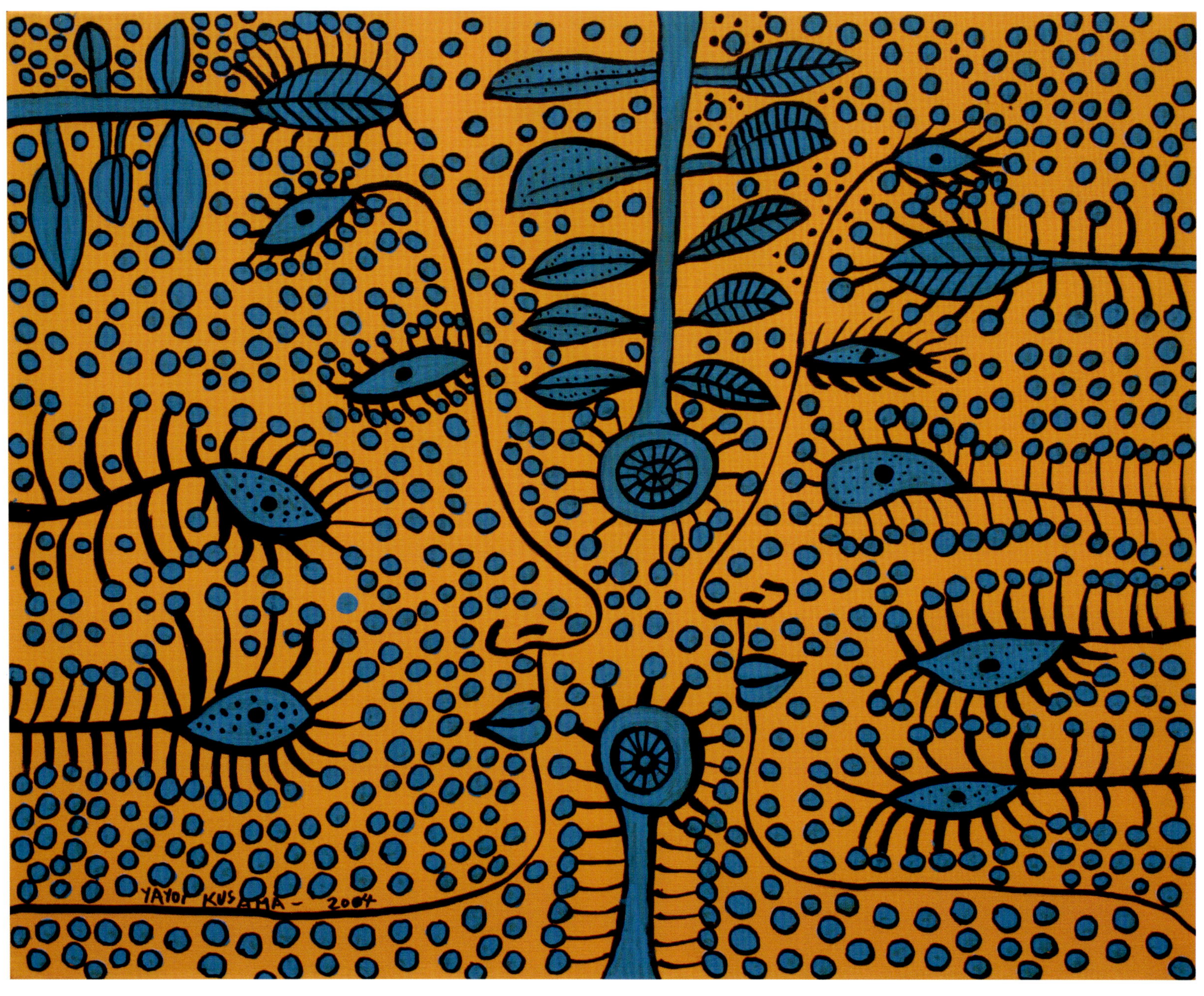

Fig. 19 (above)
Conversations in Heaven, 2004
Acrylic on canvas
20⅞ × 25⅝ in.
(53 × 65.2 cm)
Collection of the artist

Fig. 20 (opposite)
Tribute to the Sun in the Cosmos, 2010
Acrylic on canvas
63¾ × 63¾ in. (162 × 162 cm)
Collection of the artist

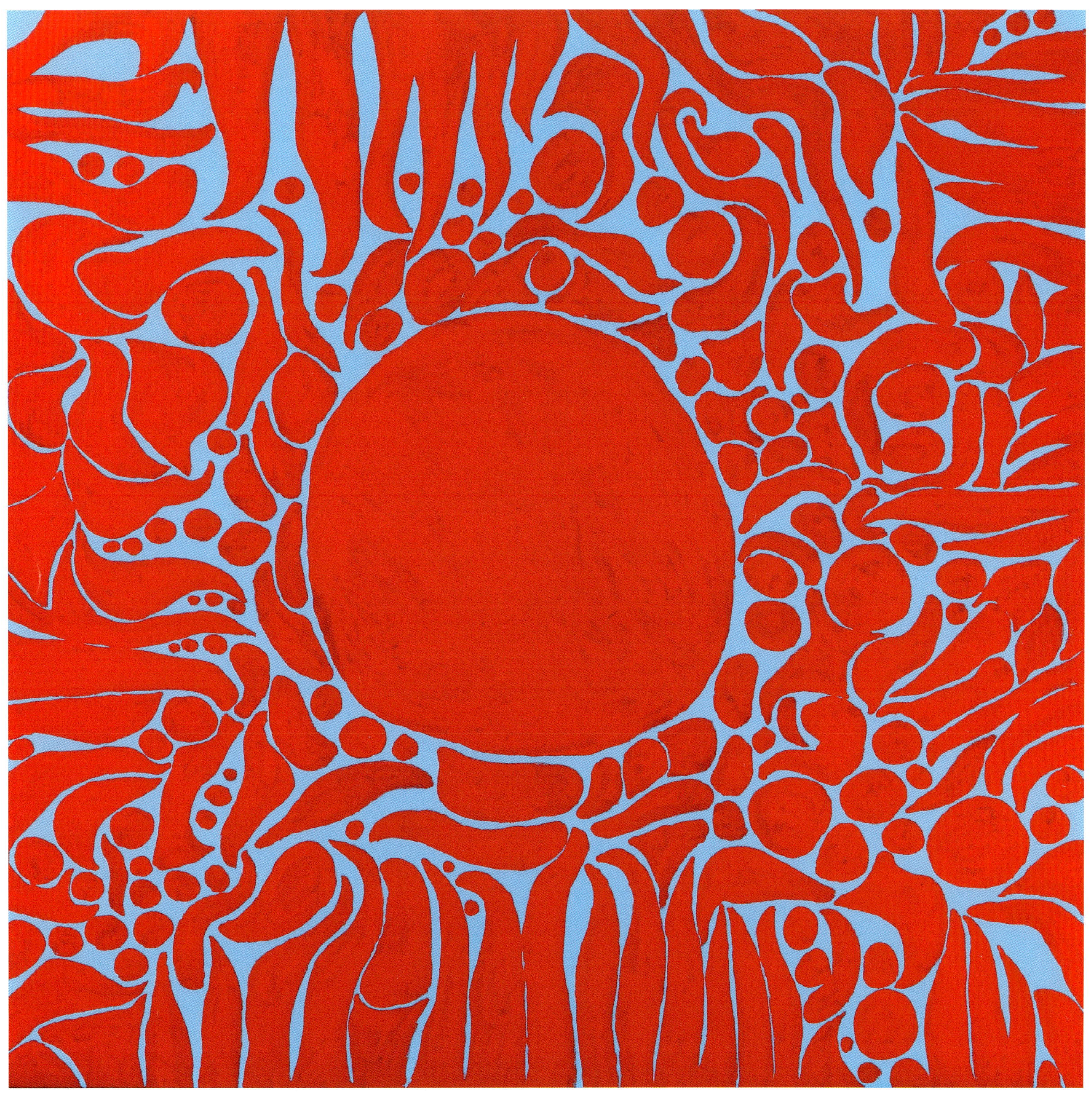

Fig. 21 (below)
Production still from
Kusama's Self-Obliteration
film, 1967

opposite
Untitled, 1953
Ink, pastel, and gouache
on paper
10¾ × 8¹⁄₁₆ in.
(27.3 × 20.5 cm)
Collection of the artist

moment when 'human nature' is about to take a strange leap toward 'cosmic nature.'"[26] In photographs documenting a 1985 performance, *Flowers of Basara* (pages 154–55), Kusama stands before blossoming cherry trees at Kuhonbutsu Jōshin-ji, a large Buddhist temple in Tokyo, wearing a deep-red, kimono-like garment with oversize sleeves. White streamers encircle her body, extending to the branches of the trees, forming a vast, three-dimensional infinity net. Kusama herself becomes the "eye" of her own infinity net, occupying the threshold between nature and the cosmos.

In Kusama's work we witness three interrelated languages: anthropomorphism, a doubling of forms that take on a human character; *visagéité* (faciality), the invisible emergence of a presence in the formation of her polka dot and infinity nets; and, finally, the bio-cosmic, in which mineral- and animal-like elements converge with outer space. At the core of Kusama's unique engagement with nature is a radical embrace of the unknown. In Kusama's words:

> *My momentary life that is supported by some invisible force exists in illusions in a brief moment of quietude of hundreds of millions of endless light years. The self-revolution which I had been pursuing as a means to live was actually a means to find death. What death signifies, its colors and special beauty, the quietude of its footprints and "nothingness" after death. I am now at a stage to creat[e] art[,] for the repose of my soul embrac[es] all of these.*[27]

In a poignant scene from her 1967 film *Kusama's Self-Obliteration* (**FIG. 21**), the artist appears wearing a straw fisherman's hat, half-submerged in a lake surrounded by a green forest in Woodstock, New York. Holding a brush, she paints red dots on the surface of the water and continues as each disperses and dissolves into tinier droplets with each ripple, one by one. The ephemerality of the dotted paint—its slowly morphing form and diffusion into a larger macrocosm—indexes the artistic fusion of creation and dissolution, the marking and unmarking of time, and the principles of connectedness and an expanded consciousness that lie at the root of Kusama's engagement with the natural world. Kusama's perception of nature is one that adapts the natural cycles of organic growth and proliferation as a means through which cosmic life is made ever-present.

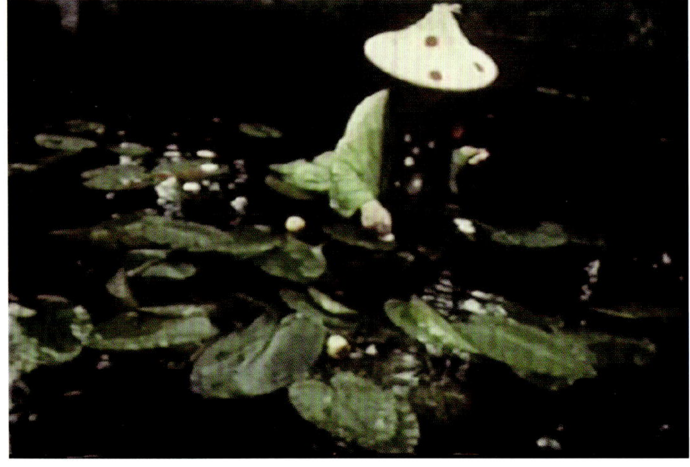

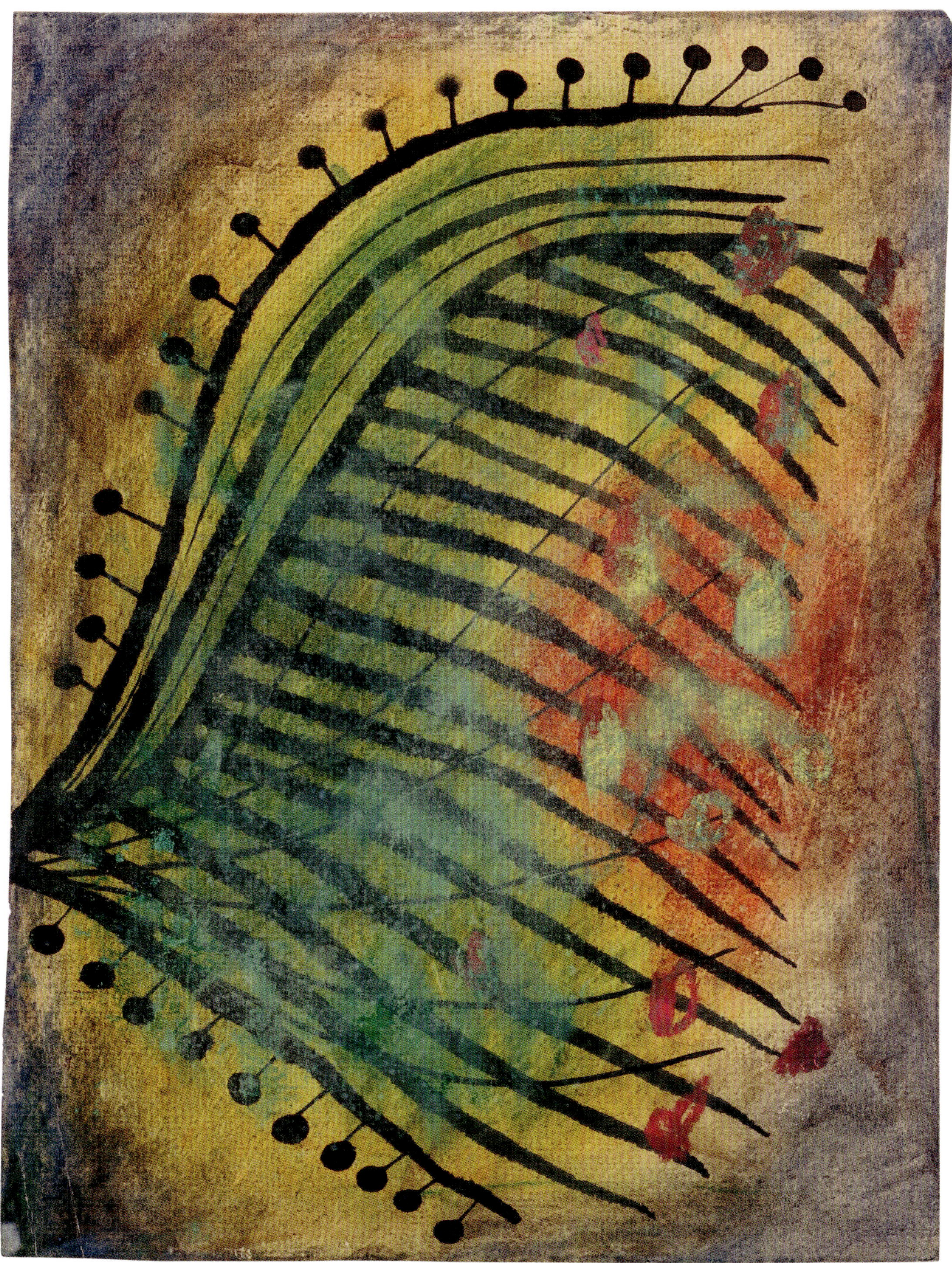

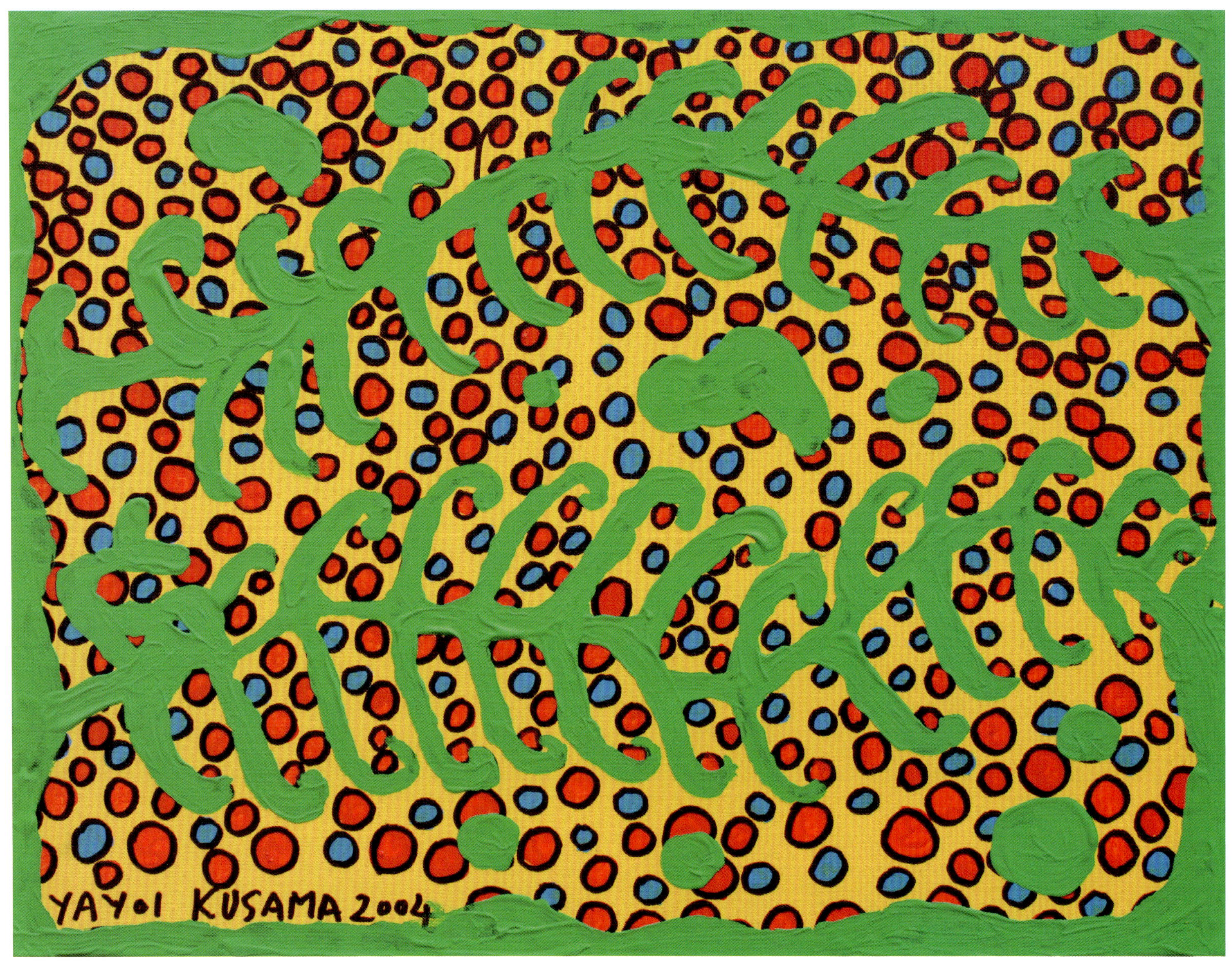

above
The Prairie in the Summer, 2004
Acrylic and felt pen on canvas
12½ × 16⅛ in. (31.8 × 41 cm)
Collection of the artist

opposite
The Path of Life, 2017
Acrylic on canvas
76⅜ × 76⅜ in. (194 × 194 cm)
Collection of the artist

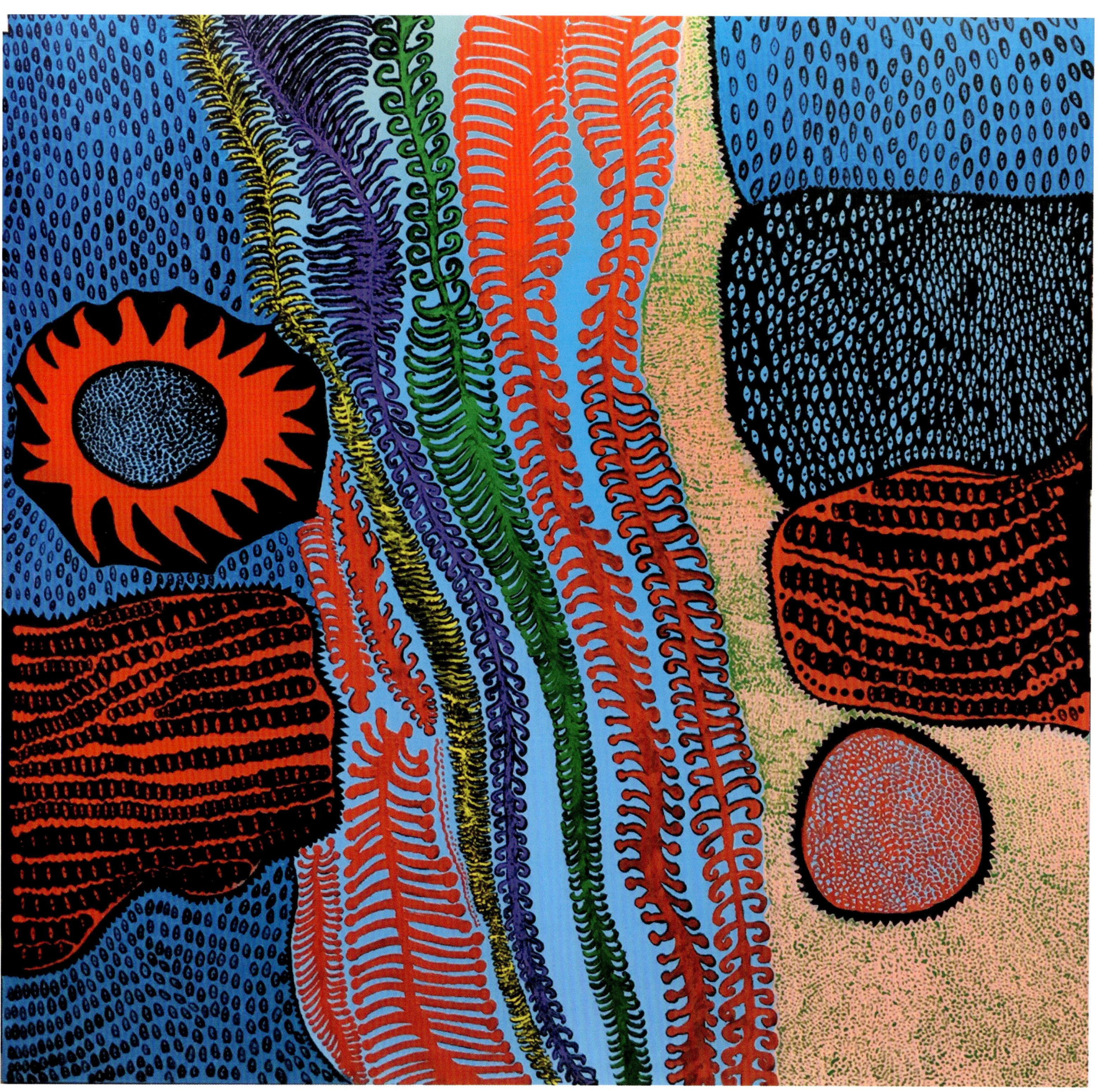

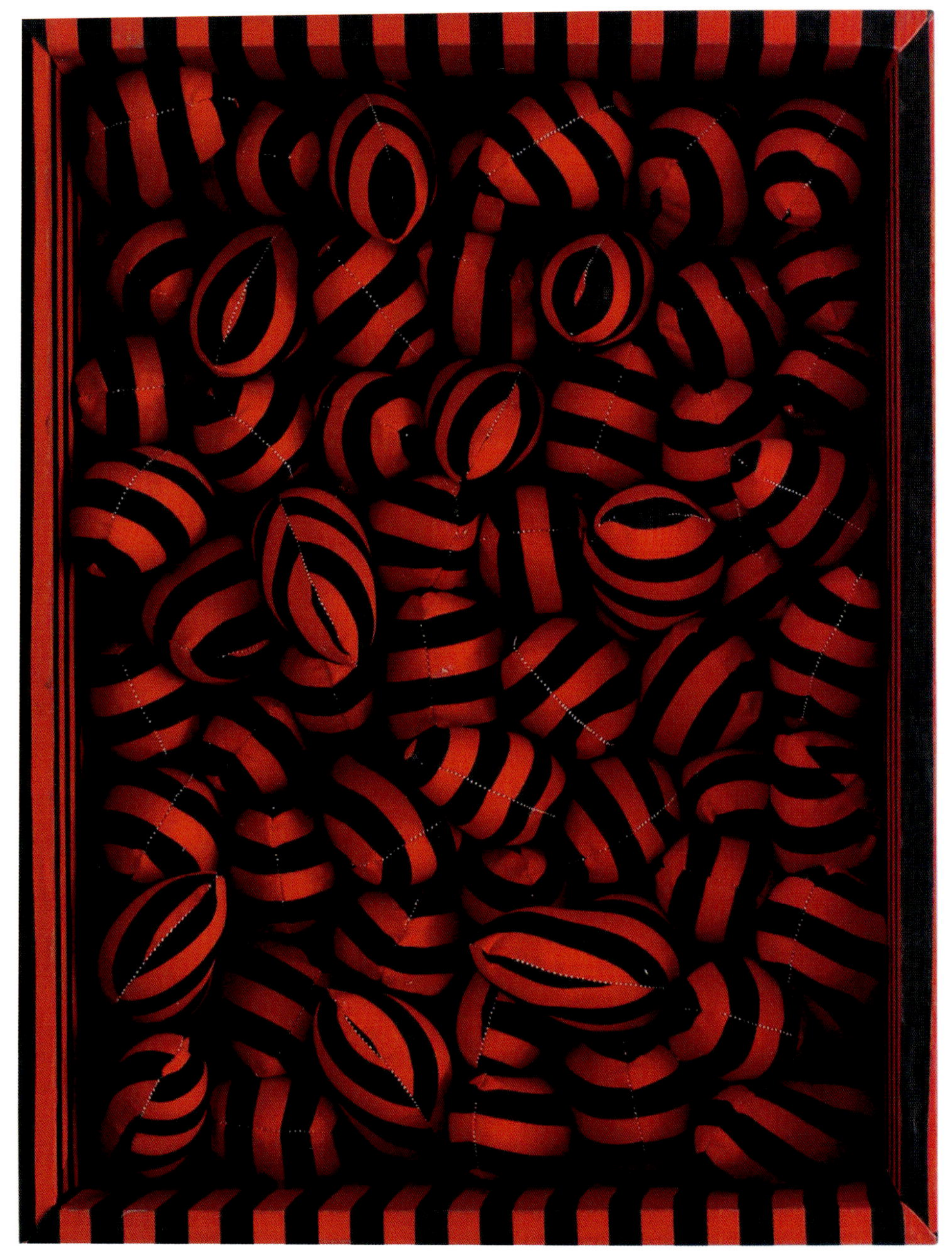

above
Summer, 1980
Sewn and stuffed fabric, fabric and wood box
15½ × 11⅝ × 4¾ in.
(39.5 × 29.5 × 12.2 cm)
Private collection, Japan
Courtesy of Ota Fine Arts

opposite
Blue Flower, 1988
Mixed media
11¾ × 8 × 4⅛ in.
(30 × 20.2 × 10.5 cm)
Takahashi Ryutaro Collection, Yokohama, Japan

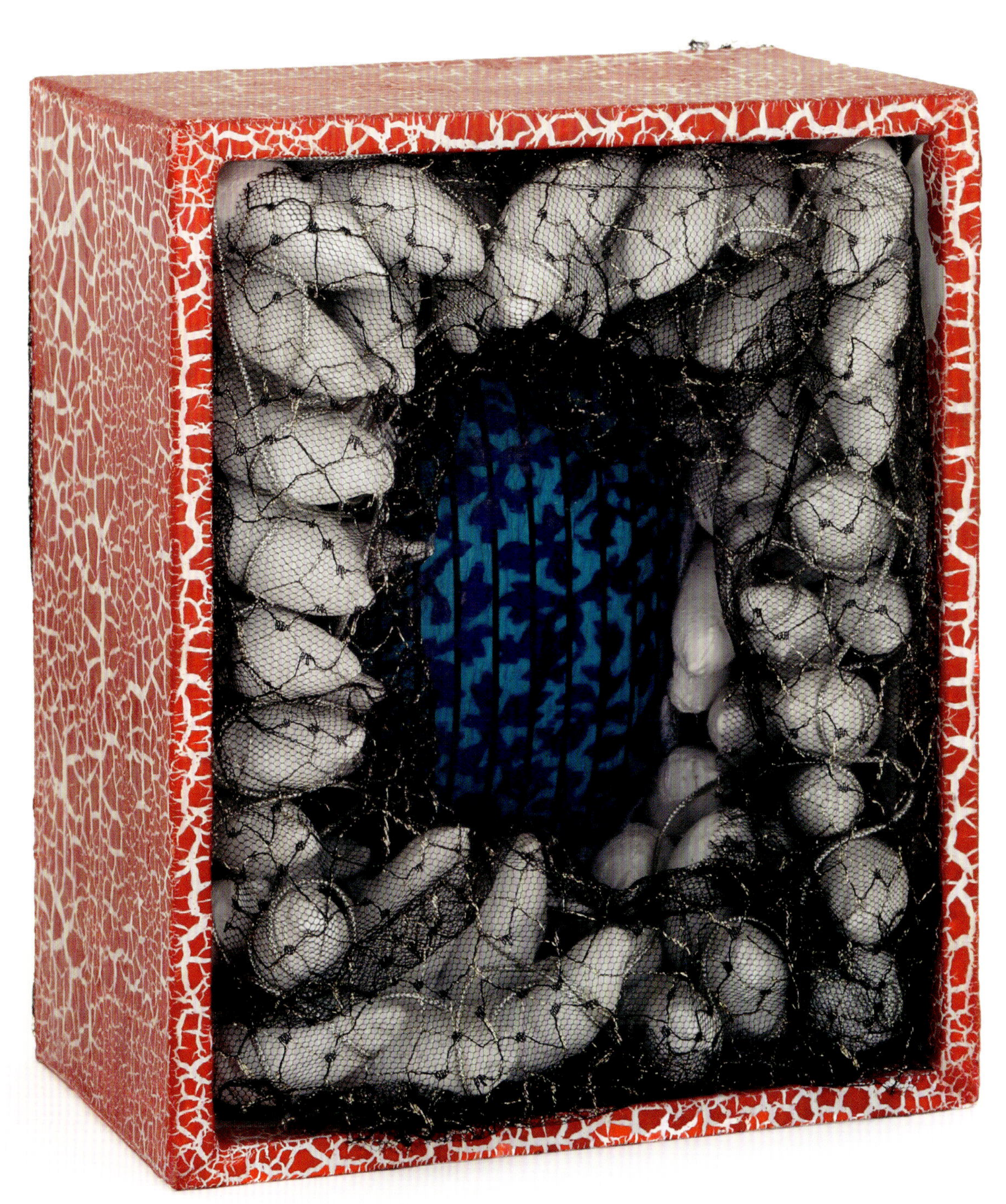

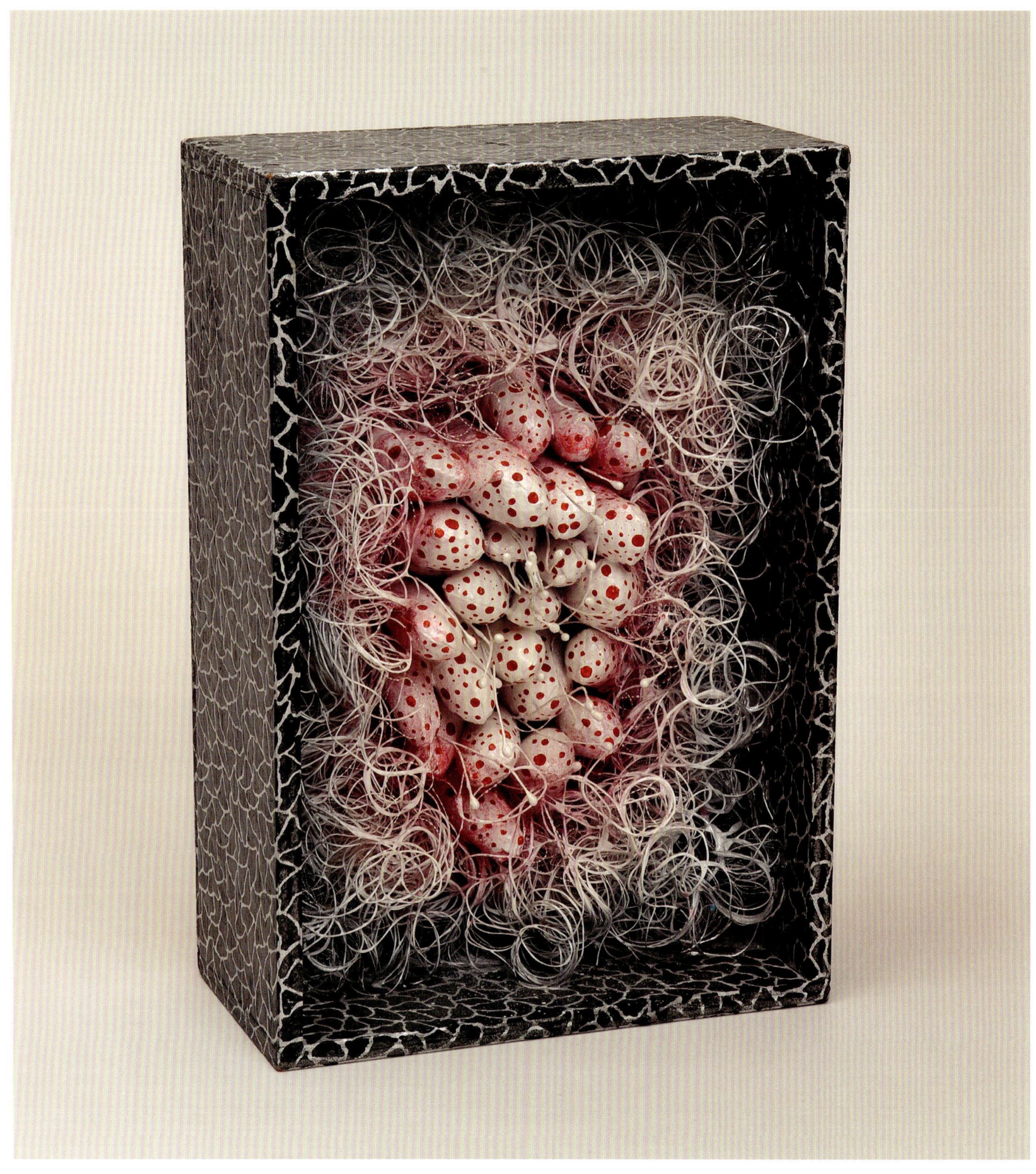

above
Flower, 1985
Mixed media
11¾ × 8 × 4⅛ in.
(30 × 20.2 × 10.5 cm)
Collection of Ota Fine Arts

opposite
Moonlit Bedding, 1988
Mixed media
15½ × 10⅝ × 4¾ in.
(39.5 × 27 × 12 cm)
Private collection
Courtesy of Ota Fine Arts

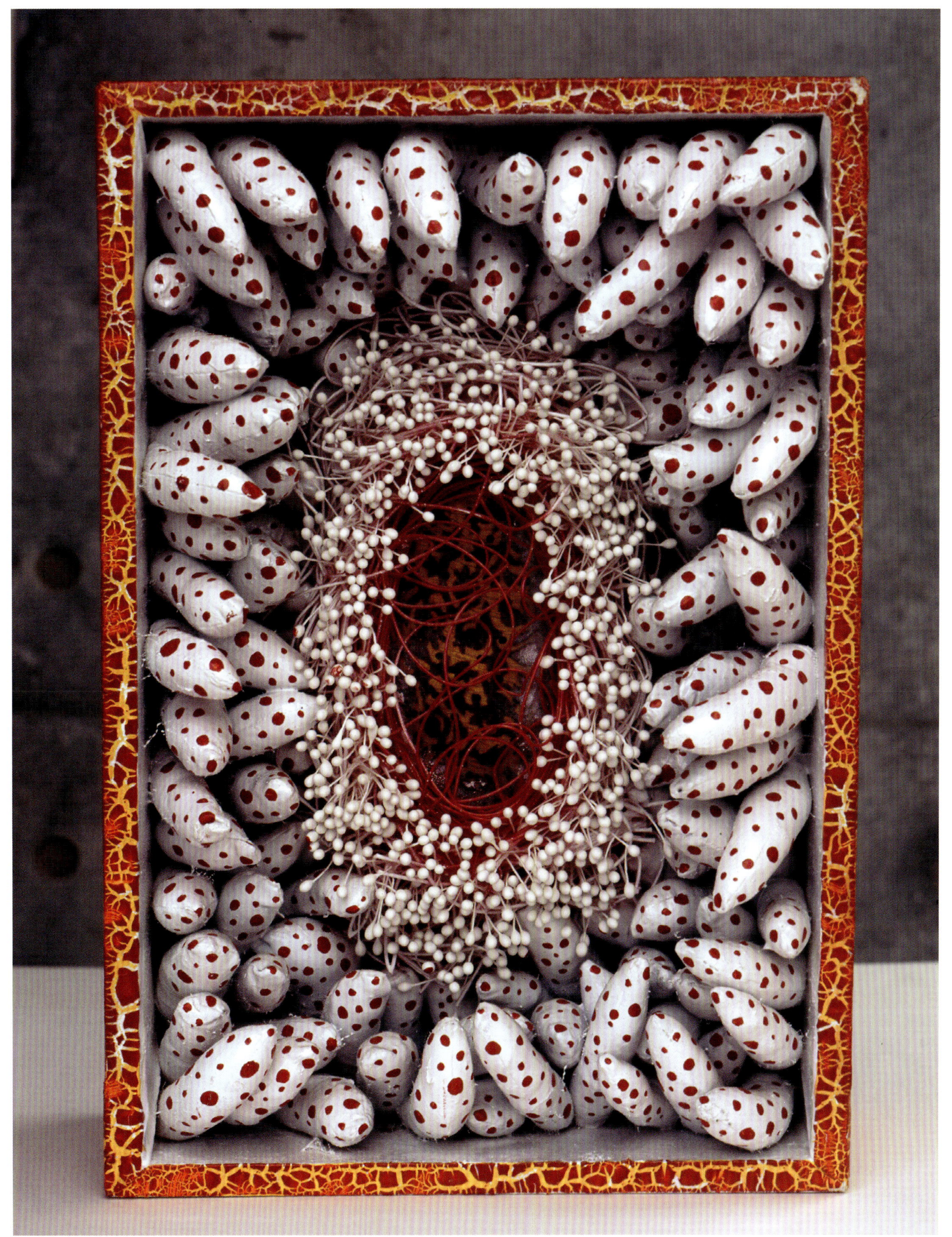

All About the Appearance of the Heart, 2018
Acrylic on canvas
76⅜ × 76⅜ in. (194 × 194 cm)
Collection of the artist

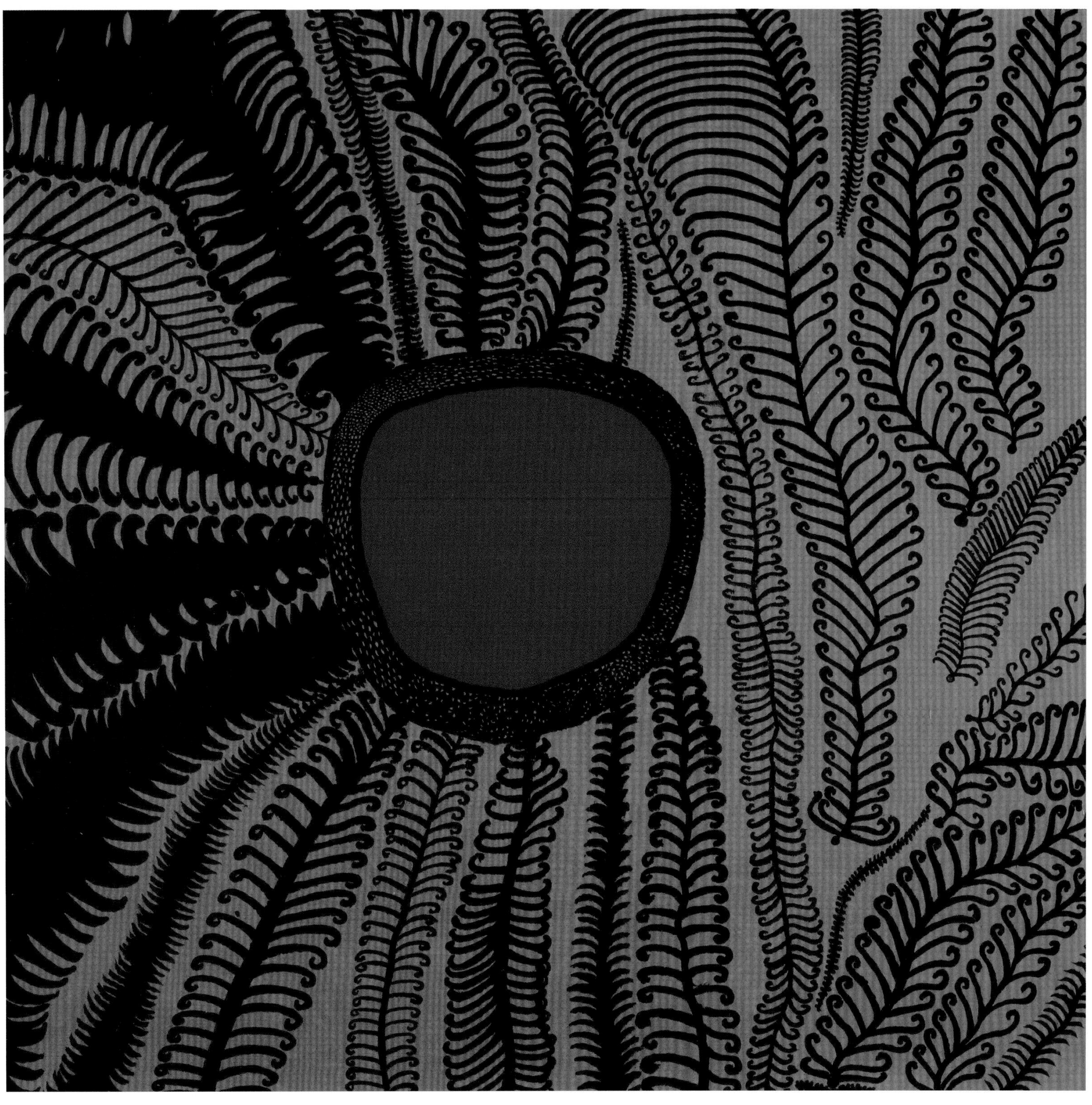

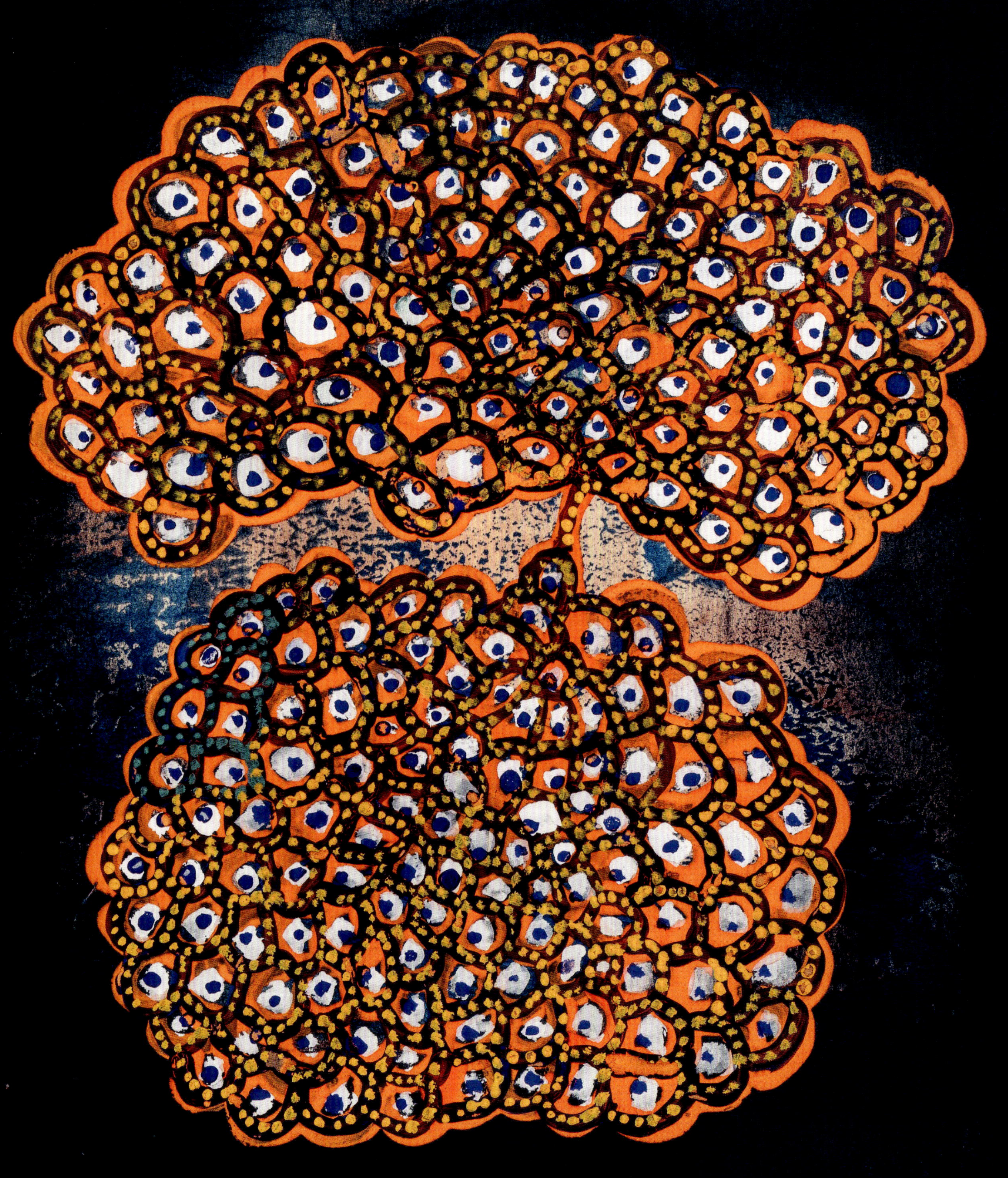

"VISION OF REPETITION"

BUILDING PATTERNS IN PLANTS

previous
T.6, 1953
Gouache on paper
13 × 10⅜ in. (33 × 26.4 cm)
Private collection, Chicago

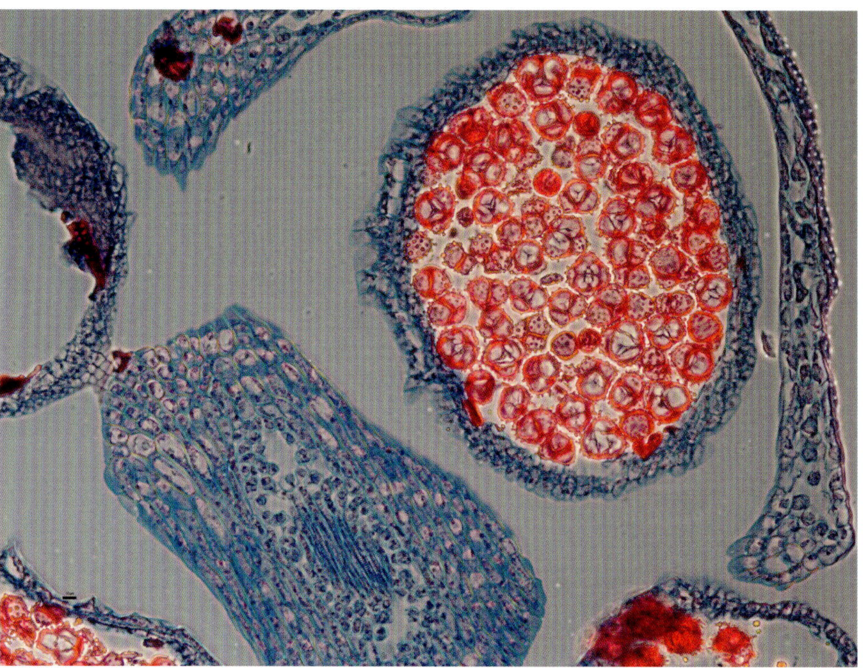

Fig. 1 (right)
Histochemical staining illustrates the patterns present in reproductive structures of a spikemoss (*Selaginella moellendorffii*).

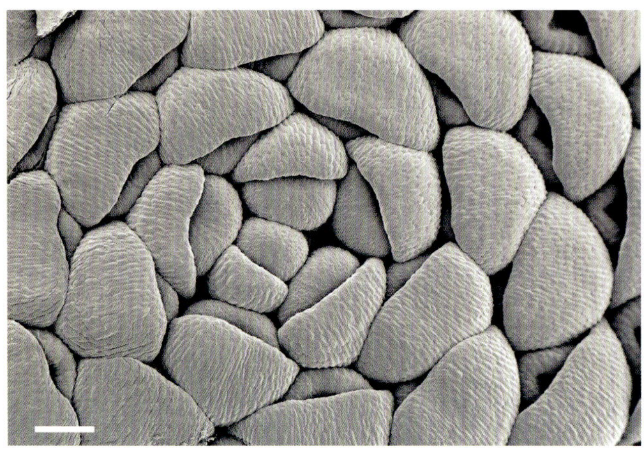

Fig. 2 (below)
Scanning electron microscopy (SEM) image of flowers arranged in a spiral around a stem of a dahlia inflorescence. At maturity, the dahlia inflorescence resembles a single large flower termed a pseudanthium (false flower). Scale bar = 100 µm

YAYOI KUSAMA'S ART CONSISTENTLY CALLS THE VIEWER'S ATTENTION to patterns, connections, and cycles found in nature that are not always visible. She portrays plants in astounding ways, as abstract (and not so abstract) shapes accumulating, dividing, and expanding: a personal vision that includes boldly depicting cell-like forms (pages 90 and 100) and creating a dizzying array of patterns on leaves, stems, and petals—inspiring a renewed appreciation for the mysteries of the natural world. In her art and her writings, Kusama considers the ways in which every living organism is connected, part of a larger, cosmic whole. Curators and critics have cited philosophy and psychology in analyzing the meaning behind her work. But Kusama's worldview is not only conceptual, not only imagined. As a botanist viewing Kusama's art, I know that the bold patterns she depicts often actually exist in nature. When I study plant development, or magnify any part of a plant thousands of times, otherwise hidden patterns and connections are revealed (**FIG. 1**).

Patterns can be seen in the arrangement of petals in flowers and flowers on stems. These patterns—as well as the form of cellular structures seen only on the microscopic level—occur as the plant develops (**FIG. 2**). They are fixed, unchanged, and reproduced from one generation to the next, indicating that these patterns are determined genetically. But how are these patterns built? Do the same genes underlie similar patterns in diverse species? Or do different genes underlie similar patterns? And ultimately, what can these patterns teach us about evolution and the connectedness of all living organisms?

COSMIC NATURE: THE CONNECTEDNESS OF ALL

There is grandeur in this view of life, with its several powers, having been originally breathed into a few forms or into one; and that, whilst this planet has gone cycling on according to the fixed law of gravity, from so simple a beginning endless forms most beautiful and most wonderful have been, and are being, evolved.

—Charles Darwin, 1859[1]

Life is estimated to have originated billions of years ago and has since evolved into millions of unicellular and multicellular species.[2] Many of the living organisms we are familiar with—brown algae, red algae, green algae, land plants, lichens, fungi, invertebrates, and vertebrates—are eukaryotic species, which are composed of cells containing DNA inside distinct nucleii. There are nearly 2 million known eukaryotic species on Earth. However, there are an estimated 7 million additional eukaryotic species, meaning that scientists have only just begun to identify the multitude of living things all around us (**FIG. 3**).[3] All of these species come in a seemingly endless variety of forms, from unicellular microscopic species to multicellular species as diverse as ginkgo trees, button mushrooms, and zebras. Humans are just one of these species. But most amazing is that all life has a single common origin, which is revealed in the comparisons of genomes—all the hereditary information of an organism—across living forms. The ability to sequence genomes, allowing scientists to know the order and composition of every single base of DNA in an organism, at an ever-increasing rate, has provided more insight into that single origin of life and how it evolved.[4] The DNA of all organisms is composed of the same four bases, or nucleotides, which are abbreviated as A, T, C, and G. If all life is built from only four different bases, then how is it that distinct organisms evolved? It happens through changes in the composition and order of those DNA bases and the proteins they produce. The pattern and sequence of DNA bases, which produce a particular amino acid, combine in specific patterns and sequences to yield distinct proteins. The workhorses in development, proteins are themselves the result of patterns and are responsible in turn for the patterns we see in living things.

Each multicellular organism starts as a single cell. Through cell division, pattern formation, growth, and differentiation, that single cell eventually becomes a multicellular adult organism with distinct organs in particular patterns and in specific forms. This process is known as development. Development is studied through time and space to understand *how* a single cell becomes a multicellular

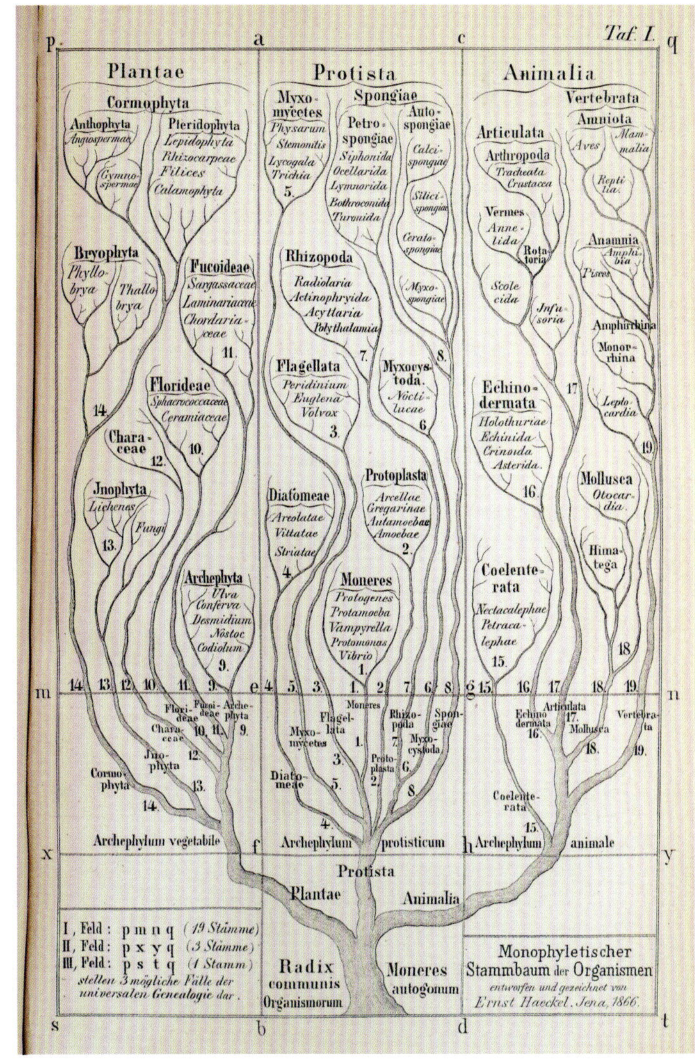

Fig. 3
Ernst Haeckel (1834–1919)
Generelle morphologie der organismen, vol. 2, plate I
(Berlin: G. Reimer, 1866)
LuEsther T. Mertz Library
The New York Botanical Garden

Fig. 4 (below)
Flower forms
Top (left to right):
tulip, iris, coneflower
Bottom (left to right):
dahlia, squash, orchid

Fig. 5 (opposite)
Floral diagrams from a late nineteenth-century botany textbook by H.B. Spotton (1844–1933). Each diagram depicts the plan of a flower in cross section, showing the positions of sepals, petals, stamens, and carpels.

organism. For example, in plants all zygotes initially appear similar, and even after initial rounds of cell division, any four-celled embryo looks just like any other. It is only after further cell division, pattern formation, and differentiation that one species can be discerned from another. Animals and plants share similar developmental mechanisms. To understand how these species generate distinct forms, we can study where and when in development their forms begin to diverge. This can be done by studying not only the visible changes in form, but also the invisible genes that underlie those forms.

Every cell in an organism has the same genome—the same instructions encoded as DNA. Developmental genes set up patterns in the developing organism such as the location of insect legs or the arrangement of flower petals or specify the identity of cells, for example, whether the cell produces hair. Many of the well-understood developmental regulators are particular types of proteins known as transcription factors, which turn other genes on or off. Only a very small fraction of any genome (approximately 5 percent) are transcription factors.[5] Yet they are major players in the developmental process. Studies of developmental regulators reveal that they are shared across highly divergent plant species.[6] How is it possible that similar proteins construct such different organisms? When and where those proteins are turned on or off, and their interactions with other proteins, determine the difference between a tulip and a rose. The study of the development of organisms in an evolutionary framework allows scientists to understand how the diversity of life is generated. This is called evolutionary developmental biology, or evo-devo.[7]

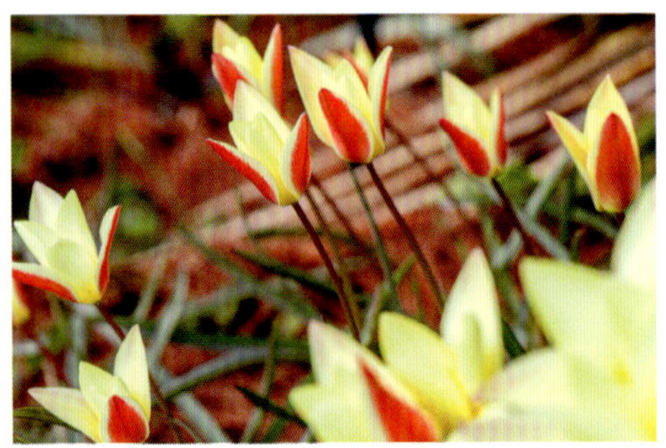
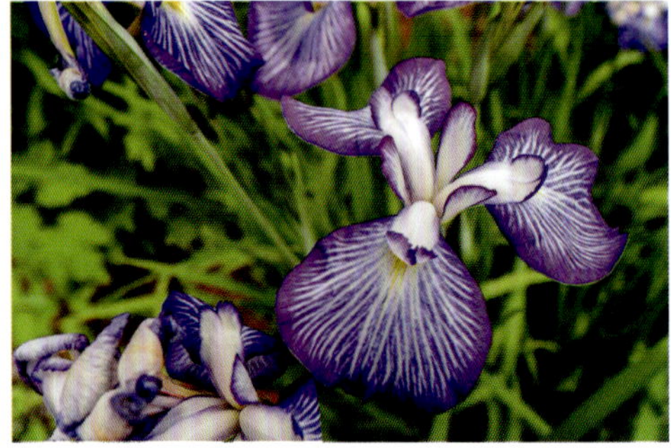
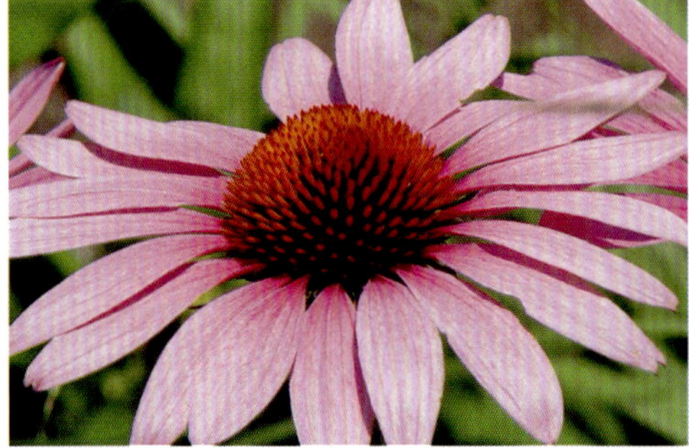
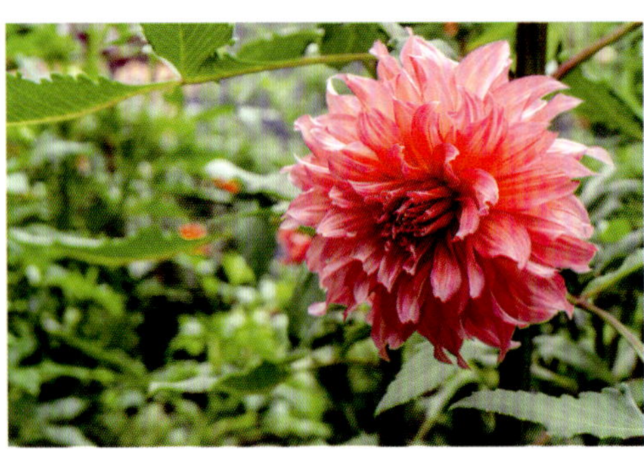
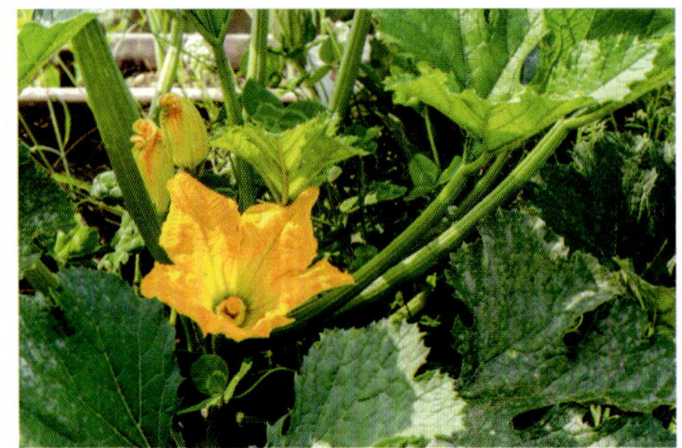
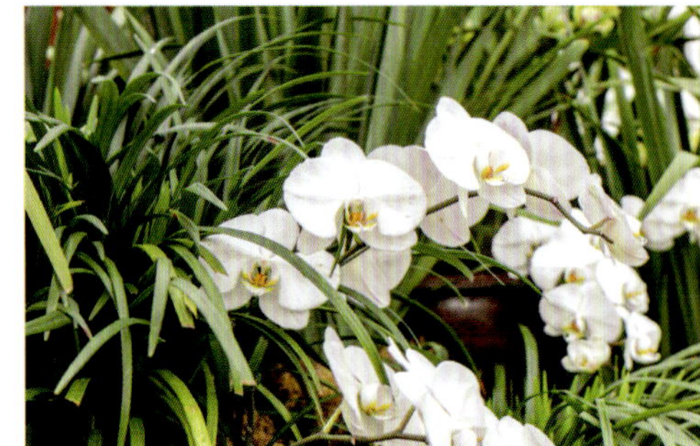

FLOWERS, FLOWERS, FLOWERS: AN EVO-DEVO ILLUSTRATION OF PATTERN FORMATION

Long before starting to create artworks I had been in the thrall of a vision of "repetition" which, along with "multiplication," was to become the foundation of my art.

—Yayoi Kusama, 2011[8]

In her early, botanically accurate sketches (pages 32–44), Kusama demonstrates a sophisticated understanding of plant forms, while her more recent monumental, stylized flower sculptures (pages 22–23) can be seen as drawing creative inspiration from her lifelong study of plants. Even Kusama's hulking soft sculptures, with gloves and other objects representing the sexual organs of flowers (page 55), show evidence of deep familiarity with natural forms, in which the artist has induced mutations of her own making.

Flowers come in a multitude of forms, colors, and sizes (**FIG. 4**). But all flowers have a common floral ground plan, or Baüplan: the sterile, mostly showy parts (sepals and petals) comprise the outermost structures of the flower, while the reproductive organs are within. The male reproductive structures (stamens) surround the the female structures (carpels), which are nearly always located in the center (**FIG. 5**).

In the 1990s, developmental genetic studies of flowers revealed that a set of related yet distinct proteins act together in different combinations to determine whether a floral organ develops as a sepal, a petal, a stamen or carpel.[9] Molecular genetic studies investigated these proteins sequentially to understand how each is necessary to build the different floral organs. Turning on or off these proteins could cause one floral organ to form in place of another.[10] This change of one organ into another is called a homeotic transformation, a term coined by English biologist William Bateson (1861–1926).[11] American geneticist Richard Goldschmidt (1878–1958) hypothesized that significant mutations, such as natural homeotic mutations, could generate "hopeful monsters" and help explain the evolution of new species.[12]

One of the most surprising facts about the molecular genetics of flowers is that the same genes can build morphologically diverse flower in different species. This was first demonstrated in *Arabidopsis thaliana* (mouse-ear cress) and *Antirrhinum majus* (snapdragon) where evolutionarily related (homologous) genes build the sepals, petals, stamens, and carpels in each species (**FIG. 6**).[13] These plants produce very different flowers, yet they still have the same four basic floral organs. However, what was even more surprising was that the same genes build the floral organs of grass flowers, whose

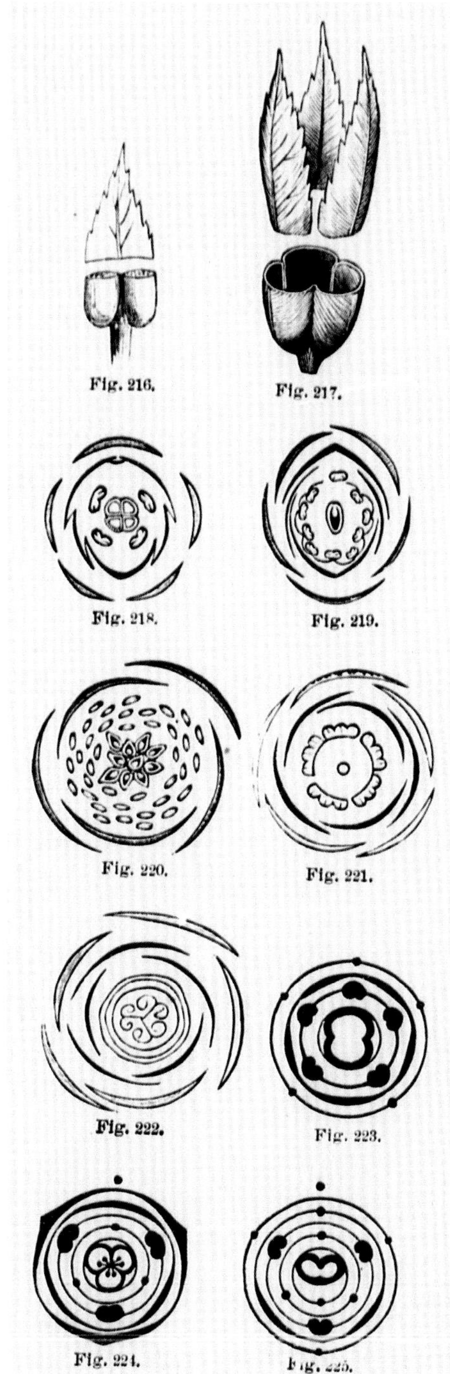

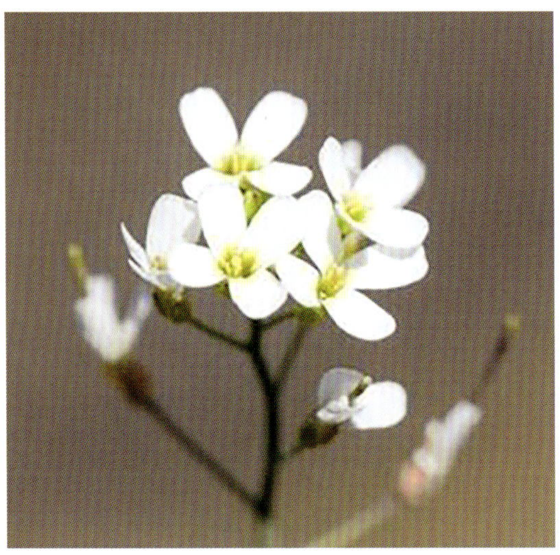
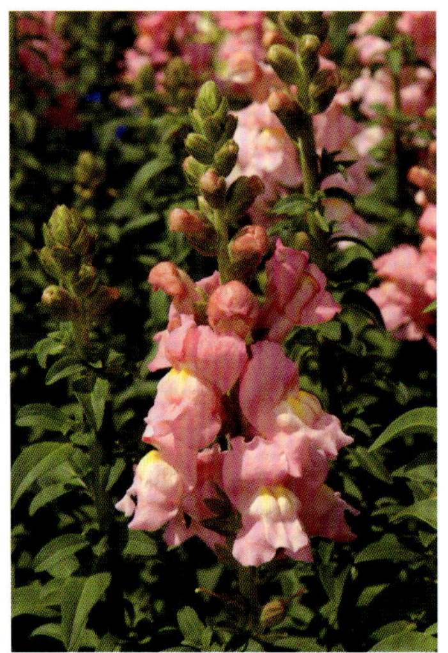
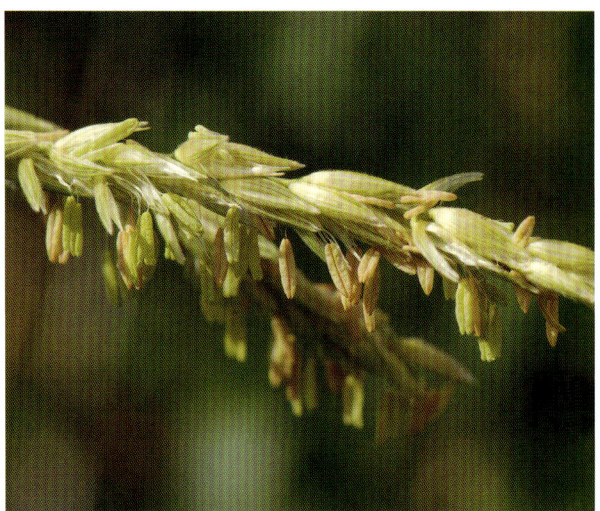

structure is so different that you would never recognize their petals as petals. In fact, they were given a different name—lodicules.[14] Scientists were not surprised that the same genes build reproductive structures in mouse-ear cress, snapdragon, and corn, a grass. But it was surprising that the same genes build the lodicules. The appearance of the floral organs does not matter. What *does* matter is the structural pattern found in flowers, and that building this pattern across the more than 350,000 known flowering plant species is generally conserved and triggered by the same genes.

Of course, there are exceptions to the floral Baüplan. The sterile organs of tulips, a favorite subject in Kusama's work, are not differentiated into sepals and petals, but instead have showy organs called tepals in their place. Molecular genetic studies show that the gene that builds petals in other flowering plants builds the tepals.[15] In many peonies and roses the stamens have undergone a homeotic transformation into petals. We can hypothesize that the gene necessary to build petals has been turned on in the stamens, resulting in a flower with petals in their place. One of the most remarkable deviations from the floral Baüplan is found in *Lacandonia schismatica*, the only flowering plant with male reproductive structures surrounded by those that are female.[16] Developmental genetic studies showed that the protein that builds stamens is present in *Lacandonia schismatica*, as it is in all flowering plants, yet it is turned on only in the center of the flower, which is why this plant's stamens form in the center and carpels do not.[17] In other words, the genes are conserved, but changing where and when they are turned on changes the pattern formation in the flower. *Lacandonia schismatica* is likely one of Goldschmidt's hopeful monsters.

HOW THE PUMPKIN GOT ITS SPOTS: AN EVO-DEVO ILLUSTRATION OF PATTERNS

In the examination of the common function of all developments there emerges the fact that one of the prime essentials in the orderly spacing and patterning is a communication between parts.

—John Tyler Bonner, 1958[18]

Kusama's signature spotted pumpkins are often cited for their whimsical motifs. But if you look closely, you can see that those spots are not merely decorative. They are not random; they form patterns, and none overlap. Many similar-looking microscopic patterns can be found throughout the natural world (**FIG. 7**), including the patterning of stomata (the pores that plants "breathe" through) and the hairs on a leaf. Studied under a microscope, we can see that the development of stomata or hairs does not generally occur on adjacent cells. Instead, there is a pattern. The question in studying development is how such a pattern is generated. There is an order or logic at play.

As surmised by American biologist John Tyler Bonner (1920–2019) in 1958, and confirmed in developmental genetic research, there is a "communication between parts." Whether that communication is between the leaf and the stem from which it emerges, between epidermal cells to determine which might produce a hair, or among cells that may (or may not) develop a spot.[19] These patterns are not random and are nearly universal. Surpisingly, some of these complex patterns can develop from a simple two-component system, which was theorized in 1952 by English mathematician Alan Turing (1912–54), who called it a reaction-diffusion mechanism.[20] In Turing's

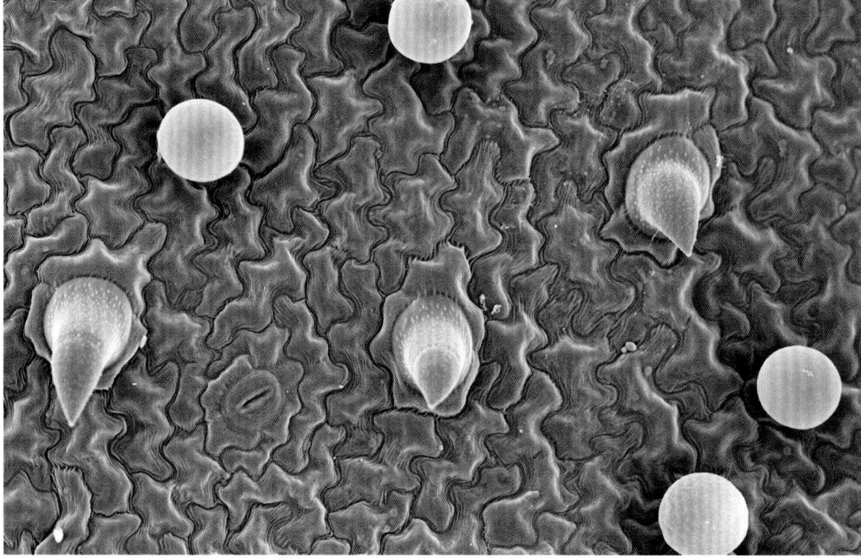

Fig. 6 (opposite)
Mouse-ear cress (*Arabidopsis thaliana*) and snapdragon (*Antirrhinum majus*) share many genes but their flowers look very different. Yet their form is more easily recognizable as such than the flowers of corn (*Zea mays*).

Fig. 7 (below)
SEM image showing the patterns of different hairs and stomata on a leaf of basil (*Ocimum basilicum*). Scale bar = 100 μm

system, there is an activator and a repressor. That is, one is a protein that turns on a gene (namely the gene that makes the repressor protein) and the other is a protein that turns off a gene (namely the gene that makes the activator). The reaction-diffusion system disturbs a homogenous layer of cells resulting in different activated or repressed genes in each cell. It is differences in the diffusion of each component that can produce spots, or even stripes. Therefore, from a field of identical cells, a reaction occurs in one cell, and through diffusion it sets up a very precise pattern throughout an organ, cell by cell. The Turing reaction-diffusion mechanism has been demonstrated in the patterning of animal embryos and the spots on monkey-flowers (*Mimulus* spp.).[21] It is this communication—and cooperation—between cells that can pattern the natural world.

YAYOI KUSAMA'S COSMIC WORLDVIEW HAS CAPTIVATED AUDIENCES for decades. As my colleagues at The New York Botanical Garden embarked on the project of bringing her work to our gardens and galleries, they—and I—were struck by the ways in which the artist's repetitive forms and patterns called to mind the patterns found in plants on many scales (**FIG. 8** and page 101). From the structural patterns of flowers, to the patterns of the proteins that build those flowers, to the patterns of DNA bases that build those proteins, organisms take shape from a series of patterns on top of patterns. Kusama's lifelong project, from carefully observed documentation of peonies to fantastically adorned monumental flower sculptures, is one of awareness and attunement to the mysteries of the natural world.

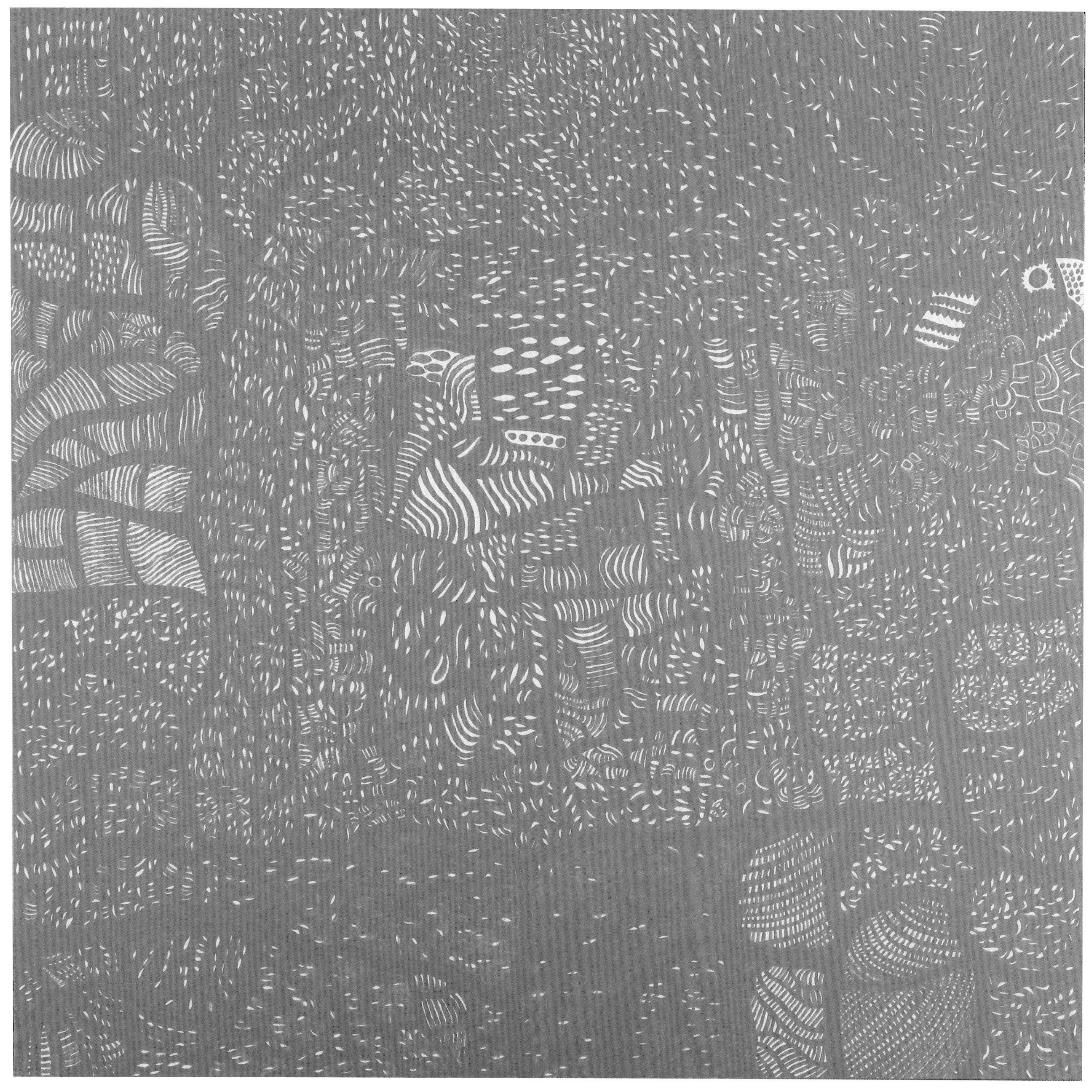

Fig. 8
The Moving Moment When I Went to the Universe, 2017
Acrylic on canvas
76⅜ × 76⅜ in. (194 × 194 cm)
Collection of the artist

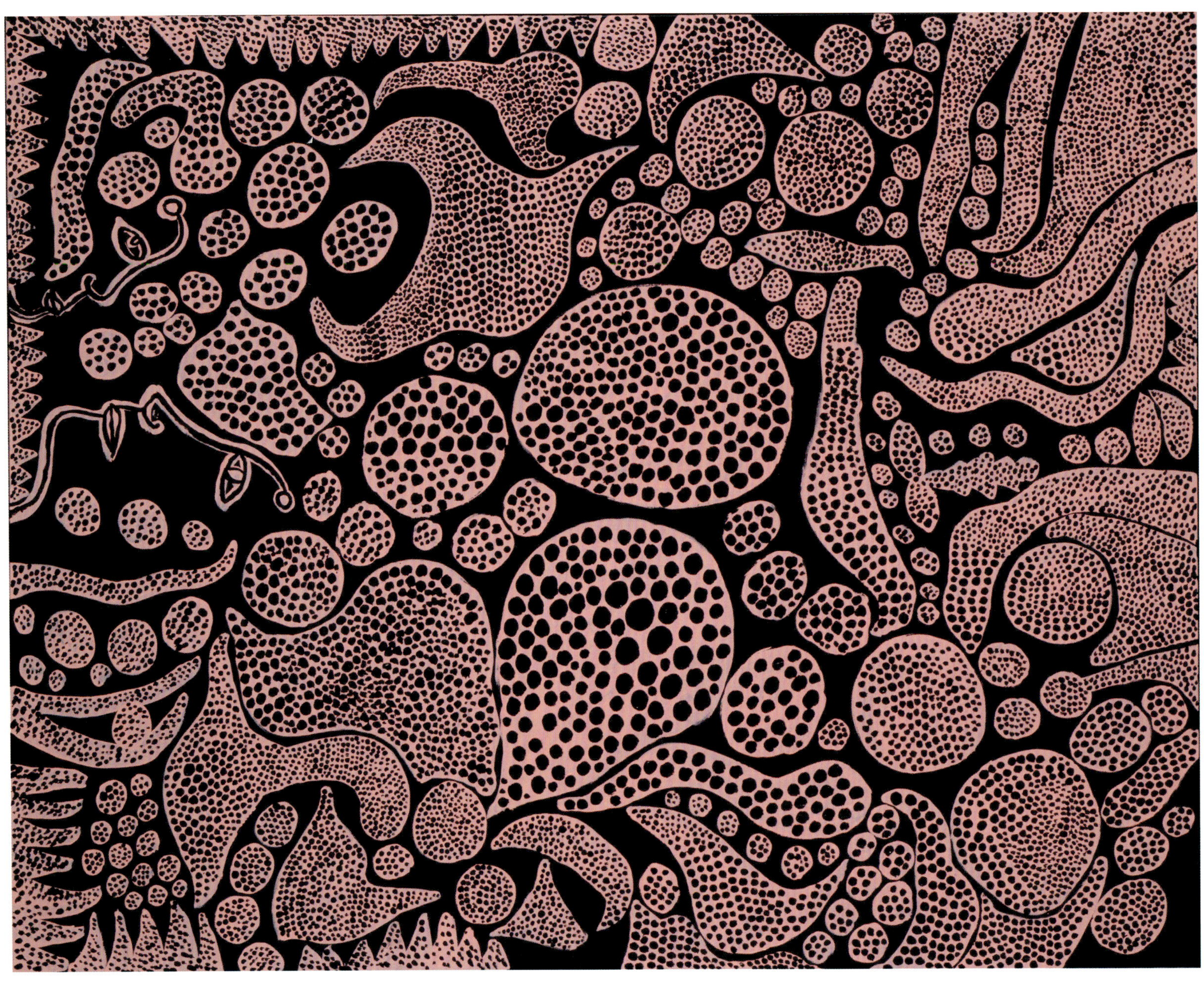

above
Shining Stars in Pursuit of the Truth are Off in the Distance Beyond the Universe, The More I Sought the Truth the Brighter They Shone, 2009
Acrylic on canvas
51¼ × 63¾ in. (130.3 × 162 cm)
Collection of the artist

opposite
Blue Wind, 2011
Acrylic on canvas
51¼ × 63¾ in. (130.3 × 162 cm)
Collection of the artist

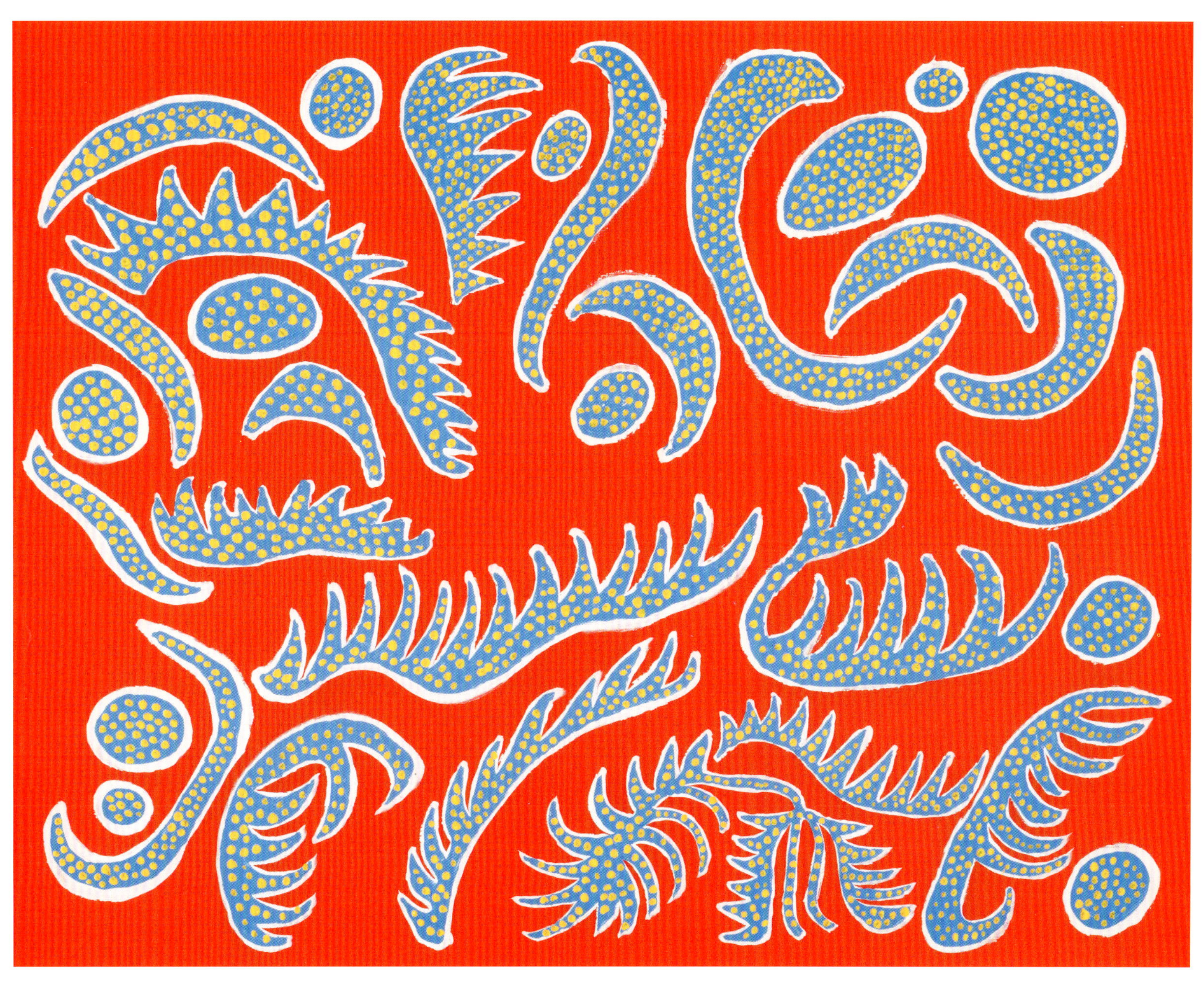

following
Life, 2015
Installation view, The New York Botanical Garden, 2021
Fiberglass-reinforced plastic, tiles, and resin
10 elements, installation dimensions variable
Courtesy of Ota Fine Arts and David Zwirner

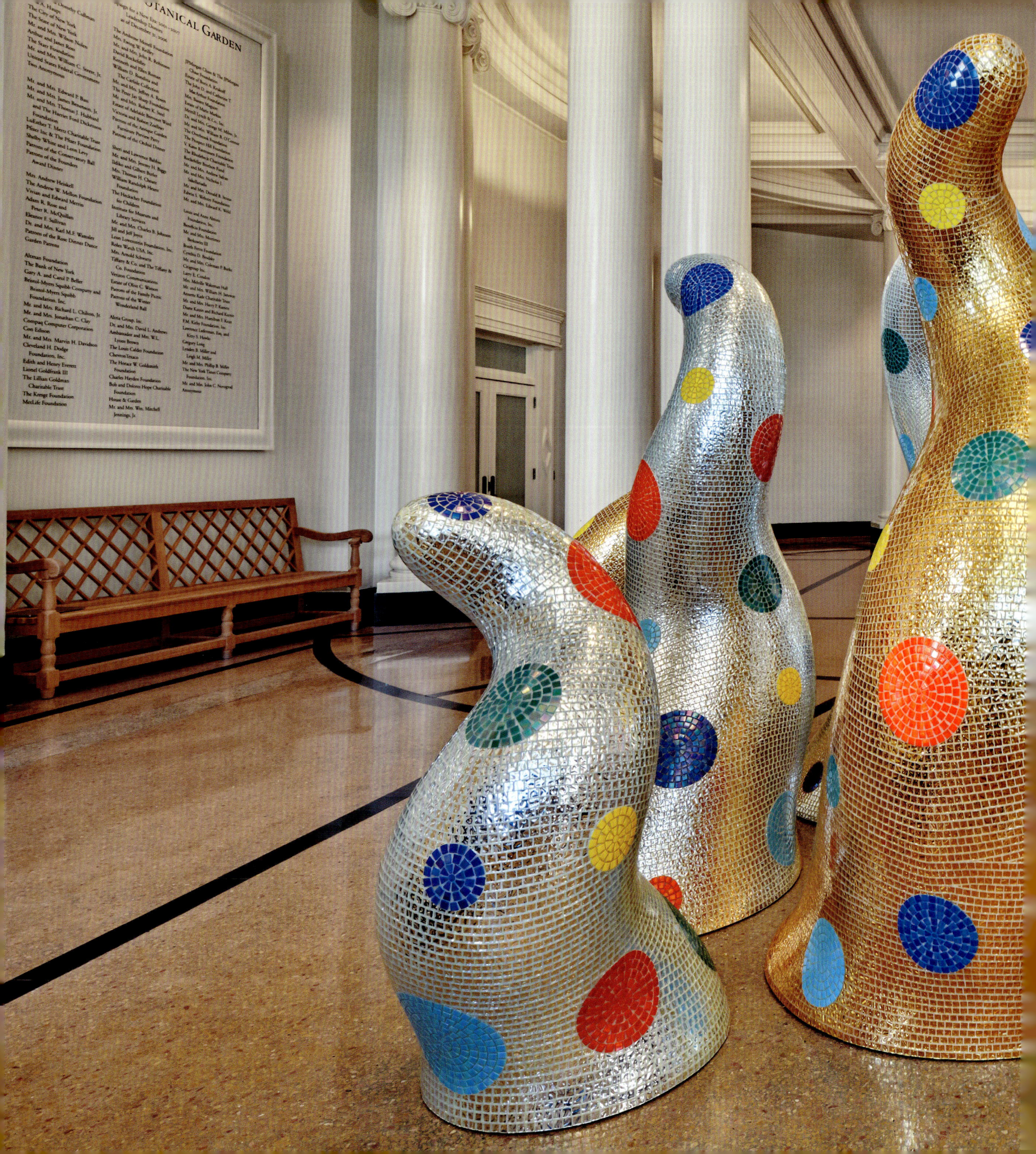
GARDEN
Leadership Donors
as of December 31, 2006
The City of New York
The State of New York
Mr. and Mrs. Wilson Nolen
Arthur and Janet Ross
The Starr Foundation
Mr. and Mrs. William C. Steere, Jr.
United States Federal Government
Two Anonymous
Mr. and Mrs. Edward P. Bass
Mr. and Mrs. James Benenson, Jr.
Mr. and Mrs. Thomas J. Hubbard
and The Harriet Ford Dickenson
Foundation
LuEsther T. Mertz Charitable Trust
Pfizer Inc & The Pfizer Foundation
Shelby White and Leon Levy
Patrons of the Conservatory Ball
Patrons of the Founders
Award Dinner
Mrs. Andrew Heiskell
The Andrew W. Mellon Foundation
Vivian and Edward Merrin
Adam R. Rose and
Peter R. McQuillan
Eleanor F. Sullivan
Dr. and Mrs. Karl M.F. Wamsler
Patrons of the Rose Dinner Dance
Garden Patrons
Altman Foundation
The Bank of New York
Gary A. and Carol P. Beller
Bristol-Myers Squibb Company and
Bristol-Myers Squibb
Foundation, Inc.
Mr. and Mrs. Richard L. Chilton, Jr.
Mr. and Mrs. Jonathan C. Clay
Compaq Computer Corporation
Con Edison
Mr. and Mrs. Marvin H. Davidson
Cleveland H. Dodge
Foundation, Inc.
Edith and Henry Everett
Lionel Goldfrank III
The Lillian Goldman
Charitable Trust
The Kresge Foundation
MetLife Foundation
The Carlisle Collection
The Peter Jay Sharp Foundation
Patrons of the Orchid Dinner
William Randolph Hearst
Foundation
The Heckscher Foundation
for Children
Institute for Museum and
Library Services
Mr. and Mrs. Charles B. Johnson
Jill and Jeff Joyce
Rolex Watch USA, Inc.
Mrs. Arnold Schwartz
Tiffany & Co. and The Tiffany &
Co. Foundation
Verizon Communications
Estate of Olive C. Watson
Patrons of the Family Picnic
Patrons of the Winter
Wonderland Ball
Altria Group, Inc.
Dr. and Mrs. David L. Andrews
Ambassador and Mrs. W.L.
Lyons Brown
The Louis Calder Foundation
ChevronTexaco
The Horace W. Goldsmith
Foundation
Charles Hayden Foundation
Bob and Dolores Hope Charitable
Foundation
House & Garden
Mr. and Mrs. Wm. Mitchell
Jennings, Jr.

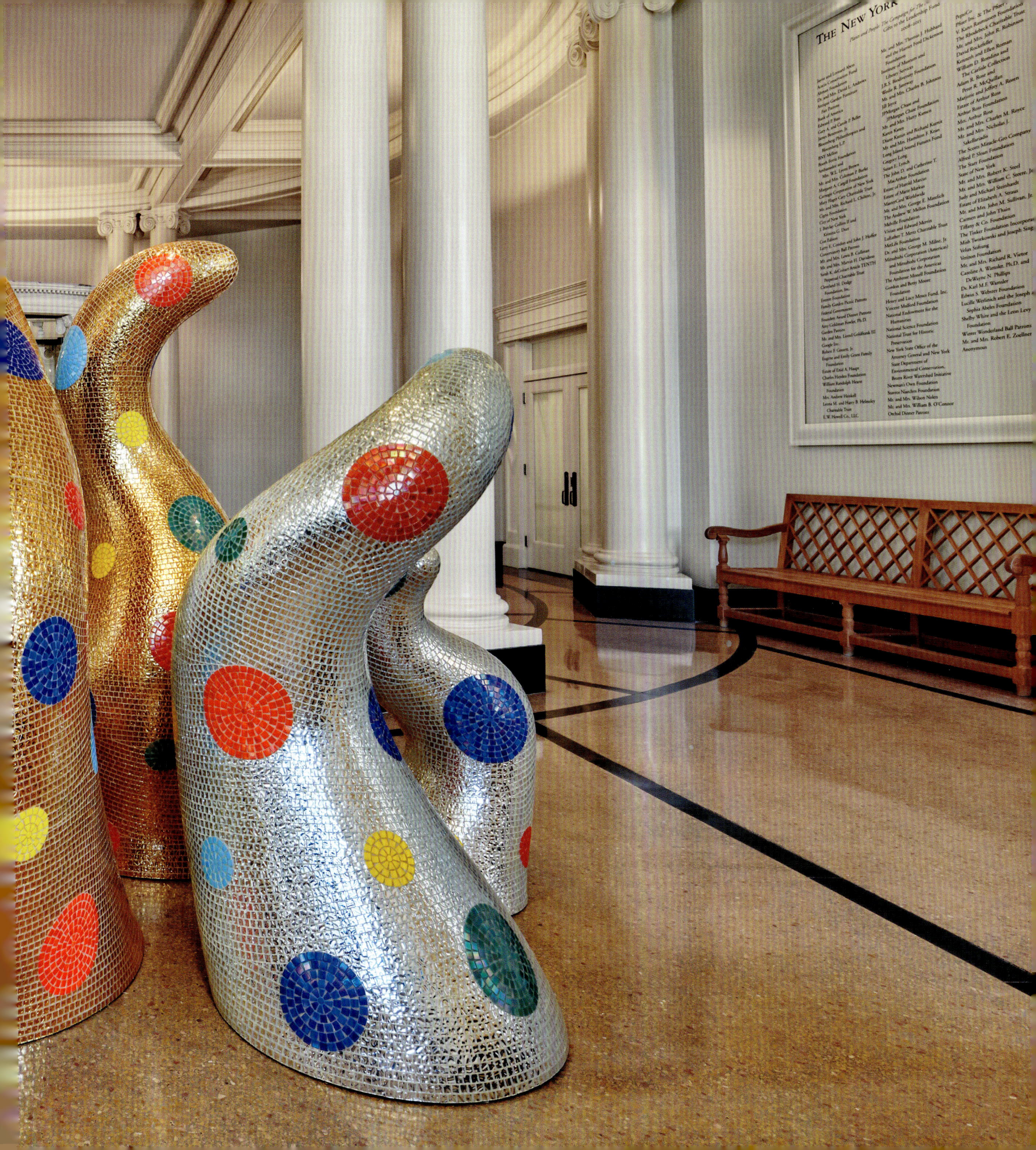
THE NEW YORK

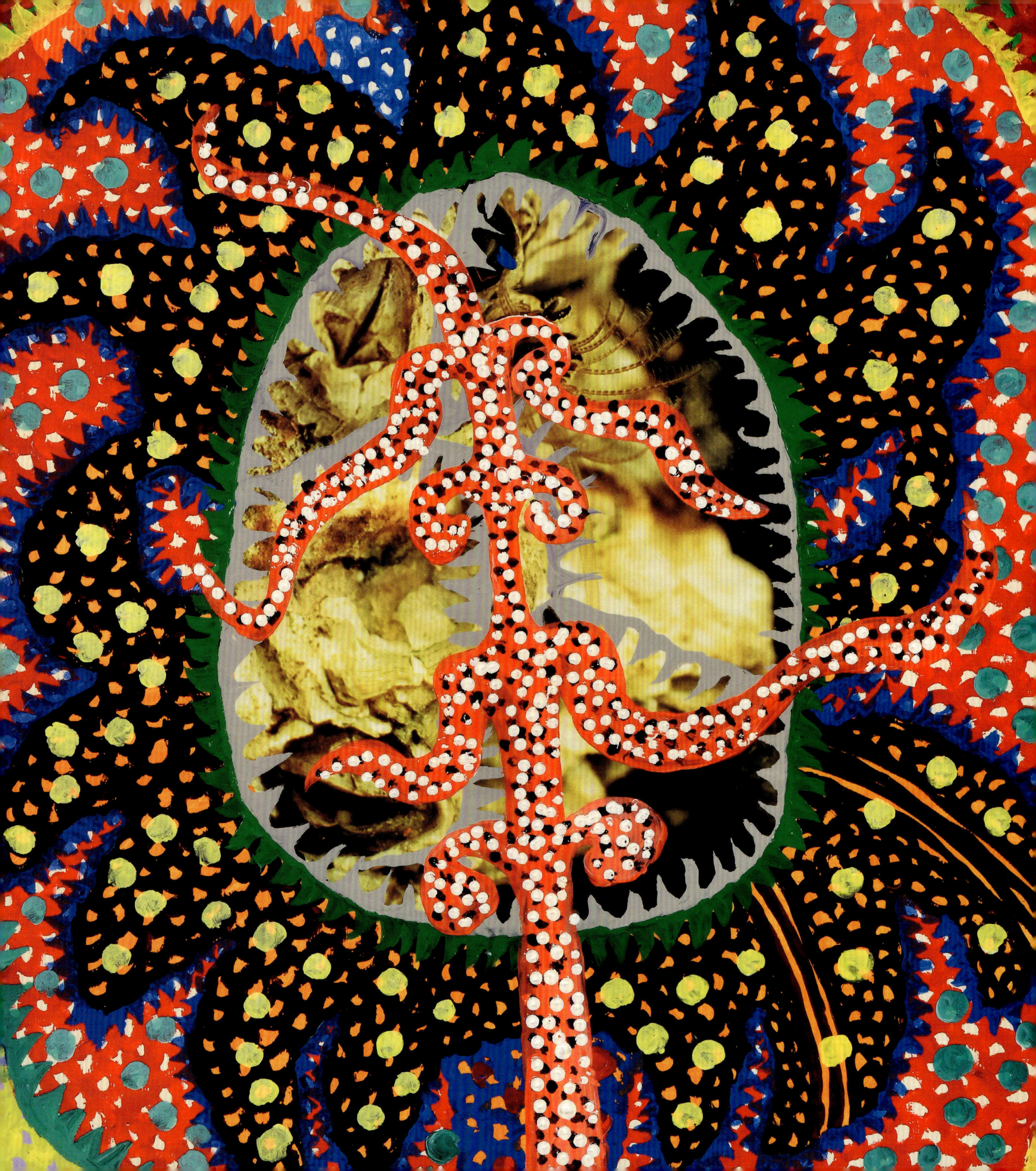

Jenni Sorkin

BOTANICALS FOR THE EYE

YAYOI KUSAMA'S FLOWER POWER

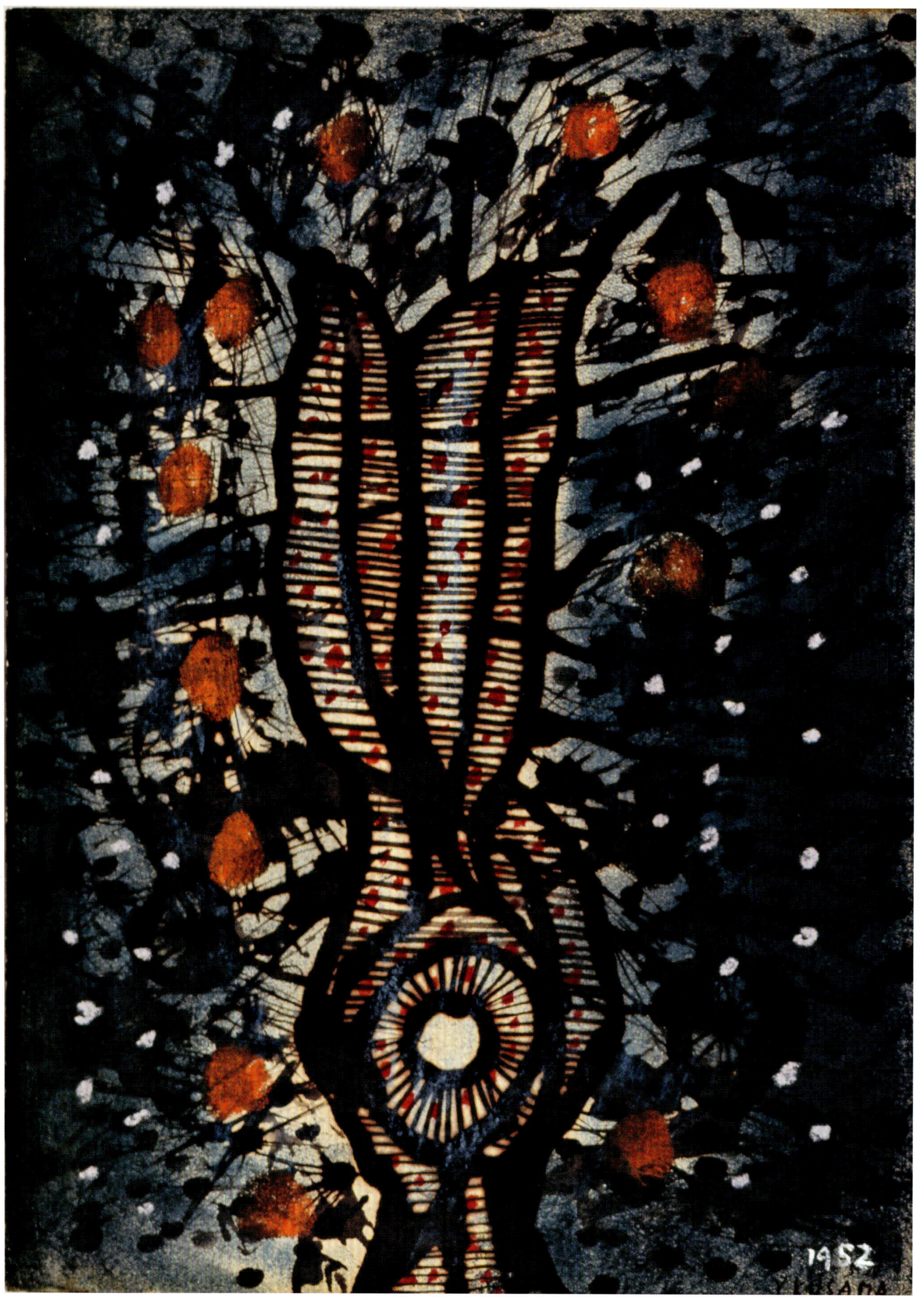
1952

DERIVED FROM PLANTS SUCH AS LAVENDER OR MINT, BOTANICALS are substances that are valued for their cosmetic or healing properties. Instead of using fibers, oils, or pulp derived directly from plant materials, Yayoi Kusama's installations and objects are botanicals for the eye: aesthetic preparations of fantastical organic forms, flower sculptures, and floral patterns that cover walls and furniture. These obsessive variants underscore her distinctive artistic sensibility, or what British art historian Sir Herbert Read once described as "radical and hypnotic repetitive energies."[1] With origins in the 1960s notion of "flower power," an American protest slogan coined to express utopian idealism, nonviolence, and passive opposition to the Vietnam War, Kusama's practice has been embraced globally in recent decades due to its inclusivity and visual pleasure.

previous
Pistils Swaying in the Wind (detail), 1978

Fig. 1 (opposite)
Tree, 1952
Gouache and pastel on paper
10 × 7 in. (25.5 × 18 cm)
Collection of the artist

Fig. 2 (below)
Odilon Redon
(French, 1840–1916)
Cyclops (Le cyclope), 1914
Oil on cardboard
mounted on panel
25⅞ × 20¾ in. (65.8 × 52.7 cm)
Kröller Müller Museum,
Otterlo, Netherlands
KM103.098

EARLY WORKS: 1952–56

Kusama's rootedness in flowers and trees as subject matter commenced early in her career, in her first mature works on paper. Between 1952 and 1956, she made an ongoing series of mixed-media pastel-and-ink drawings that burst with a mystical, exaggerated form of naturalism reminiscent of French Symbolism: elongated stalks, roots, and tree limbs; curvaceous hatched lines and spiraling, stylized leaves; flowers and seed pods magnified into cell-like specimens. All point to an evocative self-portraiture in which the self is tightly cloistered, hemmed in within the boundaries of the frame. For instance, *Tree* (1952; **FIG. 1**) becomes centered on an ocular form from which roots and fingerlike leaves emerge, suggesting a *hamsa*, or eye symbol embedded in a human palm. But Kusama's symbolic tree is less spiritual than physiological in its shape-shifting, a presence that is all-knowing or all-seeing. In this sense, the drawing recalls French Symbolist painter Odilon Redon's *Cyclops* (*Le cyclope*) (1914; **FIG. 2**), in which the one-eyed monster tenderly guards his stolen nymph.

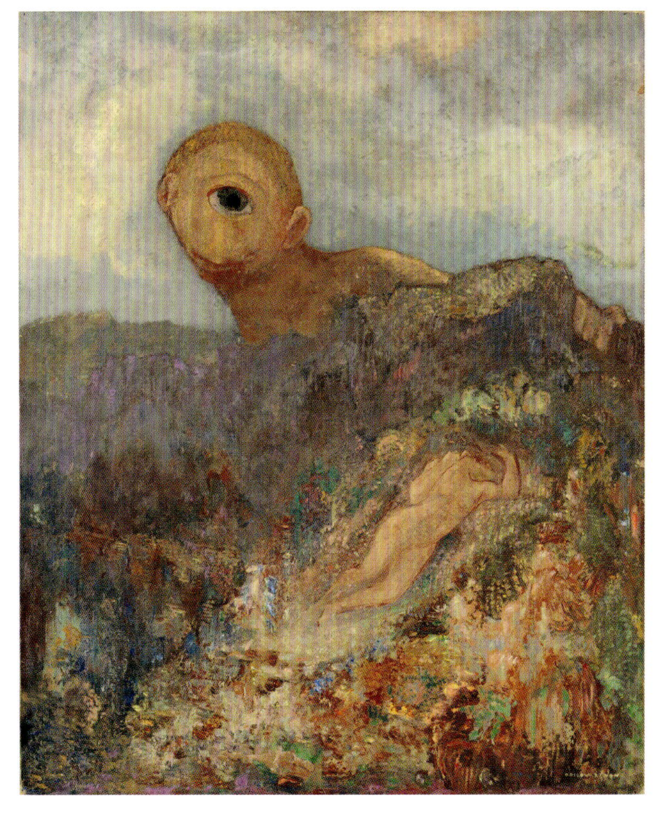

Redon (1840–1916) is an important, but perhaps overlooked, predecessor for Kusama's own investment in flowers as subject matter. The darkness of his vision—brought to life in surreal paintings of mythological creatures, narrative sequences, and alien flora and fauna that stand at the compelling precipice between dreams and night terrors—calls to mind Kusama's inner world. Her own visions, shaped through an ongoing biographical lens for her artistic production, have formed the basis of her dots and nets, a hallucinatory projection of her interior world as a means of shaping the exterior one. The radiant glow of her layered colors and the lush lyricism in early works such as *The Earth* (1953) and *Leaves* (1954; **FIG. 3**) bear a strong resemblance to Redon's own pictorial vocabulary of highly detailed fantasia, rendered during the dawning of photographic development and lens-based magnification.

Nature itself became a muse and source of inspiration, one of the primary vehicles for Redon's self-conscious construction as an artist. In 1891 he wrote of his own sense of "mental ebullience" in drawing from nature, after endeavoring to copy "a pebble, a blade of grass, a hand, a profile."[2] Few of his peers made such intensely romantic compositions in which a vase full of dark blossoms became a stand-in for human mortality. In 1931 critic Katharine Grant Sterne recounted that Redon painted each floral arrangement only after it had died, intent on capturing what she called the "particular charm of desiccation."[3]

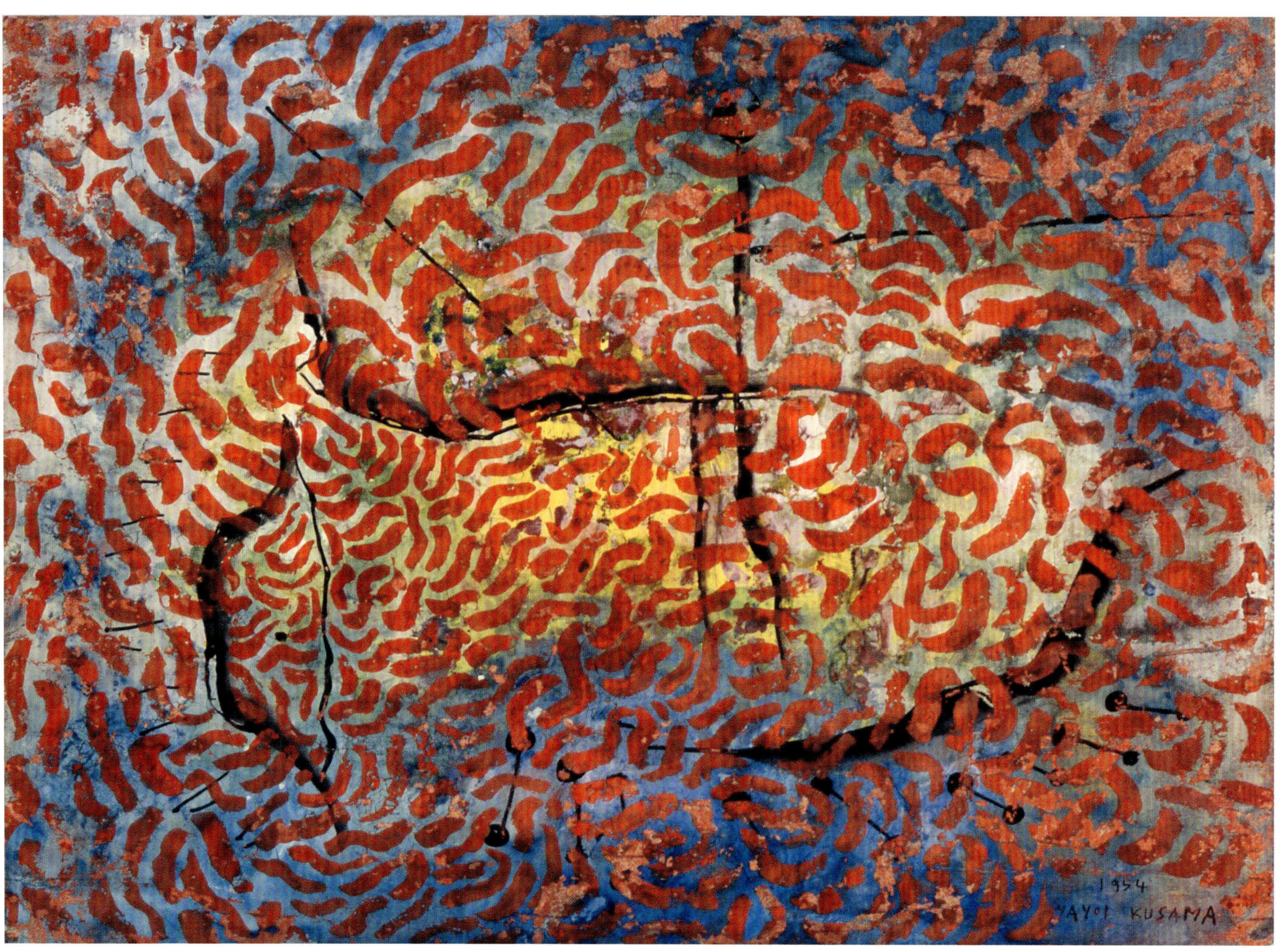

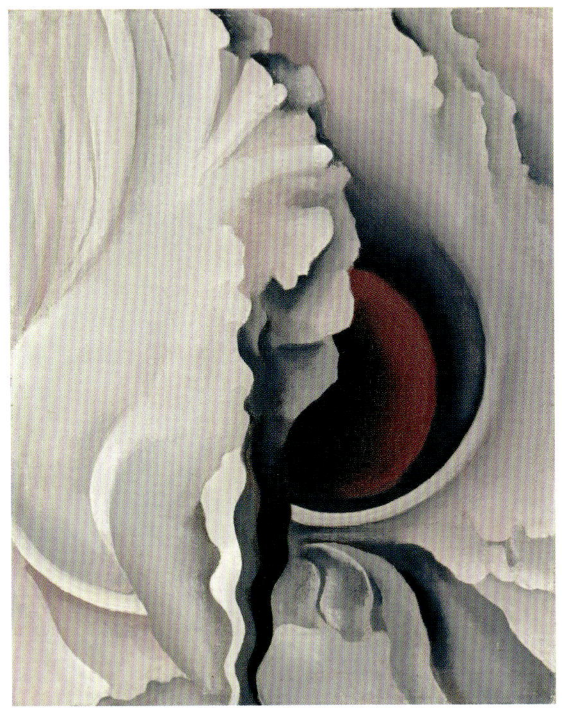

Fig. 3 (opposite)
Leaves, 1954
Gouache on paper
7⅞ × 10¾ in. (20.1 × 27.3 cm)
Collection of the artist

Fig. 4 (above)
Georgia O'Keeffe
(American, 1887–1986)
The Black Iris, 1926
Oil on canvas
9 × 7 in. (22.9 × 17.8 cm)
Georgia O'Keeffe Museum, Santa Fe
Gift of the Burnett Foundation, 2007.1.19

In contrast, while Kusama's early images float upon darkness, leaching color from fuzzy-edged forms against shadowy black backgrounds, her forms and imagery are strong affirmations of life, celebrating the flower as an agent of growth: germination, transformation, opening outward into the light. The affinity between both bodies of work is the intensely private psychological world rendered in semi-surreal visions. The dreamlike imagery in both is arresting as a quasi-landscape of the mind, shedding layers of the self to get to archetypal imagery such as spirals, lozenges, eyes, seeds, and pods, all biomorphic constructions that suggest the possibility of rebirth.

Beyond Redon, an early encounter with Georgia O'Keeffe's (1887–1986) flowers marked Kusama's own personal transformation: from a young, aspiring artist in provincial Japan into a daring adventurer willing to take a chance and leave her native country for the first time in 1957. After she happened upon a book of O'Keeffe's cow skulls and lush, highly detailed flower paintings, such as *The Black Iris* (1926; **FIG. 4**), Kusama wrote directly to the artist. O'Keeffe responded in kind, with generosity of spirit and encouragement, which Kusama strongly credits: "Her letter gave me the courage I needed to leave for New York."[4] In so doing, Kusama drew power and strength from the wisdom she found in O'Keeffe's formidable response and inspiration in the older artist's singular approach to subjects found in nature.

COUNTERCULTURAL MOMENTUM

Between 1958 and 1973, Kusama lived in New York City, where she was inspired by the countercultural sensibility that overtook American youth: freedom of speech and freedom of assembly fueled the Civil Rights Movement and a rejection of blind faith in the government. Despite her status as a foreigner, Kusama was emboldened by these new ideas, and she took an active part in protests against the Vietnam War, staging an infamous demonstration in 1968 on the Brooklyn Bridge, in which nude participants were covered in her signature polka dots (**FIG. 5**). This was a means of underscoring her philosophy of self-obliteration, in which the dots would blot out the individual, making all people equal. In an open letter to President-elect Richard Nixon, she poignantly demanded, "Honor those whose lives have been ended by ending the war!"[5]

The secondary effects of the countercultural revolution were the fashion, music, and lifestyle shifts that signaled hippie and protest culture more generally: young women wearing flowers in their long,

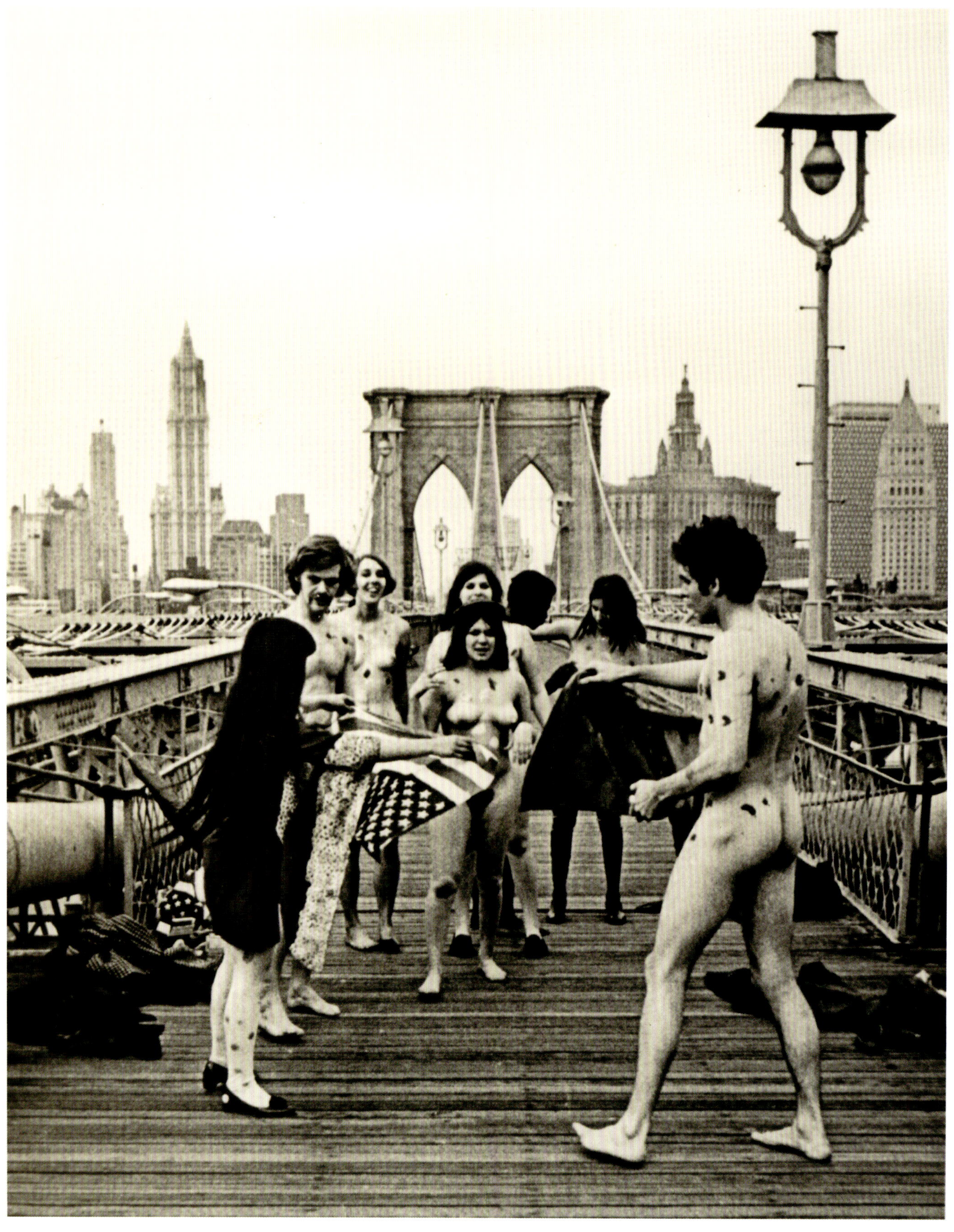

straight hair; folk music sing-alongs; and the collectivity of gathering for the common good—be-ins and love-ins followed on the heels of politically minded sit-ins. In the art world, this translated to experiential events such as happenings and performances, in which the actions of artists took precedence over objects themselves. Here, too, Kusama made an impact beginning in 1967, staging happenings, fashion shows, and her own *Love-In Festival* in Central Park in 1968 (**FIG. 6**). Once again, dots offered the materiality of a universal surface, or facade, flattening out all bodies, regardless of shape, color, or size, as a simultaneous gesture of communitarianism and rebellion.

With the body, whether nude or clothed, at the center of such works, covered over in unifying polka dots, Kusama originated a proto-feminist Pop sensibility through her fashion shows, installations, happenings, and sculptural objects. This also included designing garments with holes cut in the genital area that strategically uncovered the body, or even a single garment for two, such as a wedding gown she created for *Homosexual Wedding* in 1968, over which she presided, said to be the first ever in the United States.[6]

Another, lesser-known slogan from the 1960s, coined during the Free Speech Movement in Berkeley, California, also utilized the flower as a central metaphor, a phrase that positions the human body itself as a stem, or complex root system, signifying presence and grace under pressure: "I am a human being—please do not fold, bend, spindle, or mutilate" (**FIG. 7**). First used as an action of student protest, it is an assertion of authenticity and sense of self. The latter part of the phrase, "fold, bend, spindle, or mutilate," refers directly to early computer punch cards, increasingly used as time cards for laborers and identification for workers and students in the postwar period, and the necessary care one must use when feeding them into a machine to be counted or tallied. Writing in 1992, historian Steven Lubar framed the history of punch cards and the institutional turn toward mechanizing systems as a means of social control, in that such increasing systemization turned people into codes and numbers, inevitably overlooking their individual humanity.[7]

Through later works, the syncopation in Kusama's organic, stuffed forms from the mid-1980s, such as *Summer* (1985; **FIG. 8**) and *Pollen* (1986), embodies the transition between the singular flower form and the sheer repetition of floral patterning that transforms into monstrous proportions, fully realized as nonhuman tentacles or maniacal pistils. These works are markedly different from the 1960s phallic assemblages that, like mushrooms, seemed to grow overnight, covering everyday objects such as boats or furniture. Instead, the 1980s forms appear as alien vegetation, exotic stalks, and flowers that somehow live beyond their native habitats, like trophies secured from other worlds.

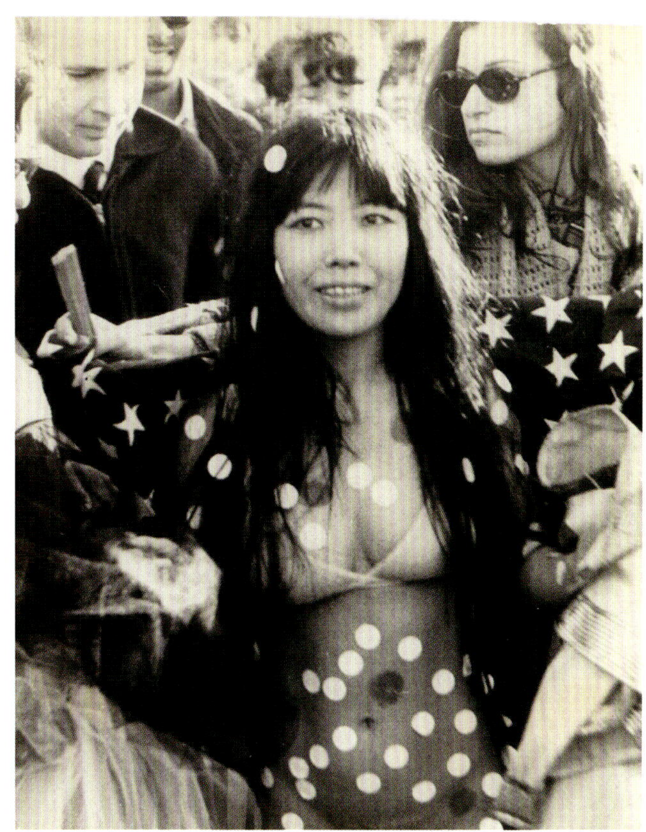

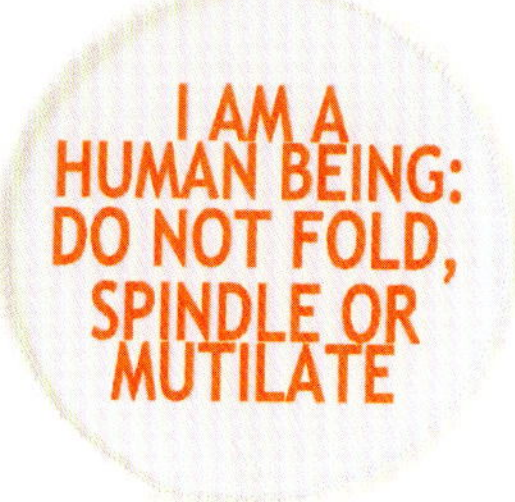

Fig. 5 (opposite)
"Anti-War" Naked Happening and Flag-Burning at Brooklyn Bridge, New York, 1968

Fig. 6 (top)
Love-In Festival Happening, Central Park, New York, 1968

Fig. 7 (above)
Free Speech Movement patch, ca. 1960s

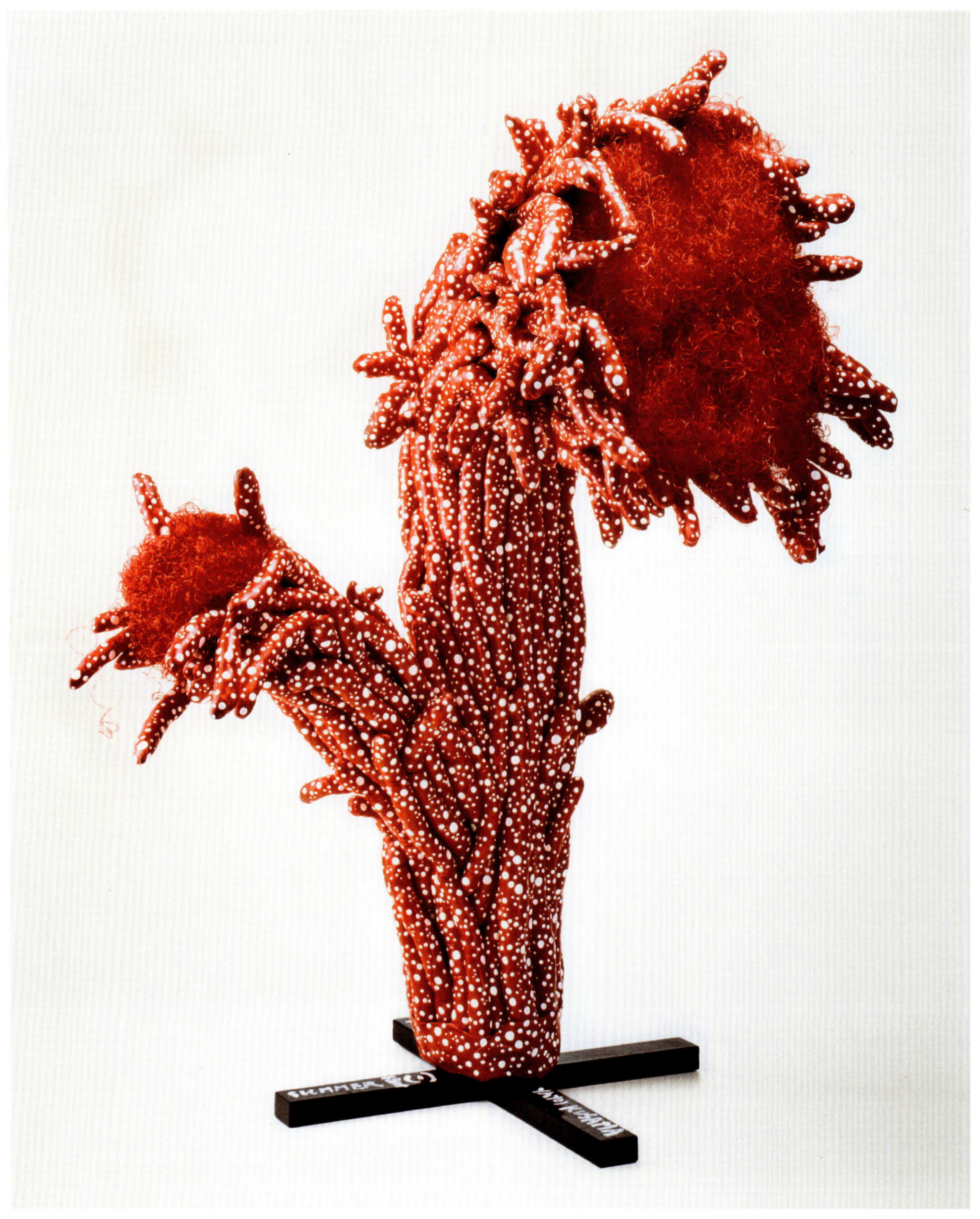

Fig. 8 (opposite)
Summer, 1985
Mixed media
70 × 47¼ × 39⅜ in.
(178 × 120 x100 cm)
Fukuoka Prefectural
Museum of Art

Fig. 9 (below)
Narcissus Garden, 1966
Installed at the 33rd Venice
Biennale, 1966

Despite her ingenuity as a forward-thinking innovator in the artistic vanguard, there was no enduring critical acknowledgment of the significance of her work for many years. Or, as curators Yuko Hasegawa and Pamela Miki wrote in 2006, "although she was recognised and highly regarded as an artist who broke new ground in various fields, Kusama failed to establish herself within the context of European and American modernism."[8] I would argue, however, that it was the establishment that failed Kusama, not the other way around. That is, she lacked the critical attention and recognition seamlessly accorded to her male peers in New York, such as Claes Oldenburg and Andy Warhol, who both became commercially and critically successful, even though her own forays into soft sculpture and repeating images proliferating across gallery walls in the form of wallpaper predated theirs.[9]

In 1966, though she was not invited to the Venice Biennale, Kusama self-organized and staged the performative exhibition *Narcissus Garden*. This was an unsponsored event; she was not invited to show within the exhibition site itself (**FIG. 9**). With a handmade sign that read "Your Narcissism for Sale," she stood

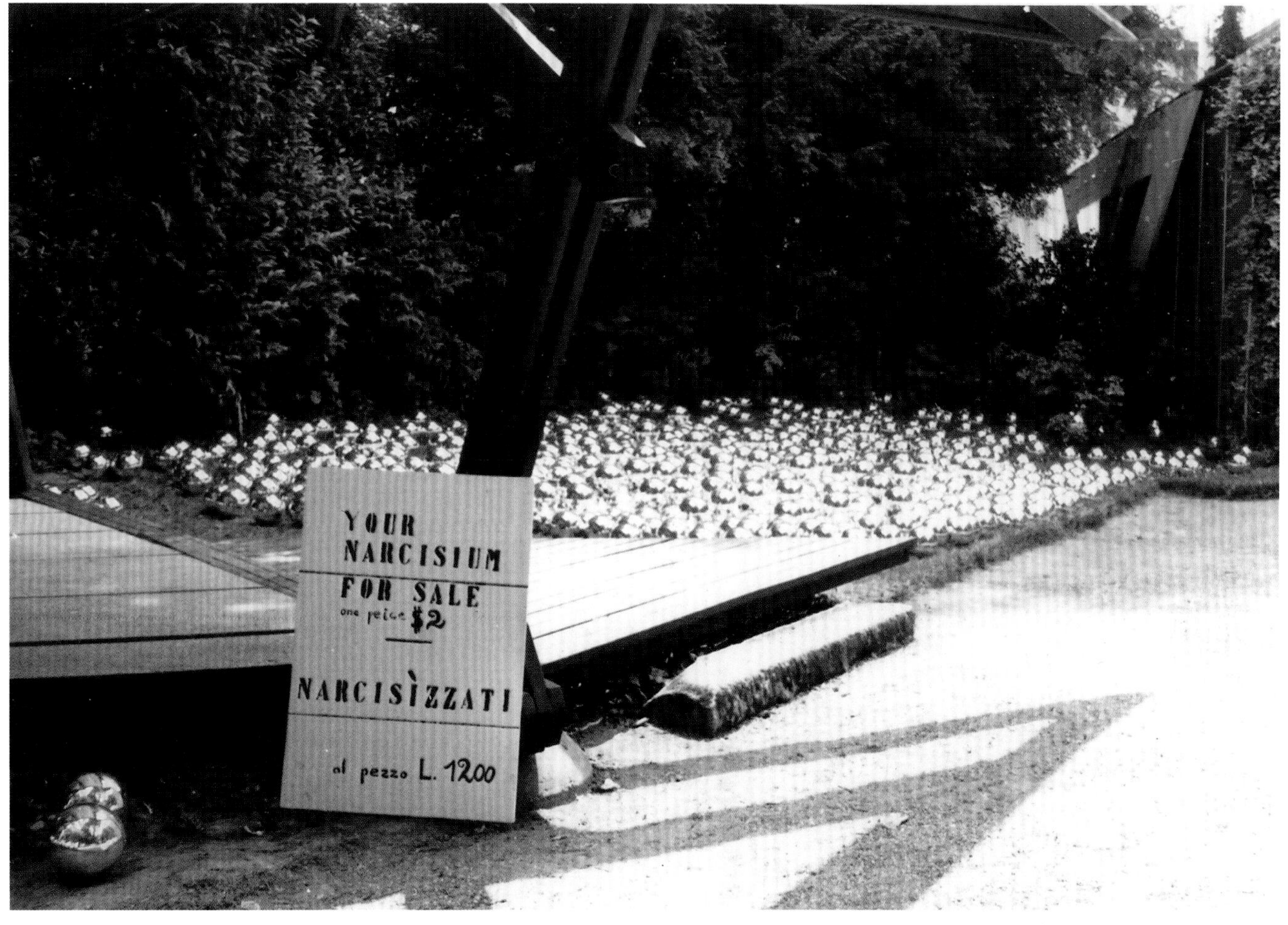

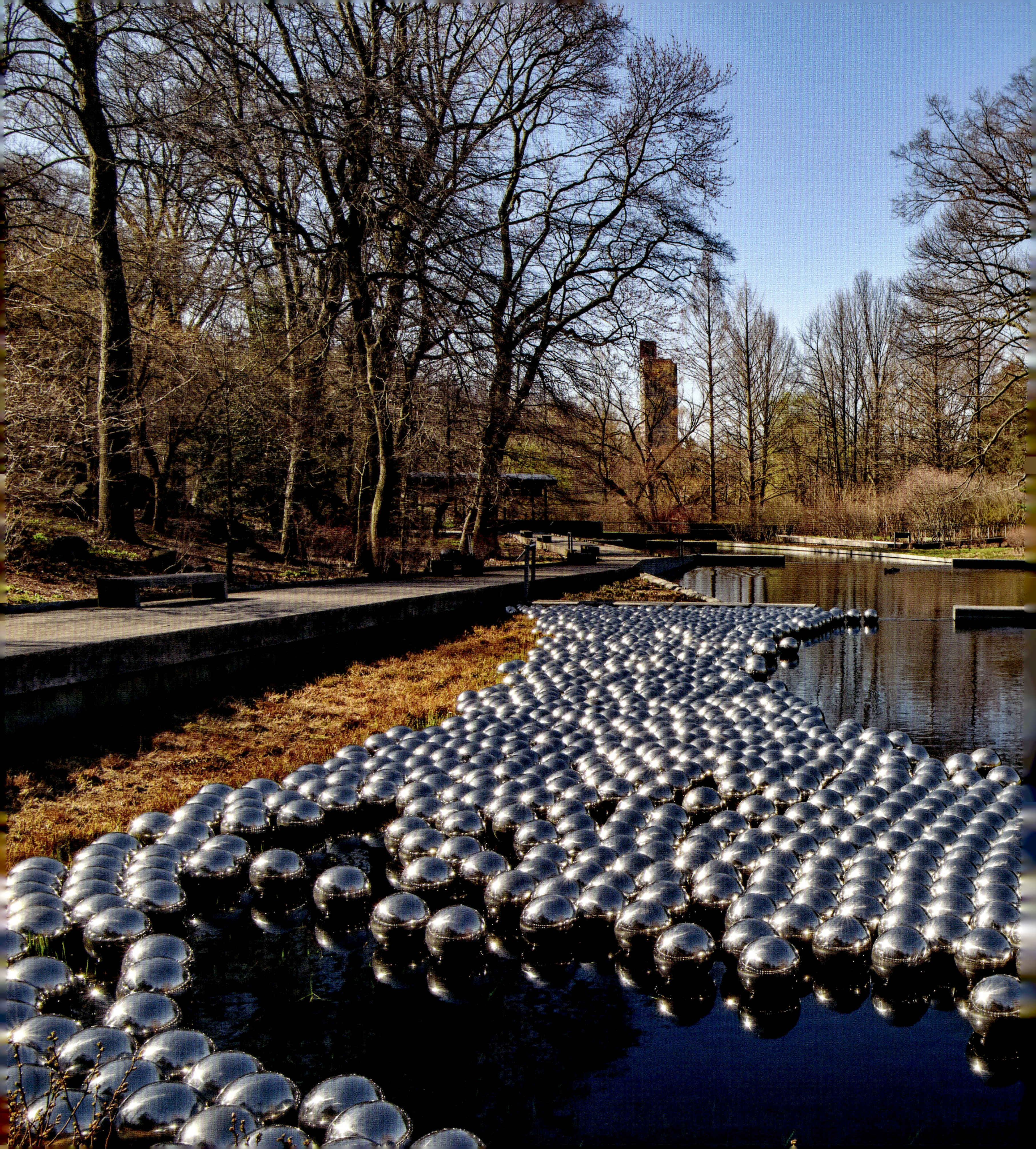

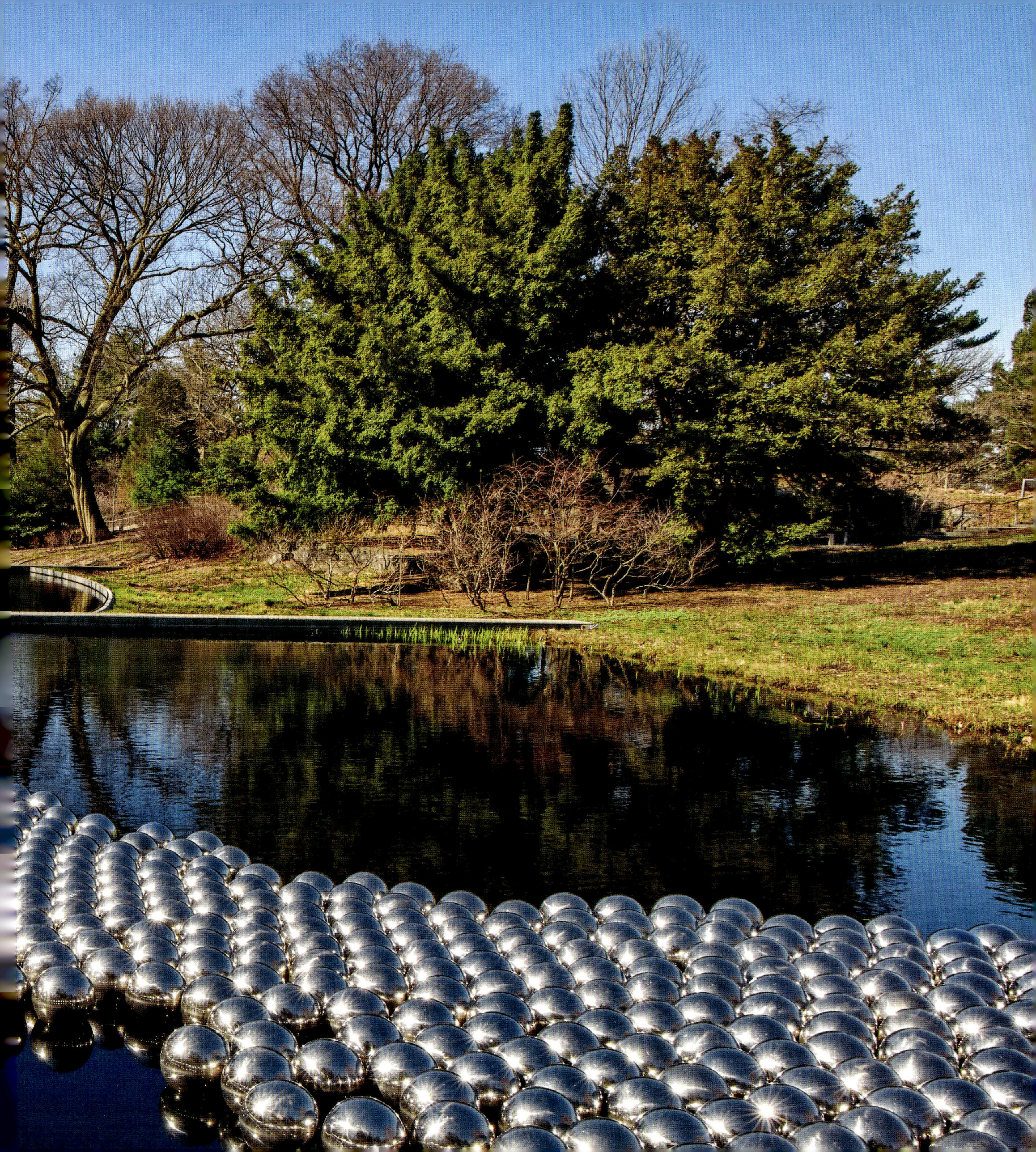

Fig. 10 (previous)
Narcissus Garden, 1966/2021
Installation view, The New York Botanical Garden, 2021
1,400 stainless steel spheres
Installation dimensions variable
Courtesy of Ota Fine Arts

among fifteen hundred mirrored orbs, which she sold for two dollars apiece, as a magnanimous gesture of affordability, but also to comment on exclusion and art world elitism, including the experience of art itself as an activity associated with the wealthy. Part protest, part manifesto, Kusama's baubles enacted twentieth-century French psychoanalyst Jacques Lacan's notion of the "mirror stage," a critical reinterpretation of Freudian psychoanalytic theory, in which children register self-recognition in seeing themselves in a mirror for the first time as a toddler.[10] The particularity of Kusama's own circumstances as an artist add a further layer of analysis: in encouraging the viewer to purchase a dimensional mirror, the "mirror stage" in *Narcissus Garden* quite literally reflected the transactional nature of self-representation—a critique of the viewer and of the artist's own position in the art world, blatantly excluded from its networks and opportunities. Kusama's own interpretation of narcissism, projecting reflective surfaces into a garden setting, is one more affirmation, like her outdoor happenings, that human self-absorption and greed drive the relationship between people and the natural world. In the 1966 press release for *Narcissus Garden*, Kusama wrote that "the silver ball is also a representative of the moon, of sunshine, of peace."[11] This investigation of nature and the cosmos as impervious to human fallibility is one of the key concerns that underscores her oeuvre as an expansive and continuous practice of joining the cosmos, or entering into a dialogue with matter at large (**FIG. 10**).

COSMIC ENERGY

Many decades later, "flower power" is still particularly applicable as a theory of Kusama's work: in contemporary terms, it is the transference from the artist to her public of the principles of compassion, beauty, and the sustained attention to life and liberty, favoring a humanistic impulse toward the environment. Using natural light, human-scale enclosures, colored glass-filled holes, and mirrored surfaces, her signature mirrored installations, such as *Infinity Mirrored Room—Illusion Inside the Heart* (2020; pages 118–19), installed at The New York Botanical Garden, are intent on offering an experience that parallels the natural world: mimicking the glory of an expansive field of wildflowers that stretches past the horizon line, or the underwater phosphorescence observed by scuba divers or the infinite space of the cosmos. It is the sublime that Kusama seeks to convey, the experience of not just one sun, but thousands of lit suns, without regard for the light of day or the darkness of night. Her installations propose an exuberant artifice cultivated to emulate, and to exceed, nature: an experiential reality lit from within, such as her mirrored lighted spaces, which emanate bright colors and flickering lights that blink on and off, like a city without people. This is especially residual in the recent months experienced in urban environments during the pandemic, redolent of a strange emptiness. The cutouts, or portals, allow a pair of viewers to engage with the work, seeing their own reflections, and serve as a reminder that everyday, ordinary people are pertinent to activating Kusama's artworks. It is this fact that underscores her humanist impulses toward her now-global audiences.

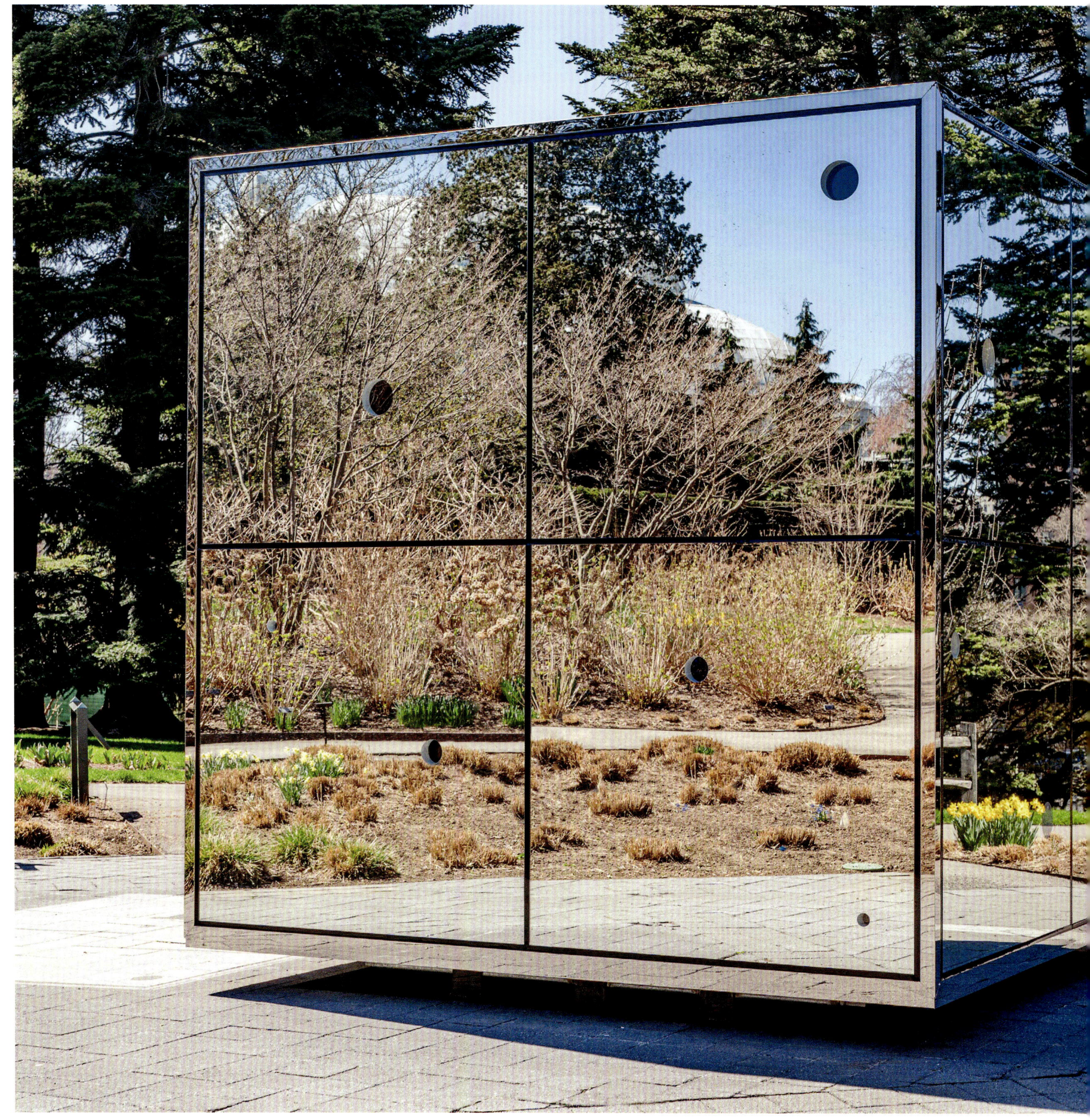

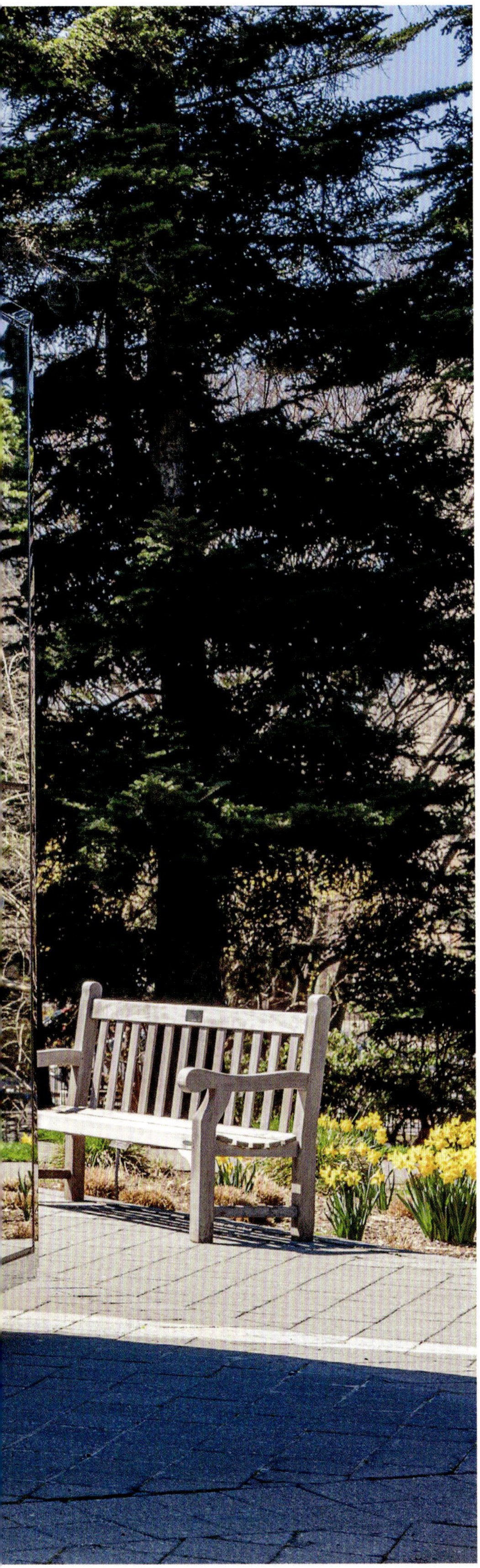

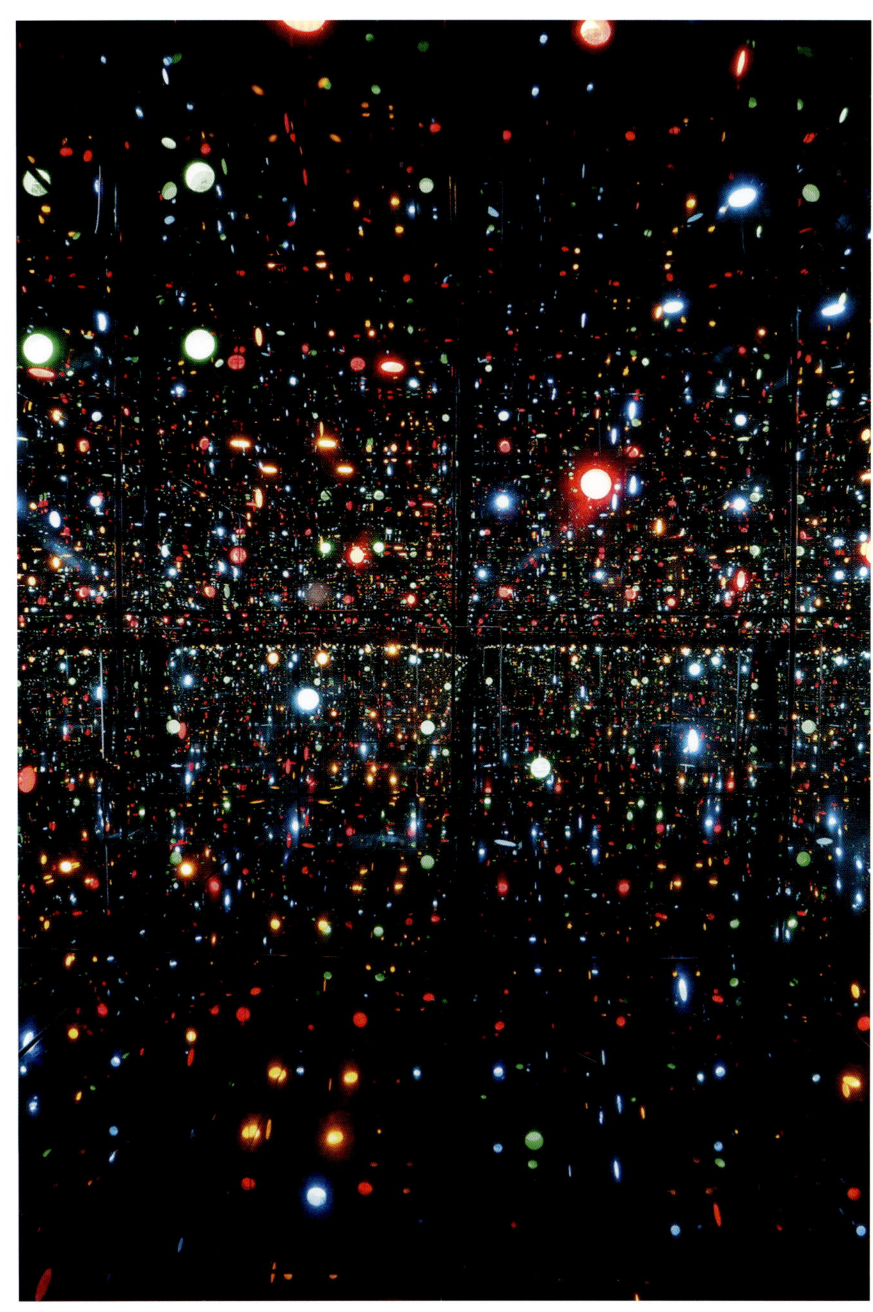

Infinity Mirrored Room—
Illusion Inside the Heart,
2020
Installation view, The New York Botanical Garden, 2021
Mirror-polished stainless steel, glass mirrors, and colored glass
118⅛ × 118⅛ × 118⅛ in.
(300 × 300 × 300 cm)
Courtesy of Ota Fine Arts, Victoria Miro, and David Zwirner

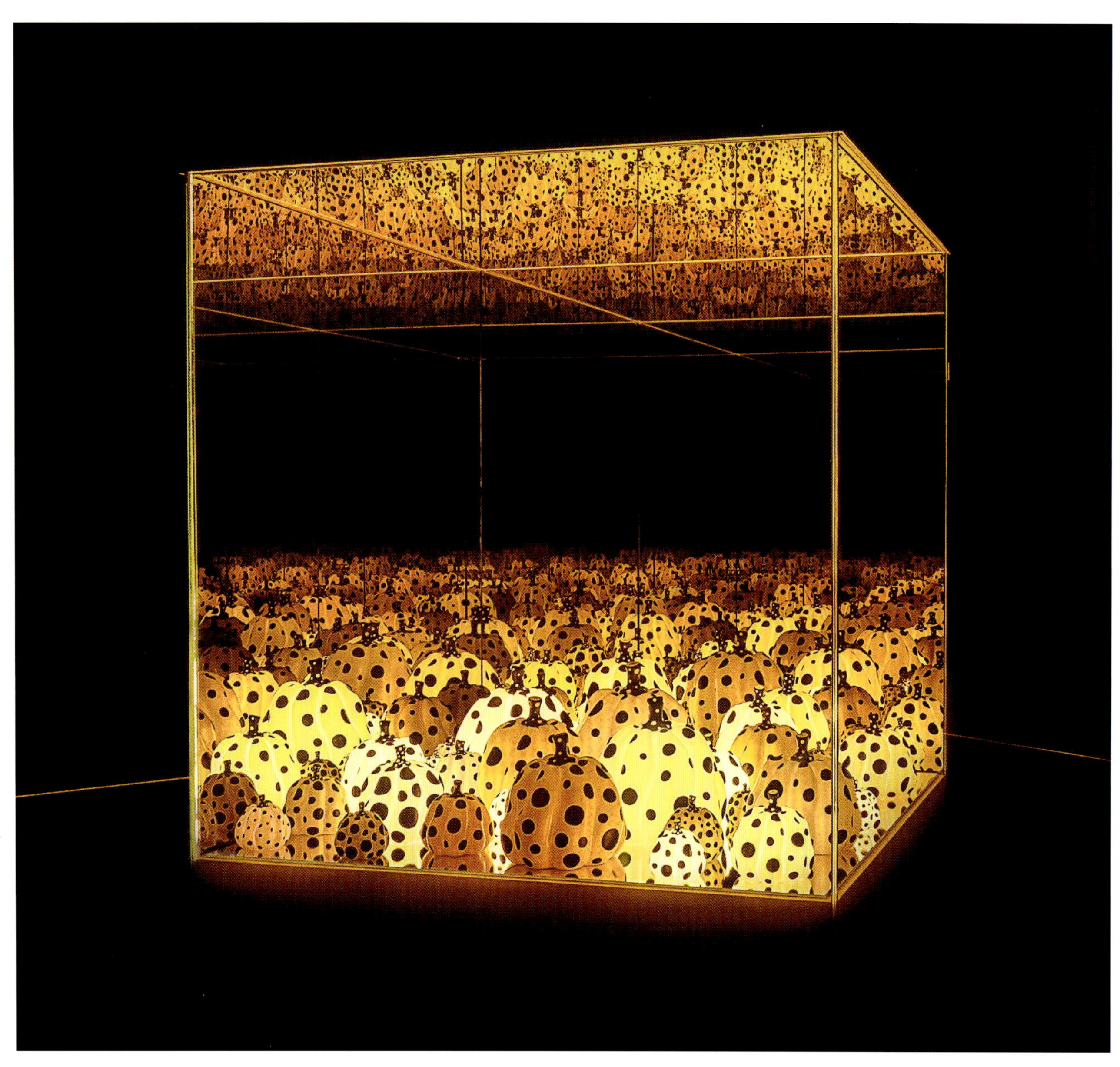

Pumpkins Screaming About Love Beyond Infinity, 2017
Installation view, The New York Botanical Garden, 2021
Mirrors, acrylic, glass, LEDs, and wood panels
59 × 59 × 83½ in.
(150 × 150 × 212 cm)
Courtesy of Ota Fine Arts

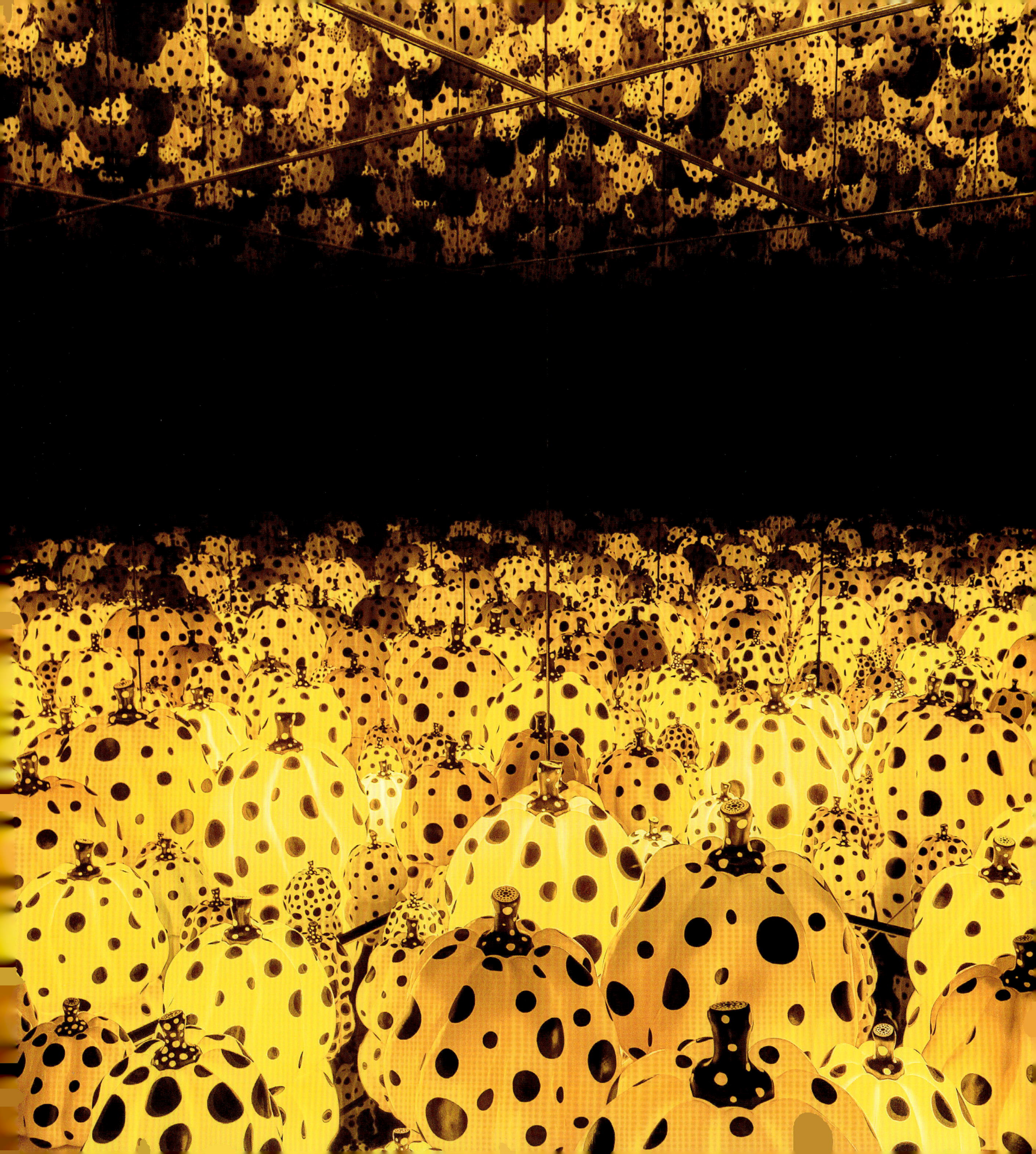

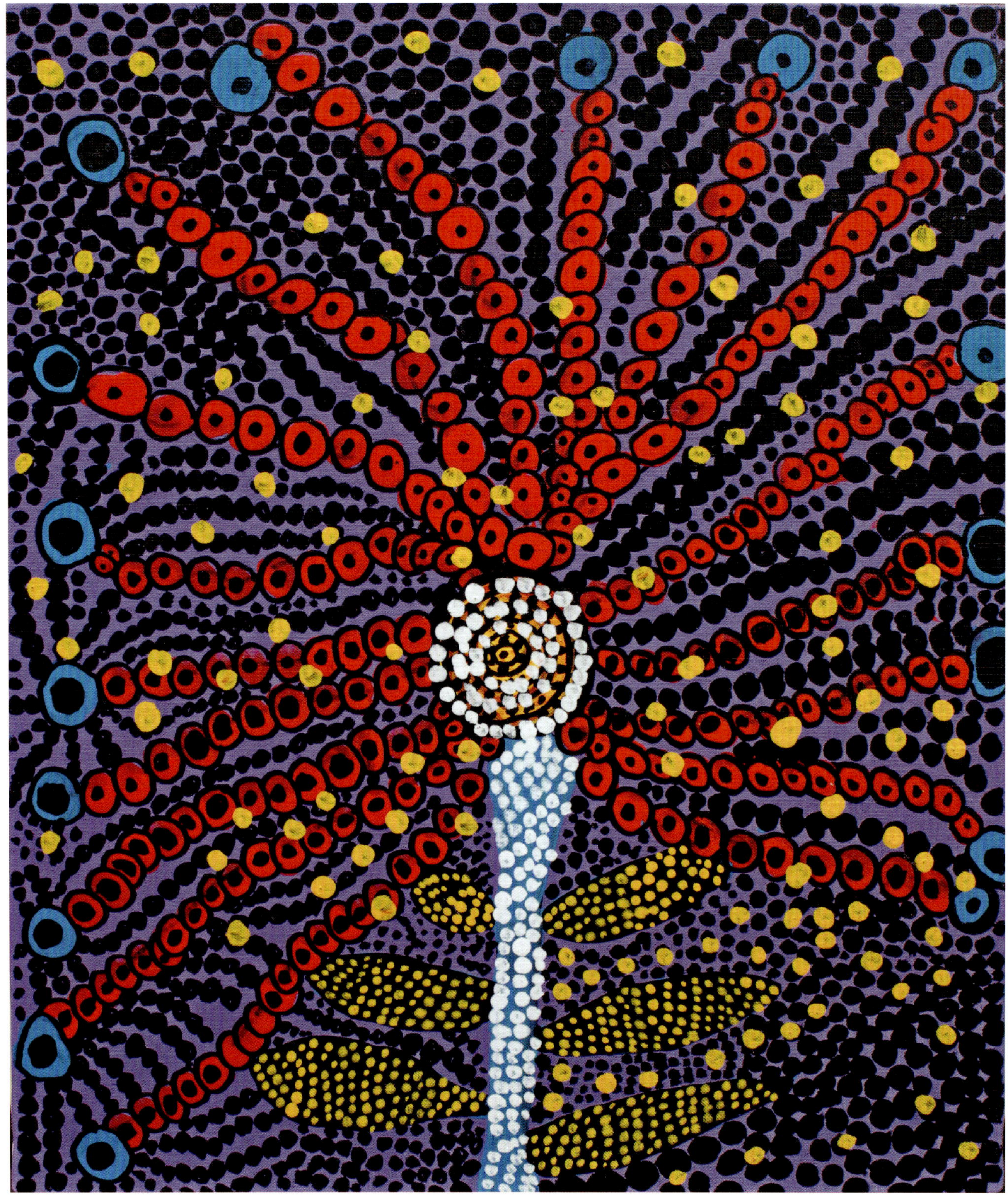

above
Flower Bloomed in My Heart, 2004
Acrylic and felt pen on canvas
17⅞ × 15 in. (45 × 38 cm)
Collection of the artist

opposite
Pistils Swaying in the Wind, 1978
Collage and acrylic on cardboard
25⅞ × 20¼ in. (65.6 × 51.3 cm)
Collection of the artist

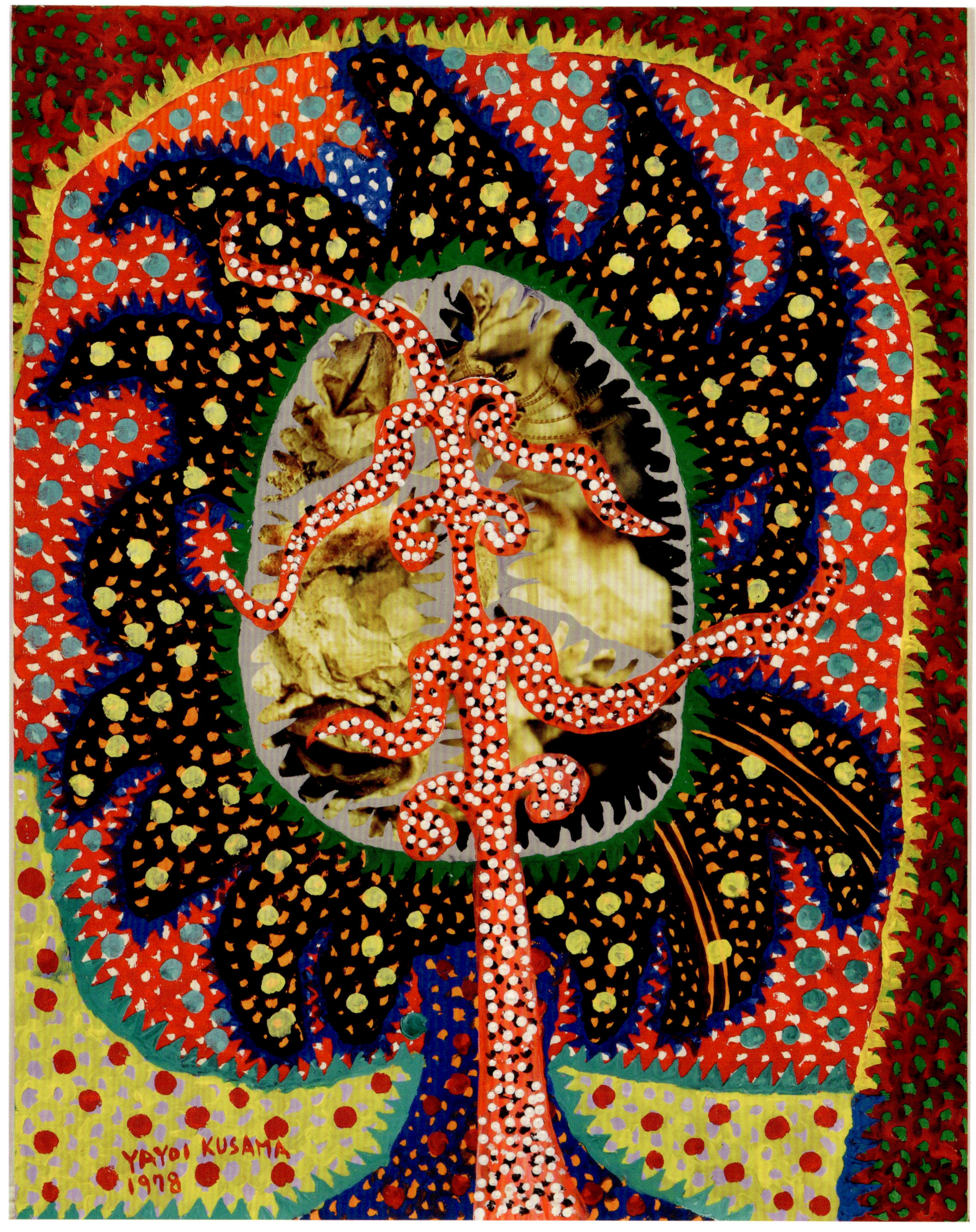
YAYOI KUSAMA
1978

Butterflies' Nest, 2004
Acrylic and felt pen
on canvas
15 × 17⅞ in. (38 × 45.5 cm)
Collection of the artist

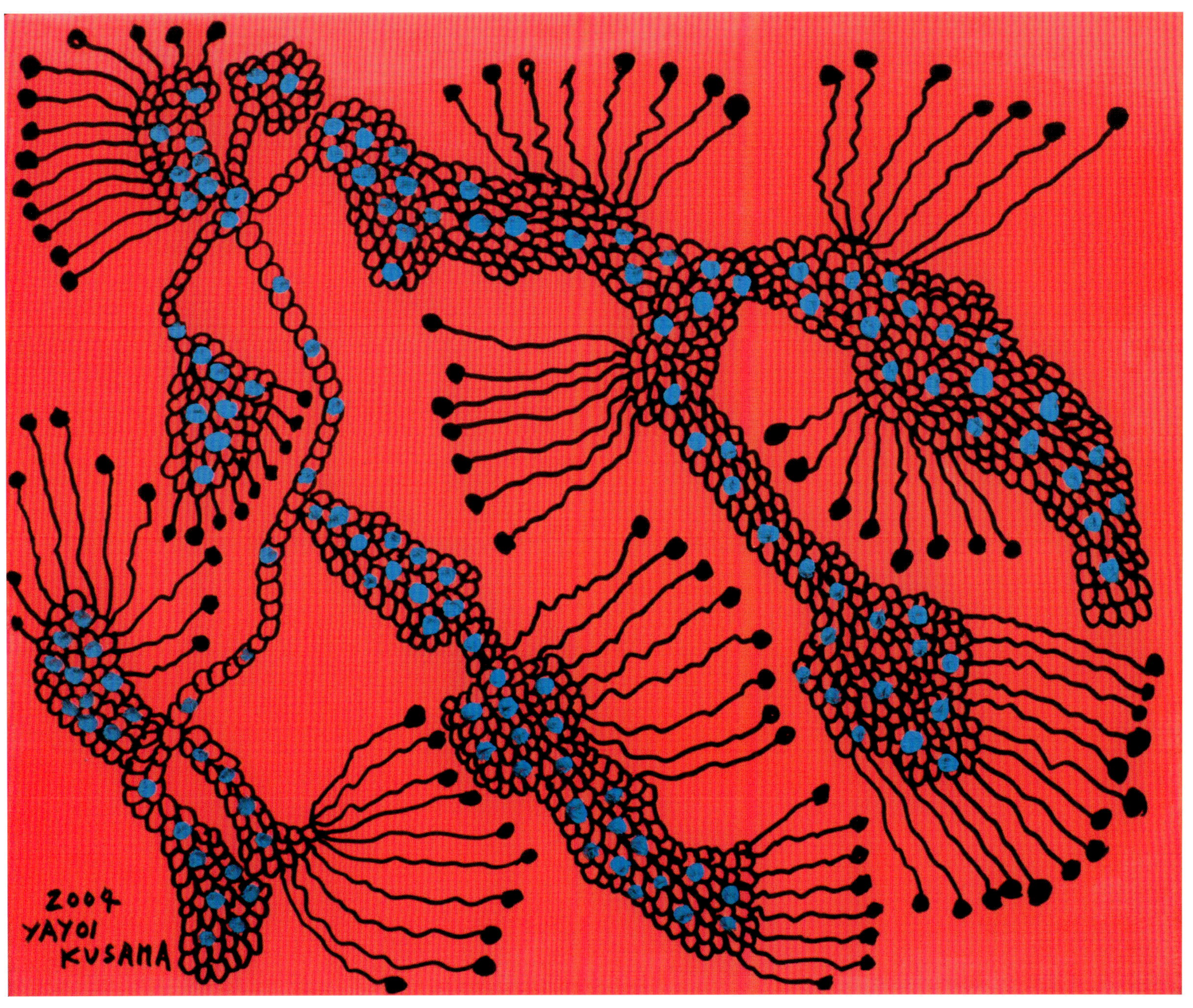
2004
YAYOI
KUSAMA

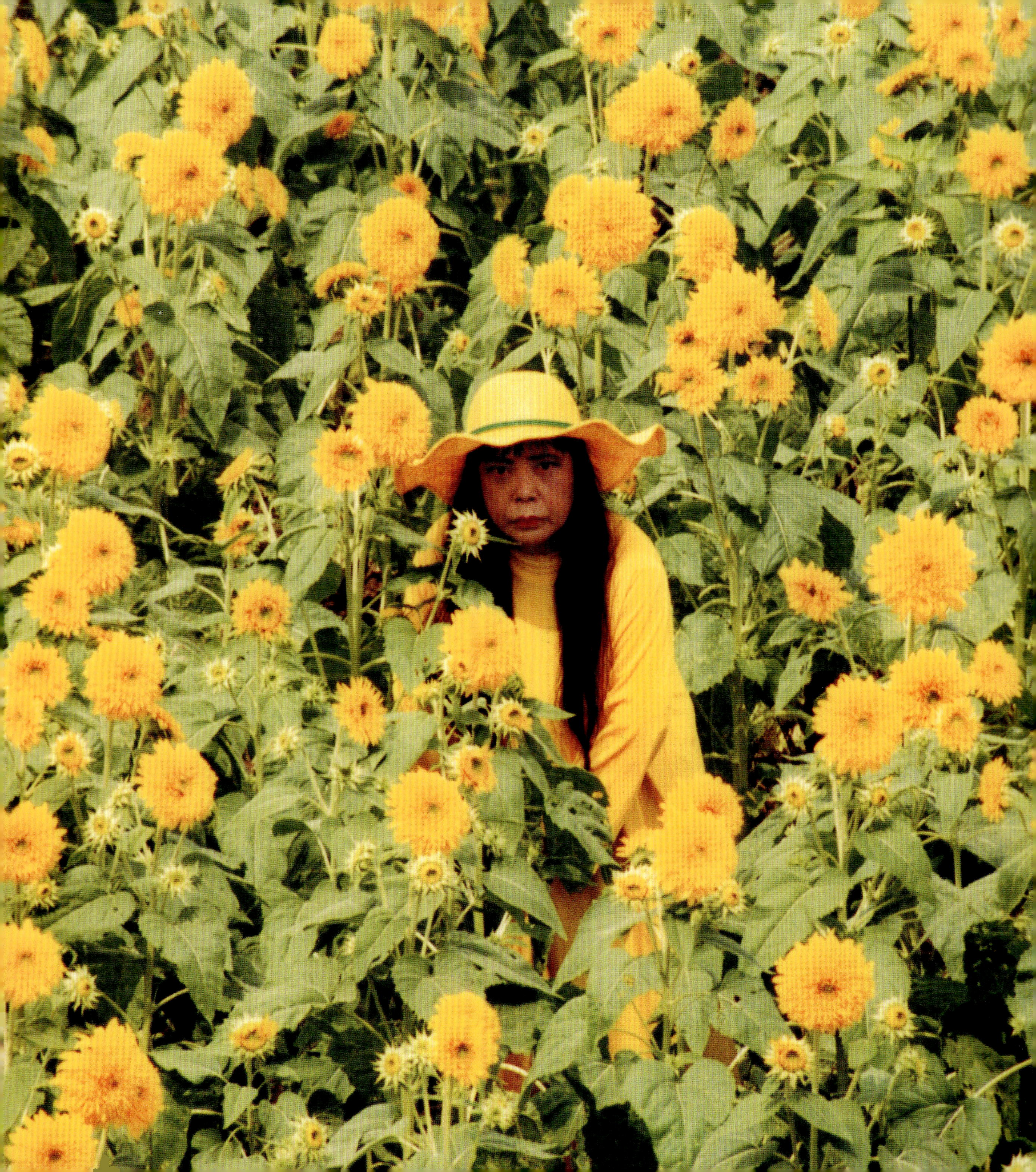

“FORGET YOURSELF AND BECOME ONE WITH NATURE!”

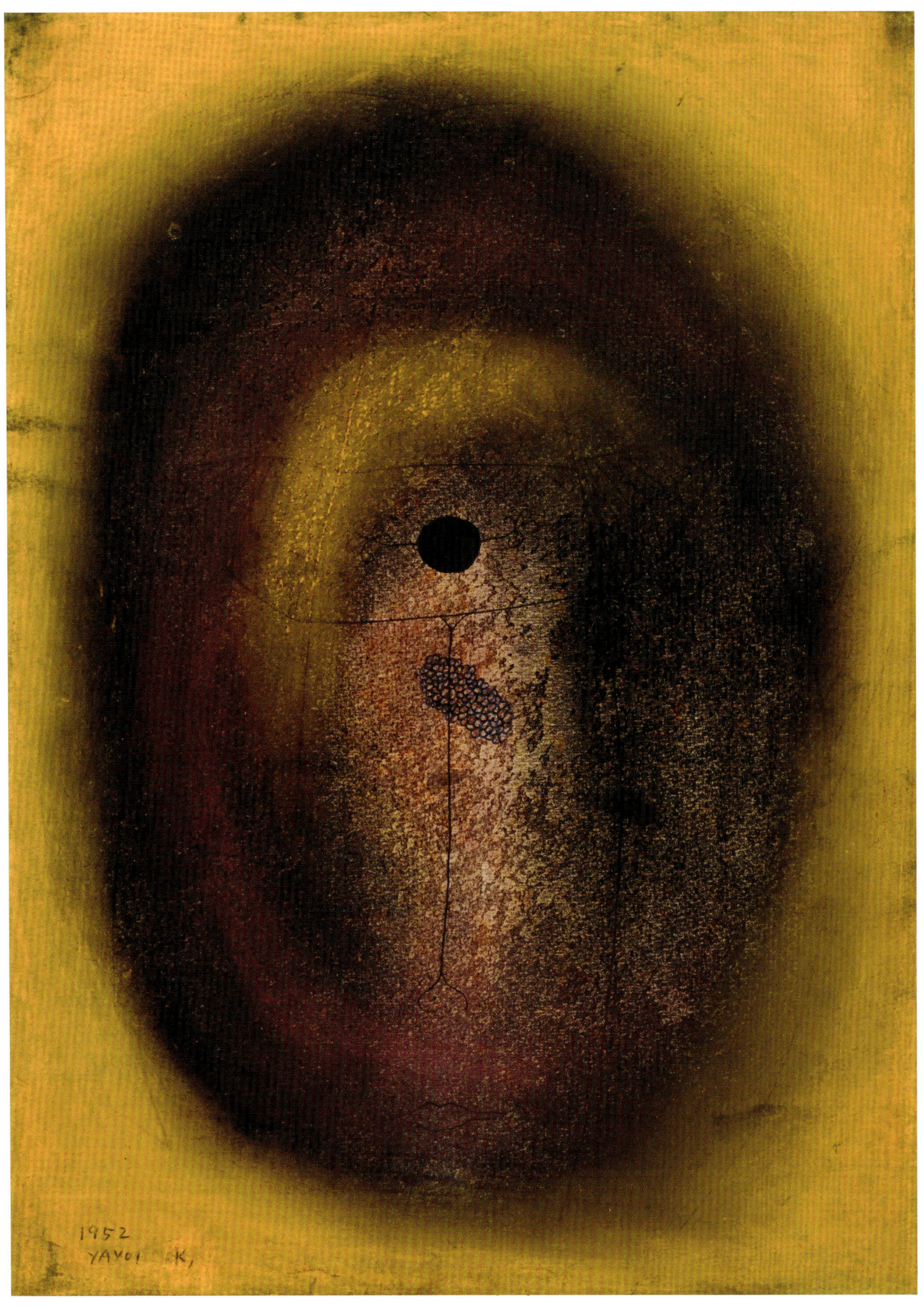
1952
YAYOI K,

WHEN YAYOI KUSAMA WAS TWENTY-THREE, SHE MADE A PASTEL-AND-INK drawing titled *A Seed* (1952; **FIG. 1**). It was one of hundreds of abstract works on paper inspired by nature that she created during this period. An oval form hovers on a yellow ground, its reddish-brown outer covering pulsing toward the edges of the paper. Inside the luminous hollow is a black dot: the embryo, a collection of cells waiting to expand into root and shoot. Kusama would have known such rudimentary botany because her family owned a seed nursery, and her childhood memories were formed in the acres of flowers that they grew. It would be one of innumerable dots Kusama would paint, sculpt, repeat, magnify, and electrify over the next seven decades of her prolific artistic career. Picturing a vortex of deep space that is simultaneously organic and psychic, prolific and generative, *A Seed* also presages Kusama's lifelong fascination with the interconnected worlds of human and nonhuman life forms.

In a 1968 interview about those early works, Kusama describes her fixation on the "forever" aspect of nature, something she saw as a kind of "mysterious energy or feeling in the infinity."[1] It is an energy that "comes up growing and growing, never stops." Polka dots multiply, she says, like "millions of stars in the sky or millions of stone[s] in the river or millions of sand [particles] of the seaside." Imagine, then, what Kusama saw in her local universe of plants and trees. A single *shirakaba (Betula platyphylla)*, a white birch species that is ubiquitous in her hometown of Matsumoto, may produce a quarter of a million seeds every year. Most are carried off by the wind, never to grow. It takes the keen observational skills and imagination of a scientist, mystic, or artist to fathom the creation, four hundred million years ago, of a seed.[2] Kusama has the mind of all three.

Kusama's entire life's work can be seen as a series of acts of creative subversion—and also of farsighted revolution. The political thrust of her activism—one that rebelled against racial and sexual inequality, against the presidency of Richard Nixon and the Vietnam War, against monolithic orthodoxies—takes on new urgency in the context of our contemporary concerns.[3] Beyond these causes, however, her intuitions about the unity of nature and consciousness now suggest an uncanny prescience of current critical examinations of the Anthropocene and its multiple unfolding political, environmental, and health crises, trends in twenty-first-century thinking that span physics, philosophy, cosmology, and other disciplines. In the context of today's resurgent interest in mysticism and metaphysics, Kusama's call to awareness—"Forget yourself and become one with nature!"—also relates to a broader and urgent reckoning: the pressing need to dismantle monolithic supremacist thinking by recouping knowledge systems from non-Western and premodern

previous
Flower Obsession (Sunflowers), 2000
Performance, Ibaraki, Japan

Fig. 1 (opposite)
A Seed, 1952
Pen and pastel on paper
13⅝ × 9⅞ in. (34.5 × 25 cm)
Collection of the artist

Fig. 2
Pacific Ocean, 1960
Oil on canvas
72 × 72 in. (183 × 183 cm)
Museum of Contemporary Art, Tokyo

thought. Kusama's "yearning for an eternity of eternal eternity"[4] is adamantly nature-centric and holistic; it overturns our long-held rules of anthropocentricism, dualism, and mechanistic materialism. She dispels the Cartesian split of mind from matter and unsettles the Enlightenment's establishment of a mechanistic worldview, encouraging instead insight into our true natural order, one in which we coexist in a vibrating web of interconnected phenomena. For Kusama, art manifests consciousness, and consciousness manifests what she most venerates—the "vast, eternal universe."[5]

***KUSAMA: COSMIC NATURE* IS A BRILLIANT STROKE ON THE PART OF** The New York Botanical Garden. Of all the themes scholars and curators have discussed over the decades—Kusama's self-described neuroses, her antiestablishment rage, her presaging of one avant-garde movement after another—none of us ever named what was right before us all along: Kusama's use of nature as method.[6] Her cosmic vision of nature has driven her imagination through every chapter of her career and in every medium, and it explains her hallucinatory experiences as born not of trauma alone but of mystical experiences, too.

Her pursuit was clear from early on. From the mid-1940s, Kusama filled sketchbooks with intensely observed botanical drawings, and in 1950, she painted a self-portrait as a face superimposed over a blood-red sunflower (pages 32–44 and 58). The features—eyes, nose, mouth—are embedded in the disc florets, literally fusing her human anatomy with a plant. She titled her inky watercolors, mimetic or not, after parts of plant anatomy: *Flower Bud No. 6* (1952), *Leaves* (1954; page 108). The Pacific Ocean, viewed from her airplane window on the bumpy flight from Tokyo to Seattle in 1957, inspired her overall compositions of rippling, arc-like brushstrokes, a signature style that would evolve into her *Infinity Nets* (**FIG. 2**). A nudist happening that she staged at the Statue of Liberty in July 1968 embodied the counterculture of the *Whole Earth Catalog*, that manifesto of the holistic ethos of the day. The flyer for Kusama's event read, "Forget yourself and become one with nature! Obliterate yourself with polka dots!"[7] By the late 1980s and early 1990s, when she created works such as *Between Heaven and Earth* (1987) and the similarly titled *Heaven and Earth* (1991; **FIG. 3**), massive soft-sculpture installations of engorged tendril forms, Kusama had decided the universe was hers to remake. The vivid dare of her claim to a cosmic vision of nature has intensified over recent decades, driving her entwined psychological and creative lives. As feminist psychoanalyst Juliet Mitchell wrote, "In her experience as a flower, Kusama is a

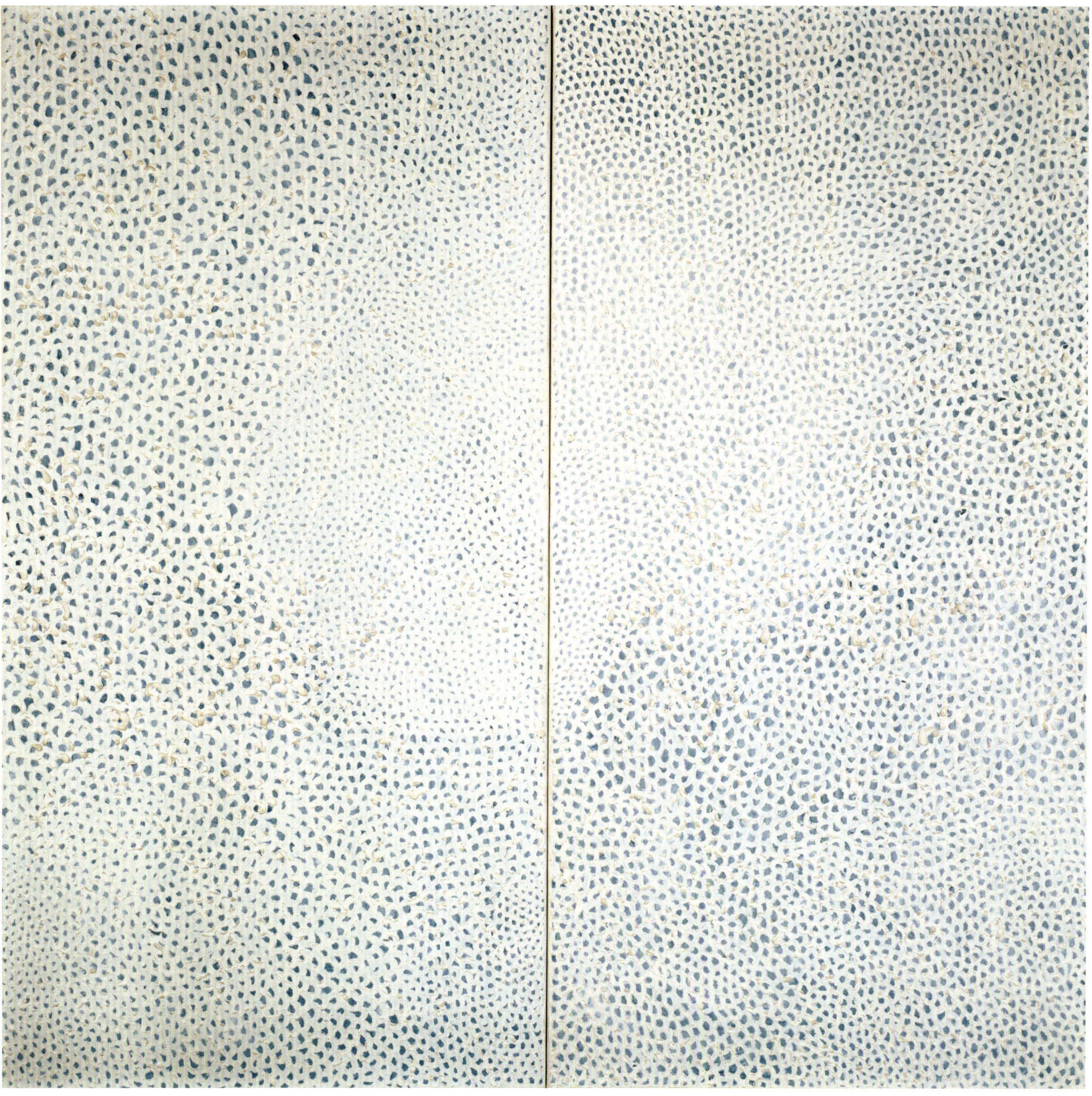

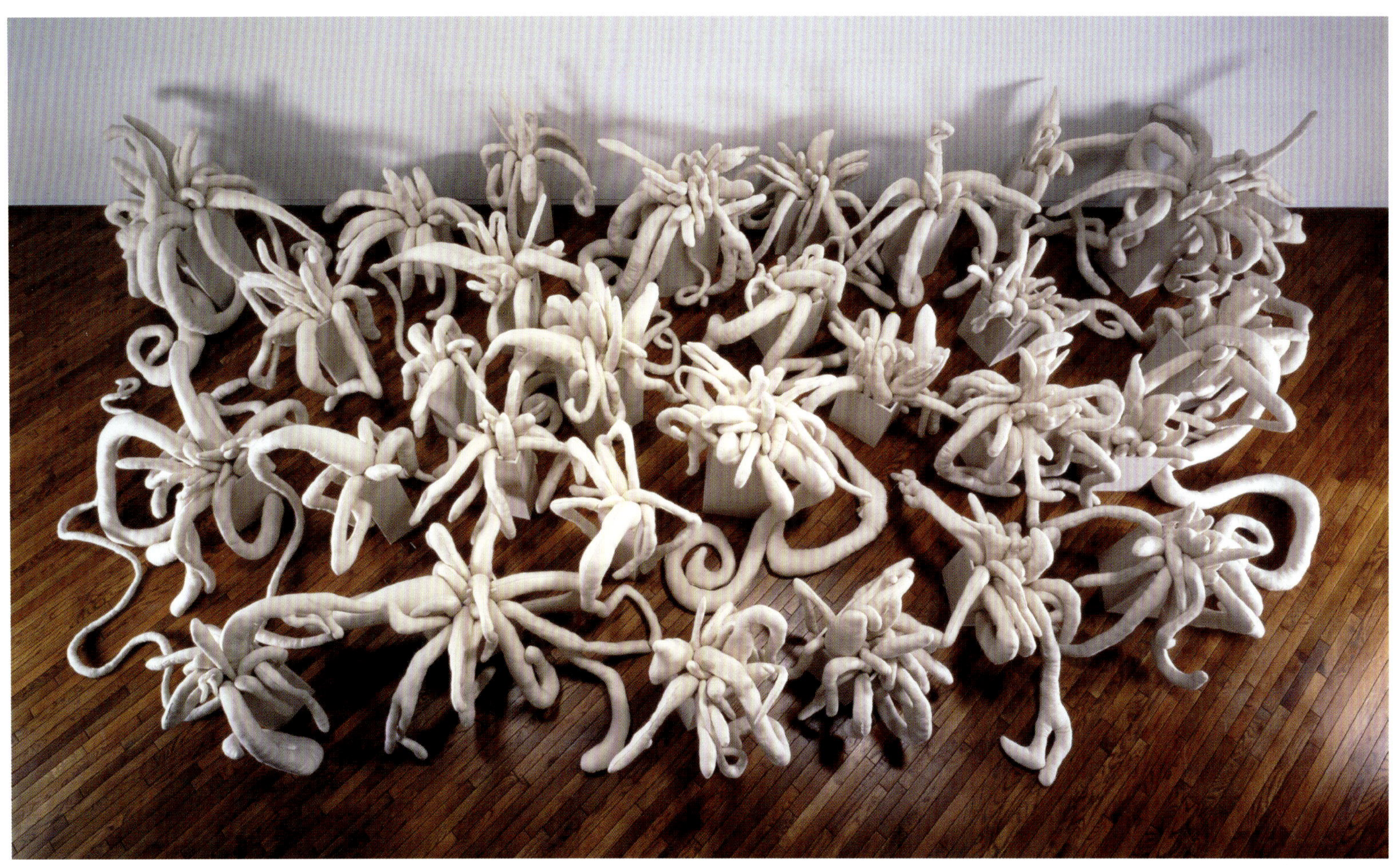

flower."[8] In scores of staged photographs throughout her career, Kusama poses in colors and patterns that simulate the proliferating dots of her flower, nets, or pumpkin environments, as if to literally embody the natural forms that dominate her imagery (**FIG. 4**).

But something more radical might be at work in Kusama's insistent production of a cosmology the terms of which have grown increasingly transcendent. What does it mean to push aside the entire inheritance of the Enlightenment and its stridently anthropocentric worldview? Or to disrupt the mechanistic notion of nature that has shaped modern science since Galileo Galilei, René Descartes, and Isaac Newton with an alternative vision of a cosmos animated by a conscious nature? It would be easy to read such audacity as a deliberate affront to the dominion of Western epistemology if Kusama identified herself as its antithesis, by waving the flag of Japanese otherness or casting her statements in fashionable Zen rhetoric. Quite the opposite. She was keenly aware of how critics positioned her Japanese identity in postwar New York and famously rejected the artist and critic Sidney Tillim's description of her work as "Zen." Kusama resisted and rejected what "Japan" stood for, claiming that its "shackles, the conventions, the prejudice" made the place feel "too small, too servile, too feudalistic, too scornful of women"for an artist to thrive.[9] However, she complicated this position as she also "performed" the exotic Japanese woman—wearing a flashy kimono at openings and notably at the 1966 Venice Biennale *Narcissus Garden* installation—which reflects a subversive strategy that satirizes tradition and the Western Orientalist gaze.[10]

The origins of Kusama's visceral attention to nature can be found rather in her genius at forecasting ideas that have changed the way we know the world. By assuming reciprocities among art, science, and mysticism, she subverts the modern Western intellectual canon and its host of governing assumptions. I suggest that we see Kusama's art through a new lens of panpsychism, the theory that the universe is conscious and everything in it, from quarks to plants to humans to stars, is vitally interconnected. Recently, this ancient and long-contested doctrine has taken on new currency. In 2017 the *Stanford Encyclopedia of Philosophy* revised its entry on the term and noted:

> *Panpsychism is the view that mentality is fundamental and ubiquitous in the natural world. The view has a long and venerable history in philosophical traditions of both East and West, and has recently enjoyed a revival in analytic philosophy. For its proponents panpsychism offers an attractive middle way between physicalism on the one hand and dualism on the other.... Panpsychism, strange as it may sound on first hearing, promises a satisfying account of the human mind within a unified conception of nature.*[11]

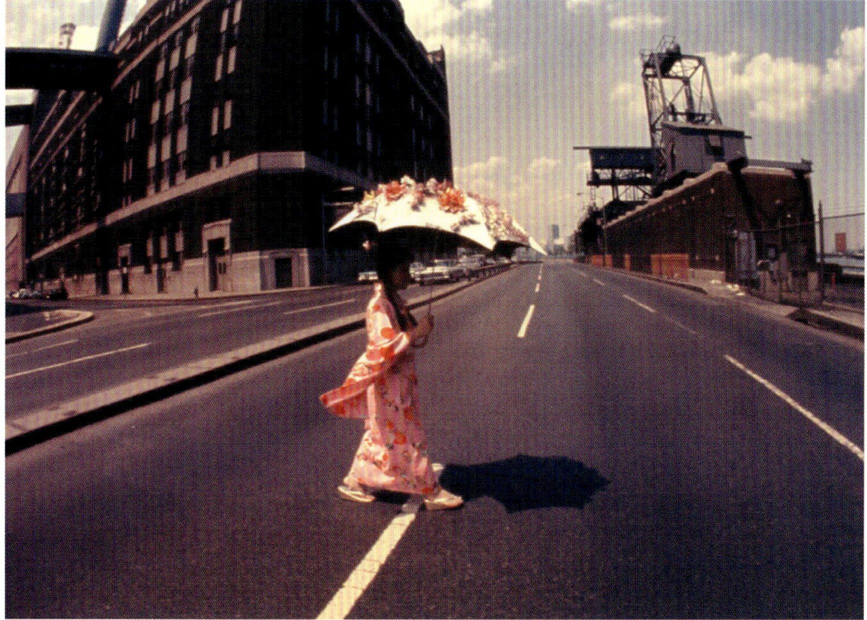

Fig. 3 (opposite)
Heaven and Earth, 1991
40 wooden boxes, muslin, and 285 stuffed muslin forms
Display dimensions variable

Fig. 4 (below)
Walking Piece (detail), 1966
24 slides
Installation dimensions variable
Collection of the artist

Fig. 5 (below)
Kusama in Seattle, 1957

Fig. 6 (opposite)
Kusama with a no-longer-extant, 33-foot-long *Infinity Net* painting (title unknown), 1961. Stephen Radich Gallery, New York

In the context of recent critical examinations of the Anthropocene, panpsychism offers both a restoration of a nature-centric humanity and an aspiration toward an ecologically wise future of the planet. Kusama's endless fascination with nature and her almost shamanistic approach are, in fact, radical expressions of an ecocritical worldview. As I have argued elsewhere, Kusama has always been ahead of the cultural zeitgeist.[12] Now, with the rise of panpsychism, we can choose a whole new way to appreciate and interpret Kusama's art. As she said, "Forget yourself and become one with nature!"

SCHOLARS HAVE TRIED TO PINPOINT THE ORIGINS OF WHAT A Japanese critic called Kusama's "metaphysical mysterious work" early in her career.[13] Her training in *nihonga* (traditional Japanese-style painting) undoubtedly grounded her practice in the astute observation of nature as a way to transcend the self. This artistic approach was linked to Zen Buddhism, whose notion of *mu* (nothingness or void) as the substance of one's mind and the universe was pervasive in elite Japanese culture at the time. Kusama's friendship with leading Surrealist poet and critic Shūzo Takiguchi, who wrote for her 1952 exhibition brochure, illuminated for her how art might tap psychic imagery far beyond the rational mind. In her 1955 essay, "Ivan the Fool," Kusama wrote that she wanted to express things that are "deep in the bottom of life" such as "tempests, buds, wounds, and genitalia that provoked my anxiety" and "the hidden, shadowy part of life on earth."[14]

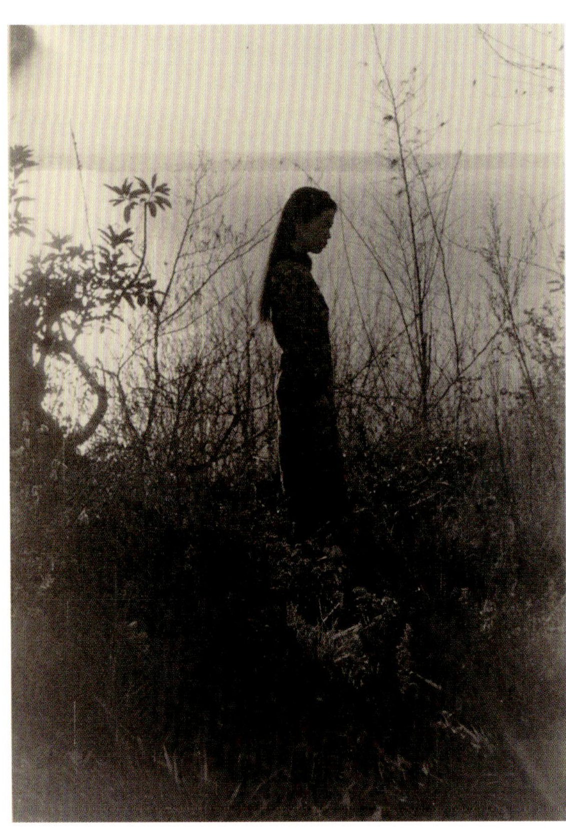

In these early writings, Kusama was calling upon the "power" of art to seek "spiritual freedom in eternity." If only artists could mine the "inexplicable," she wrote, "people [would] see the world of yonder."[15] Her interest in the Pacific Northwest School in Seattle helped Kusama articulate a "mysticism born out of mechanical civilization."[16] Kenneth Callahan, Morris Graves, and Mark Tobey, who were dubbed the "Mystic Painters of the Northwest" by *Life* magazine in 1953, pursued the spiritual cosmos in abstract art inspired by their sympathy with and proximity to East Asian and Native American cultures.[17] Reckoning with the devastation of World War II, and aghast at American enmity toward Japan, these artists believed in the need to restore universalism to humanity by connecting to the vast awe of nature. Kusama's US career was launched when their dealer, Zoë Dusanne, offered her a solo show in Seattle in 1957 (**FIG. 5**).[18]

When she arrived in New York City in 1958, the language she used was unabashedly cosmic. Kusama titled her first series of allover white paintings *Infinity Nets*. These canvases, one of which

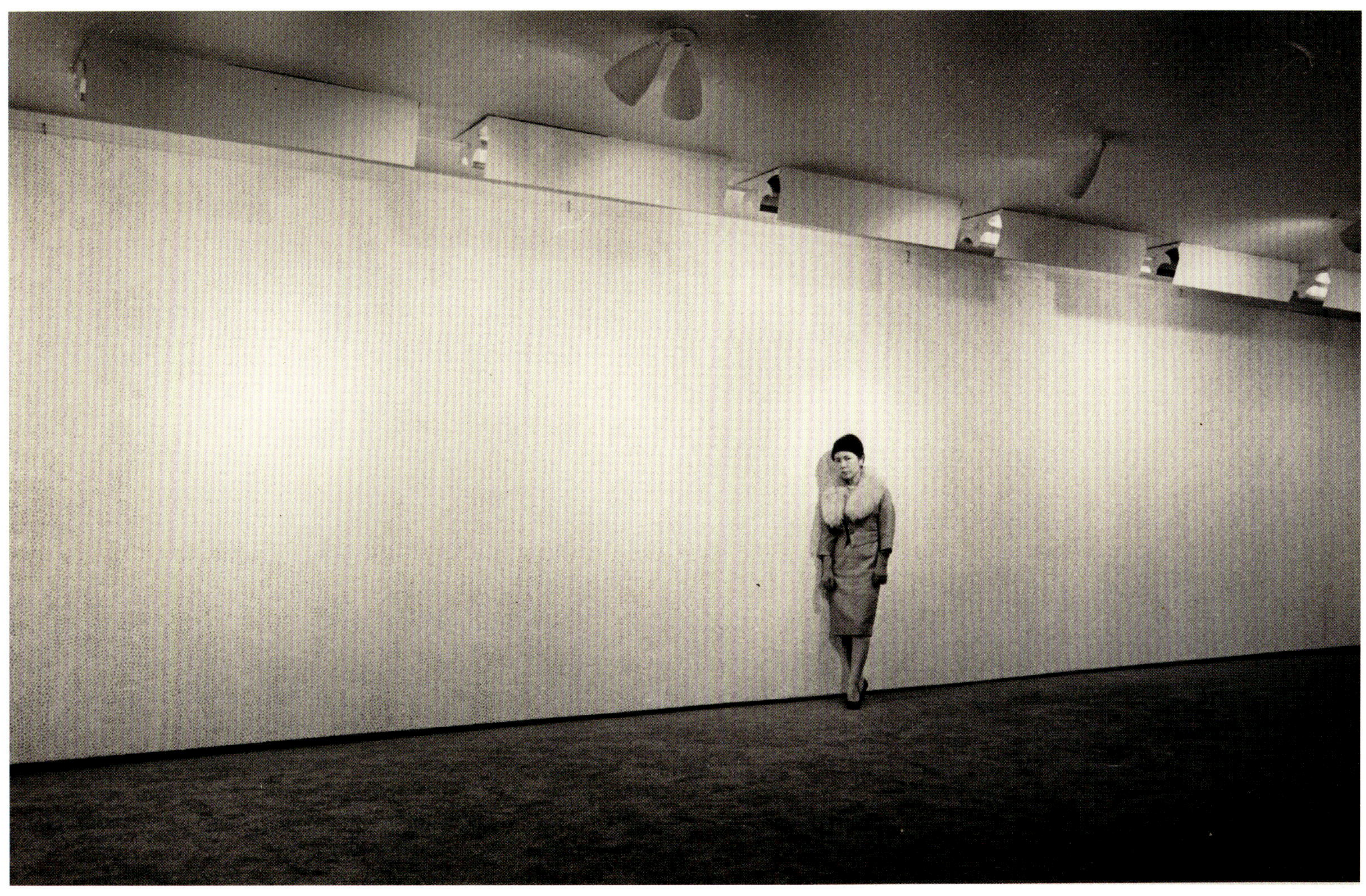

was thirty-three feet long (**FIG. 6**), were composed of a single arc, or dot, brushed in orb-like patterns across the entire surface. "My net paintings," Kusama said, are "without beginning, end or center."[19] Formally, the image and its process of creation represented a systematic singularity of idea and execution, drawing acclaim from the then art critic Donald Judd (who would later write the manifesto for Minimalist art, "Specific Objects"). But what Judd saw as "shallow" space configured of two parallel planes—the dark-wash ground and the "solid lace" surface—can also be read as its contrary: waves of deep space. He acknowledged Kusama's affinity with the abstract sublime by comparing her to Mark Rothko, Clyfford Still, and Barnett Newman, but he shied away from describing her art in spiritual terms.[20] Judd's insistence on the modernist rhetoric of the flatbed picture plane in Abstract Expressionist discourse actually prevented him from seeing Kusama's pictorial space as an evocation of psychically charged cosmic infinity. *Infinity Nets*, the series that became a lifelong touchstone of Kusama's art, emphatically offers the kind of immersion in durational time and expansive imagery that goes well beyond "objecthood." It is art as a medium for ecstatic contemplation. In her autobiography, Kusama looks back over her decades-long obsession with sublime experience:

> *My desire was to predict and measure the infinity of the unbounded universe, from my own position in it, with dots—an accumulation of particles forming the negative spaces in the net. How deep was the mystery? Did infinite infinities exist beyond our universe?*[21]

In the 1960s, Kusama's impulse to intuit and reflect the psychic connection between herself, her environment, and the universe, as if consciousness pervaded everything, was also part of the cultural zeitgeist. Along with Graves and Tobey, Ad Reinhardt was the most learned of the artists moving away from American Abstract Expressionism via a deep dive into Asian aesthetics and philosophy. His notebooks, written as a direct extension of his studio practice, are filled with transcriptions from Hindu and Buddhist texts, quotations on Asian aesthetics, and excerpts from the *Tao Te Ching*. They served as thresholds for his practice and acted as meditational asides on the workings of his inner eye: "The Tao is through and through mysterious and dark."[22] While Kusama did not court simplistic Zen, Buddhist, or Daoist readings of her work, she gladly promoted herself as a chosen medium of all things eternal, infinite, and cosmic. In a letter to Georgia O'Keeffe, with whom she carried on a correspondence for some years, she once described her art as "my Oriental mystic symbolism."[23]

Kusama's artwork, poetry, and other writings have long been ascribed to her psychosis, most famously her hallucinations of being dissolved in an infinity of nets, flowers, or dots. She would often describe how, as a child, she heard her own voice as that of a dog; and how she saw and heard violets talking to one another in a field. She was afflicted by visions of repetitive and proliferating matter saturating her physical being. As she recalled:

> *One day I was looking at the red flower patterns of the tablecloth on a table, and when I looked up I saw the same pattern covering the ceiling, the windows and the walls, and finally all over the room, my body and the universe. I felt as if I had begun to self-obliterate, to revolve in the infinity of endless time and the absoluteness of space, and be reduced to nothingness.*[24]

In 2021, as The New York Botanical Garden presents Kusama's work through the lens of nature, we can offer a fresh reading of this creative spirit. What if hers were not the notations of a psychotic all these years, but were rather those of a *self-made panpsychist*?[25]

After all, panpsychism offers a unified field theory of the universe and material existence, and it poses consciousness as a quality inherent in all, from quarks and stars to butterflies and chrysanthemums.[26] Consciousness is not merely a cognitive function, but is, as one panpsychist puts it, a "solidarity with non-human people, the feeling of recognition and interconnectedness of everything in the universe."[27] No artist of our time has imagined and reflected this vision more obsessively than Kusama in such works as her *Infinity Mirrored Rooms* (pages 118–21). In these environments, reflections of the viewer refract across infinite space. In a flash, differentiation between body, mind, and one's surroundings vanishes. Like James Watson and Francis Crick's 1953 three-dimensional double helix structure of DNA, Kusama's *Infinity Mirrored Rooms* could be imagined as a physical model of a panpsychist worldview.

PANPSYCHIST DOCTRINES APPEAR IN PRE-SOCRATIC THOUGHT IN ancient Greece. Thales of Miletus—a thinker whom Aristotle regarded as the first Greek philosopher—claimed that "the universe is alive and full of spirits." Later thinkers credited him for positing the "ubiquity of animation."[28] Democritus proposed that all matter consisted of multi-shaped atoms "interlocking" to form an infinity of ever more complex shapes. Such early probes into the nature of reality could not resolve whether consciousness was an elemental feature of the world or could be reduced even further to more fundamental elements.

Two millennia later, philosophical questions such as these lay at the center of the scientific revolution. The "mechanistic" explanation of the world, starting with Galileo's mathematization of nature, advanced all kinds of theories about the actual physics of the universe, but the theorists were at a loss as to what to make of experience: what was it, of what did it consist, and how was it to be understood? All of this would still be ascribed to the wonders of the soul. For these early scientific thinkers, there was nature's realm, one that included man and all his superior faculties; and there was God, whose province was all things sensorial and metaphysical. Descartes and Newton went along with this schema, encouraging a stern doctrine of dualism that ordained a gulf between mind and matter, soul and machine. This dualism has dominated Western philosophical discourse and debate ever since. According to this view, consciousness was a subjective phenomenon: God, angels, and all mental experiences—including human reason, purpose, meaning, poetry, and art—exist outside the material universe, and hence beyond the realm of empirical reality. This construct further entrenched the dichotomy of subject and object and established humans as the sole thinking agents in a world of inert matter. *Cogito, ergo sum.*

In Europe during the Enlightenment era, occasional panpsychist views flourished in opposition to the prevailing philosophies of dualism, idealism, and materialism. Baruch Spinoza (1632–77) and Gottfried Wilhelm Leibniz (1646–1716), for example, were keen to provide a more unified and animated model of nature. Spinoza saw mind and matter as being the entwined attributes of God's eternal, infinite, and unique *substance*. In part 2 of the *Ethics* (1677), he wrote:

> *a circle existing in nature and the idea of the existing circle, which is also in God, are one and the same thing . . . therefore, whether we conceive nature under the attribute of Extension, or under the attribute of Thought . . . we shall find one and the same order, or one and the same connection of causes.*[29]

For his part, Leibniz elaborated with a system of metaphysics based on *monads*—not one, but an infinity of individual entities that make up the universe. He posited that each monad was a unique, dynamic, and soul-like being, carrying within it the complete information of the entire universe. For Leibniz, the universe was the grand synchrony of monads existing by the grace of God's determined harmony.

Leibniz's monadism spurred the popularity of panpsychism in the nineteenth and early twentieth centuries, when thinkers such as William James developed ideas that would admit psychic elements into the basic structure of reality. But the most significant defense of a panpsychist philosophy was made by British mathematician and philosopher Alfred North Whitehead (1861–1947). His insight that the fundamental nature of reality consists of dynamic and interdependent *processes* characterized by creativity and spontaneity was a radical departure from modern Western philosophy, the logic of which had long rested on the separate entities of matter, time, and space. Whitehead's speculative cosmology embraced ideas supported by research in the area of quantum mechanics that were developing around the same time, in the early 1920s, in Göttingen, Germany. Where rigid determinism had been the rule, randomness, unpredictability, and "energy quanta" now inspired a holistic reimagining of the universe. Whitehead's "process philosophy" posited that "there is urgency in coming to see the world as a web of interrelated processes of which we are integral parts, so that all of our choices and actions have consequences for the world around us."[30]

From the 1930s, when Kusama was coming of age, mainstream philosophers dismissed panpsychism as a wacky theory. Aversion to metaphysics dominated modern philosophy as much as it did modern art, especially after Pop, Minimalism, and Conceptualism hit their stride. It is no surprise that Kusama's happenings of the late

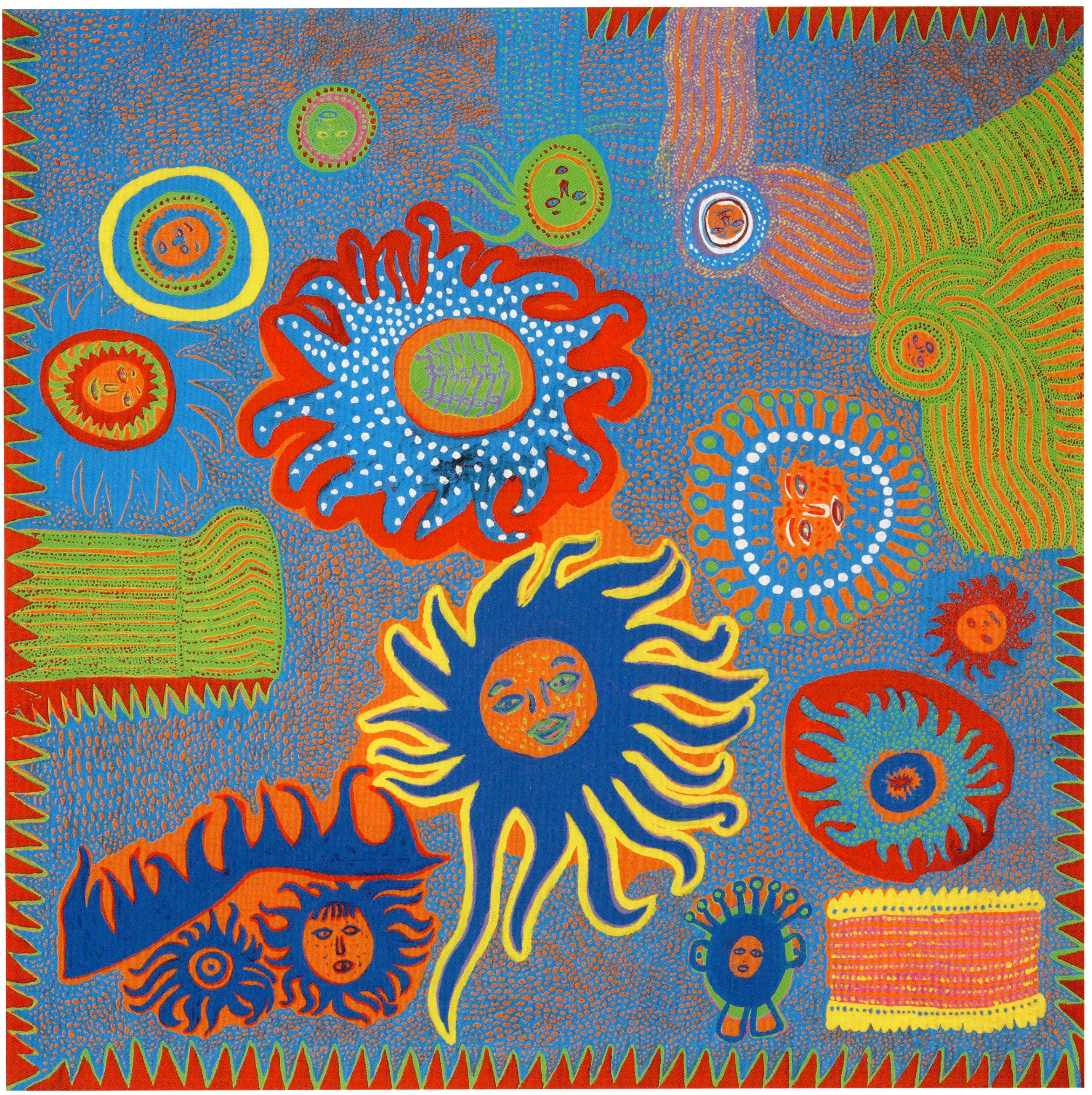

Fig. 7
I Want to Go to the Universe, 2013
Acrylic on canvas
76⅜ × 76⅜ in. (194 × 194 cm)
Collection of the artist

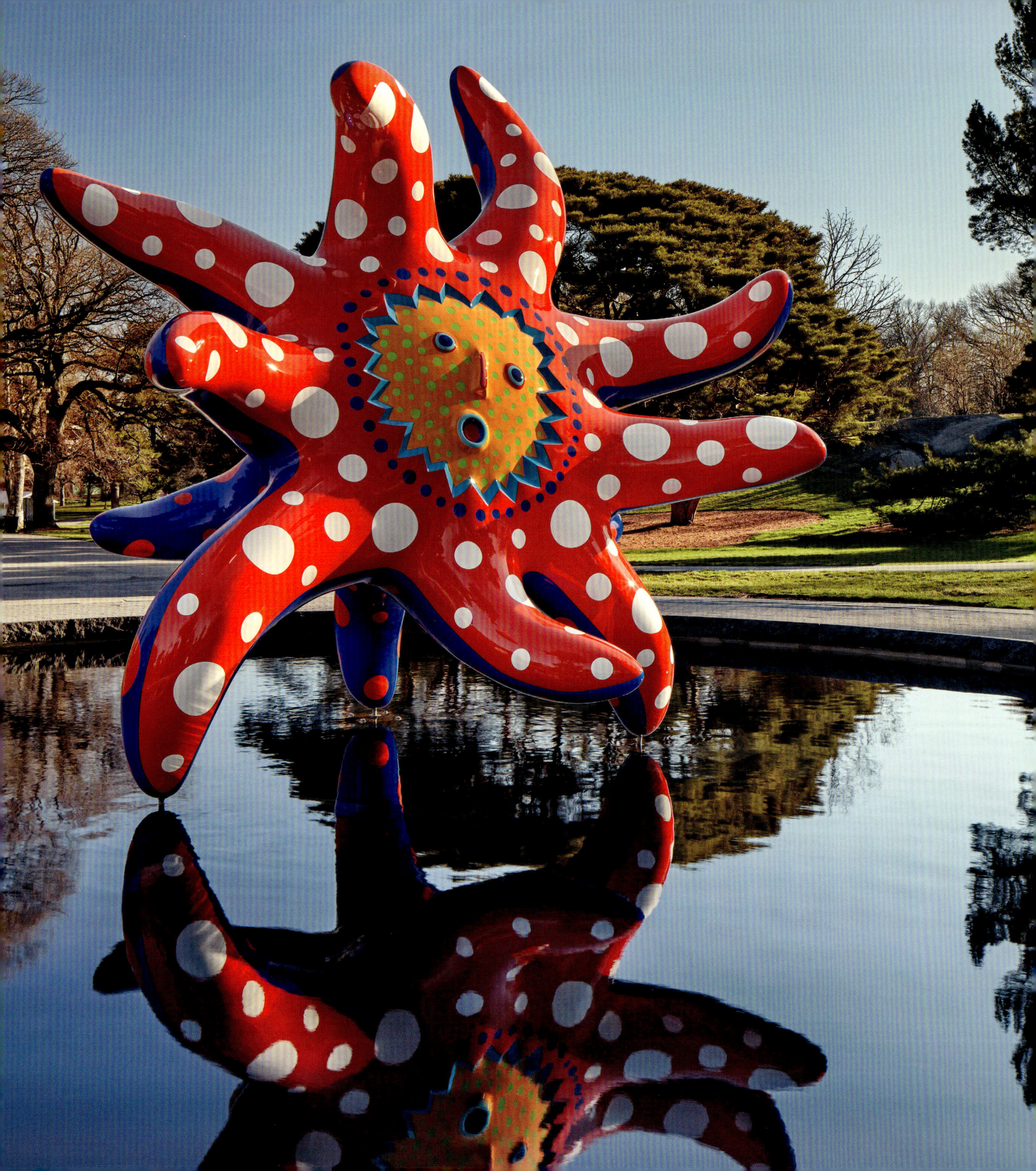

1960s were mostly dismissed by the highbrow art establishment at the time as publicity stunts, political antics, or incoherent displays. Where did the "the Priestess of Polka Dots" belong, when in 1968 she was staging a nudist happening on the streets of New York and painting the dancing bodies with polka dots as a way of enacting her vision of "the ever-advancing stream of eternity"? Hers was anti-establishment protest laced with cosmic theory:

> *The polka dot has the form of the sun, signifying masculine energy, the source of life. The polka dot has the form of the moon, symbolizing the feminine principle of reproduction and growth. Polka dots suggest multiplication to infinity. Our earth is only one polka dot among millions of others.... We must forget ourselves with polka dots! We must lose ourselves in the ever-advancing stream of eternity!*[31]

Panpsychism has resurfaced in recent cultural debate through the popular writings of philosophers David Chalmers, Philip Goff, and Thomas Nagel, among others.[32] These thinkers take different tacks, but all agree that consciousness is an intrinsic aspect of nature and not merely an accident of evolution. In *Mind and Cosmos*, Nagel despairs about the "respective inadequacies of materialism and theism as transcendent conceptions" and dismisses dominant neo-Darwinian naturalism being premised on the idea of a "mindless universe."[33] He argues instead for an expanded conception of the natural order, one that is not atomic but *holistic*, one whose entirety, from the big bang to "the endless generation of insects and spiders in their enormous, extravagant populations," manifests *consciousness*. In a radical, Kusama-like statement, Nagel declares, "Each of our lives is a part of the lengthy process of the universe gradually waking up and becoming aware of itself."[34]

Alternative cosmologies have also contributed to the revival of unified-field theories of the universe. Philosopher Yuk Hui, who draws on innovative Confucian thinkers as well as twentieth-century French thinkers Jean-François Lyotard, Gilbert Simondon, and Bernard Stiegler, offers a radical way to think about the cosmology of ancient China—and, by extension, Japan and Korea, the cultures of which were influenced by China. His neologism "cosmotechnics" offers a conceptual tool to "overcome the conventional opposition between technics and nature, and to understand the task of philosophy as that of seeking and affirming the organic unity of the two."[35] In the Western canon, religion encompasses ethics and dogma, while technics applies to science and technology. But in Daoist tradition, Hui argues, there is no opposition; rather, there is a *resonance* and *harmony* between the cosmic order and the moral order, and between humans and "other cosmological beings," including celestial

Fig. 8
I Want to Fly to the Universe, 2020
The New York Botanical Garden, 2021
Urethane paint on aluminum
157⅜ × 169⅜ × 140⅛ in.
(400 × 430 × 356 cm)
Courtesy of Ota Fine Arts, Victoria Miro, and David Zwirner

bodies (**FIG. 7**).[36] This "Unity of Heaven and Earth" (天人合一) is expressed as Qi, the energy force that flows through all existing beings, and Dao, the Way of cosmic forces evident in nature. Kusama's large-scale cast-aluminum sculpture *I Want to Fly to the Universe* (2020; **FIG. 8**) conjures this notion. A star-shaped form combining features of a flower and human face, one side colored night and the other day, is a literal display of how human, earthly, and celestial worlds are structurally reversible.

As an episteme, Daoism encompasses cosmology, divination, biology, medicine, chemistry, alchemy, magic, and astrology, as well as moral sentiment. Philosophical Daoism traces its origins to Laozi, an extraordinary thinker who worked during the sixth century BCE, according to Chinese sources. Its vision was crystallized in the mind-bending writings of Zhuangzi, who lived two centuries later. Thereafter, Daoism evolved through several syncretic iterations of doctrine and, over the millennia, became an umbrella for a range of folk, naturalistic, and mystical religious practices. Its view of human consciousness as a vessel of the natural properties pulsing through the cosmos also influenced the unique development of Buddhism in China, particularly Chan (Zen) Buddhism.

Drawing on Eastern and Western, ancient and modern, philosophical discourses, Hui critiques the limitations of Western anthropocentric thought, its assumption of universal reason, and its teleological construction of the modern. "The 'internal resonance' we seek here," Hui writes, "is the unification of the metaphysical categories of Qi and Dao, which must be endowed with new meanings and forces proper to our epoch."[37] Kusama's art does just that. While she may never use the terms "Qi" and "Dao," her notions of infinity, eternity, and self-obliteration resonate with the Daoist cosmology. In 2009 she set out to create what she envisioned would be her final work, a massive series of large-scale acrylic-on-canvas paintings called *My Eternal Soul*. Initially, she planned to create one hundred paintings in this series, which, when shown side by side, floor to ceiling, produce a dazzling mural-size environment. From the start, Kusama both retrieved imagery from her earliest works on paper—biomorphic and botanical imagery of her early Surrealist watercolors and the calligraphic arcs of her Pacific Ocean paintings of the late 1950s—and forged a new inventory of pictorial motifs using line, form, and vibrant color. The quivering speed of the artist's brushwork traces her furtive imagination, whose images she attributes to an urge to mark, or even touch, cosmic infinity. Her poetic titles belie the bold aspiration of her reach: *Tribute to the Sun in the Cosmos* (2010; page 79), *Women Who Went Sightseeing to the Universe* (2017; page 148), *Adoration for Eternal Space* (2018; **FIG. 9**).

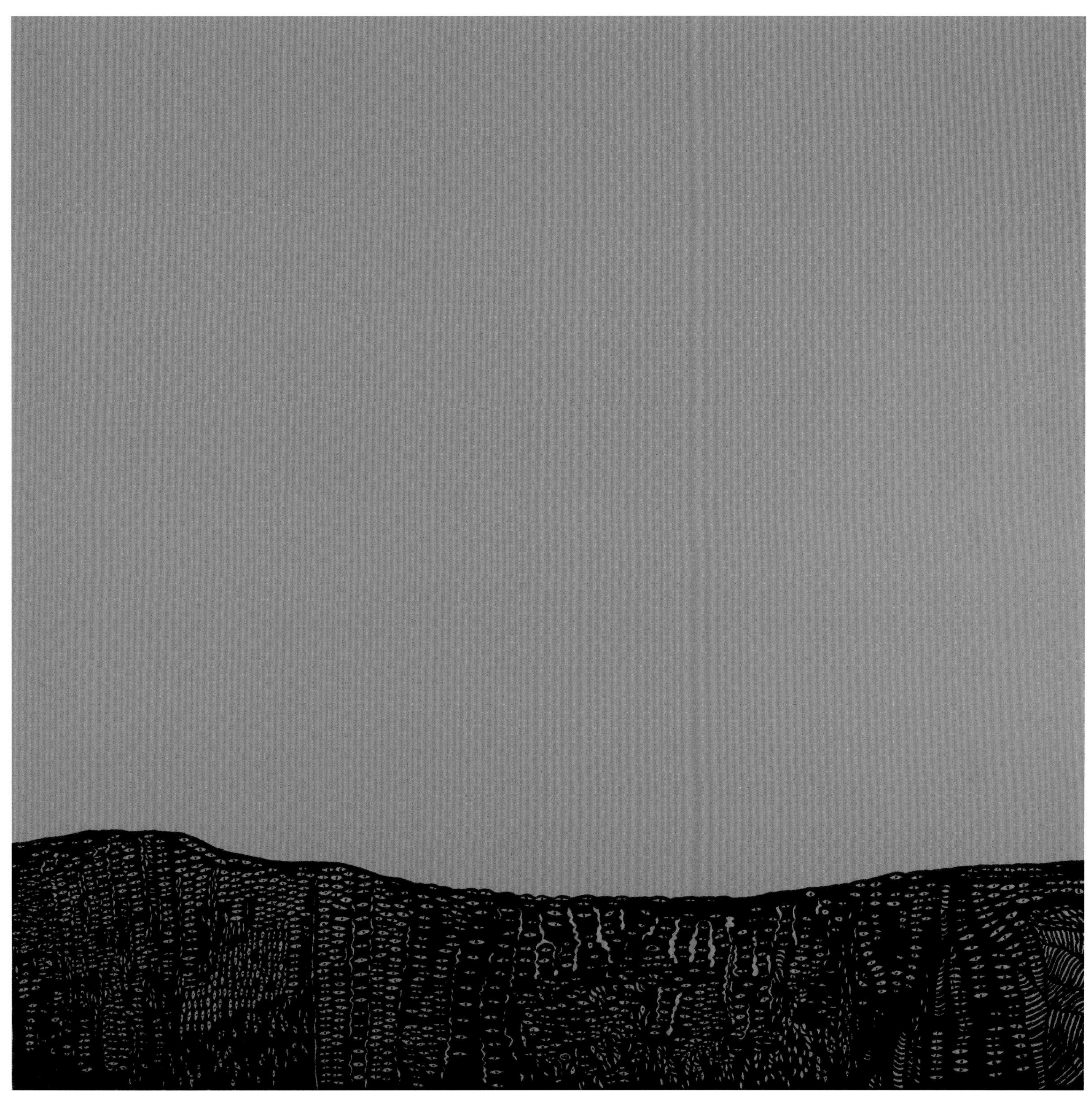

Fig. 9
Adoration for Eternal Space, 2018
Acrylic on canvas
76⅜ × 76⅜ in. (194 × 194 cm)
Collection of the artist

In Zen, *mu* (無; nothingness or void) is interchangeable with the Dao. By the time Kusama came to the United States in the late 1950s, cautiously bearing a spiritual inheritance, translations of the *Daodeqing* and the *Zhuangzi* were already popular in avant-garde circles. Artists, writers, and musicians such as John Cage, Allen Ginsberg, Allan Kaprow, and Alison Knowles, among many others, found inspiration in the ancient sages' outrageously irrational yet sublime views of the natural and supernatural worlds. Such encounters profoundly changed the course of Fluxus, Minimalism, and certain strands of Conceptual Art that Kusama could not have missed.[38] There were also stirrings in the field of physics that linked East Asian metaphysics to Whitehead's panpsychism. Most notably, the 1975 international bestseller *The Tao of Physics: An Exploration of the Parallels between Modern Physics and Eastern Mysticism*, by physicist Fritjof Capra, inspired speculation about resonances between a harmonious universe conceived by modern scientists in the West and the continuously interactive world conceived by mystics in the premodern East.[39] This sustained engagement among the American vanguard with Asian aesthetics and cosmologies roughly coincided with Kusama's time in New York City. Against this backdrop, her obsession with dissolving boundaries between the self, one's environment, and nature resonates with the broader zeitgeist. Conjuring a sense of infinity at once terrifying and transcendent, Kusama forged her own cosmic order in such bodies of work as the *Infinity Nets*, soft-sculpture *Accumulations*, *Infinity Mirrored Rooms*, and her happenings and performances. "When we obliterate nature and our bodies with polka dots, we become part of the unity of our environment," Kusama wrote of her body-painting happenings. "I become part of the eternal, and we obliterate ourselves with love."[40]

In "Heaven and Earth," Zhuangzi talks about the omnipresence of the Dao in terms that seem to presage, in clear and colloquial language, by a few millennia, the observations of our contemporary panpsychist scientists on the omnipresence of consciousness:

> *Master Dongguo asked Zhuangzi, "This thing called the Way (Dao)—*
> *where does it exist?"*
> *Zhuangzi said, "There is no place it doesn't exist."*
> *"Come," said Master Dongguo, "you must be more specific!"*
> *"It is in the ant."*
> *"As low a thing as that?"*
> *"It is in the panic grass."*
> *"But that is lower still!"*
> *"It is in the tiles and shards."*
> *"How can it be so low?"*

"It is in the piss and shit!"
Master Dongguo made no reply.[41]

More recently, panpsychism has come to inflect the art world once again. In 2020 the Camden Art Centre in London launched *The Botanical Mind: Art, Mysticism and The Cosmic Tree*, an online project and exhibition.[42] It proposed "alternative perspectives on Western scientific rationalism," including panpsychism, to argue for "the significance of the plant kingdom to human life, consciousness, and spirituality across cultures and through time."[43] Drawing on contemporary trends in art, science fiction, anthropology, ethnology, philosophy, theory, and ecology, the project traces the recent emergence of a school of thought called "the ontological turn" or the "nonhuman turn." Central to this new "planetary ecological imaginary" is the idea of plant intelligence. These ideas draw largely from *Plant Signaling & Behavior*, a scientific journal that focuses on the relatively new field of plant neurobiology, which proposes models for the phenomenological framework of plant intelligence.[44] Plants, after all, dominate every terrestrial environment, comprising 80 percent of the biomass on Earth.[45]

The Camden project also engaged with *How Forests Think*, a book by anthropologist Eduardo Kohn that challenges our very idea of what it means to be human by linking our species to the whole web of the living world.[46] Based on years of fieldwork among the Runa people of Ecuador's Upper Amazon, Kohn's book claims that forests are vital ecosystems with conscious networks that have the ability to communicate between life forms. In this concept, humans and nonhumans live in active awareness of one another. Attuned, humans develop modes of relating to the plant and animal worlds that operate outside embedded cognitive and linguistic norms. This "animist ontology" and "multi-species ethnography" upends centuries of anthropocentrism. It also puts the kibosh on all those governing Cartesian assumptions about an inert universe that exists outside and entirely separate from the all-perceiving human brain.

For Kusama, such knowledge is by no means new; she has communicated with plants since early childhood.[47] A recent tribute is the painting *Flowers Speak* (2016; **FIG. 10**) from the *My Eternal Soul* series. This hallucinatory painting appears as a flattened field of composite flowers, disks, and ovaries forming mouthlike openings, as if poised to speak, surrounded by radiating rays and bracts. Her mirrored *Pumpkins Screaming About Love Beyond Infinity* (2017; pages 120–21) presents a patch of polka-dotted glass pumpkins that light up like orbs and reflect infinitely across a room of mirrors. However imaginary, Kusama's work consistently depicts a view of nature in which distinctions between the earthly and cosmic realms are moot. What emerges instead is riotous splendor.

IN HIS REVIEW OF THOMAS NAGEL'S *MIND AND COSMOS* IN THE *New Yorker*, Richard Brody postulated that "the book's widest implications involve art and how it helps us to understand the world . . . It would be a key source of the very definition of life. Aesthetics will be propelled to the forefront of philosophy as a crucial part of metaphysical biology."[48] Once again, Kusama is ahead of global cultural shifts. For more than seventy years, in her art and her writings, she has expressed her very being as that of a vulnerable sensorium for cosmic effects—in all their magnificence and brutality. Her approach—nature as method—resonates with both ancient and contemporary philosophies that regard the human and natural worlds as a holistic dynamic animated by consciousness, an all-encompassing metaphysical biology. With this thought experiment, we arrive at a new truth about Kusama. She is all three: scientist, mystic, and artist, offering glimpses of nature in all its cosmic glory.

> *O my dearest and most generous love, my loves.*
> *I would see the beauty of all the love in the cosmos,*
> *showing itself red, and again sparkling yellow.*
> *Now blue, floating through breaks in the clouds,*
> *all commingling at this very moment inside my body.*
> *Infusing it, to my amazement, with that sizzling, colorful fragrance.*
> *All these, and the body itself, flashing through the universe.*
> *Let us speak of life lovingly.*
> *Such is my prayer for this existence of ours.*[49]

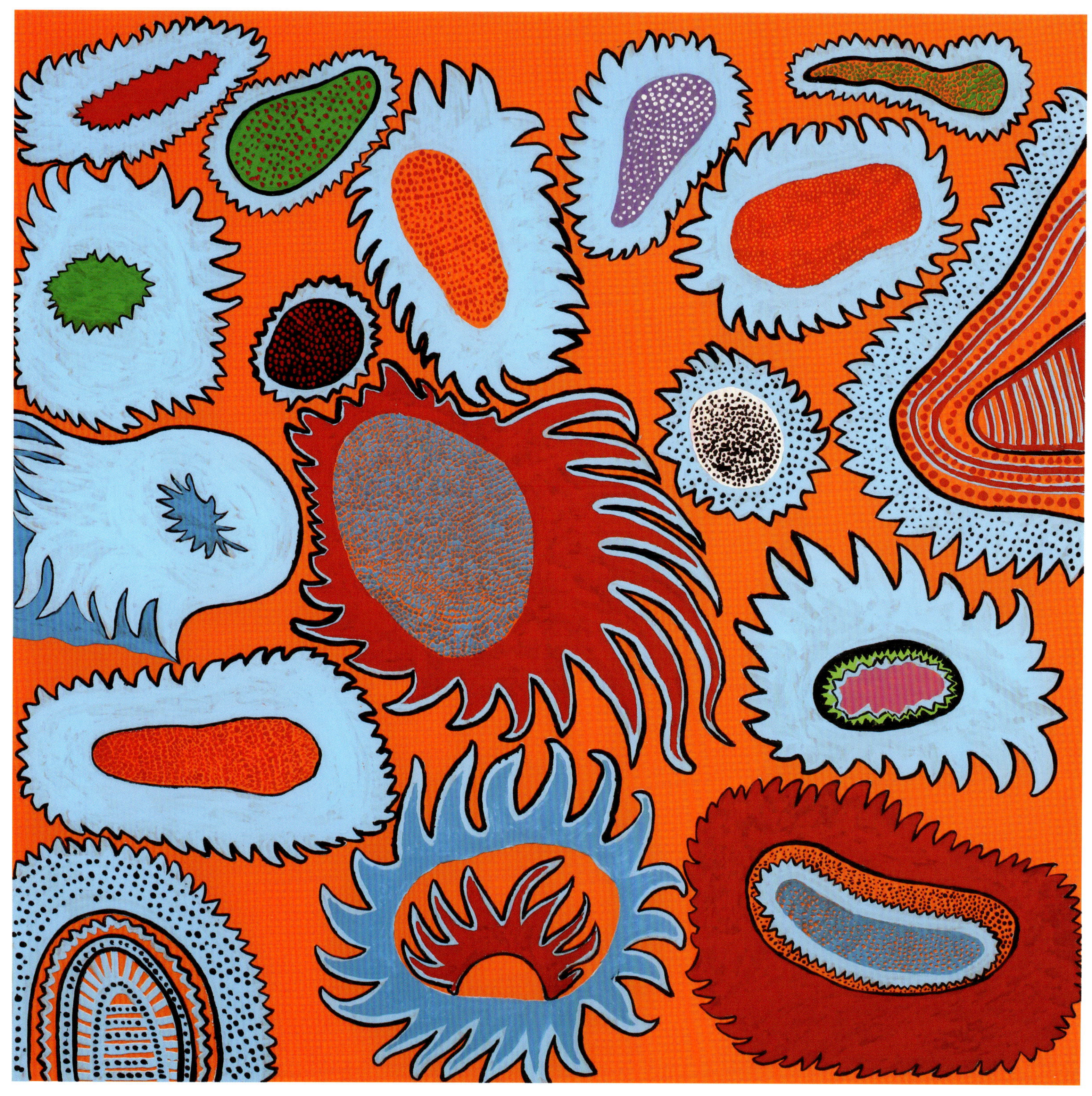

Fig. 10
Flowers Speak, 2016
Acrylic on canvas
76⅜ × 76⅜ in. (194 × 194 cm)
Collection of the artist

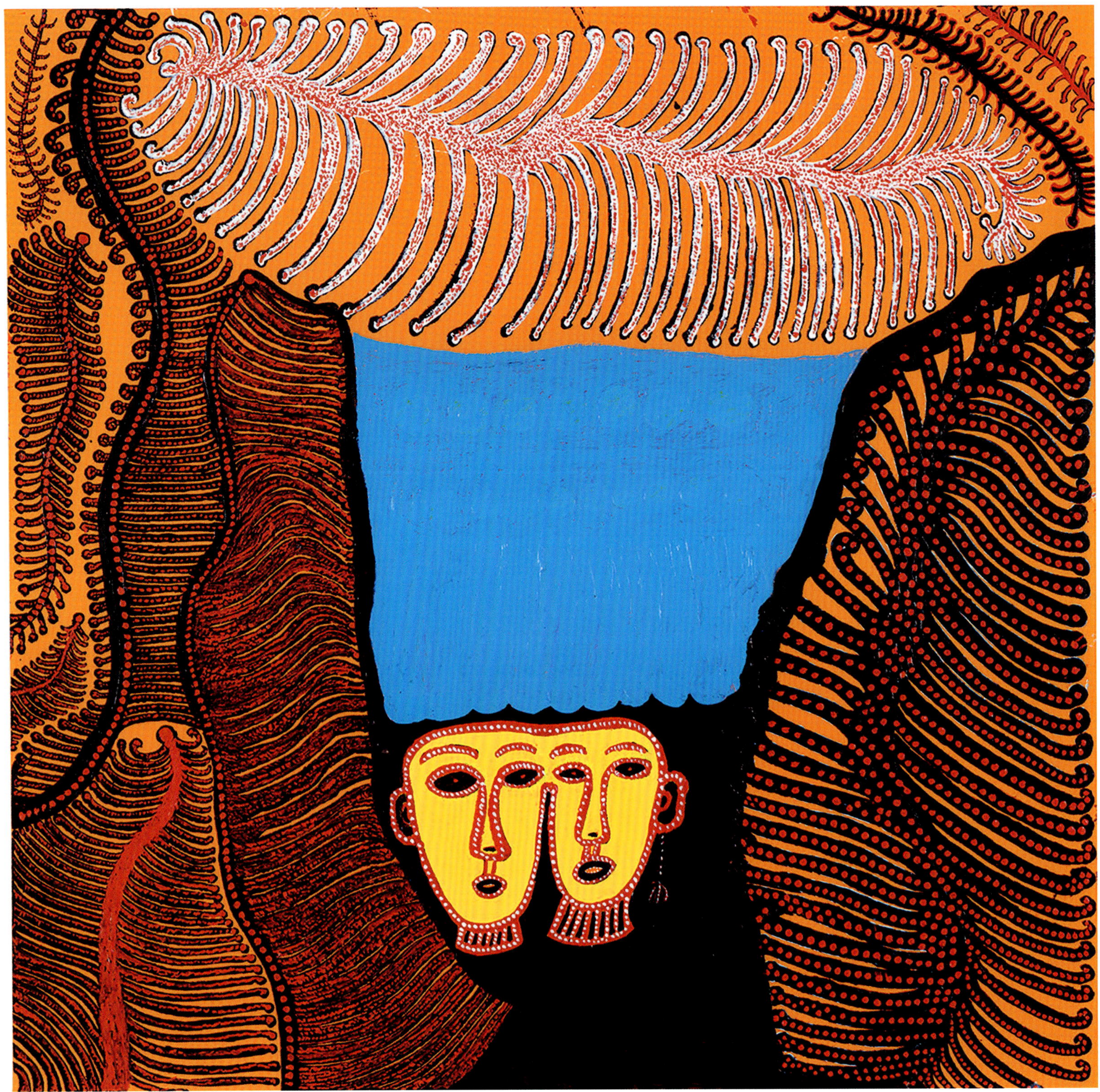

above
Women Who Went Sightseeing to the Universe, 2017
Acrylic on canvas
76⅜ × 76⅜ in. (194 × 194 cm)
Collection of the artist

opposite
Peace Shall Come as Far as the Ends of the Universe, 2016
Acrylic on canvas
76⅜ × 76⅜ in. (194 × 194 cm)
Collection of the artist

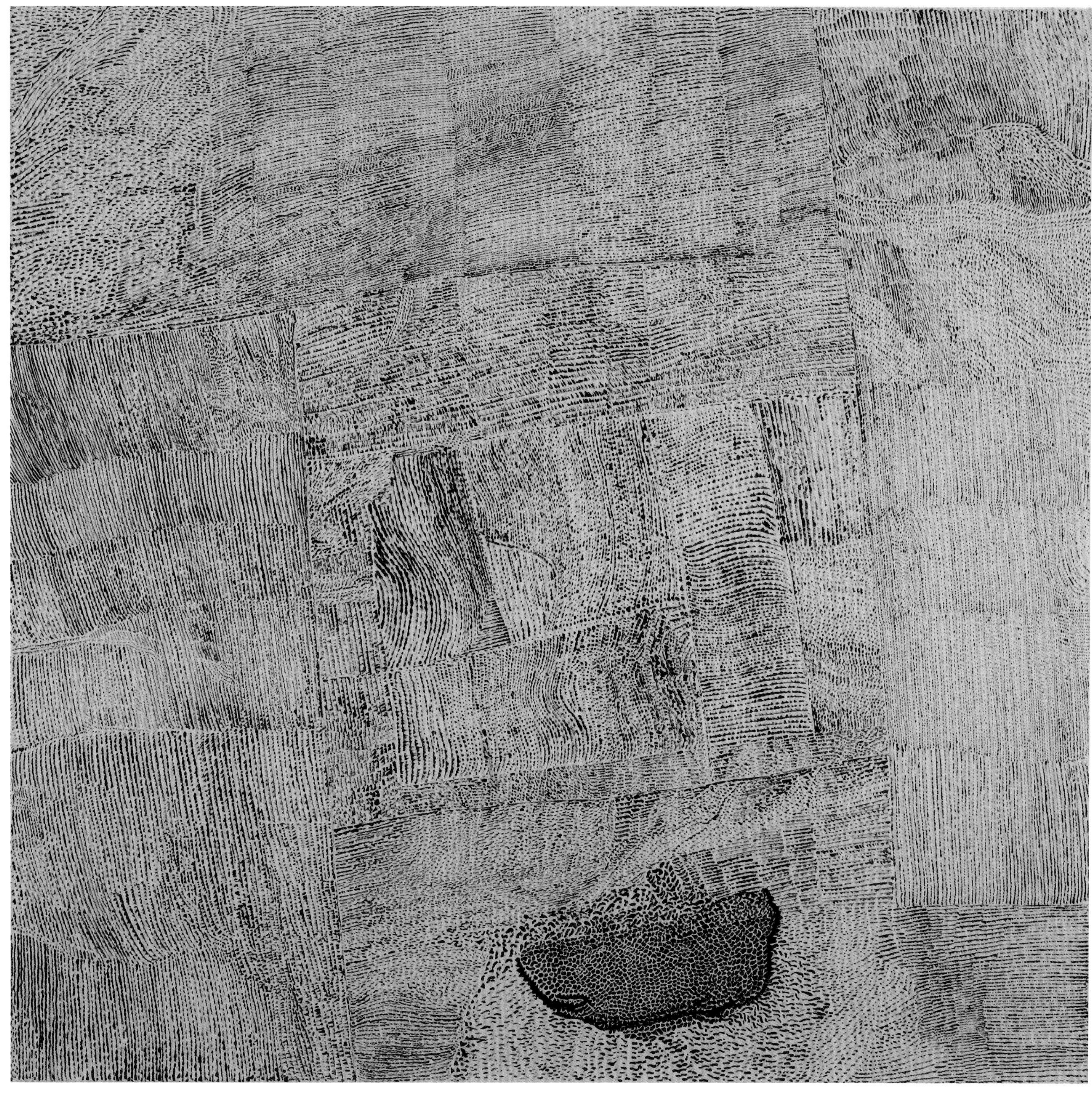

NATURE AND COSMOS IN THE WORK OF YAYOI KUSAMA

Chronology

Alex A. Jones

The profound relationship of Kusama's art to the natural world has often been overlooked in American scholarship, which has most successfully framed her work in relation to the development of avant-garde art in the 1960s. Kusama's influence on Pop, performance, and installation art has been an important revelation for art historians, but one that is mostly traced through the work the artist made during her years in New York City (1958–73), which by now comprise only one chapter of her long career. Art historical analysis does less to illuminate Kusama's work following her return to Japan in 1973, at which point she mostly insulated herself from the international art scene. From this hermetic position, Kusama has continued to work prolifically over the past four decades, and her artistic interests have turned more explicitly toward nature and the cosmos—themes that, in fact, motivated her earliest artistic endeavors.

The following chronology examines Kusama's entire life through this thematic lens, revealing an artist who has always been engaged with the forms of plants, the spiritual unity of nature, and the interplay of life and death.

1929

Born on March 22, 1929, in Matsumoto, Nagano Prefecture, Japan

My family was an old one, of high social standing, having for the past century or so managed wholesale seed nurseries on vast tracts of land. Each day a crowd of workers came to collect the seeds of violets or zinnias or whatever it might be, for resale all over Japan. We had six large hothouses, which were so rare in those days that sometimes groups of schoolchildren came on field trips to look at them. Propertied and wealthy, my family supported local painters and had a standard understanding of art. But the prospect of their youngest child becoming a painter was a different matter altogether (opposite top). [1]

1941–1945

Peony Sketches and *Harvest*

During World War II, like many Japanese schoolchildren, Kusama works in fields to plant crops and, later, in a factory sewing parachutes.[2] She contracts pneumonia from the cold factory environment and, during her convalescence in spring 1945, makes many drawings of flowers in her sketchbooks (pages 32–44). Later the same year, the sixteen-year-old artist completes a *nihonga* painting, *Harvest* (page 37), which is accepted into a juried group show in Nagano City.[3] The exhibition travels to Tokyo, Nagoya, Osaka, and Kyoto.

1949

Lingering Dream

Lingering Dream (page 57), a *nihonga* painting of decaying sunflowers, is included in the annual salon of Sōzō Bijutsu, an association of *nihonga* artists formed in 1948.[4] *Lingering Dream* is one of Kusama's last and most accomplished works using traditional Japanese painting techniques. After this time, she employs Western-style oils and increasingly abstract motifs. Curator Akira Tatehata notes that Kusama's training in *nihonga*, a discipline that emphasizes "linear rendering from nature," is crucial to her ability to observe and give form to her own reality.[5] Other scholars regard *Lingering Dream* as a key developmental work and a Symbolist representation of the artist's inner world.[6]

1955

Artist Statement

Kusama frames her work as an interplay of cosmic dualities in an artist statement published in a Tokyo-based magazine of contemporary art, *Geijutsu Shinchō* [New trends in art]:

I sing within one part of the living shadow covering the Earth, within one constant manifestation of its whole. Just as concealment reveals everything, or as the little hole in the peach reveals the existence of the worm, so by a similar method I want to lay bare the mystery. I want to live hidden in the world that lies midway between mystery and symbol.[7]

1957

Move to the United States

In November Kusama flies to Seattle, where she mounts a solo exhibition of works on paper at Zoë Dusanne Gallery. In June 1958, she moves to New York City. Kusama later reflects on her need to leave Japan:

For art like mine—art that does battle at the border of life and death, questioning what we are and what it means to live and die—[Japan] was too small, too servile, too feudalistic, and too scornful of women. My art needed a more unlimited freedom, and a wider world.[8]

1959

Infinity Nets

Kusama debuts her first major body of work made in New York, a series of abstract paintings known as *Infinity Nets*. Presented in solo shows in New York (*Obsessional Monochrome*, Brata Gallery), Boston (*Recent Paintings by Yayoi Kusama*, Nova Gallery), and

Washington, DC (*Infinity Nets*, Gres Gallery), the paintings garner immediate critical acclaim. Reviewers describe Kusama's paintings using metaphors of nature, characterizing their allover pattern as "small, cell-like apertures,"[9] "tiny dark pebble shapes,"[10] and "a net floating on the ocean, a veil shimmering across reality."[11] At least five paintings made around this time bear the title *Pacific Ocean* (page 131), connecting Kusama's technique also to the roiling, oceanic expanse she crossed to launch her career in the United States.

1964

Driving Image Show

Driving Image Show opens at Castellane Gallery in New York and subsequently tours multiple venues in the United States and Europe. British art historian Sir Herbert Read, who met Kusama through her Washington dealer, Beatrice Perry, provides a curatorial statement that notes the biomorphic aspect of Kusama's art as well as its central concept of infinity:

Those early paintings, without beginning, without end, without form, without definition, seemed to actualize the infinity of space. Now, with perfect consistency, she creates forms that proliferate like mycelium and seal the consciousness in their white integument.[12]

Kusama reprints Read's statement widely, later distributing flyers bearing the text during her unauthorized installation at the 1966 Venice Biennale.

1965

Floor Show

Kusama's November solo show at Castellane Gallery in New York includes her first mirrored installation, *Infinity Mirror Room—Phalli's Field*, as well as the large sculpture *My Flower Bed* (**below**), which appears on the cover of *Art Voices*, accompanied by a statement from the artist:

Filled with loneliness, unable to sleep, I curl up for the night in My Flower Bed because flowers are tender and loving. Now I am an insect that returns to its flower during the night; the petals close over me as the mother's womb protects the unborn child.... Until dawn, the flowers in My Flower Bed will sway in the night breeze and caress me gently, for the night is the time of love and sex.[13]

In a review of the show, however, critic Michael Benedikt references the simultaneously threatening, monstrous character of *My Flower Bed*:

Blatantly sinister was the sculpture My Flower Bed, *a large bloom made out of thousands of overlapping red gloves, with a glove trunk, and springing forth from a bed composed of old*

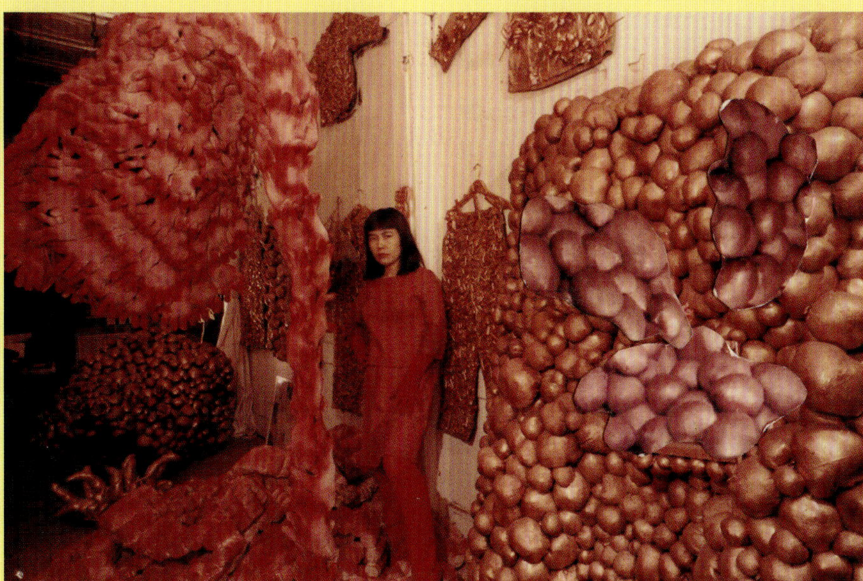

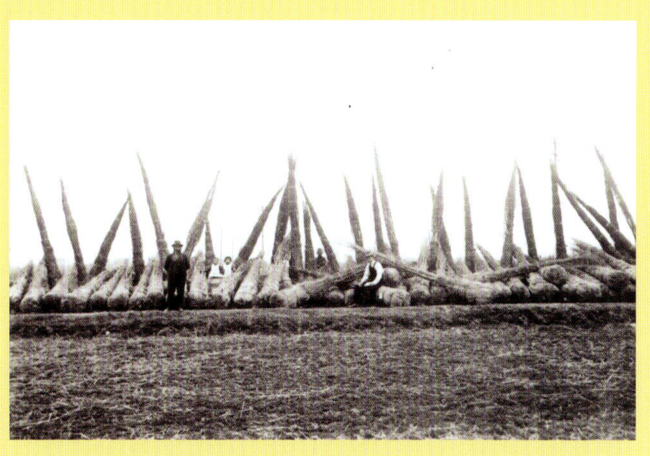

above
Willow trees prepared for shipment from the Kusama family nursery, Matsumoto, Japan, ca. 1920s

left
Photo-collage by Kusama from 1966 showing the artist in her studio with sculptures, including *My Flower Bed*.

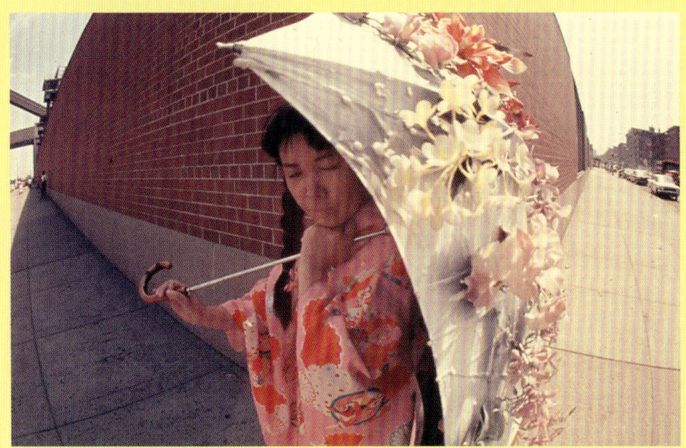

bedsprings covered in red cotton cloth. This acknowledged openly the deepest quality underlying all of Yayoi Kusama's work, an almost helpless fascination with the processes of growth, repetition, and proliferation.[14]

1966

Narcissus Garden

Kusama's first outdoor installation is an unauthorized display at the 1966 Venice Biennale featuring fifteen hundred manufactured silver spheres on the grass outside the Italian Pavilion (page 113). The mirrored plastic orbs reflect the sky as well as visitors and the artist herself, who sells them for two dollars each, a scandalously low price intended as a critique of the escalating art market. *Narcissus Garden* has since been reprised numerous times as both an indoor and an outdoor installation.

Walking Piece

Americans think of Japanese girls as hothouse flowers. For this reason, Kusama surprises them. She is rugged and strong—a veritable human dynamo of creative energy and artistic achievement.[15]

This statement is published in a profile on Kusama by Gordon Brown just months prior to a performance called *Walking Piece* (**top left**), in which the artist is photographed walking the streets of New York wearing a bright-pink floral kimono and carrying an umbrella adorned with artificial flowers. Although *Walking Piece* was not necessarily conceived in direct response to Brown's backhanded Orientalism, his words may have carried ironic significance for Kusama, who grew up among greenhouses of exotic blooms and depicted herself as a flower in early paintings. In earlier works such as *Lingering Dream* and *My Flower Bed*, Kusama already demonstrated that the exotic beauty of flowers could be a tool for survival, or even bait for prey. Art historian Midori Yoshimoto analyzes *Walking Piece* as a carefully calculated manipulation of Kusama's ethnicity and gender:

Like her performance at the Venice Biennale, her exotic outfit heightened her Asian identity and "otherness" in American society. She took advantage of being seen as an outsider in order to make herself stand out and attract attention.[16]

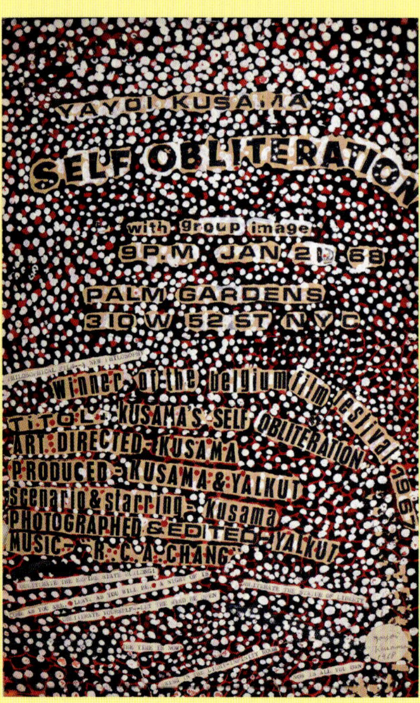

1967

Kusama's Self-Obliteration

Kusama releases a psychedelic film made in collaboration with filmmaker Jud Yalkut (**left**). Filmed in Woodstock, New York, it depicts Kusama covering the surface of a pond, a tree, a horse, and her own body with polka dots, as well as covering a man's naked body with leaves. In the second part of the film, Kusama paints on nude dancers in her mirrored room from *Kusama's Peep Show (or Endless Love Show)* (1966), suggesting a unification of nature and performer through the polka dot. Kusama explains her philosophy of dots in an interview with Yalkut for the *New York Free Press*:

My performances are a kind of symbolic philosophy with polka dots. A polka dot has the form of the sun which is a symbol of the energy of the whole world and our living life, and also the form of the moon, which is calm, round, soft, colorful, senseless and unknowing. Polka dots can't stay

above
Walking Piece (detail), 1966
24 slides
Installation dimensions variable
Collection of the artist

right
Original collage for poster for *Kusama's Self-Obliteration*, filmed by Jud Yalkut, 1967

opposite top
Body-Festival flyer, 1967

opposite bottom
Soul Going Back to Its Home, 1975
Collage with ink and pastel on paper
21⅝ × 15⅝ in. (54.8 × 39.7 cm)
Setagaya Art Museum

alone; like the communicative life of people, two or three and more polka dots become movement. Our earth is only one polka dot among a million stars in the cosmos. Polka dots are a way to infinity. When we obliterate nature and our bodies with polka dots, we become part of the unity of our environment. I become part of the eternal and we obliterate ourselves with love.[17]

Body Festivals

Kusama stages a series of weekend body-painting performances in Washington Square Park and other locations in New York during the Summer of Love. She promotes these happenings with flyers that feature cartoon images of herself and cryptic poetry promoting peace and cosmic unity. One flyer for Sunday, August 20 (**top right**), reads:

EXPLORE ALL POSSIBILITIES OF OUR TIME

THIS NOW LIFE IN INFINITE ORDER OF THE SUN, MOON, STARS AND

EARTH WITH THE APPLE OF EVE

LIFE THE PUZZLE?

*LEARN** UNLEARN ** RELEARN ***

LET US AMUSE OURSELVES FOR A TIME, IN OUR TIME

MASK IN PAINT

*FORGET THE ONENESS, *LONELINESS, FOR A TIME*

TOGETHER IN THE POLKA DOT TIME.

1968

Anatomic Explosions

The message of Kusama's body painting performances becomes more overtly political. She stages numerous happenings at prominent public locations, including the New York Stock Exchange, Statue of Liberty, and Board of Elections, where dancers strip naked and are painted with polka dots. A widely distributed press release invites the public to "Forget yourself and become one with nature. Lose yourself in the ever-advancing stream of eternity. Self-obliteration is the only way out."[18] In Kusama's "Open Letter to My Hero, Richard M. Nixon," dated November 11, 1968, the artist ties her philosophy of polka dots to the protests against the Vietnam War:

Our earth is like one little polka dot, among millions of other celestial bodies, one orb full of hatred and strife amid the peaceful, silent spheres. Let's you and I change all that and make this world a new Garden of Eden. . . . You can't eradicate violence by using more violence.[19]

1973

Return to Japan

Kusama returns to Japan. She settles in Shinjuku, Tokyo, and begins to produce poetry, works on paper, and ceramics. In a 2000 interview, curator Akira Tatehata speaks with Kusama about the stark transition in tone from her New York artworks to those she begins producing after her return to Japan, citing the latter as far more literary, intimate in scale, and closely related to her early drawings and paintings. Kusama connects the lyrical sensibility of these works to writing poetry and fiction, to her depression, and to the cultural differences between New York and Japan:

I could not survive in New York otherwise. You cannot live there with a lyrical frame of mind. . . . In Japan, I write poetry. In New York, there was no mood for poetry; every day was a struggle with the outside world.[20]

1975

Message of Death from Hades

Kusama's first major solo show after moving to Tokyo is held at Nishimura Gallery. *Message of Death from Hades* features a new series of mixed-media collages of plants, insects, and birds. In 1991 prominent art critic Toshiaki Minemura reflects on the series of collages as an important moment of growth for Kusama:

With the 1975 collages as a turning point, Kusama must have undergone a decisive change in her consciousness. This has been proven by the titles of her subsequent work and her novels. Soul Going Back to Its Home [**right**] *was the harbinger of her later artistic endeavors.*[21]

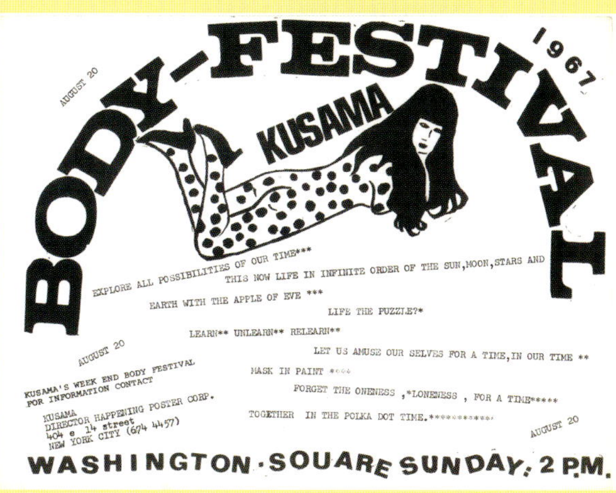

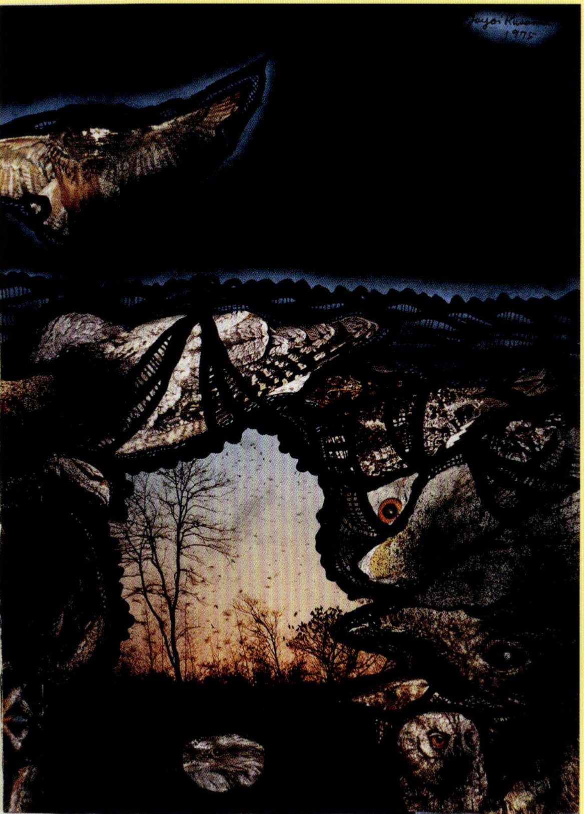

following
Flowers of Basara
Happening, Jōshin-ji temple, Tokyo, 1985

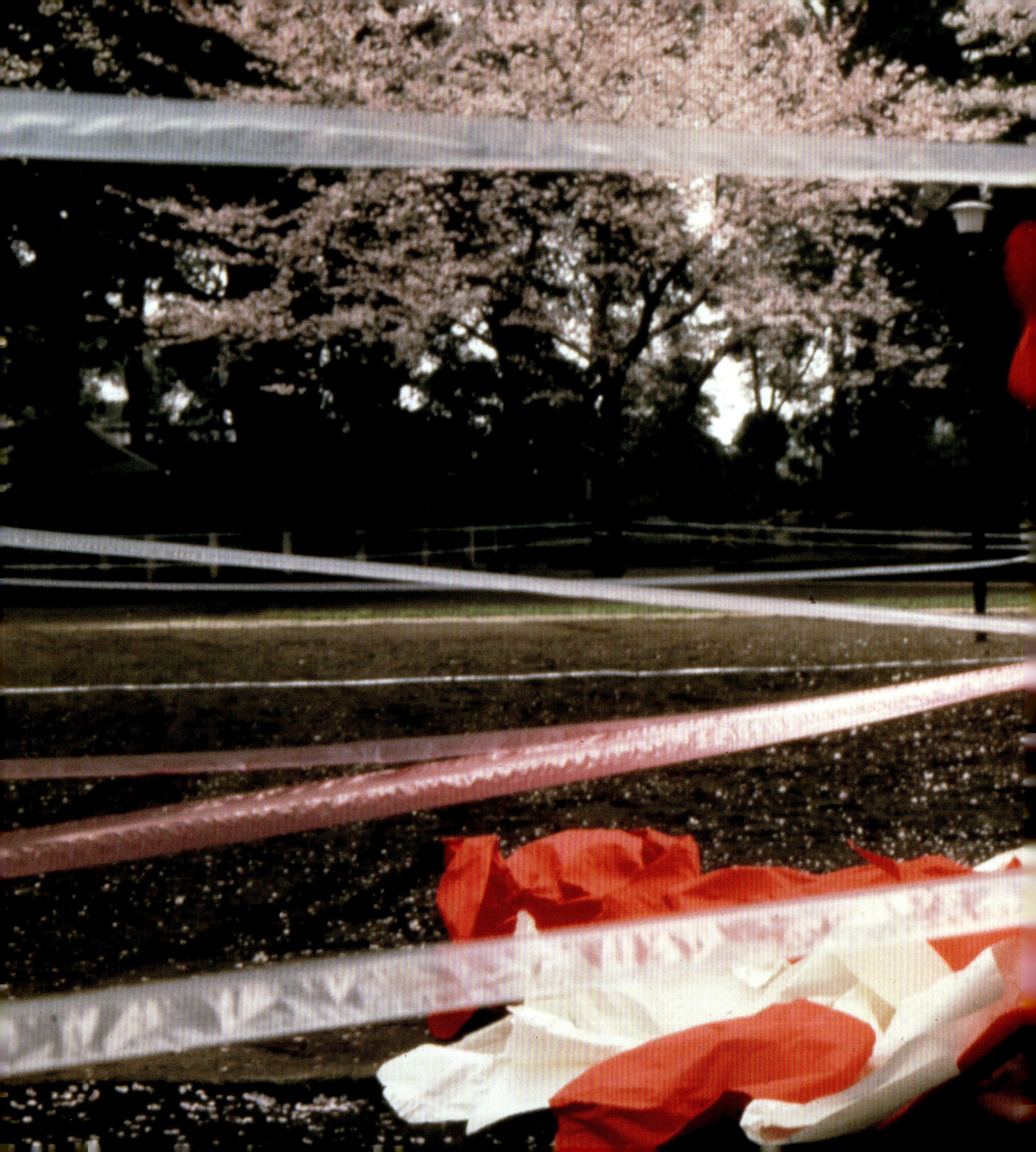

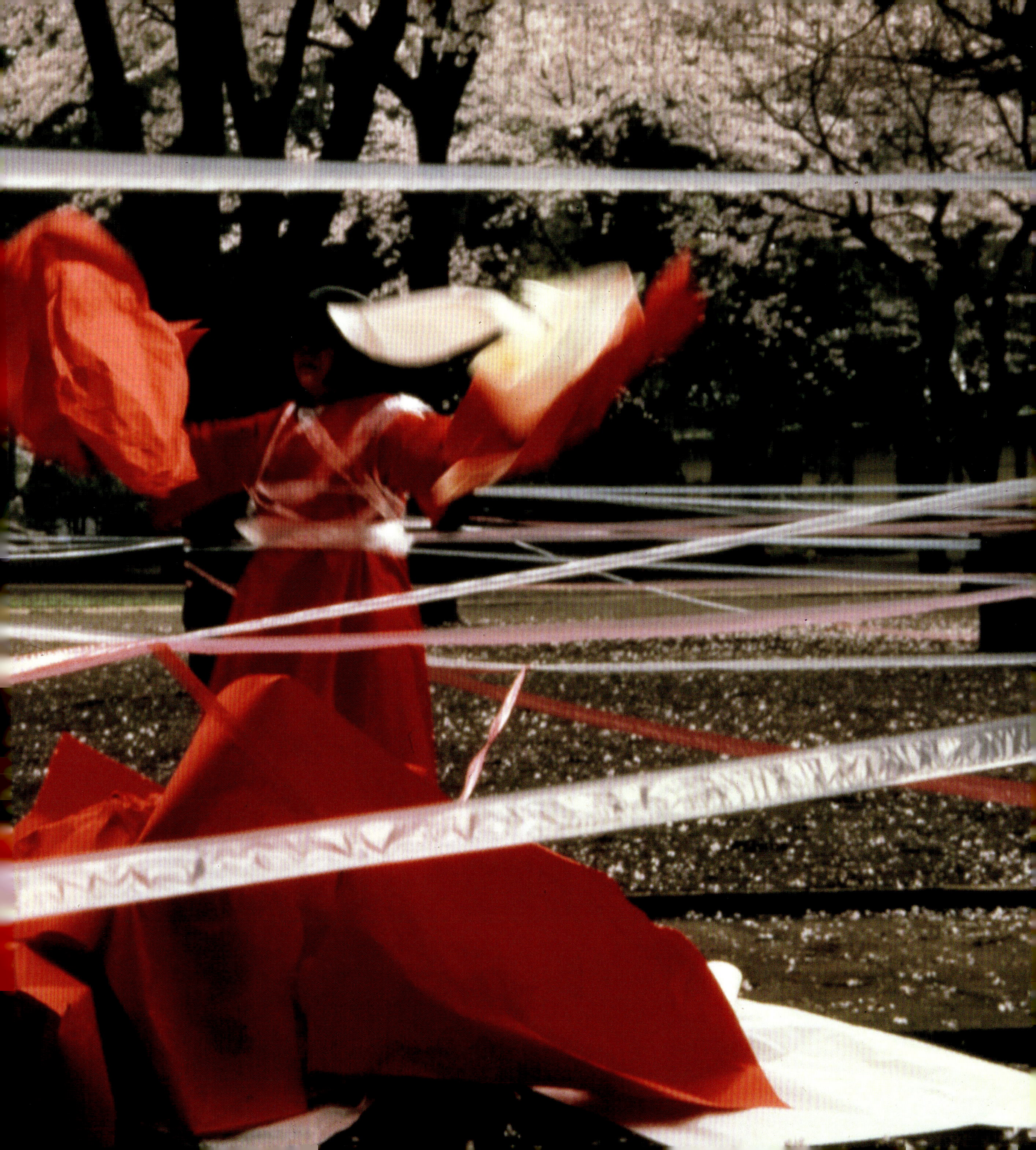

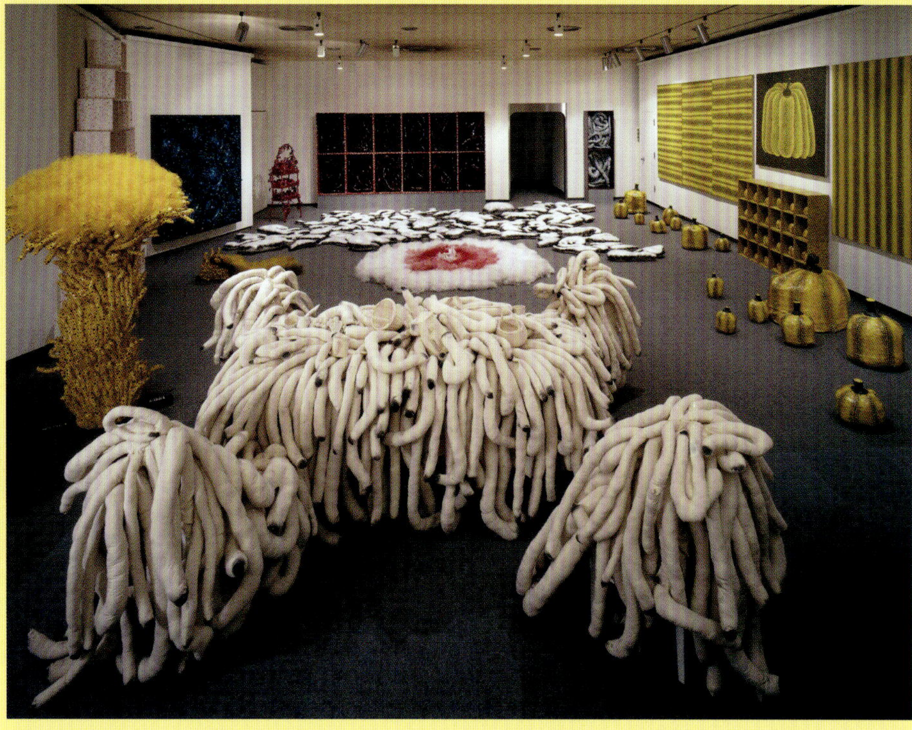

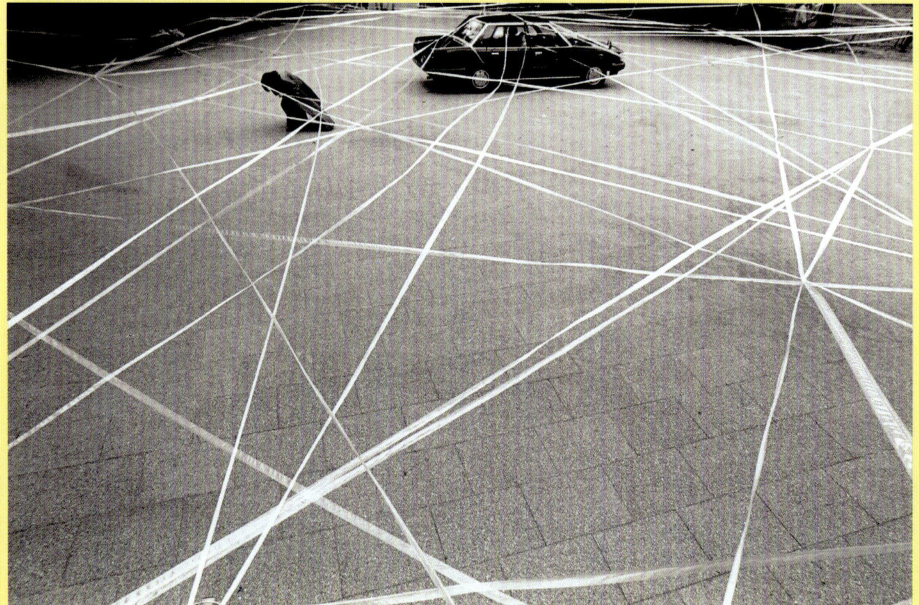

1978

Manhattan Suicide Addict

Kusama's first novel, *Manhattan Suicide Addict*, receives positive critical response from avant-garde literary circles in Tokyo. The novel's plot concerns a young male prostitute and his madam—a Japanese woman—in New York City, but it is also a surreal mirroring of Kusama's own experience living in New York. Imagery throughout the novel explores the sexual symbolism of plants, which is a recurring motif in Kusama's prolific literary output over the next two decades.

1984

Biomorphic Sculpture

In her second solo exhibition with Tokyo's Fuji Television Gallery, Kusama debuts a new series of sculptures with a distinctly biomorphic character (**top left**). Many of these works return to the idiom of sprawling, stuffed fabric protuberances used in Kusama's earlier sculptures and environments, including *Infinity Mirror Room—Phalli's Field* (1965), but in a manner that is now distinctly plantlike, as in *Summer* (1985; page 112). Numerous paintings and sculptures of pumpkins, a subject Kusama began to represent around 1981, also feature prominently in the exhibition. Critic Yūsuke Nakahara supplies a catalogue essay, offering a take on the sexual metaphor of Kusama's fabric protuberances that is less Freudian than cosmic:

The appearance that these massed rod-shaped forms are thrusting into space suggests union with space. Spilling out into space, the surface becomes one with space. Thus, Yayoi Kusama's work presents a sexual metaphor in which space is a female principle and the discrete object is a male principle. The sexual union of the object and space brings about the "self-obliteration" of the object.[22]

1985

Flowers of Basara

In April 1985, Kusama stages a happening at Joshin-ji temple in

Tokyo, titled *Flowers of Basara*, her first public outdoor performance in about a decade. Dressed in flowing red robes, Kusama weaves a huge "web" of red and white plastic streamers around blossoming cherry trees in a symbolic gesture of interconnectedness.

1986

Infinity Explosion

Kusama performs another version of *Flowers of Basara* at Okurayama Memorial Hall in Kanagawa (pages 154–55, **opposite bottom**). She also has a solo exhibition at Fuji Television Gallery: *Infinity Explosion*, featuring new biomorphic sculptures (**top right**). A catalogue essay by art critic Toshiaki Minemura characterizes the artist's obsession with the concept of infinity as a cosmological idea, comparing the scale of her ideas to that of two philosophers of the infinite, Giordano Bruno and Georg Cantor.

Also in spring of 1986, several *Accumulation* sculptures by Kusama are included in a survey of contemporary Japanese art at the University of California San Diego (*Japanese Art Today*, May 16–June 22). Praising Kusama's work above the rest, one reviewer compares the effect of her stuffed tubers to botanical monsters: "Her pods evoke memories of *The Invasion of the Body Snatchers*. One can almost see them growing."[23]

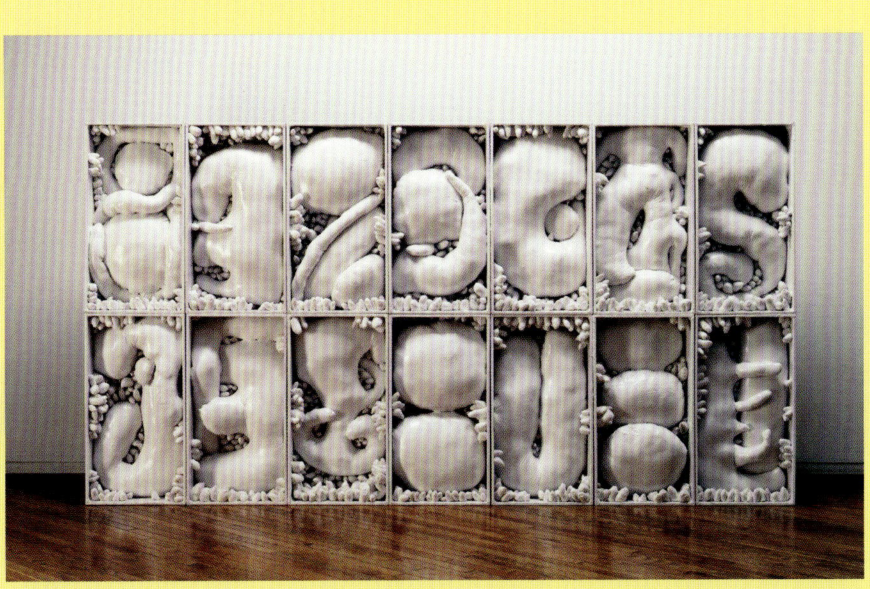

1989

A Retrospective

Kusama's first major international retrospective, organized by the Center for International Contemporary Arts in New York, asserts her influence on American art in the 1960s. Curator Alexandra Munroe evaluates Kusama's status as both influential insider and eccentric outsider to international contemporary art movements, and she also notes the shift of tone in the artist's later sculptures:

The familiar repetitive pattern and organic tubular shapes no longer connote monotony and aggression but rather abundant growth. . . . Like the lovers on a Hindu temple frieze, these fleshy forms writhe and climb in ecstatic union with one another.[24]

This retrospective revives American critical and commercial interest in Kusama. Reviewing it for *Artforum*, Bill Berkson emphasizes the strength of her recent biomorphic sculptures, using imaginative prose to describe the lifelike quality of *Leftover Snow in the Dream* (1982; **below**):

Several white podlike forms swell against the walls of 14 abutted, upright bins. If a pinprick were applied, the whole ripe conglomerate might burst, spurting its juices clear across the room.[25]

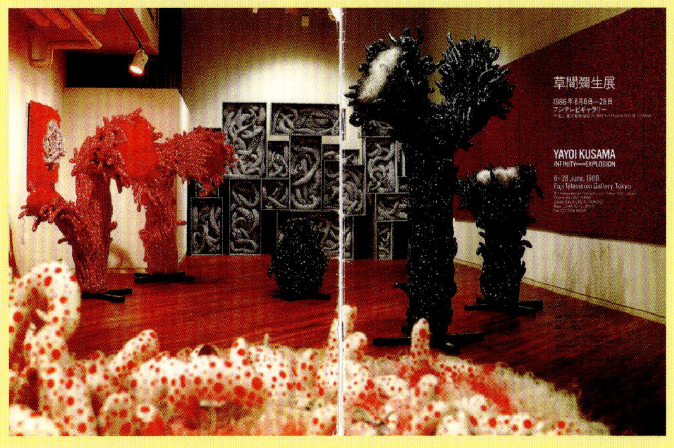

opposite top
Installation view, *Obsession*, Fuji Television Gallery, Tokyo, 1984

opposite bottom
Flowers of Basara happening, Okurayama Memorial Hall, Kanagawa, ca. 1986

above
Installation view, *Infinity Explosion*, solo exhibition at Fuji Television Gallery, Tokyo, 1986

left
Leftover Snow in the Dream, 1982
Plasticine, wood, and paint
70⅝ × 130¾ × 8¾ in.
(179.3 × 332 × 22.3 cm)
Courtesy of Ota Fine Arts

following
Flower Obsession, 1994
Performance at Noko Island, Fukuoka, Japan

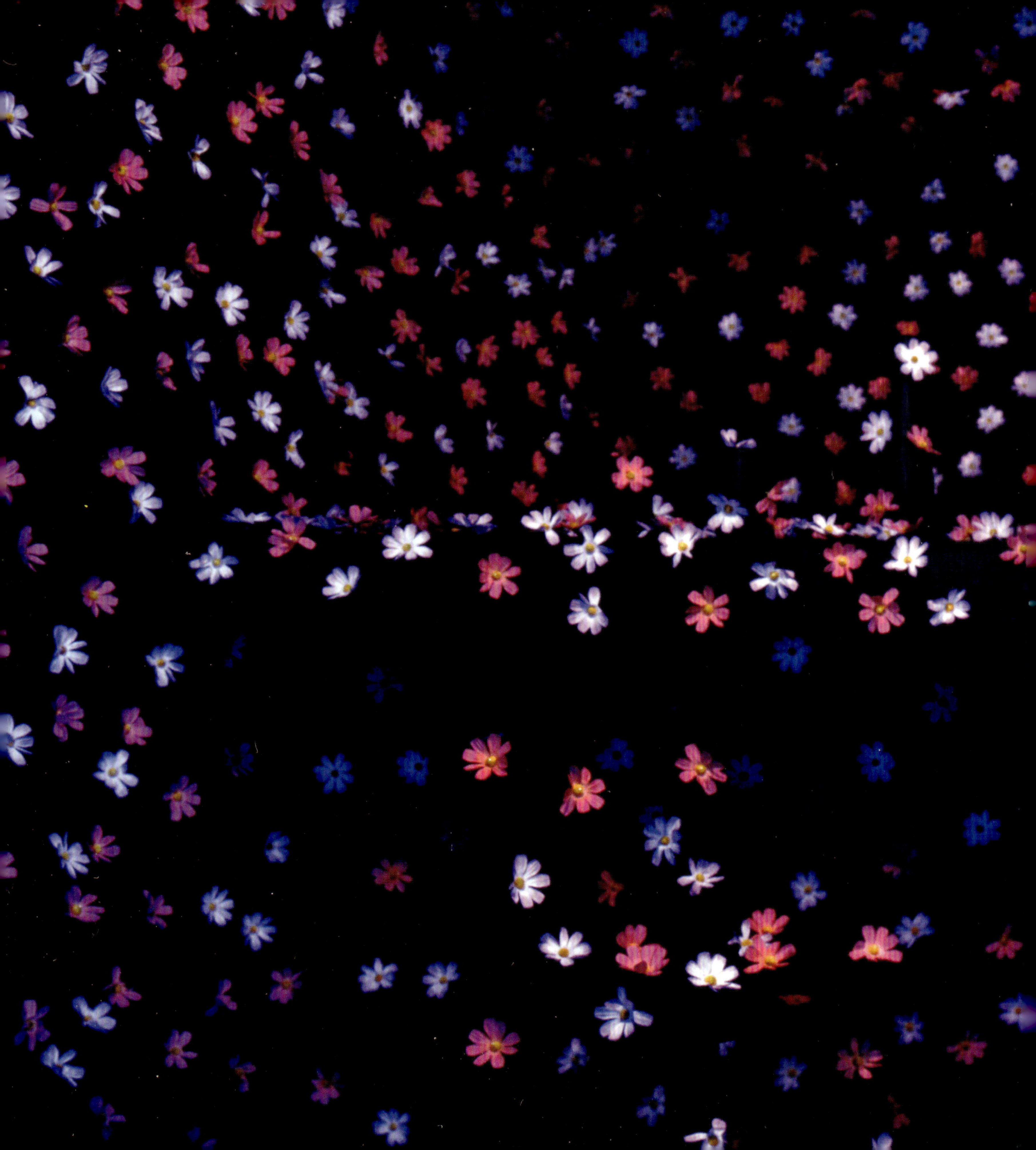

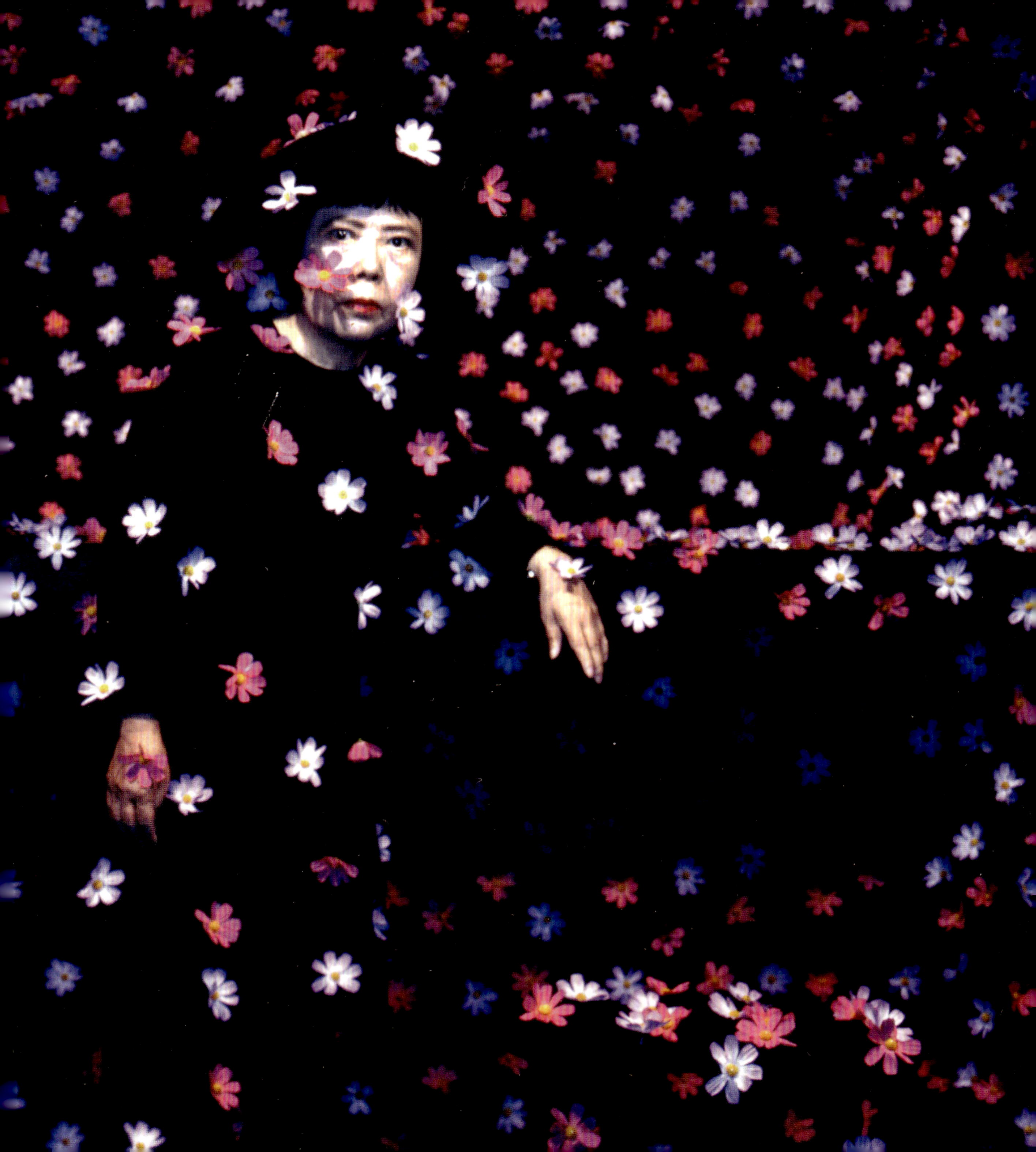

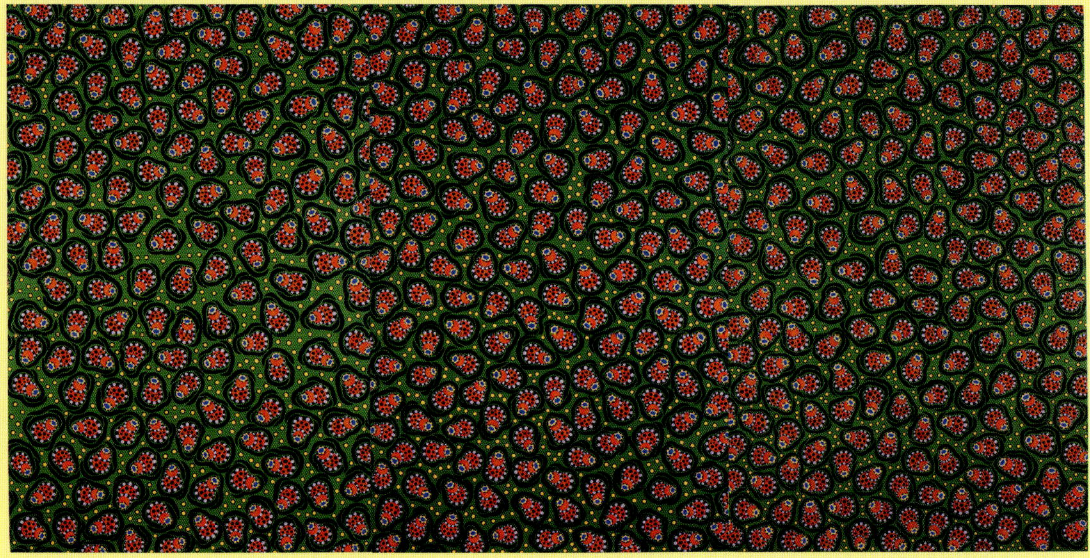

above
Awe of Life, 1989
Acrylic on canvas
76⅜ × 153½ in.
(194 × 390 cm)
Oita City Art Museum

opposite top
Pumpkin, 1994
Fiberglass-reinforced plastic, urethane paint, and metal
Permanent installation, Benese Art Site, Naoshima, Japan

opposite bottom
Kusama with *Flowers of Shangri-La*, Kirishima Open-Air Museum, Yūsui, 2000

1991

Between Heaven and Earth

Kusama debuts *Mirror Room* (*Pumpkin*) and numerous biomorphic soft sculptures at Fuji Television Gallery, as well as new paintings with colorful, graphic motifs that evoke cell structures and microorganisms that foreshadow her later series *My Eternal Soul* (**above**). In the same year, Kusama publishes *Foxgloves of Central Park*, a semiautobiographical novella about a Japanese immigrant to New York who suffers from hallucinations triggered by plants and eventually finds healing in a progressive psychiatric facility that employs art and gardening as therapy. Imagery in the novel mirrors Kusama's sculptural experiments in the conflation of plant and human form:

One day, as Shimako pulled a young daikon from the earth, the radish's long root entwined itself around the palm of her hand. It covered her hand completely. Startled, she tried to pry it off, only to find it stuck to her other hand as well. Try as she might, she could not get it off her hands. In fact, her entire field of vision began to fill with daikon radishes.[26]

1992

Print Works

A monograph presents Kusama's print works of the 1980s and early 1990s, most of which feature animal and plant subjects. A short essay by critic Akira Asada personifies Kusama's creative energy as a life force, driven toward its own replication and self-destruction:

"It" multiplies. . . . "It" divides, links, and diffuses. In order to cover up the universe with its own "being?" Yes, however, not only so with it. At the moment that dots like cancer cells seem to fill up every inch of space, through the dizzying reversal between figure and ground, positive and negative, and substance and shadow, the dots as substance obliterate themselves and make the insubstantial mesh of a white net appear between them. OBLITERATION at the end of MULTIPLICATION.[27]

1993

Venice Biennale

Kusama represents Japan at the Venice Biennale. A large solo exhibition includes recent biomorphic sculptures, as well as *My Flower Bed* (1962), which is a clear predecessor to these works. Most notably, the exhibition features *Infinity Mirror Room—Pumpkin*, an immersive polka-dotted environment formed around a group of papier-mâché pumpkins endlessly reflected inside a peep-in mirrored box.

1994

Pumpkin

Kusama installs her first permanent outdoor sculpture, *Pumpkin*, in the exhibition *Open Air '94, "Out of Bounds" Contemporary Art in the Seascape* at Benesse Art Site on Naoshima, Japan (**opposite top**). During the exhibition, the work is selected for permanent display in the location. Kusama later writes about her affinity for the subject: ***What appealed to me most was the pumpkin's generous unpretentiousness. That and its solid spiritual balance.***[28] On the other hand, Yūsuke Nakahara speculates that the artist's attraction is related to:

the unique configuration of irregular protuberances and indentations which characterize the pumpkin's surface. . . .

The outer skin of the pumpkin represents, shall we say, a surface in the throes of hanran (insurrection).[29]

The benign (or rebellious) pumpkin has since become one of Kusama's most ubiquitous sculptural motifs, including examples in fiberglass, bronze, mosaic concrete, and stainless steel, which have been displayed in sculpture parks around the world.

1998

Violet Obsession

The first compilation of Kusama's poetry translated into English is published in a volume titled *Violet Obsession*. Many of the poems address Kusama's intense emotional identification with nature, and some include references to specific plant species, such as *Fastia japonica* (Japanese paperplant) in the poem "AGAINST THE GLASS, SLEEPLESS NIGHT," originally written in Japanese in 1983:

the sound of heavy rain against
glass doors
fastia leaves crying in the rain
O sleepless night begone
the wind pierces my heart and moves on
let me sleep O Nature

I'm wide awake, my eyes won't shut
inside my head it's cold and wet with
raindrops
I want you to let me sleep
what is this madness in my heart?
O raging storm outdoors subside
a while for me[30]

2000

Flowers of Shangri-La

The first of Kusama's monumental flower sculptures, *Flowers of Shangri-La* (**below**), is permanently installed at the Kirishima Open-Air Museum in Yūsui, Japan. A reviewer later notes that Kusama's giant flower sculptures, a series known as *Flowers That Bloom at Midnight*, "linger delicately on a threshold between joy and horror with their vibrant immediacy, overwhelming presence, and saccharine, poxlike patterning."[31]

2001

Narcissus Sea

The Yokohama Triennale of Contemporary Art, Japan's first large-scale international art fair, includes two thousand mirrored orbs floating in the Yokohama Canal (page 164). Titled *Narcissus Sea*, it is the first installation of Kusama's *Narcissus Garden* in water. The artist reflects:

The mirror balls bobbed and rolled in the waves. Light glinted off them, and their perfectly spherical surfaces reflected the sky and the clouds and the surrounding water and landscape.

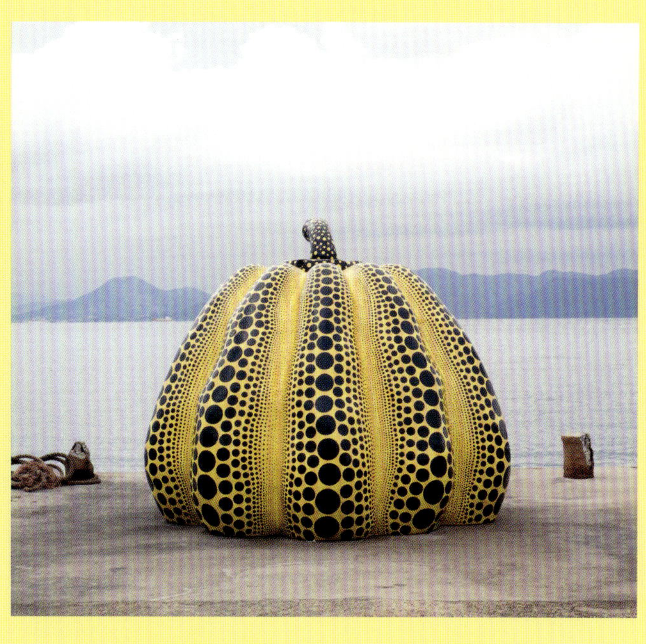

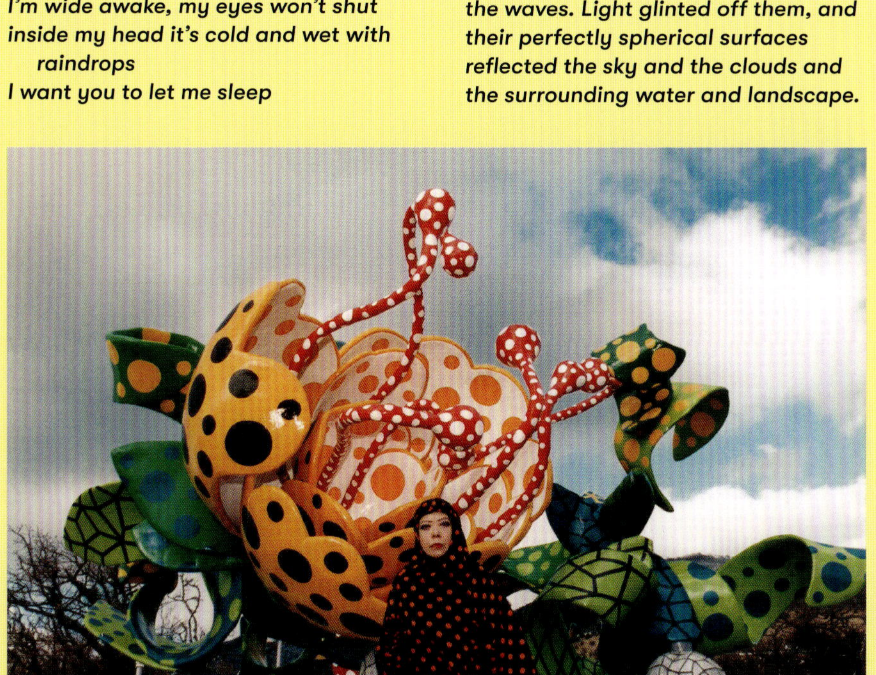

following
Installation of *Narcissus Garden* at Fort Tilden, Queens, New York, 2018

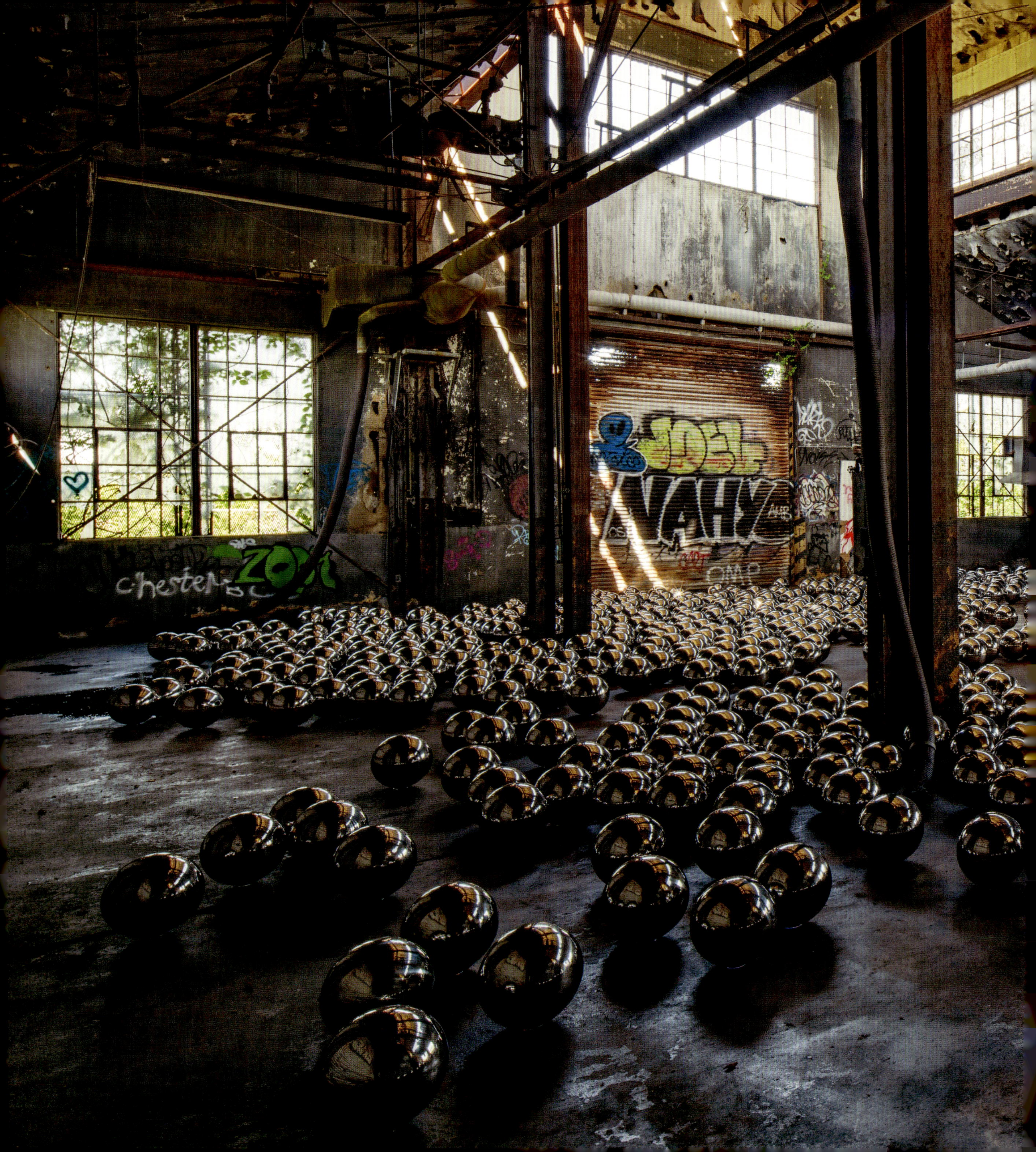
JOEL
VAHY
chester

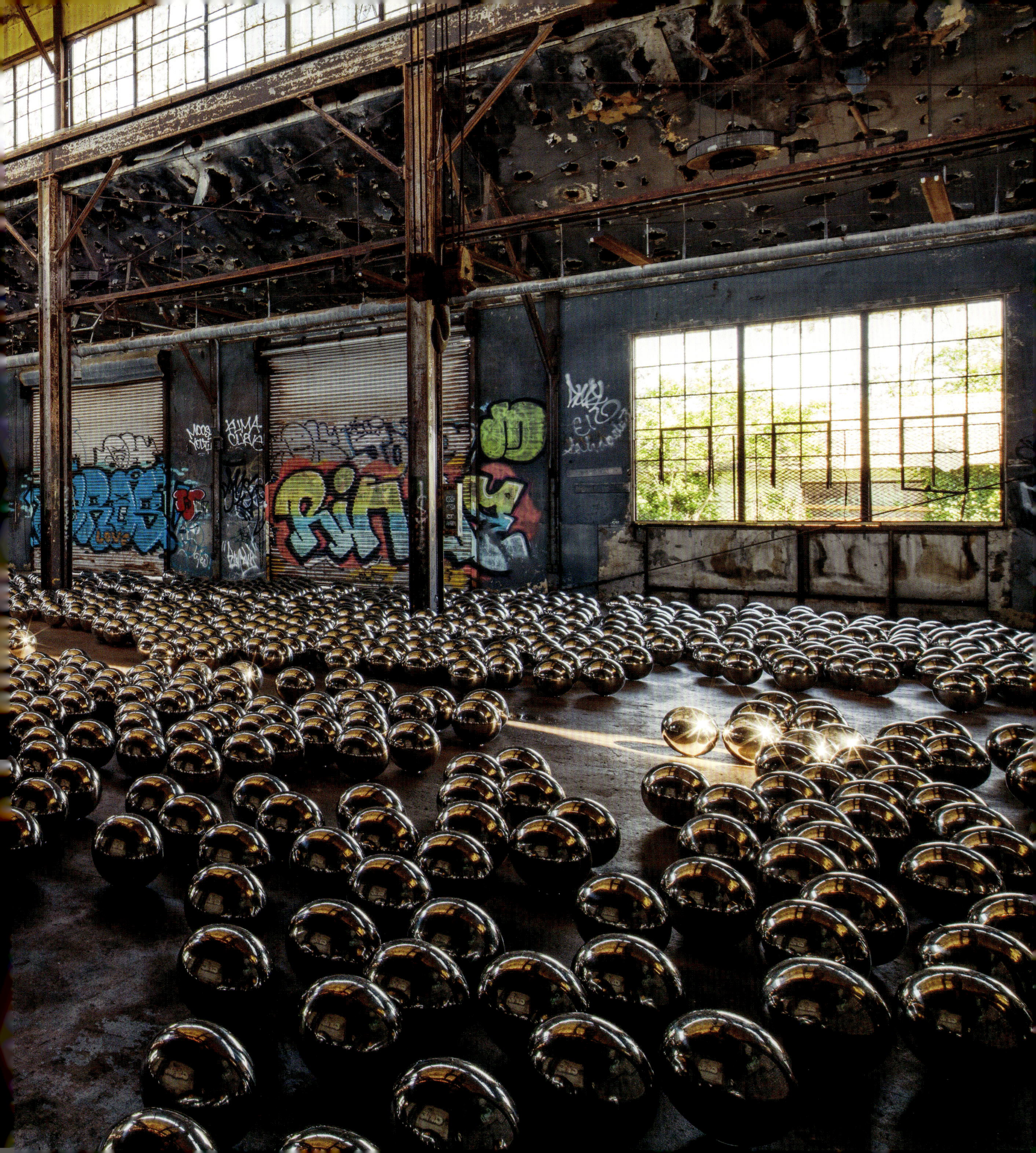

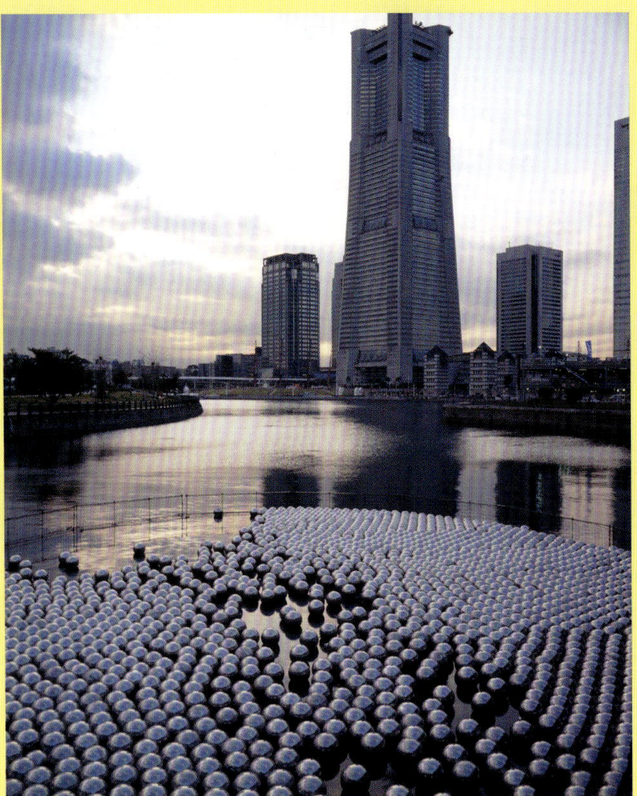

Onlookers watched an endless, silvery sea of mirrors bubble into existence. The ceaseless movement of the water pushed the globes together and pulled them apart with gentle clicks and squeaks, constantly transforming the shape of the work. It was a startling but dazzling sight: a mysterious sort of entity reproducing endlessly at the water's edge.[32]

2002–2007

The Visionary Flowers

Kusama installs several more permanent, large-scale flower sculptures around the world, beginning with *The Visionary Flowers* (2002) at Matsumoto City Museum of Art, followed by *Tulips of Shangri-La* (2003) on the Esplanade François Mitterrand in Lille, France, and *Hymn of Life—Tulips* (pages 22–23) at Beverly Gardens Park in Beverly Hills, California.

2006

Ascension of Polka Dots on the Trees

For the Singapore Biennale, Kusama wraps trees in white-on-red polka-dotted fabric, echoing earlier polka-dotted trees seen in the film *Kusama's Self-Obliteration* (1967; **opposite bottom**) and a smaller-scale display mounted at the Kirishima Open-Air Museum in 2002. Like *Narcissus Garden*, *Ascension of Polka Dots* has since been installed in numerous locations around the world (**opposite top**).

2009

Flowers That Bloom at Midnight

Kusama's solo exhibition at Gagosian Gallery in Beverly Hills features large-scale fiberglass flower sculptures called *Flowers That Bloom at Midnight*. Critic Leslie Camhi reflects on the duality of life and death present in these sculptures, which are at once comedic and monstrous:

Six legendary ginkgo trees (an ancient species) were among the rare survivors of the atomic blast on Hiroshima, and are still alive today. In this sense, Kusama's flower sculptures, the late blossoming of her ever-fertile mind, will long outlast her, to bloom perpetually in the light of day.[33]

2009–PRESENT

My Eternal Soul

O Time: hold still a while. I have so much more work to do. There are so many things I want to express.[34]

Kusama's most recent body of work is an ongoing series of large, vividly colored paintings collectively titled *My Eternal Soul*. Begun in 2009, the series currently comprises more than seven hundred works. Art historian Jenni Sorkin notes, "In contrast to the cheerful color palette of bright, matte shades, many of the *My Eternal Soul* titles are profoundly dark, and are rooted in the artist's literary expression."[35] Kusama identifies death and afterlife as the primary subject of these paintings, explaining her desire to create "art which gives meaning to death, tracing the beauty of colours and space in the silence of death's footsteps and the 'nothingness' it promises."[36] The biomorphic patterns in the paintings also often echo motifs found in her works on paper from the early 1950s. Curator Masahiro Yasugi observes:

The trajectory of Kusama's 70-year career forms a circle, or perhaps a spiral, marking the completion of one round trip and signalling a return t o her original point of departure, and therefore might be seen as a major turning point.[37]

2016

Where the Lights in My Heart Go

Kusama produces her first outdoor mirror room, *Where the Lights in My Heart Go*, which debuts at Victoria Miro Gallery in London. The stainless steel walls of the room are perforated with numerous tiny holes, so that sunlight passing into the otherwise darkened room creates an impression like being surrounded by stars. In the same year, Kusama's *Narcissus Garden* is installed on the property of Philip Johnson's Glass House in New

above
Installation of *Narcissus Sea* in the Yokohama Canal, Yokohama Triennale of Contemporary Art, 2001

opposite top
Installation of *Ascension of Polka Dots on the Trees*, Marseille-Provence, European Capital of Culture, 2013

opposite bottom
Production still, *Kusama's Self-Obliteration*, 1967

Canaan, Connecticut. At a site where the architecture was designed to facilitate maximum visual integration with the surrounding bucolic landscape, the silver orbs are used to highlight an experience of the natural world. The spheres reflect the sky and surrounding greenery, and their movement emphasizes natural drifts and currents in the pond where they are installed.

2018

Narcissus Garden

Narcissus Garden is installed in an abandoned train garage at Fort Tilden, a former military base in Queens, New York as part of the *Rockaway!* public art fair presented by MoMA PS1 (pages 162–63). As the announcement for the event describes it:

The mirrored metal surfaces reflect the industrial surroundings of the now-abandoned building, drawing attention to Fort Tilden's history as well as the devastating damage inflicted on many buildings in the area by Hurricane Sandy in 2012.[38]

The installation harks back to Kusama's performances of the late 1960s, in which she occupied public spaces to protest war and environmental destruction.

2018

I Want You to Look at My Prospects for the Future: Plants and I

The Yayoi Kusama Museum in Tokyo presents an exhibition that surveys botanical subjects in Kusama's work from the formative *Lingering Dream* (1949) to recent paintings such as *Alone, Buried in a Flower Garden* (2014; page 20). The show includes a variety of self-portraits that conflate the artist's identity with flowers, and includes a poem from 1978 titled "Violet Obsession," which narrates a formative moment of hallucinatory connection with flowers:

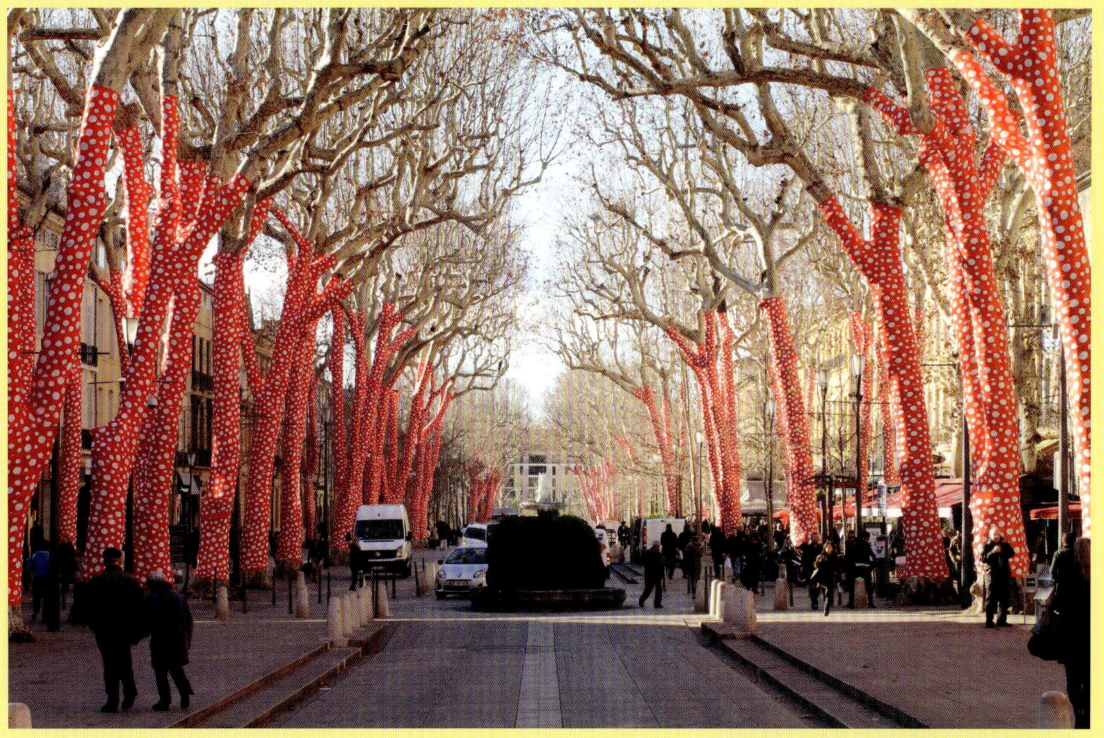

VIOLET OBSESSION

one day suddenly my voice
is the voice of a violet
calming my heart holding my breath
they're all for real, aren't they
all these things that happened today

violets came out of the tablecloth
crawled up and on to my body
one by one they stuck there
violets sumire *flowers*
they came to lay claim to this love of mine

full to the brim with danger
I stand petrified in the fragrance
just look even on the ceiling and pillars

violets adhere
youth is hard to hold on to
violets, please don't talk to me
give me back my voice, now a violet voice
I don't want to grow up not yet
all I ask is one more year
just leave us alone that long[39]

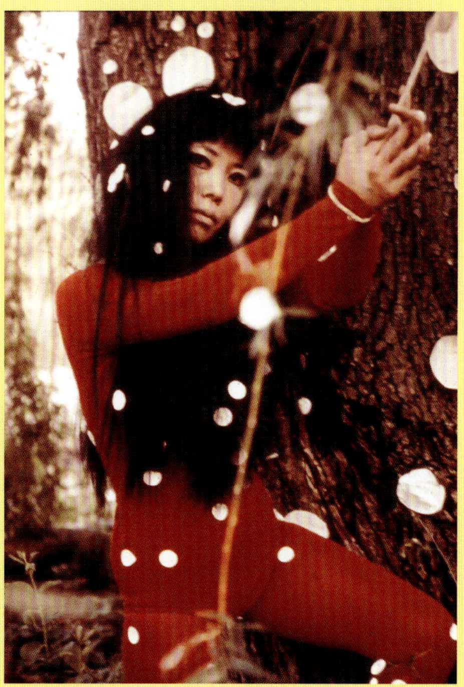

following
Dancing Pumpkin (detail), 2020
Installation view, The New York Botanical Garden, 2021

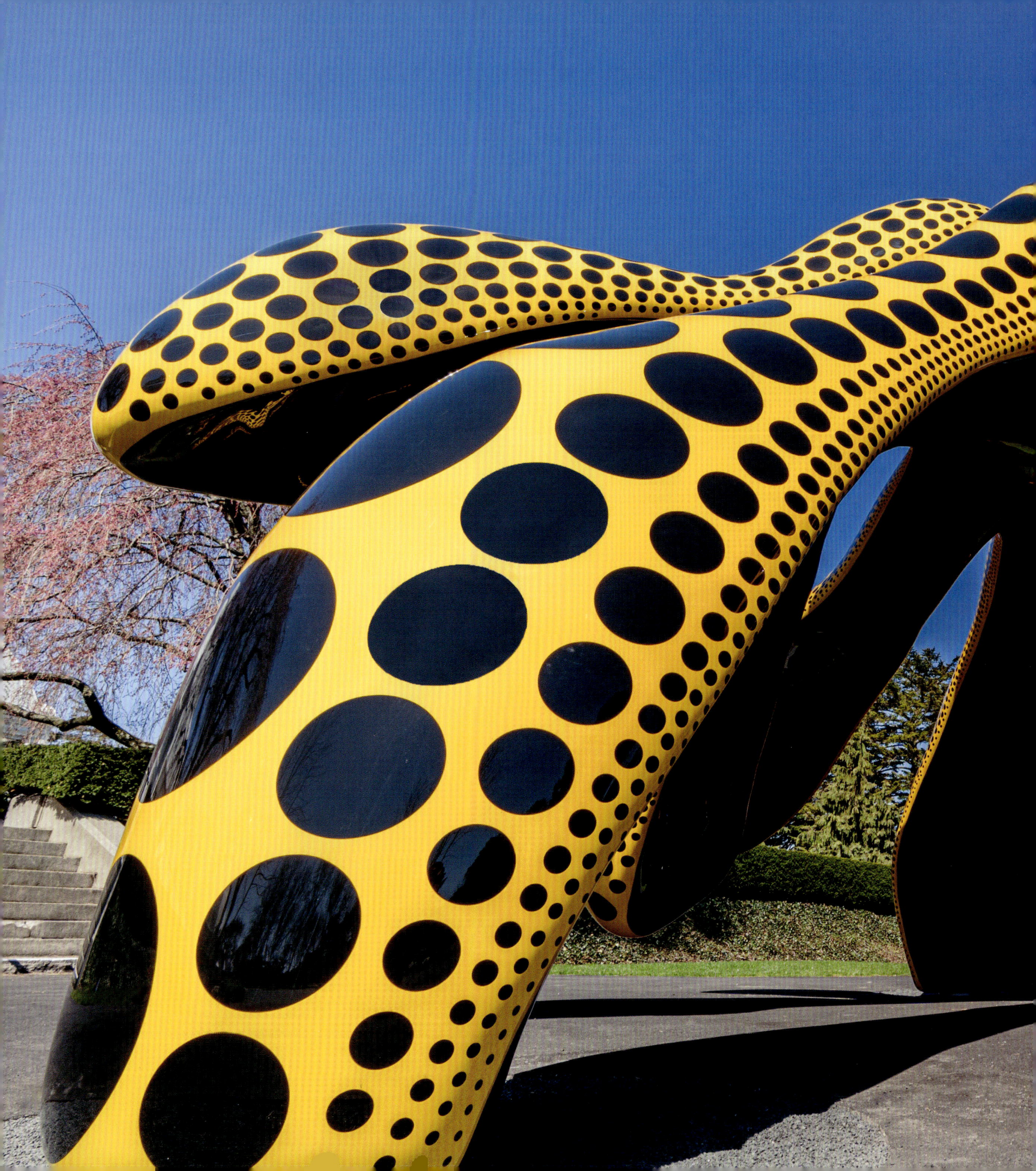

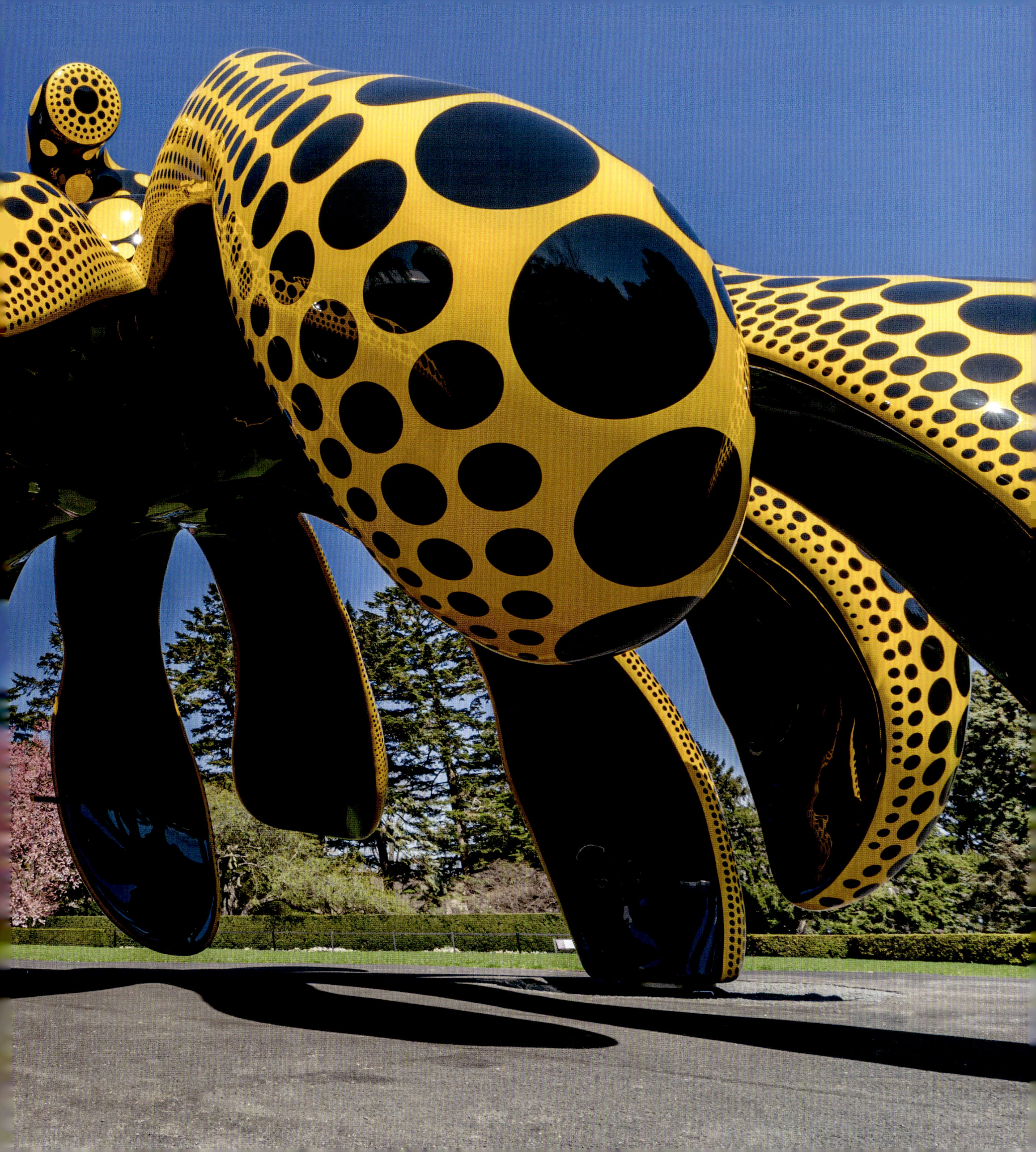

Exhibition Checklist

Untitled (Flower Sketches), 1945
Pencil in notebook
8½ × 11⅞ in. (21.5 × 30 cm)
Collection of the artist

Leaf of Japanese Medlar, 1948
Pencil on paper
21⅛ × 15⅜ in.
(53.7 × 39.2 cm)
Collection of the artist

Self-Portrait, 1950
Oil on canvas
13⅜ × 9½ in. (34 × 24 cm)
Collection of the artist

Flower Bud No. 6, 1952
Cover image, *Mizue*
Tokyo: Bijutsu Shuppansha, May 1954

A Seed, 1952
Pen and pastel on paper
13⅝ × 9⅞ in. (34.5 × 25 cm)
Collection of the artist

The Night, 1953
Pastel and gouache on paper
15 × 12⅛ in. (38 × 30.8 cm)
Collection of the artist

T.6, 1953
Gouache on paper
13 × 10⅜ in. (33 × 26.4 cm)
Private collection, Chicago

Untitled, 1953
Ink, pastel, and gouache on paper
11⅝ × 8⅞ in. (29.5 × 22.5 cm)
Collection of the artist

Untitled, 1953
Ink, pastel, and gouache on paper
10¾ × 8¹⁄₁₆ in.
(27.3 × 20.5 cm)
Collection of the artist

No. 3 P.B., 1960
Oil on canvas
62¾ × 56¼ in.
(159.4 × 142.9 cm)
Private collection, Chicago

Narcissus Garden, 1966/2021
1,400 stainless steel spheres
Installation dimensions variable
Courtesy of Ota Fine Arts

Walking Piece, 1966/2021
24 slides converted to multi-screen digital projection
Photographs by Eikoh Hosoe
Installation dimensions variable
Collection of the artist

Flower Petals, 1975
Pastel, ink, and fabric on paper
21½ × 15¼ in.
(54.5 × 38.6 cm)
Collection of the artist

Pistils Swaying in the Wind, 1978
Collage and acrylic on cardboard
25⅞ × 20¼ in.
(65.6 × 51.3 cm)
Collection of the artist

Early Spring, 1979
Ink and watercolor on paper
20⅛ × 26 in. (51.1 × 65.8 cm)
Collection of the artist

Summer, 1980
Sewn and stuffed fabric, fabric and wood box
15½ × 11⅝ × 4¾ in.
(39.5 × 29.5 × 12.2 cm)
Private collection, Japan
Courtesy of Ota Fine Arts

Dandelions, 1984
Acrylic on canvas
17⅞ × 20⅞ in. (45.5 × 53 cm)
Collection of the artist

Lilies, 1984
Acrylic on canvas
17⅞ × 20⅞ in. (45.5 × 53 cm)
Collection of the artist

Wild Flowers, 1984
Acrylic on canvas
17⅞ × 20⅞ in. (45.5 × 53 cm)
Collection of the artist

Flower, 1985
Mixed media
11¾ × 8 × 4⅛ in.
(30 × 20.2 × 10.5 cm)
Collection of Ota Fine Arts

Blue Flower, 1988
Mixed media
11¾ × 8 × 4⅛ in.
(30 × 20.2 × 10.5 cm)
Takahashi Ryutaro Collection, Yokohama, Japan

Moonlit Bedding, 1988
Mixed media
15½ × 10⅝ × 4¾ in.
(39.5 × 27 × 12 cm)
Private collection
Courtesy of Ota Fine Arts

Summer Flowers, 1988
Acrylic on canvas
17⅞ × 20⅞ in. (45.5 × 53 cm)
Collection of the artist

Flower, 1993
Pastel, acrylic, pen, and collage on paper
21¼ × 26¾ in.
(54.1 × 67.8 cm)
Collection of the artist

Ascension of Polka Dots on the Trees, 2002/2021
Printed polyester fabric, bungees, and aluminum staples installed on existing trees
Site-specific installation, dimensions variable
Collection of the artist

Butterflies' Nest, 2004
Acrylic and felt pen on canvas
15 × 17⅞ in. (38 × 45.5 cm)
Collection of the artist

Conversations in Heaven, 2004
Acrylic on canvas
20⅞ × 25⅝ in.
(53 × 65.2 cm)
Collection of the artist

Flower Bloomed in My Heart, 2004
Acrylic and felt pen on canvas
17⅞ × 15 in. (45 × 38 cm)
Collection of the artist

The Prairie in the Summer, 2004
Acrylic and felt pen on canvas
12½ × 16⅛ in. (31.8 × 41 cm)
Collection of the artist

Pumpkin TWOTOEL, 2004
Acrylic and felt pen on canvas
17⅞ × 20⅞ in.
(45.5 × 53 cm)
Collection of the artist

Hymn of Life—Tulips, 2007
Mixed media
3 elements, installation dimensions variable
Collection of the City of Beverly Hills

Tribute to the Sun in the Cosmos, 2010
Acrylic on canvas
63¾ × 63¾ in.
(162 × 162 cm)
Collection of the artist

I Want to Go to the Universe, 2013
Acrylic on canvas
76⅜ × 76⅜ in.
(194 × 194 cm)
Collection of the artist

Alone, Buried in a Flower Garden, 2014
Acrylic on canvas
76⅜ × 76⅜ in.
(194 × 194 cm)
Collection of the artist

Land of Glory, 2014
Acrylic on canvas
76⅜ × 76⅜ in.
(194 × 194 cm)
Collection of the artist

Life, 2015
Fiberglass-reinforced plastic, tiles, and resin
10 elements, installation dimensions variable
2 elements, H. 89⅜ in.
(227 cm); Diam. 43¼ in.
(110 cm)
2 elements, H. 78¾ in.
(200 cm); Diam. 37⅜ in.
(95 cm)
2 elements, H. 59⅞ in.
(152 cm); Diam. 29½ in.
(75 cm)
2 elements, H. 49¼ in.
(125 cm); Diam. 23⅝ in
(60 cm)
2 elements, H. 40½ in.
(103 cm); Diam. 19⅝ in.
(50 cm)
Courtesy of Ota Fine Arts and David Zwirner

Pumpkin, 2015
Sewn and stuffed fabric, acrylic, and metal
19⅝ × 25⅝ × 23⅝ in.
(50 × 65 × 60 cm)
Collection of the artist

Starry Pumpkin, 2015
Fiberglass-reinforced plastic, tiles, and resin
71¼ × 79½ × 80 in.
(181 × 202 × 203 cm)
Courtesy of Ota Fine Arts

Peace Shall Come as Far as the Ends of the Universe, 2016
Acrylic on canvas
76⅜ × 76⅜ in. (194 × 194 cm)
Collection of the artist

Pumpkin, 2016
Sewn and stuffed fabric, acrylic, and metal
18⅞ × 17¾ × 17¾ in.
(48 × 45 × 45 cm)
Collection of the artist

The Sun Has Gone Down, I Am Scared as Much as Being Alone, 2016
Sewn and stuffed fabric, acrylic, and metal
18⅞ × 17¾ × 17¾ in.
(48 × 45 × 45 cm)
Collection of the artist

Suppressing the Burning Desire for Death, 2016
Sewn and stuffed fabric, acrylic, and metal
19½ × 19½ × 19½ in.
(50 × 50 × 50 cm)
Collection of the artist

Flower Obsession, 2017/2021
Glasshouse, furniture, household objects, plastic stickers, and silk flowers
Dimensions variable
Courtesy of Ota Fine Arts

The Path of Life, 2017
Acrylic on canvas
76⅜ × 76⅜ in.
(194 × 194 cm)
Collection of the artist

Pumpkins Screaming About Love Beyond Infinity, 2017
Mirrors, acrylic, glass, LEDs, and wood panels
59 × 59 × 83½ in.
(150 × 150 × 212 cm)
Courtesy of Ota Fine Arts

Women Who Went Sightseeing to the Universe, 2017
Acrylic on canvas
76⅜ × 76⅜ in.
(194 × 194 cm)
Collection of the artist

All About the Appearance of the Heart, 2018
Acrylic on canvas
76⅜ × 76⅜ in.
(194 × 194 cm)
Collection of the artist

Flower Bud Opening to the Heavens, 2018
Sewn and stuffed fabric, acrylic paint, and metal
H. 35½ in. (90 cm);
Diam. 28 in. (71 cm)
Collection of the artist

Flower E, 2018
Sewn and stuffed fabric, acrylic paint, and metal
H. 19⅝ in. (50 cm);
Diam. 16⅞ in. (43 cm)
Collection of the artist

Flower F, 2018
Sewn and stuffed fabric, acrylic paint, and metal
H. 30¾ in. (78 cm);
Diam. 26¾ in. (68 cm)
Collection of the artist

My Soul Blooms Forever, 2019
Urethane paint on stainless steel
5 elements, installation dimensions variable
71¼ × 49⅞ × 25⅞ in.
(181 × 126.7 × 65.7 cm)
97⅝ × 62¼ × 49⅞ in.
(248 × 158 × 126.7 cm)
109¼ × 55⅝ × 43 in.
(277.5 × 141.3 × 109.3 cm)
90⅜ × 44½ × 35 in.
(229.5 × 113 × 89 cm)
85½ × 44¼ × 40 in.
(217.1 × 112.3 × 101.7 cm)
Courtesy of Ota Fine Arts, Victoria Miro, and David Zwirner

Dancing Pumpkin, 2020
Urethane paint on bronze
196⅞ × 116⅞ × 117¼ in.
(500 × 296.9 × 297.8 cm)
Courtesy of Ota Fine Arts, Victoria Miro, and David Zwirner

I Want to Fly to the Universe, 2020
Urethane paint on aluminum
157⅜ × 169⅜ × 140⅛ in.
(400 × 430 × 356 cm)
Courtesy of Ota Fine Arts, Victoria Miro, and David Zwirner

Infinity Mirrored Room—Illusion Inside the Heart, 2020
Mirror-polished stainless steel, glass mirrors, and colored glass
118⅛ × 118⅛ × 118⅛ in.
(300 × 300 × 300 cm)
Courtesy of Ota Fine Arts, Victoria Miro, and David Zwirner

Further Reading

General Reading

Karia, Bhupendra, ed. *Yayoi Kusama: A Retrospective*. With an essay by Alexandra Munroe and appendices by Reiko Tomii. New York: Center for International Contemporary Arts, 1989. Exhibition catalogue.

Kusama, Yayoi. *Infinity Net: The Autobiography of Yayoi Kusama*. Translated by Ralph F. McCarthy. English paperback edition. London: Tate, 2013.

Macellari, Elisa. *Kusama: The Graphic Novel*. London: Laurence King, 2020.

Minemura, Toshiaki. "The Soul Going Back to Its Home." In *Yoyoi Kusama Collage, 1952–1983*. Tokyo: Nabis Gallery; Fuji Television Gallery, 1991. Exhibition catalogue.

Morris, Frances, ed. *Yayoi Kusama*. With contributions by Jo Applin, Juliet Mitchell, Mignon Nixon, Rachel Taylor, and Midori Yamamura. London: Tate, 2012. Exhibition catalogue.

Shibutami, Akira, Masahiro Yasugi, and Yuji Maeyama, eds. *Eternity of Eternal Eternity*. Tokyo: Asahi Shimbun, 2012. Exhibition catalogue.

Suzuki, Sarah. *Yayoi Kusama: From Here to Infinity*. New York: Museum of Modern Art, 2017.

Tatehata, Akira, Laura Hoptman, Udo Kultermann, and Catherine Taft. *Yayoi Kusama*. 2nd ed. London: Phaidon, 2017.

Yamamura, Midori. *Yayoi Kusama: Inventing the Singular*. Cambridge, MA: MIT Press, 2015.

Yoshimoto, Midori. "Performing the Self: Yayoi Kusama and Her Ever-Expanding Universe." In *Into Performance: Japanese Women Artists in New York*. New Brunswick, NJ: Rutgers University Press, 2005.

Yoshitake, Mika, ed. *Yayoi Kusama: Infinity Mirrors*. With contributions by Melissa Chiu, Alexander Dumbadze, Alex Jones, Gloria Sutton, and Miwako Tezuka. Washington, DC: Hirshhorn Museum and Sculpture Garden; New York: DelMonico Books/Prestel, 2017. Exhibition catalogue.

Zelevansky, Lynn, Laura Hoptman, Akira Tatehata, and Alexandra Munroe. *Love Forever: Yayoi Kusama, 1958–1968*. Los Angeles: Los Angeles County Museum of Art, 1998. Exhibition catalogue.

Readings on Kusama, Nature, and the Cosmos

Asada, Akira. "Multiplication and Reversal." In *Yayoi Kusama: Print Works*, 27. Tokyo: Abe, 1992.

Benedikt, Michael. "New York Letter: Light Sculpture and Sky Ecstasy." *Art International* 10, no. 9 (September 1966): 46–47.

Camhi, Leslie. "New Sculpture." In *Yayoi Kusama*, edited by Louise Neri and Takaya Goto, 214–39. New York: Rizzoli International Publications, 2012.

Castellane, Richard. "On Kusama." In *Yayoi Kusama: Early Drawings from the Collection of Richard Castellane*, by Richard Castellane and David Moos, 44–45. Birmingham, AL: Birmingham Museum of Art, 2000. Exhibition catalogue.

Cremer, Jan. "On the Cover." *Art Voices* 4, no. 4 (1965): 5.

Guattari, Félix, and Toshiaki Minemura. *Yayoi Kusama: Infinity ∞ Explosion*. Tokyo: Fuji Television Gallery, 1986. Exhibition catalogue.

Kataoka, Mami. "Yayoi Kusama: An Infinite Consciousness Directed at the Cosmos." In *Look Now, See Forever*, edited by Reuben Keehan. Brisbane: Queensland Art Gallery, Gallery of Modern Art, 2011. https://play.qagoma.qld.gov.au/looknowseeforever/essays/infinite-consciousness-directed-at-the-cosmos/. Exhibition catalogue.

Koplos, Janet. "The Phoenix Returns." *Art in America* 87, no. 2 (February 1999): 92–97.

Kusama, Yayoi. *I Want You to Look at My Prospects for the Future: Plants and I*. Tokyo: Yayoi Kusama Museum, 2018. Exhibition catalogue.

———. "Kusama Opens a Shining Door to the 21st Century." In *Yayoi Kusama: Soul Burning Flashes*. Tokyo: Fuji Television Gallery, 1988. Exhibition catalogue.

———. *Violet Obsession: Poems*. Edited by Alexandra Munroe. Translated by Hisako Ifshin and Ralph F. McCarthy with Leza Lowitz. Berkeley, CA: Wandering Mind Books, 1998.

Nakazawa, Shinichi. "Jōdō shokubutsu (Les végétaux affectives)" [Affective Plants]. In *Kusama Yayoi*. Kitakyushū: Kitakyushū Municipal Museum of Art, 1987.

Seki, Naoko. *In Full Bloom: Yayoi Kusama, Years in Japan*. Tokyo: Museum of Contemporary Art, Tokyo, 1999. Exhibition catalogue.

Solomon, Andrew. "Dot Dot Dot: The Lifework of Yayoi Kusama." *Artforum* 35, no. 6 (February 1997): 66–73, 100, 104, 109.

Tatehata, Akira. "A Passage to Another World." In *Yayoi Kusama: My Solitary Way to Death*. Tokyo: Fuji Television Gallery, 1994. Exhibition catalogue.

Turner, Grady T. "Yayoi Kusama." *Bomb*, no. 66 (Winter 1999): 62–69. https://bombmagazine.org/articles/yayoi-kusama/.

Williams, Gilda. "Infinite Nature." In *Yayoi Kusama: Pumpkins*. London: Victoria Miro Gallery, 2014. Exhibition catalogue.

Yasugi, Masahiro. "The Path to Eternity: Yayoi Kusama's Paintings of the '00s," in *Eternity of Eternal Eternity*, edited by Akira Shibutami, Yasugi, and Yuji Maeyama, 146. Tokyo: Asahi Shimbun, 2012. Exhibition catalogue.

Contributors

Joanna L. Groarke, Editor, is Director of Public Engagement and Library Exhibitions Curator at The New York Botanical Garden, where she is part of the team that develops Garden-wide exhibitions and interpretive materials. She has developed exhibitions and programs for more than fifteen years for institutions including The New York Botanical Garden; the Irish Arts Center, New York; and Tufts University Art Galleries, Somerville, Massachusetts.

Mika Yoshitake, PhD, Guest Curator and Editor, is an independent curator with expertise in postwar Japanese art. As a curator at the Hirshhorn Museum and Sculpture Garden (2011–18), she organized the North American tour of *Yayoi Kusama: Infinity Mirrors* (2017–19) among numerous other exhibitions. She is currently guest curator at the Los Angeles County Museum of Art (LACMA) for the international tour of *Yoshitomo Nara* (2021–22) and Pacific Standard Time 2024's *Breath(e): Towards Climate and Social Justice* at the Hammer Museum in Los Angeles. A recipient of the AICA-USA award for *Requiem for the Sun: The Art of Mono-ha* (2012), Yoshitake also curated *Parergon: Japanese Art of the 1980s and 1990s* (2019) at Blum & Poe, Los Angeles.

Barbara Ambrose, PhD, is Director of Laboratory Research and Associate Curator of Plant Genomics at The New York Botanical Garden, where she also serves as Editor-in-Chief of *Botanical Review*. She is a specialist in plant morphology, genomics, and evolution and development.

Karen Daubmann is Vice President for Exhibitions and Audience Engagement at The New York Botanical Garden, where she leads the development of Garden-wide exhibitions. She has more than twenty years of experience in planning and implementing botanical garden exhibitions, previously at Phipps Conservatory and Botanical Gardens, Pittsburgh; Olbrich Botanical Gardens, Madison, Wisconsin; and Walt Disney World, Resort, Orlando.

Alex A. Jones is a writer and independent scholar living in Brooklyn, New York. She studied art history and theory at the Maryland Institute College of Art, Baltimore, and worked as curatorial research assistant on *Yayoi Kusama: Infinity Mirrors*, organized by the Hirshhorn Museum and Sculpture Garden (2017).

Alexandra Munroe, PhD, is Senior Curator, Asian Art, and Senior Advisor, Global Arts, at the Solomon R. Guggenheim Museum, New York, where she has led the Asian Art Initiative since 2006, presenting groundbreaking exhibitions and scholarly publications on Asian art in a global context. She also serves as Director, Curatorial Affairs, of the future Guggenheim Abu Dhabi. Prior to the Guggenheim, Munroe was Vice President of Arts and Culture at the Japan Society, New York. In 1989, at the Center for International Contemporary Arts (CICA), New York, she curated *Yayoi Kusama: A Retrospective*, the first critical survey of Kusama's work.

Jenni Sorkin, PhD, is Associate Professor of History of Art & Architecture at the University of California, Santa Barbara. She writes on the intersections between gender, material culture, and contemporary art, working primarily on women artists and underrepresented media. Her books include *Art in California* (Thames & Hudson, forthcoming), *Live Form: Women, Ceramics, and Community* (University of Chicago Press, 2016), and the catalogue for the exhibition *Revolution in the Making: Abstract Sculpture by Women, 1947–2016*, in which Yayoi Kusama was included.

Endnotes

Kusama in the Garden

1 • Yayoi Kusama, "The Struggle and Wanderings of My Soul," undated, Kusama Archive. Excerpt adapted in *Infinity Net: The Autobiography of Yayoi Kusama*, trans. Ralph F. McCarthy (London: Tate, 2013), 69.

2 • Ibid., 76.

"Provisions of Nature" • The Botanical Art of Yayoi Kusama

1 • Yayoi Kusama, "My Holy Land of Dreams for a Bright Future," in *Yayoi Kusama: Print Works*, exh. cat. (Tokyo: Abe, 1992), 52–53.

2 • *Infinity Net: The Autobiography of Yayoi Kusama*, trans. Ralph F. McCarthy (Tate, 2013), 75–76.

3 • Ibid., 61.

4 • See *Untitled (Flower Sketches)* contained in a sketchbook dating to 1945 in the collection of the artist. I would like to thank Takako Hara, Museum Registrar at The New York Botanical Garden, for her translations of the artist's sketchbook notes in Japanese, which appear throughout this essay.

5 • Midori Yamamura, *Inventing the Singular* (Cambridge, MA: MIT Press, 2015), 9–12; *Infinity Net: The Autobiography of Yayoi Kusama*, 26, 62.

6 • Kusama worked in the Kureha Textile Factory. She still painted and drew whenever possible. Midori Yamamura, "Rising from Totalitarianism: Yayoi Kusama, 1945–1955, Formative Years," in *Yayoi Kusama*, ed. Frances Morris, exh. cat. (London: Tate, 2012), 168–75.

7 • Laura Hoptman, "Yayoi Kusama: A Reckoning," in *Yayoi Kusama*, ed. Catherine Taft (London: Phaidon Press, 2017); Miwako Tezuka, "Chronology," in *Yayoi Kusama: Infinity Mirrors*, ed. Mika Yoshitake, exh. cat. (Washington, DC: Hirshhorn Museum and Sculpture Garden; New York: Delmonico Books/Prestel, 2017), 191.

8 • I am indebted to Deanna Curtis, Thain Senior Curator of Woody Plants and Landscape Project Manager, and Todd A. Forrest, Arthur Ross Vice President for Horticulture and Living Collections, The New York Botanical Garden, for their assistance in identifying the species Kusama depicts in her sketches.

9 • Yamamura, "Rising from Totalitarianism"; Yamamura, *Inventing the Singluar*, 13.

10 • Yamamura, *Inventing the Singular*, 13–14; Arūnas Gelūnas, "Making Art in the Japanese Way: *Nihonga* as a Process and Symbolic Action," *Acta Orientalia Vilnensia* 5 (December 2004), 44–47; Bert Winther-Tamaki, "Embodiment/Disembodiment: Japanese Painting During the Fifteen-Year War," *Manumenta Nipponica* 52, no. 2 (Summer 1997), 145.

11 • Chelsea Foxwell, "Introduction: *Nihonga* and the Historical Inscription of the Modern," in *Making Modern Japanese-Style Painting: Kano Hōgai and the Search for Images* (Chicago: University of Chicago Press, 2015), 2–3.

12 • Chronology, *Infinity Mirror Room*, 191; Yamamura, *Inventing the Singular*, 19.

13 • Yamamura, *Inventing the Singular*, 18.

14 • Michiyo Morioka and Paul Berry, introduction to *Modern Masters of Kyoto: The Transformation of Japanese Painting Traditions;* Nihonga *from the Griffith and Patricia Way Collection*, exh. cat. (Seattle: Seattle Art Museum, 1999), 22; Akira Tatehata, "Early Work," in *Yayoi Kusama*, ed. Louise Neri and Takaya Goto (New York: Rizzoli International Publications, 2012), 48.

15 • An evergreen tree or shrub that is often grown ornamentally in Japan, China, and parts of Europe, *Eriobotrya japonica* was formerly known as Japanese-medlar because it was believed to be related to the genus *Mespilus*, known commonly as medlar. It is sometimes referred to as Japanese plum, because of its edible yellow fruit. The artist labeled the drawing by hand: "Leaf of 'Biwa.' December 25, 1948. At Fushimi, Fukakusa. Department of Art and Painting. Kusama Yayoi." Trans. by Takako Hara.

16 • Akira Tatehata, "Kusama as Autonomous Surrealist," in Lynn Zelevansky, et. al., *Love Forever: Yayoi Kusama, 1958–1968*, exh. cat. (Los Angeles: Los Angeles County Museum of Art, 1998), 62.

17 • *Infinity Net: The Autobiography of Yayoi Kusama*, 113.

18 • Tatehata, "Kusama as Autonomous Surrealist," 67–68.

19 • *Infinity Net: The Autobiography of Yayoi Kusama*, 26.

20 • Arthur Lubow noted that circles, concentric rings, and dots occur in many of Kusama's early paintings, suggesting that many of the works from the period before she departed for the United States "could well be the visual record of hallucinations." He does not seem to be referring to the artist's earliest sketches. Lubow, "Prologue," in *Yayoi Kusama*, eds. Louise Neri and Takaya Goto, 28. Tatehata similarly makes connections between early works with repetitive forms and later infinity net paintings. See "Interview: Akira Tatehata in Conversation with Yayoi Kusama," in *Yayoi Kusama*, ed. Louise Neri and Takaya Goto, 8.

Cosmic Nature • Embracing the Unknown

1 • Félix Guattari, "Les riches affect des Madame Yayoi Kusama / Kusama Yayoi no hōjō no kanjō" [Yayoi Kusama's fertile emotion], in *Infinity ∞ Explosion* (Tokyo: Fuji Television Gallery, 1986), n.p. Translation by author.

2 • Shinichi Nakazawa, "Jōdō shokubutsu (Les végétaux affectives)" [Affective plants], in *Kusama Yayoi* (Kitakyushū: Kitakyushū Municipal Museum of Art, 1987), 12. Translation by author.

3 • Ibid., 12.

4 • Yayoi Kusama, *Sumire kyōhaku* [Violet obsession] (Tokyo: Sakuhin-sha, 1998), 94–95.

5 • Yayoi Kusama, quoted in Louis Guzzo, "Japanese 'Doll' Speaks through Her Paintings," *Seattle Times*, December 8, 1957.

6 • Founded in 1905, the family's Nakatsutaya seed nursery has been in business for 115 years to this day. Kusama recalls how the nursery extended all the way from the train station to her home. Kusama studio, conversation with author, 2019.

7 • Yayoi Kusama, "Kabocha no naka no watashi" [Myself Inside a Pumpkin], *Hanga geijutsu*, no. 103 (1999): 80. Translation by author. During the war when food was scarce, Kusama recalled, people from Tokyo came to visit her family's nursery in exchange for pumpkins and filled their sacks until they were on the verge of falling over.

8 • Ibid., 81.

9 • Ibid., 80. *Nihonga* was a technique in which artists used pulverized mineral pigments, adhered to the surface with *nikawa* animal-based glue. During this time, Kusama also employed a "bone drawing" (*kotsugaki*) technique of outlining in sumi ink before adding colors, seen in early paintings such as *Harvest* (1945).

10 • Tsuneyuki Tokue, ed., *Midori no chikara: Nihon kingendai kaiga ni miru shokubutsu no hyōgen* [The power of green: Expression of plants in Japanese modern and contemporary painting], exh. cat. (Tatebayashi: Gunma Museum of Art, Tatebayashi, 2003). Translation by author.

11 • In 1950, the Japanese art journal *Sansai* ran a series of features on new *nihonga* techniques by the artist Hoshun Yamaguchi. Practitioners of modern *nihonga* sought a new painterly line in their depictions of nature, and many artists began to incorporate Fauvist color and Cubist sense of space into their work. Cited in Izumi Nakajima, "Kusama Yayoi no 'Netto peintingu'—seijiteki-ni" [On Yayoi Kusama's Net Paintings—towards Politics], in *Anchi akushon: Nihon sengo kaiga to josei gaka / Anti-Action: Postwar Japanese Art and Women Artists* (Tokyo: Brücke, 2019), 157.

12 • This centripetal vortex is more pronounced in another historic work: *Accumulation of the Corpses (Prisoner Surrounded by the Curtain of Depersonalization)* from 1950.

13 • Kusama, quoted in *Seattle Times*, December 8, 1957.

14 • Nakajima, "Kusama Yayoi no 'Netto peintingu.'" Translation by author.

15 • Ibid.

16 • Kusama, cited in ibid., 176 n47. Translation by author. Kusama encountered Pacific Northwest artists such as Graves during a major exhibition in Tokyo, *30 Artists Japan-US Exchange Exhibition* (January 1951), which also paralleled the 3rd *Yomiuri Independent* exhibition (famous for introducing the work of Jackson Pollock). Nakajima cites how Kusama had written to Georgia O'Keeffe wanting to search for "symbolic mysticism from the Eastern mysticism of the Pacific Northwest," but O'Keeffe commented that she didn't really understand Eastern mysticism.

17 • Nakazawa, "Jōdō shokubutsu," 14.

18 • Yayoi Kusama, "The Struggle and Wanderings of My Soul," undated, Kusama Archive. Excerpt adapted in *Infinity Net: The Autobiography of Yayoi Kusama*, trans. Ralph F. McCarthy (London: Tate, 2013), 69.

19 • *Visagéité* (faciality) is derived from Gilles Deleuze and Félix Guattari, *A Thousand Plateaus: Capitalism and Schizophrenia*, trans. Brian Massumi (London: Continuum, 1987), which was published in the same year as Nakazawa's essay. The concept is defined as the ability "to discern details of the face without wishing to idealise its aura or charm . . . that calls into question the power of facial images. [Rather than] a site of psychological inquiry or of a reassuring human essence. . . it is the spirit in a corporeal form, a bodily and vital breath whose end is that of *undoing the face*. In sum, a forceful reconsideration is made of the face work in philosophy, aesthetics, and political theory." Tom Conley, *The Deleuze Dictionary*, ed. Adrian Parr (Edinburgh: Edinburgh University Press, 2010), 102.

20 • Nakazawa, 14.

21 • Ibid.

22 • This is in reference to Herbert Read's statement for Kusama's 1964 *Driving Image Show*, in which he likened her *Infinity Nets* to mycelium: "Those early paintings, without beginning, without end, without form, without definition, seemed to actualize the infinity of space. Now with perfect consistency, she creates forms that proliferate like mycelium and seal the consciousness in their white integument. It is an autonomous art, the most authentic type of super reality. This image of strange beauty presses on our organs of perception with terrifying persistence." Herbert Read, statement for *Kusama: Driving Image Show*, Castellane Gallery, New York (1964). Beatrice Perry Papers, New York, March 13, 1964.

23 • Guattari, "Les Riches Affect des Madame Yayoi Kusama," n.p.

24 • Video Gallery SCAN was an innovative platform in Tokyo for presenting new, experimental video art founded by artist Fujiko Nakaya in 1980.

25 • Nakazawa, 15.

26 • Nakazawa, 14.

27 • Kusama, "The Struggle and Wanderings of My Soul," undated, Kusama Archive.

"Vision of Repetition" • Building Patterns in Plants

Images presented by the author were generated by scanning electron microscopy (SEM) or histochemical staining. For histochemical staining, thin slices of plants are treated with different stains that react with the chemistry of the cells, producing differential color reactions depending on whether the cell is composed of particular proteins or lipids. Scanning electron microscopes (SEM) are able to magnify tens of thousands of times with a high resolution, as the SEM uses electrons for imaging the sample instead of light. Many images have scales in the micrometer (u) range, where 1 μm = 0.000001 m.

I thank Tynisha L. Smalls for excellent technical assistance in preparing plant material for microscopy. The SEM and associated processing equipment are supported by NSF-MRI grant 1828479 to Barbara A. Ambrose, Damon Little, Fabián Michelangeli, and The New York Botanical Garden. I am very grateful to Joanna L. Groarke, Lawrence Kelly, and Sally Armstrong Leone for their edits and comments on earlier versions of this essay.

1 • Charles Darwin. *On the Origin of Species by Means of Natural Selection* (London: John Murray, 1859).

2 • Stephen Jay Gould, "The Evolution of Life on the Earth," *Scientific American* 271, no. 4 (October 1994): 84–91.

3 • Camilo Mora, Derek P. Tittensor, Sina Adl et al., "How Many Species Are There on Earth and in the Ocean?," *PLOS Biology* 9, no. 8 (August 23, 2011): e1001127, https://doi:10.1371/journal/pbio.1001127; Cody E. Hinchliff, Stephen A. Smith, James F. Allman et al., "Synthesis of Phylogeny and Taxonomy into a Comprehensive Tree of Life," *Proceedings of the National Academy of Sciences* 112, no. 41 (October 13, 2015): 12764–69, https://doi:10.1073/pnas.1423041112.

4 • Cody E. Hinchliff, Stephen A. Smith, James F. Allman et al., "Synthesis of Phylogeny and Taxonomy into a Comprehensive Tree of Life," *Proceedings of the National Academy of Sciences* 112, no. 41 (October 13, 2015): 12764–69, https://doi:10.1073/pnas.1423041112.

5 • J. L. Riechmann, J. Heard, L. Reuber et al., "Arabidopsis Transcription Factors; Genome-Wide Comparative Analysis among Eukaryotes," *Science* 290, no. 5499 (December 15, 2000): 2105–10, https://doi:10.1126/science.290.5499.2105.

6 • Per K. I. Wilhelmsson, Cornelia Mühlich, Kristian K. Ullrich et al., "Comprehensive

Genome-Wide Classification Reveals That Many Plant-Specific Transcription Factors Evolved in Streptophyte Algae," *Genome Biology and Evolution* 9, no. 12 (December 2017): 3384–97, https://doi:10.1093/gbe/evx258.

7 • Brian K. Hall, "Evo-Devo: Evolutionary developmental mechanisms," *International Journal of Developmental Biology* 47 (2003): 491-5. Gerd B. Müller, "Evo-devo: Extending the evolutionary synthesis," *Nature Review Genetics* 8 (December 2007): 943–9. Sean B. Carroll. *Endless Forms Most Beautiful: The New Science of Evo Devo*, W.W. Norton & Company, 2006.

8 • *Infinity Net: The Autobiography of Yayoi Kusama* (London: Tate, 2013), 205.

9 • John L. Bowman, David R. Smyth, and Elliot M. Meyerowitz, 1989. "Genes Directing Flower Development in Arabidopsis," *The Plant Cell* 1, no. 1 (January 1989): 37–52; John L. Bowman, David R. Smyth, and Elliot M. Meyerowitz, 1991. "Genetic Interactions among Floral Homeotic Genes of Arabidopsis," *Development* 112, no. 1 (May 1991): 1–20; Enrico S. Coen and Elliot M. Meyerowitz, 1991. "The War of the Whorls: Genetic Interactions Controlling Flower Development," *Nature* 353, no. 6339 (September 5, 1991): 31–37, https://doi:10.1038/353031a0. Martin F. Yanofsky, Hong Ma, John L. Bowman et al., "The Protein Encoded by the *Arabidopsis* Homeotic Gene *AGAMOUS* Resembles Transcription Factors," *Nature* 346, no. 6279 (July 5, 1990): 35–39, https://doi:10.1038/346035a0. Thomas Jack, Laura L. Brockman, and Elliot M. Meyerowitz, "The Homeotic Gene *APETALA3* of *Arabidopsis Thaliana* Encodes a MADS Box and Is Expressed in Petals and Stamens," *Cell* 68, no. 4 (February 21, 1992): 683–97, https://doi:10.1016/0092-8674(92)90144-2.

10 • Martin F. Yanofsky, Hong Ma, John L. Bowman et al., "The Protein Encoded by the *Arabidopsis* Homeotic Gene *AGAMOUS* Resembles Transcription Factors," *Nature* 346, no. 6279 (July 5, 1990): 35–39, https://doi:10.1038/346035a0. Thomas Jack, Laura L. Brockman, and Elliot M. Meyerowitz, "The Homeotic Gene *APETALA3* of *Arabidopsis Thaliana* Encodes a MADS Box and Is Expressed in Petals and Stamens," *Cell* 68, no. 4 (February 21, 1992): 683–97, https://doi:10.1016/0092-8674(92)90144-2. Beth A. Krizek and Elliot M. Meyerowitz, "The Arabidopsis Homeotic Genes *APETALA3* and *PISTILLATA* Are Sufficient to Provide the B Class Organ Identity Function," *Development* 122, no. 1 (January 1996): 11–22.

11 • William Bateson, *Materials for the Study of Variation Treated with Especial Regard to Discontinuity in the Origin of Species* (London: Macmillan, 1894).

12 • Richard Goldschmidt, *The Material Basis of Evolution* (New Haven, CT: Yale University Press, 1940).

13 • Enrico S. Coen and Elliot M. Meyerowitz, 1991. "The War of the Whorls: Genetic Interactions Controlling Flower Development," *Nature* 353, no. 6339 (September 5, 1991): 31–37. https://doi:10.1038/353031a0.

14 • Barbara A. Ambrose, David R. Lerner, Pietro Ciceri et al., "Molecular and Genetic Analyses of the *Silky1* Gene Reveal Conservation in Floral Organ Specification between Eudicots and Monocots," *Molecular Cell* 5, no. 3 (March 2000): 569–79, https://doi:10.1016/s1097-2765(00)80450-5.

15 • Cindy Callens, Matthew R. Tucker, Dabing Zhang et al., "Dissecting the Role of MADS-Box Genes in Monocot Floral Development and Diversity," *Journal of Experimental Botany* 69, no. 10 (April 27, 2018): 2435–59, https://doi:10.1093/jxb/ery086.

16 • Barbara A. Ambrose, Silvia Espinosa-Matías, Sonia Vázquez-Santana et al., "Comparative Developmental Series of the Mexican Triurids Support a Euanthial Interpretation for the Unusual Reproductive Axes of *Lacandonia schismatica* (Triuridaceae)," *American Journal of Botany* 93, no. 1 (January 2006): 15–35, https://doi.org/10.3732/ajb.93.1.15.

17 • Elena R. Álvarez-Buylla, Barbara A. Ambrose, Eduardo Flores-Sandoval et al., "B-Function Expression in the Flower Center Underlies the Homeotic Phenotype of *Lacandonia Schismatica* (Triuridaceae)," *Plant Cell* 22, no. 11 (November 2010): 3543–59.

18 • John Tyler Bonner, *The Evolution of Development*, Cambridge University Press, 1958.

19 • Erin Sparks, Guy Wachsman, and Philip N. Benfey, "Spatiotemporal signalling in plant development," *Nature Review Genetics* 14, no. 9 (September 2013): 631–44. Luis Matías-Hernández, Andrea E. Aguilar-Jaramillo, Riccardo Aiese Cigliano et al., "Flowering and trichome development share hormonal and transcription factor regulation," *Journal of Experimental Botany* 67, no. 5 (2016): 1209–19.

20 • Alan Turing, "The Chemical Basis of Morphogenesis," *Philosophical Transactions of the Royal Society B* 237, no. 641 (August 14, 1952): 37–72, https://doi.org/10.1098/rstb.1952.0012

21 • Rory L. Cooper, Alexandre P. Thiery, Alexander G. Fletcher et al., "An ancient Turing-like patterning mechanism regulates skin denticle development in sharks," *Science Advances* 4 (2018): 1–10. Shigeru Kondo and Takashi Miura, "Reaction-diffusion model as a framework for understanding biological pattern formation," *Science* 329, no. 5999 (September 24, 2010): 1616–20. Stefanie Sick, Stefan Reinker, Jens Timmer et al., "WNT and DKK determine hair follicle spacing through a reaction-diffusion mechanism," *Science* 314, no. 5804 (December 2006): 1447–50. Jeremy B. A. Green and James Sharpe "Positional information and reaction-diffusion: two big ideas in developmental combine," *Development* 142 (2015): 1203–11. Andrew D. Economou, Atsushi Ohazama, Thantrira Porntaveetus, et al., "Periodic stripe formation by a Turing mechanism operating at growth zones in the mammalian palate," *Nature Genetics* 44, no. 3 (February 2012): 348–51. Baoqing Ding, Erin L. Patterson, Srinidhi V. Holalu et al., "Two MYB Proteins in a Self-Organizing Activator-Inhibitor System Produce Pigmentation Patterns," *Current Biology* 30, (March 9, 2020): 802–14. Amit N. Landge, Benjamin M. Jordan, Xavier Diego et al., "Pattern formation mechanisms of self-organizing reaction-diffusion systems," *Developmental Biology* 460 (2020): 2–11.

Botanicals for the Eye • Yayoi Kusama's Flower Power

1 • Sir Herbert Read, introduction to *Obsession: Yayoi Kusama* (Tokyo: Fuji Television Gallery, 1982), n.p.

2 • Odilon Redon, "To Myself (1857–1915)," in *To Myself: Notes on Life, Art, and Artists*, trans. Mira Jacob and Jeanne L. Wasserman (New York: George Braziller, 1986), 23–24. For the most recent English-language publication on Redon, see Jodi Hauptman, *Beyond the Visible: The Art of Odilon Redon* (New York: Museum of Modern Art, 2005).

3 • Katharine Grant Sterne, "Odilon Redon Viewed Again," *Parnassus* 3, no. 3 (March 1931), 8.

4 • "Interview: Yayoi Kusama," by Rosanna Greenstreet, *Guardian*, Q&A: Life and Style, May 21, 2016, https://www.theguardian.com/lifeandstyle/2016/may/21/yayoi-kusama-interview-artist.

5 • Yayoi Kusama, "Open Letter to My Hero, Richard Nixon," November 11, 1968, Jack S. Blanton Museum of Art Archive, University of Texas, Austin.

6 • Tamasin Doe, "Joining the Dots," *Guardian*, January 28, 2000, Fashion, https://www.theguardian.com/lifeandstyle/2000/jan/28/fashion1.

7 • Steven Lubar, "'Do Not Fold, Spindle or Mutilate': A Cultural History of the Punch Card," *Journal of American Culture* 15, no. 4 (Winter 1992), 43–55.

8 • Yuko Hasegawa and Pamela Miki, "The Spell to Re-integrate the Self: The Significance of the Work of Yayoi Kusama in the New Era," *Afterall: A Journal of Art, Context and Enquiry*, no. 13 (Spring/Summer 2006), 46.

9 • Midori Yamamura thoroughly argues this point throughout her excellent book, *Yayoi Kusama: Inventing the Singular* (Cambridge, MA: MIT Press, 2015).

10 • Jacques Lacan, "The Mirror Stage as Formative of the I Function as Revealed in Psychoanalytic Experience (1949)," in *Écrits: The First Complete Edition in English*, trans. Bruce Fink in collaboration with Héloïse Fink and Russell Grigg (New York: W. W. Norton, 2006), 75–81.

11 • Yayoi Kusama, "Garden of Narcissus," unpublished statement, 1966.

"Forget Yourself and Become One with Nature!"

The title "Forget yourself and become One with Nature!" comes from Kusama's press release for the "Naked Event at Statue of Liberty," 1968, cited in Midori Yoshimoto, *Into Performance: Japanese Women Artists in New York* (New Brunswick, NJ: Rutgers University Press, 2005), 74.

The author thanks her readers for their comments that improved this essay: Geremie Barmé, Joanna L. Groarke, Andrew Solomon, and Mika Yoshitake.

1 • Yayoi Kusama, interview by Arlene Jacobowitz, January 19, 1968, Brooklyn Museum interviews of artists [ca. 1965–68] file, Archives of American Art, Smithsonian Institution. The interview may have been conducted on the occasion of the museum's acquisition of works on paper dated to the early 1950s, donated by Richard Castellane. I am grateful to Zoe Diao for research assistance.

2 • I am indebted to Hope Jahren for her scientific descriptions of the natural world. See Hope Jahren, *Lab Girl* (New York: Alfred A. Knopf, 2016).

3 • Kusama was also at the epicenter of 1960s social radicalism, embracing anarchism, pacifism, nudism, free love, gay rights, the antiwar movement, and psychedelia. Kusama's happenings, experimental films, and installations of the late 1960s now stand among the most consistent body of activist protest art produced by any artist working anywhere during that paradigm-shattering era. Feminist critics have also cast Kusama as a pioneer who both performed and transgressed femininity before there was even a name for what she was doing.

4 • Yayoi Kusama, "Eternity of Eternal Eternity" (2011), in *Yayoi Kusama: Every Day I Pray for Love*, trans. Ralph F. McCarthy, et al. (New York: David Zwirner Books, 2020), 195.

5 • Yayoi Kusama, *Yayoi Kusama Ten: Tamashii o moyasu senkou* [Exhibition of Yayoi Kusama: Soul Burning Flashes] (Tokyo: Fuji Television Gallery, 1988, n.p.), cited in Yoshimoto, *Into Performance*, 72.

6 • My early writings on Kusama include, "Obsession, Fantasy, Outrage: The Art of Yayoi Kusama," in *Yayoi Kusama: A Retrospective*, ed. Bhupendra Karia (New York: Center for International Contemporary Arts, 1989); "Between Heaven and Earth: The Literary Art of Yayoi Kusama," in Lynn Zelevansky, et al., *Love Forever: Yayoi Kusama, 1958–1968*, exh. cat. (Los Angeles: Los Angeles County Museum of Art, 1998).

7 • Kusama flyer, cited in Yoshimoto, *Into Performance*, 74–75. The full quote from Kusama's release for the "Naked Event at the Statue of Liberty," on July 17, 1968, is: "Take it off, liberty! . . . Nudism is the one thing that doesn't cost anything. Clothes cost money. Property costs money. Taxes cost money. Stocks cost money. Only the dollar costs less. Let's protect the dollar by economizing! Let's tighten our belts! Let the pants fall where they may! . . . Forget yourself and become one with nature! Obliterate yourself with polka dots!"

8 • Juliet Mitchell, "Portrait of the Artist as a Young Flower," in *Yayoi Kusama*, ed. Frances Morris (London: Tate, 2012), 193.

9 • Yayoi Kusama, *Infinity Net: The Autobiography of Yayoi Kusama*, trans. Ralph F. McCarthy (London: Tate, 2013), 93.

10 • See Sidney Tillim, "In the Galleries," *Arts* 34, no. 1 (October 1959): 56; Midori Yoshimoto, "Performing the Self: Yayoi Kusama and Her Ever-Expanding Universe," in Yoshimoto, *Into Performance*.

11 • *Stanford Encyclopedia of Philosophy*, s.v. "panpsychism," revised July 18, 2017, https://plato.stanford.edu/entries/panpsychism/.

12 • See Munroe, "Obsession, Fantasy, Outrage," Munroe, *Japanese Art after 1945: Scream against the Sky* (New York: Harry N. Abrams, 1994). Kusama's work first became the subject of serious study and a recognized chapter in the history of contemporary art with *Yayoi Kusama: A Retrospective*, at New York's Center for International Contemporary Arts in 1989. Since then, she has come to enact and symbolize some of the most defining shifts in recent cultural history. Well into the 1980s, Euro-Americentrism perpetuated biases regarding what constituted avant-garde ideas and practice. As a result, artists such as Kusama, who hailed from backgrounds other than cultural metropoles, were sidelined or overlooked, dismissed as being "belated" or "derivative." The rise of postmodern and postcolonial critiques in the late 1980s and early 1990s, and that of identity politics in the arts in the 1990s, would begin to undo much of that. Kusama's triumph in the 1990s was an act of recuperation. The curatorial establishment that barely knew of her before now saw Kusama as part of a long and neglected lineage of artists struggling to be seen and heard: the artistic self was now the principal carrier of artistic content.

13 • Critic Fukushima Tatsuo wrote that Kusama's "metaphysical mysterious work . . . stands on rationalist grounds, yet shows a strong resistance to anti-humanism." Fukushima Tatsuo, "Shinpifū nasakuhin, chūmoku sareru Kusama Yayoi no koten" [Mysterious work, remarkable exhibition of Yayoi Kusama], unknown newspaper, April 6, 1955, Kusama Papers, cited and trans. Midori Yamamura, "Rising from Totalitarianism: Yayoi Kusama, 1945–1955, Formative Years," in *Yayoi Kusama*, ed., 168–75.

14 • Yayoi Kusama, "Iwan no baka" [Ivan the Fool], in *Geijutsu Shinchō* (May 1955): 164–65, cited in Yamamura, "Rising from Totalitarianism," 174.

15 • Ibid., 175.

16 • "Kodoku no gaka Kusama Yayoi raishi" [Solitary artist Yayoi Kusama visits Seattle], cited in Yamamura, "Rising from Totalitarianism," 175.

17 • Tobey had spent time in Shanghai and Kyoto in the 1930s, studying calligraphy and practicing Chan/Zen meditation, hoping to forge a syncretic aesthetic and ethical system for modern art. Tobey's comment on his *White Writing* series epitomizes this shared vision: "White lines in movement symbolize a unifying idea which flows through the compartmented units of life bringing the consciousness of a larger relativity," https://www.azquotes.com/author/25170-Mark_Tobey.

18 • The Zoë Dusanne Gallery was a leading modern art gallery in Seattle and represented the key figures of the Pacific Northwest School, including Guy Anderson, Kenneth Callahan, Morris Graves, and Mark Tobey.

19 • "[Interview with] Miss Yayoi Kusama," by Gordon Brown, *De Nieuwe Stijl* (The New Style), vol. 1 (1965): 48–53, 162–64.

20 • Donald Judd, "Reviews and Previews: New Names This Month—Yayoi Kusama," *ArtNews* 58, no. 6 (October 1959): 17.

21 • Kusama, *Infinity Net*, 23.

22 • Ad Reinhardt (undated), quoted in Barbara Rose, ed., *Art-as-Art: The Selected Writings of Ad Reinhardt* (Berkeley: University of California Press, 1975), 82–83. Reinhardt traveled extensively in Asia, earned a master's degree in Asian art history, and wrote essays on Asian art. In one essay, he praises the "timeless" art of Asia as being "vacant and spiritual, empty and marvelous," a form of expression that conveys "the timeless 'supreme principle,' the ageless 'universal formula.'" Ad Reinhardt, "Timeless in Asia," *ArtNews* (January 1961): 34, cited in ibid., 290. Taking cues from this Eastern cosmology, Reinhardt spent nearly two decades making matte black compositions of a barely visible geometric cross. For the artist, these paintings were psychically charged objects of self-transcendence. In Reinhardt's mind, art, ontology, and cosmology all pointed to a higher insight. The curator Barbara Rose wrote that the function of the black paintings demands "not merely a different order of perception" but also induces "a qualitatively different state of consciousness from normal consciousness . . . [and must be] seen as a reformulated and modernized humanism." See Barbara Rose, "The Black Paintings," in *Ad Reinhardt: Black Paintings, 1951–1967* (New York: Marlborough Gallery, 1970), 19.

23 • Yayoi Kusama to Georgia O' Keeffe, in Bhupendra Karia, "Biographical Notes," in *Yayoi Kusama: A Retrospective*, 70.

24 • Yayoi Kusama, "Waga tamashii no henreki to takakai" (The Struggle and Wanderings of My Soul), *Geijutsu Seikatsu* (Art and Life) (November 1975): 96–113, translation adapted by author in Munroe, "Obsession, Fantasy, and Outrage," 14.

25 • For example, see Philip Goff, *Galileo's Error: Foundations for a New Science of Consciousness* (New York: Pantheon, 2019); and Thomas Nagel, *Mind and Cosmos: Why the Materialist Neo-Darwinian Conception of Nature Is Almost Certainly False* (Oxford: Oxford University Press, 2012).

26 • This question was raised in Thomas Nagel, "What Is It Like to Be a Bat?," *Philosophical Review* 83, no. 4 (1974): 435–50; however, the first philosopher who came up with this idea is Timothy Sprigge. See also David Chalmers, *The Conscious Mind* (Oxford: Oxford University Press, 1996).

27 • Marco Mattei, "Cosmopsychism and the Philosophy of Hope," *Cosmic Bulletin* (commissioned for the Riga International Biennial of Contemporary Art, 2020), https://www.cosmos.art/cosmic-bulletin/2020/marco-mattei-cosmopsychism-and-the-philosophy-of-hope. See also Timothy Morton, *Humankind: Solidarity with Nonhuman People* (London: Verso, 2017).

28 • "Panpsychism in the History of Western Philosophy," in *Stanford Encyclopedia of Philosophy*, revised July 18, 2017, https://plato.stanford.edu/entries/panpsychism/index.html#PanpHistWestPhil.

29 • Spinoza, quoted in ibid.

30 • "Panpsychism in the History of Western Philosophy."

31 • Yayoi Kusama (1968), cited in Munroe, "Obsession, Fantasy, and Outrage," 29.

32 • A selective reading of recent books on panpsychism includes David J. Chalmers, *The Character of Consciousness* (Oxford: Oxford University Press, 2010), and *Constructing the World* (Oxford: Oxford University Press, 2012); Philip Goff, *Consciousness and Fundamental Reality* (New York: Oxford University Press, 2017), and *Galileo's Error*; Nagel, *Mind and Cosmos*; Yuk Hui, *The Question Concerning Technology in China: An Essay in Cosmotechnics*, Mono 3 (Falmouth, UK: Urbanomic Media, 2016), and *Recursivity and Contingency* (London: Rowman & Littlefield, 2019); Yuk Hui and Andreas Broeckmann, eds., *30 Years after Les Immatériaux: Art, Science and Theory* (Lüneburg, Germany: Meson Press, 2015).

33 • Nagel, *Mind and Cosmos*, 32. He writes: "The inescapable fact that has to be accommodated in any complete conception of the universe is that the appearance of living organisms has eventually given rise to consciousness, perception, desire, action, and the formation of both beliefs and intentions on the basis of reasons. . . . A satisfying explanation would . . . reveal mind and reason as basic aspects of a nonmaterialistic natural order."

34 • Thomas Nagel, cited in Richard Brody, "Thomas Nagel: Thoughts Are Real," *New Yorker*, July 16, 2013, https://www.newyorker.com/books/page-turner/thomas-nagel-thoughts-are-real.

35 • Hui, *The Question Concerning Technology in China*, 36.

36 • Ibid., 80.

37 • Ibid., 312.

38 • For a history of the influence of Asian aesthetics and philosophy on American art, see Munroe, *Third Mind*.

39 • Fritjof Capra, *The Tao of Physics: An Exploration of the Parallels between Modern Physics and Eastern Mysticism* (Boston: Shambhala, 1975).

40 • Yayoi Kusama, quoted in Jud Yalkut, "The Polka Dot Way of Life (Conversations with Yayoi Kusama)," *New York Free Press* 1, no. 8 (1968): 8.

41 • *The Complete Works of Zhuangzi*, trans. Burton Watson (New York: Columbia University Press, 2013), 182, cited in Hui, *The Question Concerning Technology in China*, 67.

42 • See Camden Art Centre, *The Botanical Mind: Art, Mysticism and The Cosmic Tree*, https://www.botanicalmind.online/. I am grateful to my colleague Jessica Cerasi for bringing this project to my attention.

43 • Ibid.

44 • *Plant Signaling & Behavior* is a peer-reviewed scientific journal published by Landes Bioscience, which is located in the United States. Launched in 2006, it publishes research on plant communications: pathogenic, symbiotic, and predatory interactions with plants and other species.

45 • Andrea Thompson. "Taking Stock of Life," *Scientific American* vol. 319, 2 (August 2018).

46 • Eduardo Kohn, *How Forests Think: Toward an Anthropology beyond the Human* (Berkeley: University of California Press, 2013).

47 • Animals never fascinated Kusama as much; her art and trauma are centered around the plants in her family's nursery.

48 • Brody, "Thomas Nagel."

49 • Yayoi Kusama, "The Battle of Love and Death" (2018), in Anne Wehr, ed., *Yayoi Kusama: Every Day I Pray for Love*, trans. Ralph F. McCarthy, et al. (New York: David Zwirner Books, 2020), 250.

Chronology

1 • *Infinity Net: The Autobiography of Yayoi Kusama*, trans. Ralph F. McCarthy, (London: Tate, 2013), 61.

2 • Midori Yamamura, *Yayoi Kusama: Inventing the Singular* (Cambridge: MIT Press, 2015), 12.

3 • Miwako Tezuka, "Chronology," in *Yayoi Kusama: Infinity Mirrors*, ed. Mika Yoshitake, exh. cat. (Washington, DC: Hirshhorn Museum and Sculpture Garden; New York: Delmonico / Prestel, 2017).

4 • Yamamura, *Yayoi Kusama*.

5 • Akira Tatehata, "Kusama as Autonomous Surrealist," in Lynn Zelevansky, et al. *Love Forever: Yayoi Kusama, 1958–1968*, exh. cat. (Los Angeles: Los Angeles County Museum of Art, 1998), 62.

6 • Yamamura, *Yayoi Kusama*, 22.

7 • Yayoi Kusama, "Piipuru: Koten o owatte" [People: After my solo exhibition], *Geijutsu Shinchō*, no. 6 (1955): 35.

8 • Kusama, *Infinity Net*, 93.

9 • J. K. [Jack Kroll], "Yayoi Kusama," *ArtNews* 60, no. 3 (May 1961).

10 • Stuart Preston, "Twentieth Century Sense and Sensibility," *New York Times*, May 7, 1961.

11 • Robert Taylor, "Events in Art," *Boston Sunday Herald*, December 6, 1959.

12 • Sir Herbert Read, Kusama personal archive, Tokyo, reprinted in Zelevansky, *Love Forever*, 180.

13 • Yayoi Kusama, quoted in Jan Cremer, "On the Cover," *Art Voices* 4, no. 4 (1965): 5.

14 • Michael Benedikt, "New York Letter: Sculpture in Plastic, Cloth, Electric Light, Chrome, Neon, and Bronze," *Art International* 10, no. 1 (January 1966): 99.

15 • Gordon Brown, "Yayoi Kusama, the First Obsessional Artist," *Gendai bijutsu* (November 1965), quoted in Kusama, *Infinity Net*, 47.

16 • Midori Yoshimoto, "Performing the Self: Yayoi Kusama and Her Ever-Expanding Universe," in *Into Performance: Japanese Women Artists in New York* (New Brunswick, NJ: Rutgers University Press, 2005), 45–78.

17 • Yayoi Kusama, quoted in Jud Yalkut, "The Polka Dot Way of Life (Conversations with Yayoi Kusama)," *New York Free Press* 1, no. 8 (1968).

18 • Yayoi Kusama, press release for Naked Event at the New York Stock Exchange, July 1968, Yayoi Kusama archive, Tokyo; quoted in Mignon Nixon, "Anatomic Explosion on Wall Street," *October* 142 (Fall 2012): 17.

19 • Yayoi Kusama, "Open Letter to My Hero, Richard Nixon," November 11, 1968, reprinted in *Yayoi Kusama* (London: Phaidon Press, 2017), 106.

20 • Kusama, quoted in *Yayoi Kusama*, 25.

21 • Toshiaki Minemura, "The Soul Going Back to Its Home," in *Yayoi Kusama Collage: 1952–1983*, exh. cat. (Tokyo: Nabis Gallery; Fuji Television Gallery, 1991), n.p.

22 • Yūsuke Nakahara, "The Disruption of the Surface," in *Yayoi Kusama*, exh. cat. (Tokyo: Fuji Television Gallery, 1984), n.p.

23 • Robert L. Pincus, "Exhibit Shows Today's Japanese Art," *San Diego Union*, May 22, 1986.

24 • Alexandra Munroe, "Obsession, Fantasy, and Outrage: The Art of Yayoi Kusama," in *Yayoi Kusama: A Retrospective*, ed. Bhupendra Karia (New York: Center for International Contemporary Arts, 1989), 33.

25 • Bill Berkson, "Yayoi Kusama: Center for International Contemporary Arts," *Artforum* (Summer 1990): 168.

26 • *Foxgloves in Central Park*, in *Hustlers Grotto: Three Novellas*, trans. Ralph F. McCarthy (Berkeley, CA: Wandering Mind Books, 1998), 75.

27 • Akira Asada, "Multiplication and Reversal," in *Yayoi Kusama, Print Works*, exh. cat. (Tokyo: Abe Publishing), 27.

28 • Kusama, *Infinity Net*, 76.

29 • Nakahara, "Disruption of the Surface."

30 • Yayoi Kusama, *Violet Obsession: Poems*, trans. Hisako Ifshin and Ralph F. McCarthy with Leza Lowitz, ed. Alexandra Munroe (Berkeley, CA: Wandering Mind Books, 1998).

31 • Catherine Taft, "Yayoi Kusama," *Artforum* (October 2009): 247.

32 • Kusama, *Infinity Net*, 7.

33 • Leslie Camhi, "Large Sculpture," in *Yayoi Kusama*, ed. Louise Neri and Takaya Goto (New York: Rizzoli International Publications, 2012), 214.

34 • Kusama, *Infinity Net*, 227.

35 • Jenni Sorkin, "Yayoi Kusama's Ornamental Urgency," in *Yayoi Kusama: Festival of Life*, exh. cat. (New York: David Zwirner, 2018), 11.

36 • Kusama, *Infinity Net*, "To Make Art that Will Last Forever."

37 • Masahiro Yasugi, "The Path to Eternity: Yayoi Kusama's Paintings of the '00s," in *Eternity of Eternal Eternity*, ed. Akira Shibutami, Masahiro Yasugi, and Yuji Maeyama, exh. cat. (Tokyo: Asahi Shimbun, 2012), 146.

38 • Museum of Modern Art, "Rockaway! 2018: Narcissus Garden by Yayoi Kusama" (online event announcement), https://www.moma.org/calendar/exhibitions/4995

39 • Kusama, *Violet Obsession: Poems*.

Published on the occasion of the exhibition **KUSAMA: Cosmic Nature**.

The New York Botanical Garden,
Bronx, NY: April 10–October 31, 2021

First published in the
United States in 2021 by
Rizzoli Electa, A Division of
Rizzoli International Publications, Inc.
300 Park Avenue South
New York, NY 10010
www.rizzoliusa.com

in association with

The New York Botanical Garden
2900 Southern Boulevard
Bronx, NY 10458
www.nybg.org

For Rizzoli Electa
Publisher: Charles Miers
Editor: Isabel Venero
Copyeditor: Richard Slovak
Production Manager: Alyn Evans
Managing Editor: Lynn Scrabis

For The New York Botanical Garden
Editor: Joanna L. Groarke
Editorial Director: Sally Armstrong Leone
Creative Director: Christopher Kozarich
Research Assistance: Alex A. Jones, Victoria Lewis, Kristine Paulus, Katherine Simmons

Design by pulp, ink.

2023 2024 2025 / 10 9 8 7 6 5 4 3
ISBN: 978-0-8478-6839-1
Library of Congress Control Number: 2021938494
Printed in China

Visit us online:
Facebook.com/RizzoliNewYork
Twitter: @Rizzoli_Books
Instagram.com/RizzoliBooks
Pinterest.com/RizzoliBooks
Youtube.com/user/RizzoliNY

Facebook.com/NYBotanicalGarden
Twitter: @NYBG
Instagram: @NYBG
Instagram.com/nybg
YouTube: youtube.com/c/newyorkbotanicalgardenbronx

Page 2
Dancing Pumpkin, 2020
Installation view, The New York Botanical Garden, 2021

Page 176
My Soul Blooms Forever, 2019
Installation view, The New York Botanical Garden, 2021

Photo Credits

All works and photographs are reproduced courtesy of the creators and lenders of the material depicted; the following images, indicated by page number, are those for which separate or additional credits are due. For certain archival images, we have been unable to trace copyright holders. The publishers would appreciate notification of additional credits for acknowledgment in future editions.

All works by Yayoi Kusama, except as noted below, are copyright © 2021 YAYOI KUSAMA.

All photographs of Yayoi Kusama, except as noted below, are courtesy of the artist © 2021 YAYOI KUSAMA.

2, 10, 12, 18, 23, 24–25, 27–29, 118, 120, 166–67: photos by Marlon Co, The New York Botanical Garden. 9, 133, 152: photos by Eikoh Hosoe. 14–15, 16–17, 22, 50–51, 102–03, 114–15, 140, 176: photos by Robert Benson Photography. 52: photo by Yuichi Hiruta. 67: photo by Kenneth Van Sickle. 68: image courtesy of David Zwirner, Ota Fine Arts, Victoria Miro. 84: photo by Keizo Kioku. 90: photo by Michael Tropea, Chicago. 92, 97: photos by Barbara Ambrose. 94: photos courtesy of The New York Botanical Garden. 95: The Book Work/Alamy. 96: Hakan Soderholm/Alamy (left); The New York Botanical Garden (center); Nigel Cattlin/Alamy (right). 107: photo by Rik Klein Gotink. 109: © Georgia O'Keeffe Museum / Artists Rights Society (ARS), New York. 132: photo by Norihiro Ueno. 161 (top): image courtesy of Naoshima Contemporary Art Museum. 162–63: image courtesy MoMA PS1; photo by Pablo Enriquez.

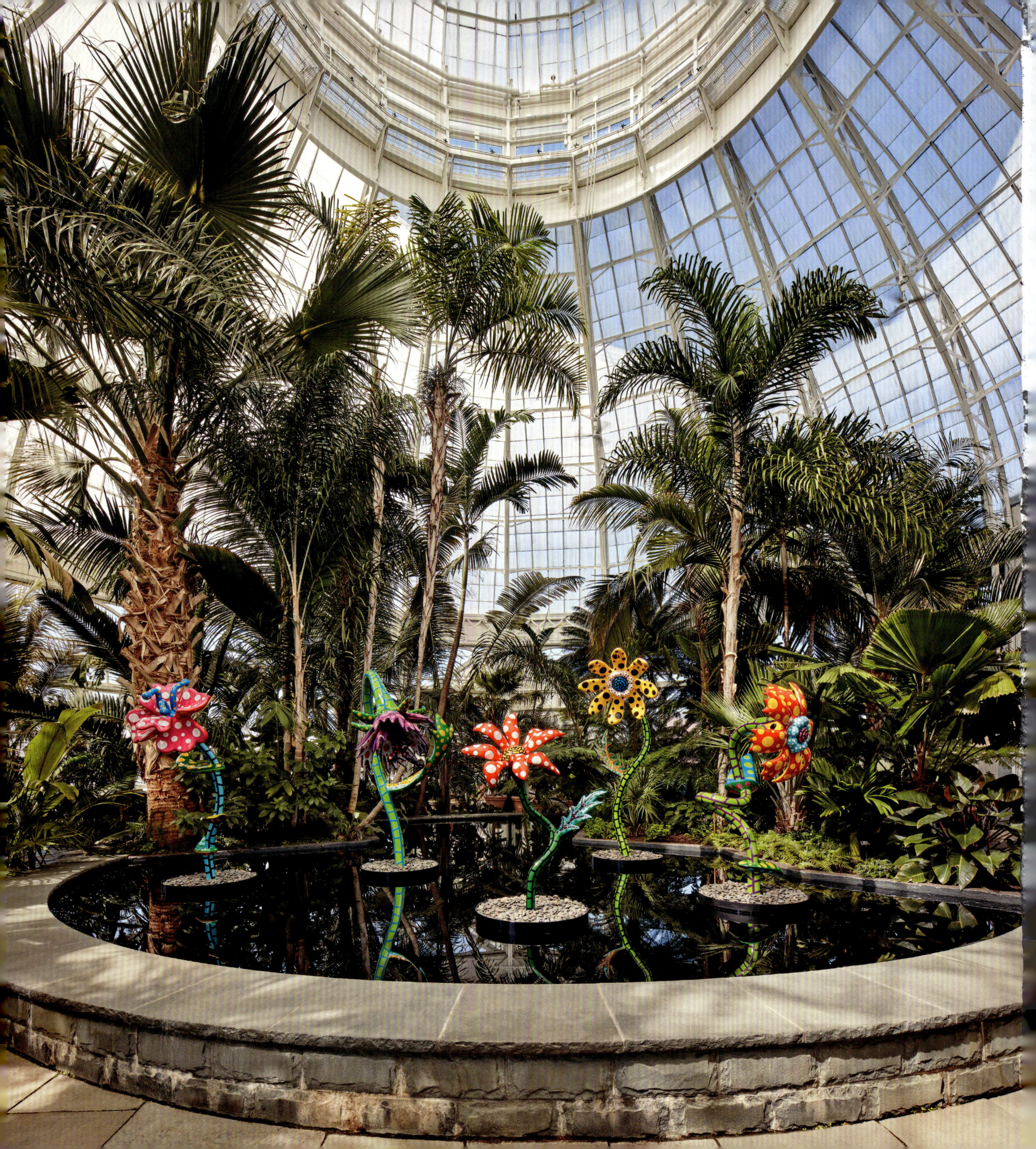